D0102832

Plowshares and Pork Barrels

Property of the
State of the Rockies Project
Walt Hecox, (719) 389-6413

Plowshares and Pork Barrels
The Political Economy of Agriculture

E. C. Pasour, Jr. and Randal R. Rucker
Foreword by Bruce L. Gardner

The INDEPENDENT INSTITUTE

Oakland, California

Copyright © 2005 The Independent Institute
All rights reserved. No part of this book may be reproduced or transmitted
in any form by electronic or mechanical means now known or to be invented,
including photocopying, recording, or information storage and retrieval
systems, without permission in writing from the publisher, except by a reviewer
who may quote brief passages in a review. Nothing herein should be construed
as necessarily reflecting the views of the Institute or as an attempt to aid or
hinder the passage of any bill before Congress.

The Independent Institute
100 Swan Way, Oakland, CA 94621-1428
Telephone: 510-632-1366 • Fax: 510-568-6040
Email: info@independent.org
Website: www.independent.org

Library of Congress Cataloging-in-Publication Data

Pasour, E. C.
    Plowshares and pork barrels : the political economy of agriculture /
E. C. Pasour, Jr. and Randal R. Rucker ; foreword by Bruce L. Gardner.
    p. cm.
Includes bibliographical references and index.

ISBN-13: 978-0-945999-03-4 (pbk. : alk. paper)
ISBN-10: 0-945999-03-8 (pbk. : alk. paper)

1. Agriculture and state–United States. 2. United States–Economic policy.
I. Rucker, Randal R. II. Title.
HD1761.P375   2005
338.1'0973–dc22

                                                          2005010937

10 9 8 7 6 5 4 3 2 1   05 06 07 08 09

The INDEPENDENT INSTITUTE

THE INDEPENDENT INSTITUTE is a non-profit, non-partisan, scholarly research and educational organization that sponsors comprehensive studies of the political economy of critical social and economic issues.

The politicization of decision-making in society has too often confined public debate to the narrow reconsideration of existing policies. Given the prevailing influence of partisan interests, little social innovation has occurred. In order to understand both the nature of and possible solutions to major public issues, The Independent Institute's program adheres to the highest standards of independent inquiry and is pursued regardless of political or social biases and conventions. The resulting studies are widely distributed as books and other publications, and are publicly debated through numerous conference and media programs. Through this uncommon independence, depth, and clarity, The Independent Institute expands the frontiers of our knowledge, redefines the debate over public issues, and fosters new and effective directions for government reform.

FOUNDER & PRESIDENT
David J. Theroux

RESEARCH DIRECTOR
Alexander Tabarrok

SENIOR FELLOWS
Bruce L. Benson
Ivan Eland
Robert Higgs
Alvaro Vargas Llosa
Richard K. Vedder

ACADEMIC ADVISORS
Herman Belz
UNIVERSITY OF MARYLAND

Thomas E. Borcherding
CLAREMONT GRADUATE
SCHOOL

Boudewijn Bouckaert
UNIVERSITY OF GHENT,
BELGIUM

James M. Buchanan
GEORGE MASON UNIVERSITY

Allan C. Carlson
HOWARD CENTER

Robert D. Cooter
UNIVERSITY OF CALIFORNIA,
BERKELEY

Robert W. Crandall
BROOKINGS INSTITUTION

Richard A. Epstein
UNIVERSITY OF CHICAGO

B. Delworth Gardner
BRIGHAM YOUNG
UNIVERSITY

George Gilder
DISCOVERY INSTITUTE

Nathan Glazer
HARVARD UNIVERSITY

Ronald Hamowy
UNIVERSITY OF ALBERTA,
CANADA

Steve H. Hanke
JOHNS HOPKINS UNIVERSITY

Ronald Max Hartwell
OXFORD UNIVERSITY

James J. Heckman
UNIVERSITY OF CHICAGO

H. Robert Heller
INTERNATIONAL PAYMENTS
INSTITUTE

Lawrence A. Kudlow
KUDLOW & COMPANY

Deirdre N. McCloskey
UNIVERSITY OF ILLINOIS,
CHICAGO

J. Huston McCulloch
OHIO STATE UNIVERSITY

Forrest McDonald
UNIVERSITY OF ALABAMA

Thomas Gale Moore
HOOVER INSTITUTION

Charles Murray
AMERICAN ENTERPRISE
INSTITUTE

William A. Niskanen
CATO INSTITUTE

Michael J. Novak, Jr.
AMERICAN ENTERPRISE
INSTITUTE

June E. O'Neill
BARUCH COLLEGE

Charles E. Phelps
UNIVERSITY OF ROCHESTER

Paul Craig Roberts
INSTITUTE FOR POLITICAL ECONOMY

Nathan Rosenberg
STANFORD UNIVERSITY

Simon Rottenberg
UNIVERSITY OF
MASSACHUSETTS

Paul H. Rubin
EMORY UNIVERSITY

Bruce M. Russett
YALE UNIVERSITY

Pascal Salin
UNIVERSITY OF PARIS,
FRANCE

Arthur Seldon
INSTITUTE OF ECONOMIC
AFFAIRS, ENGLAND

William F. Shughart II
UNIVERSITY OF MISSISSIPPI

Joel H. Spring
STATE UNIVERSITY OF NEW
YORK, OLD WESTBURY

Vernon L. Smith
GEORGE MASON UNIVERSITY

Richard L. Stroup
MONTANA STATE UNIVERSITY

Thomas S. Szasz
STATE UNIVERSITY OF N.Y.,
SYRACUSE

Robert D. Tollison
UNIVERSITY OF CLEMSON

Arnold S. Trebach
AMERICAN UNIVERSITY

Gordon Tullock
GEORGE MASON UNIVERSITY

Richard E. Wagner
GEORGE MASON UNIVERSITY

Sir Alan A. Walters
AIG TRADING CORPORATION

Walter E. Williams
GEORGE MASON UNIVERSITY

Charles Wolf
RAND CORPORATION

THE INDEPENDENT INSTITUTE
100 Swan Way, Oakland, California 94621-1428, U.S.A.
Telephone: 510-632-1366 • Facsimile: 510-568-6040
Email: info@independent.org • Website: www.independent.org

Contents

Abbreviations

AAA	Agricultural Adjustment Act
ADM	Archer Daniels Midland Corporation
AMTA	Agricultural Market Transition Act
CCC	Commodity Credit Corporation
CRP	Conservation Reserve Program
HEW	Department of Health, Education, and Welfare
HHS	Department of Health and Human Services
EBT	electronic benefit transfer
EEP	Export Enhancement Program
EPA	Environmental Protection Agency
EWG	Environmental Working Group
FAIR Act	Federal Agriculture Improvement and Reform Act
FCA	Farm Credit Administration
FCIA	Federal Crop Insurance Act
FCIC	Federal Crop Insurance Corporation
FCS	Farm Credit System
FmHA	Farmers Home Administration
FOR	Farmer-Owned Reserve
FSA	Farm Services Agency
FSCC	Federal Surplus Commodities Corporation
GATT	General Agreement on Tariffs and Trade
GDP	gross domestic product
GNP	gross national product
GSE	government-sponsored enterprise
ITA	International Trade Administration

ITC   International Trade Commission
LDPs   loan deficiency payments
NAFTA   North American Free Trade Agreement
NIRA   National Industrial Recovery Act
NRCS   Natural Resources Conservation Service
OSHA   Occupational Safety and Health Administration
PACs   political action committees
PIK   payment in kind
PL 480   Public Law 480
REA   Rural Electrification Administration
RTP   rate-of-time preference
SCS   Soil Conservation Service
Stabilization Flue-Cured Tobacco Cooperative Stabilization Corporation
TANF   Temporary Assistance to Needy Families
TRQ   tariff rate quota
USDA   U.S. Department of Agriculture
WTO   World Trade Organization

Foreword

A book on farm policy that owes more to Friedrich Hayek than to any agricultural economist may not shock the public, but it is definitely a new departure in published work on farm programs. *Plowshares and Pork Barrels* broadens the subject not only by bringing in Austrian and public-choice economics and philosophical issues, but also in taking a wide view of the scope of agricultural policy. Pasour and Rucker do not limit their discussion and analysis to traditional price supports and related forms of governmental intervention, but encompass food distribution programs, conservation of natural resources, agricultural research, and income taxation.

As a result, this book is unique in tracing noncontroversial description, data, and textbook material to a critical assessment of the entirety of farm policy issues. What makes Pasour and Rucker's approach particularly valuable is not only the facts presented and analytical findings but even more the line of argument in which it is embedded. Economic analysis of the merits of agricultural policies has generated many cost/benefit assessments of farm programs and found these programs wanting. But welfare economics is also well attuned to the market-failure aspect of economic problems, also endemic in agriculture. An exemplary summing up of the approach to policy issues in the agricultural and resource economics mainstream, in the case of rural land-use planning is: "The conclusion seems warranted that where it would work, the private market is to be preferred; but that in deciding a question of farm preservation, public action is required."[1]

For "farm preservation" others have substituted "price stability," "soil conservation," "milk marketing," and practically every other market outcome. Pasour and Rucker are not having any of this: they insist on subjecting governmental activity to the kind of skeptical investigation that we typically address to market outcomes but from which we so often exempt public action. Further, they shows what a problematical concept "public action" itself is. Their discussions on collective choice, the economics of the political process, and biases in the process are all topics vital to policy issues in agricultural economics, but too often neglected in our textbooks.

Many land-grant agriculturalists will take issue with some parts of the book. Personally I think Pasour and Rucker's skepticism about the mainstream findings of extraordinarily high returns to public investment in agricultural research is overdone. They raise many valid questions about the estimates, but those questions actually have been pretty thoroughly addressed in a huge volume of empirical work, and the findings of extraordinarily high returns appear to remain robust. The case for high returns is further strengthened by looking at the evidence on benefits of agricultural productivity gains in the less-developed countries, which this book doesn't address. And, there are reasons to believe cost-benefit studies have omitted many of the benefits of current agricultural research. For example, at the University of Maryland we are investing successfully in developing chickens and feed technologies that will result in less nutrients ending up reducing the quality of water in the Chesapeake Bay and elsewhere. These are benefits that are mainly reaped by people who are neither in the chicken business nor are chicken consumers, and are not promising for private-sector research. Nor do such benefits show up in existing benefit-cost accounting.

Readers who absorb Pasour and Rucker's political economy analysis will say, properly, that the preceding is just what you would expect from the Dean of a College of Agriculture. Nonetheless, even self-interested arguments can be right, and I do think it is important not to devalue research either public or private. I believe the most important sources of worldwide gains in less starvation, better health, longer lifespans, and improved standards of living are the results of technological progress. Therefore, while in many areas of public spending it is imprudent to spend without strong evidence that it pays, when considering policy regarding public investments in technology it is imprudent not to spend without evidence that it doesn't pay.

These remarks have been addressed to students of economics. *Plowshares and Pork Barrels* will also be informative to the general public and journalists interested in agriculture, but this broader group will see the book from a quite different perspective. The press and the public, tending to distrust governmental officials, readily accept notions of "government failure," or worse; but they also have little respect for market forces and are ready to listen to conspiratorial theories of unfavorable market outcomes. Thus they view with suspicion payment of millions of dollars to large farm operations, and other policies that the book criticizes. At the same time the majority of the nonfarm population believe that government should be active in helping agriculture. Members of this group, too, can learn much from wrestling with *Plowshare and Pork Barrels*.

Bruce L. Gardner
Professor and Interim Dean
College of Agriculture and Natural Resources
University of Maryland

Preface

This book presents a brief history of U.S. farm policy, an explanation of the political process that has given rise to the multitude of farm programs, and descriptions and economic analyses of a number of the more prominent programs. Government intervention in agriculture traces back to the creation of the land-grant colleges in the 1860s. The role of government in agriculture prior to the 1930s, however, was relatively limited, with emphasis primarily on ways to increase the productivity of crop and livestock producers. The government's role in U.S. agriculture increased dramatically under the Roosevelt New Deal with the enactment of a multitude of farm programs to regulate the production and marketing of agricultural products.

The book describes various forms of production control and price support programs for a variety of crops, including grains, cotton, milk, sugar, tobacco, wool, and peanuts. Other programs and issues discussed include subsidized food programs (including food stamps), crop insurance, subsidized credit, international trade subsidies and import restrictions, conservation, agricultural research, and taxation in agriculture. Farm programs are anticompetitive and highly complex. The analysis minimizes the discussion of the myriad details of U.S. farm programs, but instead focuses on their direct and indirect economic effects.

Public choice is the application of basic economic principles to decision-making within the political process. The first part of the book discusses basic public choice principles, relates these principles to the development of farm programs, and explains why the programs persist long after the end of the economic conditions that were used to justify them.

There are two competing explanations for farm programs—the public interest and income redistribution. Historically, it has been suggested that farm programs are a response to "market failure" problems and that the programs benefit the public at large. According to this view, the market is not able to coordinate economic activity in agriculture because of such problems as monopoly power and market instability.

The book questions this rationale as the basis for U.S. farm programs and argues that the programs are better explained by income redistribution. It is shown how agricultural groups are able to use the political process to advance their own economic interests at the expense of the public at large.

Farm programs are sold to the public as a way to help maintain the small family farm. In reality, however, the programs confer most of the benefits on individuals whose wealth and incomes are considerably greater than those of the average taxpayer footing the bill. The analysis suggests that most of the benefits are incorporated into prices of land and other specialized resources. How can farm programs that benefit the few at the expense of the many persist in a democracy? The benefits are highly concentrated on the few who can afford to expend time and effort to influence the political process, while the costs are widely dispersed among taxpayers and consumers.

What causes the political process to go awry in this manner? Information and incentive problems plague the political process. Information problems arise because of the separation of power and knowledge. Those making political decisions do not have, nor can they possibly obtain, the knowledge and information that would be required to determine the policies that would best promote the common good. Incentive problems are endemic in the political process because of the separation of power and responsibility. Those making policy and administering farm programs neither bear the costs nor receive the benefits associated with their decisions.

What norm can appropriately be used to assess the effectiveness of agricultural markets and governmental policies? Current farm programs often are justified by measuring the performance of agricultural markets against the unattainable norm of perfect competition. Perfect competition, a highly abstract and idealized concept, assumes price-taking behavior by sellers, perfect information, costless transactions, and instantaneous attainment of equilibrium. It is not surprising that economic analysts find "market failure" when real-world markets are contrasted with the ideal of perfect competition because no real-world market meets these requirements. Moreover, when perfect competition is used as a benchmark, problems facing real-world decision makers who must operate in an environment of uncertainty and imperfect knowledge are ignored. Similarly, comparisons of actual government programs with "ideal" programs will inevitably lead analysts to conclude that there is "government failure."

Throughout these pages, in contrast, the competitive entrepreneurial market process is taken as the norm in the evaluation of both agricultural markets and government programs. Here the market is viewed as a process wherein individuals are not fully informed and plans are not perfectly coordinated. In the market process approach, competition is assumed to inhere in the market of a modern economy unless constrained by nonmarket forces.

Farm programs have persisted in the United States since the 1930s despite dramatic changes in economic conditions. In 1996, Congress enacted the Federal Agricultural Improvement and Reform (FAIR) Act, which was viewed by many as representing a sweeping change in the nature of U.S. farm commodity programs. The expectation of some industry participants and observers at that time was that government's involvement in U.S. agriculture would soon end. When agricultural prices fell in the late 1990s, however, agricultural lobbying efforts resulted in the passage of annual emergency ad hoc relief legislation in each year from 1998 through 2001. The 2002 farm bill reversed some of the changes implemented in 1996, and generally increased the level of government expenditures on a wide variety of farm programs. Based on this recent experience, it seems likely that extensive government involvement in U.S. agriculture will continue into the foreseeable future.

Given this general forecast, it is noteworthy that the sixty-year old tobacco production and marketing cartel was eliminated in 2004, demonstrating that protectionist policies can be changed. Furthermore, an examination of the effects of U.S. farm programs is particularly timely because ongoing WTO negotiations clearly have important implications for these programs.

The authors are indebted to Professor Bruce Gardner of the University of Maryland for the foreword, which sets the tone of the book. Special thanks are due to Roger Strickland of the USDA's Economic Research Service for assistance in locating and providing data sources. We also thank numerous students for their assistance in tracking down data and information, including John Batastini, Katie Genadek, Jessica Kitchens, Bill Perry, and J. R. Peterson. Finally, we thank Donna Kelly for her word-processing expertise and numerous editorial suggestions.

E. C. Pasour, Jr.
Randal R. Rucker

1

The Role of Economics in Agricultural Policy Analysis

Agriculture in the United States and in other countries has been heavily regulated for many decades. During the past two decades, however, important changes have occurred in agricultural policies throughout the world. There is growing awareness that protectionist farm programs are expensive and inimical to economic progress, that they have little effect on long-run profitability of production, and that different programs frequently work at cross purposes. The inconsistencies between U.S. farm programs and free trade have been highlighted both in recent international trade agreements (for example, the General Agreement on Tariffs and Trade [GATT] and the North American Free Trade Agreement [NAFTA]) and in the two most recent U.S. farm bills—the Federal Agriculture Improvement and Reform (FAIR) Act of 1996 and the Farm Security and Rural Investment Act of 2002 (in this book referred to as the 1996 farm bill and the 2002 farm bill, respectively).

The 1996 farm bill was hailed by some as representing a major change in U.S. commodity programs. This so-called Freedom to Farm bill, which was in effect for seven years, largely dismantled the costliest price-support programs for farm commodities and permitted farmers to produce program crops with few planting restrictions. Some suggested that the FAIR Act marked the beginning of the end of government involvement in U.S. agriculture. The experience of U.S. agriculture under the FAIR Act, however, was not consistent with its advance billing. Farmers did gain increased flexibility in their planting decisions. In part because of low market prices for several major commodities, however, annual ad hoc appropriations for emergency aid were made in several recent years, and the costs to U.S. taxpayers turned out to be much larger than predicted when the 1996 farm bill was enacted.

The recently enacted 2002 farm bill (the Farm Security and Rural Investment Act) largely retains the flexibility in planting decisions implemented in the FAIR Act. Beyond that, however, the 2002 bill in many ways reverts to pre-FAIR policies. Target prices have been reinstituted, allocations for many FAIR programs have been substantially expanded, new producer groups are designated to receive government payments, and expectations are widespread that taxpayer costs will be the largest ever incurred under U.S. farm programs.

Recent trade agreements and policy changes, described throughout this book, mean that U.S. agriculture is now more closely linked than in the past to other sectors of the domestic economy and to world markets for farm products. Indeed, the effects of international trade along with the monetary and fiscal policies of the federal government may now be more important to U.S. farmers than policies designed specifically for agriculture.

In short, the farm sector cannot be considered in isolation. In many respects, the agricultural economy can be viewed as a microcosm of the entire economy. That is, economic activities in agriculture are similar to those in other sectors of the economy. Consequently, in any evaluation of the effects of various agricultural policies, it is necessary to understand how economic activity is coordinated in a market economy. First, we should consider the functions that must be performed in any type of economic system and the ways of performing these functions in a modern economy.

FUNCTIONS OF AN ECONOMIC SYSTEM

The functions of an economic system are quite general, regardless of political system and economic organization.[1] First, there is a problem of product mix. That is, the amounts to be produced of corn, wheat, milk, beef, textiles, autos, steel, and all other products must be determined. Second, and closely related, land, labor, and capital resources must be allocated to the production of the various products. In agriculture, the production of crop and livestock products is rarely restricted to a single technology. Grain producers, for example, can reduce the amount of tillage by using more herbicides and pesticides. Moreover, even with a given technology, the most profitable amount of any input generally hinges on relative prices of inputs.

Third, the economic pie must be divided, or income must be distributed in some way. It should be emphasized, however, that wealth is not merely given, nor is there a fixed amount of income to be distributed. Instead, in free societies, individuals *create* wealth through labor, cooperation, and ingenuity. Income distribution is not a separate activity, but rather an integral part of the production process—individuals respond to incentive systems that reward extra effort.

Fourth, if economic progress is to occur, capital facilities must be maintained, updated, and possibly expanded. If the expected receipts from a capital-intensive activity are less than the costs, productive facilities are likely to be depleted. And if new goods and services are to be made available, incentives must be sufficient to induce producers to assume the risks. Because productivity depends on the amount of capital investment per worker, the maintenance and expansion of capital facilities is closely related to economic growth.

Finally, goods and services must be "rationed" in the sense of adjusting consumption, both at a particular moment and over time, to the available stock. Some goods such as agricultural crops are produced seasonally and must be stored if the goods are to be available throughout the year. Regardless of whether production is seasonal or occurs throughout the year, however, the very nature of economic goods means that they are scarce and must be rationed at any point in time.

THE MARKET SYSTEM VERSUS CENTRAL DIRECTION

The economic functions just described must be performed in any type of economic system. There are basically only two methods of economic organization in a modern economy, the market system and central direction.[2] Although the comprehensive application of planning as a coordinating principle, as shown later in this chapter, is utterly unworkable, every economic system of the modern world to varying degrees involves some level of central planning. There is, however, no substitute for competitive markets in discovering, coordinating, and transmitting information throughout the production and marketing system. For this reason, a modern economy requires economic freedom and market competition just as science requires freedom and intellectual competition to progress.[3] Thus, as shown throughout this book, central planning, whether comprehensive or not, is more likely to create and protect monopoly power and privilege than it is to foster economic activity.

Abundant evidence shows that the type of political and economic system used to achieve economic and social cooperation has the potential to affect human welfare greatly. Economic incentives and private-property rights are as important in agriculture as in other activities. Prior to the breakup of the Soviet Union, for example, most of the state-owned land was organized as collective farms where the relationship between worker output and reward was tenuous at best. However, a highly disproportionate amount of food in the Soviet Union was produced on small plots of land leased to farmers by the state, on which the farmers were permitted to grow food and raise animals either for their own use or for sale. These private plots, which accounted for less than 1 percent of the agricultural land in the Soviet Union, were estimated to provide approximately one-third of total farm output.[4]

This observed link between entrepreneurial incentives and productivity is not unique. Sven Rydenfelt analyzed the economic crises in fifteen socialist countries, including Cuba, Tanzania, China, and the Soviet Union. Rydenfelt showed how socialist policies, regardless of geography, population, or natural resources, undermine a nation's single most important economic resource, the entrepreneur.[5]

In a market or private-property system, prices perform the economic coordination functions described in the previous section. Information about supply and demand conditions is coordinated and transmitted through market prices. When the expected price of soybeans increases relative to the price of corn, for example, farmers shift more land into soybean production. Similarly, changes in relative input prices bring about substitutions in input use. As the price of labor increases relative to prices of machinery and equipment, farmers substitute capital for labor. The substitution of capital for labor and land in U.S. agriculture has led to a significant increase in output per unit of labor used.

Individual incomes are determined both by one's control over productive resources and by the use made of the resources. The expectation of profits provides an inducement for individuals to engage in risky entrepreneurial activity, and the individual decision maker must frequently make choices involving trade-offs between income and risk. Resource uses yielding higher incomes in agricultural production and marketing, as in financial markets, generally involve more risk.

The present value of expected income in any future time period is determined by the discount rate. The higher the discount rate, the lower the present value of income received in a future time period. Thus, an increase in the discount rate reduces the market value of an asset yielding a given stream of expected income. For example, if the use of a particular machine increases profits by $100 per year, the market price of the machine will be lower the higher the discount rate. Thus, the interest rate—the price of credit—is a crucial variable in investment decisions affecting durable resources, including land and capital facilities.

The rationing of goods and services both in the current period and over time is also performed by the price system. U.S. agricultural programs have long been plagued by economic surpluses. The existence of a persistent economic surplus (or shortage) is evidence that the price mechanism is not allowed to perform the rationing function. Price is also important in rationing goods over time. The amount of corn stored at harvest, for example, hinges on the difference between harvest price and the expected price following storage. A farmer will store corn only if the expected increase in price is large enough to compensate for storage plus interest costs.

One of the most interesting features of the market system is that it is automatic and unconscious. The market mechanism was not deliberately created, and no one assigns market participants their roles or directs their functions. As Frank Knight puts it, "No one ever worked out a plan for such a system, or willed its existence; there is no plan of it anywhere, either on paper or in anybody's mind, and no one directs its operation."[6] Stated differently by F. A. Hayek, markets, being spontaneous in origin, are the product of "human action but not of human design."[7]

A key insight of Adam Smith's *Wealth of Nations* is that social cooperation is achieved by the price system in a decentralized market system as if by an "invisible hand." Economic cooperation occurs as individuals engage in mutually voluntary exchange. Without an order being issued, individuals are induced to use their knowledge and to cooperate with each other in ways that are broadly beneficial, but that allow individual market participants to make the "right" decision even though they may have very limited information. The New York City housewife, for example, reduces consumption of orange juice when price increases. Regardless of whether she knows that production was decreased by a Florida frost, she has the incentive to use the product more sparingly. Similarly, producers of oranges and individuals engaged in the production of inputs used in orange production and marketing are also induced to cooperate through mutually beneficial voluntary exchange.[8] The theory of the decentralized market economy shows how an overall economic order is achieved that uses a large amount of information not concentrated in any one mind, but existing only as the separate knowledge of millions of different persons.[9]

MARKET PRICES AND MARKET SOCIALISM

The alternative to this decentralized market system is *socialism* (defined as government ownership of the means of production) or some other variant of central planning that does not rely on market-price signals. If prices are not used as signals, some type of central direction involving coercion must be used to organize economic activity.

The issue of whether socialism is a viable alternative to private enterprise was hotly disputed among economic theorists for much of the twentieth century.[10] In the 1930s, socialist theorists Oskar Lange and Abba Lerner and prominent economists argued that central planners can determine economically rational product and factor prices and the efficient pattern of production in the absence of private property.[11] They demonstrated that if *given* crucial data on available resources, production possibilities, and consumer preferences, a central planning board can emulate market prices and determine the most appropriate pattern of production. Ludwig von Mises and F. A. Hayek, however, demonstrated that although market socialism may not be logically contradictory, it is practically impossible because of information problems.[12] Central planning to simulate market activity, they argued, is not operational because the necessary data cannot be obtained. The market socialism approach merely assumes away a crucial economic problem—the discovery and efficient use of knowledge. In reality, the necessary information to implement this type of central planning is *not* given to planners. Moreover, as the arguments presented later demonstrate, there is no known way that the information can be obtained through central direction.

The Mises-Hayek insights were not incorporated into mainstream economic theory, and even Nobel laureate economists failed for many years to recognize the Achilles' heel of collectivism—information.[13] These insights about central planners' inability to cope with information problems are no less relevant today than they were a half-century ago. Furthermore, information problems are just as important for piecemeal regulation, as of the farm sector, as they are for central direction of the entire economy—where the empirical evidence leaves little doubt that such problems are insurmountable.

The Cold War's nuclear standoff allowed "history's grandest economic experiment" to run virtually undisturbed for five decades.[14] The East, where collectivism was forcibly imposed, was the "experimental group," and the West, with its private-property system, constituted the control group. By the end of the 1980s, even Robert Heilbroner, the well-known proponent of democratic socialism, conceded that in the debate over the feasibility of socialism, Mises and Hayek were correct.[15] There is now a consensus that successful planning is impossible without private property and the associated market prices. Without these signals, there is no possibility of calculating costs or revenues and no way of determining the most highly valued products.

The death of socialism has discredited "politics in the large," or central planning at the national level, but it has not reduced the appeal of "politics in the small," or piecemeal economic planning.[16] Before further consideration of the problems with regard to the acquisition and use of knowledge that are inherent in noncomprehensive planning, let us first briefly review the marginal efficiency conditions of conventional welfare economics.

MARGINAL EFFICIENCY CONDITIONS AND PUBLIC POLICY

The marginal efficiency conditions of welfare economics describe the relationships that must prevail to maximize social welfare. These conditions typically are derived under the assumption of perfect competition—which requires price-taking behavior on both sides of the market, "perfect markets" with costless transactions and communication, and instantaneous information and equilibriums.[17] Price takers are market participants who do not buy or sell enough of a good or service to influence the market price. The model of perfect competition assumes away various "market imperfections," including monopoly, imperfect information, and externalities. Under these highly idealized conditions, optimizing behavior by individuals and firms brings about the most productive pattern of resource use for the entire economy.[18]

The standard marginal efficiency conditions describe the relationships that must exist among consumers, for input use among firms, and in output markets. These efficiency conditions have the potential to be useful to decision makers in agriculture and other areas as a "logic of choice." The principles are relevant, for example, in farm-management problems such as finding the most profitable amount of nitrogen per acre to use in corn production or determining the least-cost combination of grain and silage to obtain (say) one hundred pounds of milk from dairy cows. A great deal of applied work by agricultural economists deals with these marginal efficiency conditions, and the usefulness of these optimizing principles has been demonstrated in many different production and marketing contexts.

Marginal efficiency conditions, however, are of relatively little use in resolving public-policy problems. The data necessary to use the efficiency conditions for policy purposes are never "given" to a single person.[19] The economic problem of achieving a productive pattern of resource use is not a problem of how to allocate "given" resources among "given" ends. It is, instead, a problem of how to secure the best use of resources known to the various members of society for ends or purposes whose importance can be known only by those individuals. Much of the relevant information is highly specialized to particular persons in specific locations and cannot be conveyed in statistical form to a planning authority. For example, the individual farmer has unique knowledge about soil conditions of particular fields, field locations, local market conditions, his preferences in crop and livestock production, and so on.

Hayek and Mises, as previously shown, emphasized a generation ago that central planning poses insoluble problems. Even today, however, the role of markets in discovering, coordinating, and transmitting information typically is heavily discounted and not fully recognized.[20] No way has been found to overcome the information problems inherent in market socialism or in noncomprehensive central-planning approaches. Specifically, the central decision maker cannot obtain the information necessary to solve the problems inherent in central planning, whether the issue is wheat production, land-use planning, industrial policy, or socialism as such. In any type of central planning, information and incentive problems prevent the planner from achieving a pattern of resource use consistent with the marginal efficiency conditions outlined here. Incentive problems inherent in the collective-choice process are discussed in chapter 3.

IMPORTANCE OF ECONOMICS IN PUBLIC POLICY

Despite the limitations just discussed, economics has an important role to play in explaining the existence and effects of public policies. First, economic theory can help us to understand better the individual decision-making process that results in seemingly inefficient public policies.[21] Why, for example, does Congress enact a sugar program or a dairy program that benefits a small number of producers at the expense of the public at large? As shown later, the fact that the benefits of such programs are concentrated on a small number of producers but the costs are dispersed over the entire population is important in explaining farmers', consumers', and legislators' actions relating to these and many other government programs.

Second, economic theory can contribute to improvements in public policy. Public-choice theory extends the application of economic principles to analyze individuals' actions in the political process. The challenge in improving public policy is to develop an institutional framework that will induce actors in the political process to serve the general welfare, just as Adam Smith's "invisible hand" induces market participants to do so.

Third, economic theory can help trace out not only the direct effects, but also the indirect effects and unintended consequences of such public policies as price supports, subsidized credit, and other agricultural programs.[22] What, for example, are the effects of agricultural price supports on output and land prices? Why does a price-support program increase production costs? Why do government programs, once initiated, tend to grow, seemingly regardless of how economic conditions change? What are the effects of a price-support program on imports and exports of the product? In answering these and similar questions, subsequent chapters use economic theory to trace out the direct and indirect effects of various agricultural programs and policies.

THE MARKET PROCESS: COMPETITION AND ENTREPRENEURSHIP

In understanding the market effects of agricultural programs such as price supports, marketing orders, and so on, we must understand how markets operate. Throughout this book, emphasis is placed on the market as a process in which prices provide signals to consumers and producers.[23] The market is a system in which expected profits and losses influence entrepreneurial decisions. If information on goals, costs, and returns is given or known with certainty, entrepreneurship is reduced to mechanical calculation.[24] It is important to stress that entrepreneurial decisions under real-world conditions are always made under conditions of uncertainty; completely accurate information on prices, yields, weather, and so on is never given to the decision maker. Entrepreneurial success is determined not by mathematical expertise, but by the decision maker's ability to assess present conditions and to anticipate future conditions.

In the market process, entrepreneurship represents alert decision makers' attempt to create or discover and thereby to take advantage of profit opportunities not yet noticed by others. Where product prices reflect market forces and there are no government subsidies or "soft loans" to failing firms, only those firms that best anticipate market conditions survive. In this way, market forces cause resources to be deployed away from less-productive firms. Government regulation of product and input markets, as shown throughout this book, often stifles and impedes the market's discovery process.[25]

The market-process approach is quite different from that of conventional welfare economics, which contrasts the operation of real-world markets with perfect competition. Perfect competition, however, has nothing to do with real-world market activity because no real-world market can meet the required conditions. This does not mean, however, that agricultural markets are not competitive in a meaningful sense in the absence of government restrictions. In a market-process sense, competition inheres in markets because, in the absence of arbitrary restrictions, entrepreneurial activity follows the lure of expected profits. Consequently, the ability to enter a market is the key requirement in maintaining effective competition as a process in which competitors engage. Moreover, it is assumed in subsequent chapters that the major restrictions on the competitive market process in agriculture result from government programs and policies. It is shown that price-support programs, marketing orders, and other farm programs are inconsistent with freedom of exchange both domestically and internationally.

If perfect competition is taken to be the norm, as is often the case in policy analysis, then "market failure" in the form of monopolies, externalities, and information problems is inevitable because no real-world market can satisfy the conditions of perfect competition. Moreover, the use of perfect competition as a benchmark in analyzing the efficiency of real-world market activities ignores the functions and requirements of entrepreneurial decision making. Although long-run competitive equilibrium models are useful as an engine of analysis in explaining how markets work, they cannot be used to derive norms for policy aimed at making allocation more efficient.[26]

SUMMARY

In any type of economic system, five functions must be performed: (1) determine what goods and services to produce, (2) organize production, (3) determine how the economic pie is to be divided, (4) provide for economic progress, and (5) ration the available goods and services, both in the current period and over time.

There are basically only two methods of organizing economic activity in a modern economy—the private-property market system and central direction. However, there is no other known way to accommodate consumer preferences as fully as is done through decentralized competitive markets.

What is the role of economic theory in agricultural policy analysis? The marginal efficiency conditions of conventional welfare economics are useful to the individual decision maker as a logic of choice but are of limited use in the evaluation of public policies. All real-world markets will appear to fail when measured against the norm of perfect competition. The alternative is to view competition as a process in which competitors engage and to use the competitive market process as a touchstone in explaining and evaluating the effects of government policies in agriculture. Throughout this book, this view of the entrepreneurial market process is taken, both in explaining individual decisions as they affect and are affected by public policies and in tracing out the direct and indirect effects of public policies on agriculture in the United States.

The remaining chapters in this book can usefully be thought of as being composed of two distinct sections. The first section consists of chapters 2 through 5. These chapters provide basic information on several fundamental concepts, including a discussion of efficiency and equity as criteria for assessing government programs, a discussion of private versus collective choice as alternative systems for making decisions, and both a fairly general discussion of the economics of the political process and a discussion that applies the basic concepts of public-choice theory to the context of agricultural policy. An understanding of the materials in these chapters might be considered to be a prerequisite for the more focused discussion and analysis of U.S. farm programs in later chapters.

The second section consists of chapters 6 through 20. These chapters focus directly on a wide variety of issues associated with U.S. farm policy, from discussions of the basic "farm problem" and the expansion of the U.S. government's role in agriculture, to quite detailed discussions and analyses of past and present policy tools used in commodity programs. These chapters also include discussions of the nature and impacts of federal programs that affect such areas of interest as international trade, risk management, agricultural credit, conservation of natural resources, research and extension, and taxes.

Most general readers will find it useful to read and contemplate the material presented in the first section before they proceed to the second section with its more focused discussion and analyses of specific agricultural programs. Readers familiar with the concepts presented in the "prerequisite" chapters, however, might view these chapters as an entry barrier over which they can jump straight into the later chapters that deal directly with agricultural policies. Readers interested in the public-policy process, but less interested in agricultural policies may choose to focus only on the early chapters.

From the perspective of classroom use, we find that many students in the agricultural policy classes that we teach have had little exposure to much of the material in the early chapters and that it is useful to spend some time on the fundamental concepts. The second section thereafter provides institutional details on agricultural policies in relatively short and concise chapters. Many of these details are new to students. Of equal or greater importance in the second section, however, is our critical analysis of the various policies from the perspective of the information and incentive problems associated with government regulations and programs. A recurring issue in our consideration of government programs is the importance and implications of the capitalization of program benefits into asset values.

Shortly before we finished writing, the 2002 farm bill was passed. We have chosen to handle the various issues related to this new legislation in two ways. First, we include an appendix at the end of the book that provides considerable detail on the provisions of the new farm bill and how they relate to the provisions of the 1996 farm bill. Second, in those chapters where it is appropriate, we have included supplemental sections discussing the new legislation.

2

Economic Efficiency and Equity in U.S. Agriculture

Agricultural policy in the United States has been heavily influenced by productivity and equity considerations. From 1862 to 1933, the U.S. Department of Agriculture (USDA) was mainly a scientific and statistical agency limited to research, extension programs, education, and some policing activities related to food safety. During this period, the major emphasis of government policy in agriculture was to increase productivity. Although income redistribution has been the dominant concern in U.S. agricultural policy since 1933, government-subsidized research and education programs continue to be important.

Prior to the New Deal era of the 1930s, government programs in agriculture were small and seldom had much impact on the individual farmer. Franklin Delano Roosevelt's New Deal was a watershed development in government involvement in agriculture. At that time, many action programs were instituted with the goal of redistributing income to the agricultural sector.

Commonly used criteria for evaluating government programs, in agriculture as well as in other sectors of the economy, are the programs' economic efficiency and their equity impacts. As conventionally defined, economic efficiency is concerned with the size of the economic pie produced, whereas equity deals with how the economic pie is divided. The distinction between efficiency and equity is not as clear-cut as frequently implied, however, because the way the economic pie is divided affects the size of the pie. Stated differently, individual productivity is directly related to the expected reward.

ECONOMIC EFFICIENCY: AN ELUSIVE CONCEPT

It is often contended that *economic efficiency* is an objective concept in the sense that it can be empirically measured, but that *equity* is subjective. This distinction between efficiency and equity, however, does not withstand scrutiny. Economic efficiency is sometimes contrasted with technical efficiency—the ratio of output to input in physical terms. Technical efficiency is of little interest, however, because by the laws of thermodynamics the ratio of physical output to physical input is always equal to unity.[1] Therefore, efficiency is meaningful only when both resources and products are measured in value terms.

Efficiency, if it is to be a meaningful objective for decision making, is always a measure of the value of output in relation to the value of inputs used. For instance, "The 'objective' efficiency of an automobile engine can be determined only after specifying the subjectively determined goal as the forward movement of the automobile. Otherwise, every engine is 100 percent efficient in the sense that all the energy input is used, either in the forward motion of the car, overcoming the internal friction of engine parts, or in random shaking of the automobile."[2] Consequently, the efficiency of any activity will change with changes in valuation of inputs or outputs.

Consider the problem of whether it is more efficient for a homeowner to cut wood with a bow saw or with a chain saw. It depends, of course, not only on the amount of wood to be cut and the cost of the saws, but also on the subjective values associated with the use of each type of saw, the value of time, and so on. An individual who enjoys the smell of gas fumes and the roar of the motor may rationally choose to use a chain saw, whereas another individual who loves strenuous physical activity may choose to saw wood by hand. The outside observer cannot legitimately conclude that either individual is behaving inefficiently.

Similarly, it is sometimes held in agriculture that the production of beef relative to corn is inefficient because more calories of food can be produced when a given amount of land, labor, and capital inputs are devoted to corn production rather than to beef production. The inefficiency conclusion does not follow, however, because consumers place a higher value per unit (calorie) on beef than they do on corn. Again, the relative efficiency of corn production versus beef production cannot be determined on the basis of physical measurements of inputs and outputs.

The subjective nature of economic efficiency limits the outside observer's ability to identify real-world examples of economic inefficiency.[3] Efficiency measurements must be based on some norm or standard of comparison. The efficiency of real-world activities is typically measured against the economic model of "perfect competition." This is not a defensible approach, however, in evaluating the performance of real-world activities because no individuals, markets, or economic systems will ever appear to be efficient when measured against the benchmark of perfect competition. That is, no real-world market will ever conform to the ideal concept of perfect competition, which (as described in chapter 1) requires "perfect markets" and price-taking behavior on the part of individual traders. Consequently, the fact that real-world markets do not conform to the competitive norm does not imply that these markets are inefficient in an economically meaningful sense. It is inappropriate to compare real-world markets with an unattainable ideal because the *relevant alternative* to current markets is simply another *possible* institutional arrangement and not "perfectly competitive" markets.[4]

The fact that outside observers cannot measure economic efficiency does not mean that the efficiency concept has no value. Economic efficiency is a useful concept as long as the inputs and outputs are defined in terms of the decision maker's own values. Thus, in the woodcutting example, the concept might be quite useful for the homeowner buying a saw. The data on which individuals base choices, however, are inherently subjective and distinct from data that can be obtained by external observers. That is, the outside observer is not able to "read" individual preference functions.[5] Because utility is measurable only to the individual decision maker, the concept of economic efficiency is not useful as a touchstone of public policy.

EQUITY

Equity is concerned with how the economic pie *should* be divided. It is virtually impossible to make definitive statements about the fairness of public policies that benefit some people at the expense of others. Many people, consciously or unconsciously, identify their own interests with the common good, rationalizing that a government program that benefits them is also in the public interest. In this view, a farm program that increases "my" income is fair, and what's fair to "me" is fair to everyone else. Thus, people often oppose government-enforced restrictions on competition in the abstract while rationalizing and defending increases in their own income obtained through the use of government power.

As shown in chapter 6, the concept of a fair (or just) price or income has little objective meaning aside from prices and incomes determined through the competitive market process. Equity or fairness, like beauty, is at least to some extent in the eye of the beholder. A number of criteria for making welfare judgments about public policies that benefit some and harm others are discussed later, but none of them provides a value-free approach to redistribution.

The Pareto Criterion

The most widely accepted criterion for making welfare judgments is the Pareto criterion, which holds that a change is beneficial if it benefits at least one person without reducing the welfare of any other individual. Most public policies in agriculture (and in other sectors), however, benefit some people while harming others. An agricultural price-support program, for example, benefits farmers at the expense of consumers and taxpayers. Therefore, the Pareto criterion is not useful in the evaluation of actual public policies.

A number of theorists have attempted to devise a criterion for evaluating public policies that benefit some people at the expense of others. One widely discussed proposal is the compensation principle.

Compensation Principle

The compensation principle states that a policy is an improvement if the winners evaluate their gains at a higher figure than the value that the losers place on their losses. The compensation principle can be illustrated as follows. Determine the maximum amount an individual will pay rather than forgo a change that benefits her—say, $200. Then find out how much a second individual who is harmed by the change will be willing to pay to prevent that change—say, $100. If the figure paid to prevent a change is smaller, the compensation principle says that the change under consideration improves welfare because the first individual can compensate the second and still gain. The compensation principle does not require actual compensation. (If the second individual were actually compensated, the change under consideration would be an improvement under the Pareto criterion.)

This seemingly plausible principle is based on an unacceptable implicit value judgment.[6] It involves a concealed interpersonal comparison. Even if the first individual values her gain at $200 and the second individual values his loss at $100, it does not follow that there is a net gain from the change being contemplated. The compensation principle implicitly assumes that a dollar is worth the same to each individual. The second individual, a struggling student, however, may place a very high value on his $100 loss, whereas the first individual, a wealthy professor, may view her $200 gain as a pittance (or vice versa, of course). The $200 and $100 figures are not comparable, and there is no legitimate way to make such interpersonal comparisons of utility. Consequently, unless compensation actually is made, the Pareto criterion is violated by public policies that benefit some people at the expense of others. Although the compensation principle is often used in welfare analyses of tariffs, price supports, and other government restrictions on competition, any such analyses should be viewed with a healthy dose of skepticism because they inevitably involve invalid interpersonal utility comparisons.

Social Welfare Function

The *social welfare function* is another approach devised to analyze the welfare effects of policies that harm some people while benefiting others. The social welfare function is closely related to the indifference-map approach of consumer theory. An indifference map is a method of describing an individual's preferences with a set of indifference curves. An indifference curve shows the set of market baskets yielding the same amount of utility or satisfaction. Thus, the consumer is indifferent about the set of market baskets on a given indifference curve. A social welfare function can be visualized as an indifference map that ranks different combinations of utility to different members of society.[7] The same criticism applied to the compensation principle applies again here, however. There is no way to obtain the data for social indifference curves because utilities for different individuals are not comparable. The policy analyst who uses this approach must make an explicit and highly arbitrary value judgment regarding one individual's utility relative to the other's. Consequently, the social welfare function approach is of little or no use in the evaluation of public policies.

Cost-Benefit Approach versus Constitutional Approach

Despite the problems inherent in meaningfully defining efficiency and equity under real-world conditions, these problems are often ignored, and attention is focused on the technical details of cost-benefit analyses. Empirical welfare analyses frequently are based on measurements of consumer surplus and producer surplus.[8] These measurements implicitly involve the use of the compensation principle.

Consider the welfare effect of an output restriction, as depicted in figure 2.1, that increases price from P_0 to P_1 by decreasing output from Q_0 to Q_1. Area A is said to be a "transfer" from consumers to producers. The triangle B is referred to as a "welfare cost" or "deadweight loss" of the amount by which the value of lost output (area under the demand curve between Q_0 and Q_1) exceeds the value of resources saved (area under the supply curve between Q_0 and Q_1).

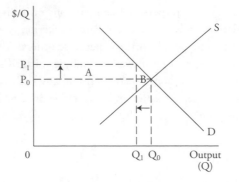

FIGURE 2.1 The welfare effects of production controls.

Such measurements based on market supply and demand curves inevitably involve interpersonal comparisons of utilities. It is implicitly assumed that a dollar is a dollar regardless of whether it is received or given up by consumers or producers (and regardless of which individuals are affected). Consequently, the measurement of areas A and B is subject to the same interpersonal utility-measurement problems as those discussed in connection with the compensation principle.

Similar problems arise in measuring the welfare effects of price supports, subsidized credit, import tariffs, marketing orders, and other government restrictions on competition in agriculture. Attempts are often made to justify the repeal of such restrictions by arguing that consumers' gain in utility will exceed producers' losses. Yet any such measurement of costs and benefits must involve interpersonal comparisons that, "to put it mildly, would be highly conjectural."[9] There is no legitimate way objectively to measure and compare the benefits afforded to or the harm endured by different groups of people. The conclusion is that all policy recommendations involve value judgments.[10] For example, there is no value-free procedure to determine whether agricultural price-support levels should be lowered or raised.

These arguments do not imply, however, that the question of how high or low government should set prices or of whether government should assist groups in restricting competition is merely a matter of opinion. Government-sanctioned restrictions on competition that infringe on individuals' rights to engage in mutually beneficial transactions are significant for both practical and ethical reasons. First, restrictions on competition hamper the operation of the market process and reduce the output of goods and services, as shown in chapter 3. Second, there is no fundamental difference between economic freedom and individual freedoms of other types, including First Amendment rights.[11] Thus, any analysis of government restrictions on competition in agriculture or in other areas must take into account both the usefulness of competitive markets and the ethical issues involved in restricting individual freedom.

One possible alternative to cost-benefit analyses is to determine appropriate government policies at the constitutional level. If economic freedoms were legally protected, at least some of the objectives that narrowly focused interest groups attempt to achieve through the political process might be ruled out on constitutional grounds.

The proposed constitutional approach involves the adoption of self-denying ordinances that limit the objectives that individuals and groups attempt to achieve through political channels. In this approach, each potential government program is not considered on its own merits; instead, broad rules are laid down as to what government may and may not do. The First Amendment, for example, adopts the general principle that "Congress shall make no law . . . abridging the freedom of speech." Milton Friedman and Rose Friedman have proposed an equivalent amendment to limit government power in the economic and social area—an "economic Bill of Rights."[12] Such a free-trade amendment would ensure that neither Congress nor any of the states shall infringe on people's right to buy and sell legitimate goods and services at mutually acceptable terms.[13] An economic-freedom amendment of this type would provide a touchstone in determining the legitimacy of government policies in agriculture and other sectors. Many of the current restrictions on competition in agriculture—including marketing orders for milk and oranges, import quotas for dairy products, and so on—are clearly inconsistent with economic freedom.

Clearly, there is a relationship between economic freedom and political and individual freedoms. Nobel laureate Ronald Coase argues that freedom of choice in making decisions among constantly changing employment, investment, and consumption opportunities is fully as important for most people as freedom of discussion and participation in government.[14] The individual retains this freedom of choice, however, only when price signals rather than central direction are used to coordinate economic activity. Consequently, a great deal of evidence shows that economic freedom is a necessary condition for political and individual freedom.[15] Moreover, if one accepts the Coase view that economic rights are similar to First Amendment rights, the implications for price supports, marketing orders, import controls, and so on are clear.

RATIONALES FOR U.S. AGRICULTURAL PROGRAMS

Two competing hypotheses explain government intervention in agriculture: the correction of "market failures" (or the advancement of "the public interest") and income redistribution. The market-failure hypothesis is consistent with arguments that government programs can enhance efficiency. Government programs that redistribute income to low-income farmers are often justified on equity grounds.

Market Failure

The public-interest justification holds that agricultural programs, instituted in response to market failure, are beneficial because they increase price and income stability arising from variability in farm product prices and yields. In the traditional welfare economics approach, where real-world agricultural markets are measured against the benchmark of perfect competition, "market failure" in the form of monopoly, market instability, imperfect information, and externalities is pervasive. As suggested earlier, however, market failure in the sense that real-world markets do not meet the conditions of perfect competition is not a sufficient reason to justify government intervention. Government programs also inevitably "fail" when measured against an idealized governmental system where there is perfect information and costless decisions, and where political markets are always in equilibrium. The relevant comparison, of course, is between real-world markets and the real-world political process.

Income Redistribution

Income redistribution is another possible rationale for government intervention in agriculture. Whereas equity-based arguments for government intervention call for redistribution to low-income farmers, the reality seems to be somewhat different. It may well be that the main motivating force behind agricultural policies has not been a desire for productivity growth and market stabilization, but rather a redistribution of wealth to commodity and other interest groups that have the greatest political clout.[16] Why, for example, are domestic producers of cheese, butter, and sugar given protection against less-expensive imports? Is it because dairy or sugar producers have low incomes (and these markets are unstable) or because they have effective political lobbies? The latter explanation appears to be more consistent with the evidence, which suggests, for example, that each of the largest Florida sugarcane growers benefits by more than $5 million per year from the U.S. sugar program.[17] In farm programs, the benefits are concentrated on a relatively small number of producers or landowners, but the costs are widely diffused among taxpayers and consumers. The sugar program, for example, is estimated to increase sweetener costs by approximately $5.60 per U.S. consumer per year.[18] Later chapters discuss more fully this bias inherent in the political process that favors small groups at the expense of the public at large.

Therefore, the only conclusion to come to is that the actual purpose of government programs in agriculture (and other sectors) may be quite different from the purposes indicated in congressional testimony and enabling legislation. It is thus important not to assume that government programs are beneficial, as is often done by individuals who hold the "public-interest" view of U.S. farm policies. In contrast to the conventional market-failure approach, a view that agricultural policies are redistributionist is taken throughout this book. In subsequent chapters, before a description and analysis of U.S. farm policies is given, the nature of decision making in the political process—public-choice theory—is briefly described and specifically related to agricultural programs. The operation of the political process is shown to provide additional support for the redistributionist view of U.S. farm policies.

SUMMARY

Agricultural programs in the United States have been justified on the basis of economic efficiency and equity considerations. Economic efficiency is concerned with the amount of output, whereas equity is related to the way the output gets divided—income distribution. Because economic efficiency inescapably involves subjective valuation, the concept provides little guidance in resolving public-policy issues.

The Pareto criterion, which holds that a policy is better if one or more people are benefited without harming anyone, is the most widely accepted criterion for making welfare judgments. The Pareto criterion is of little practical value, however, because there are losers as well as gainers for all significant public policies. No satisfactory procedure has been developed to compare the costs and benefits of government policies that benefit one group at the expense of other groups.

The constitutional approach has been offered as a possible alternative to cost-benefit analysis in the evaluation of government programs. In the proposed approach, the Constitution would be the touchstone in determining whether a particular program is an appropriate government activity. This approach is rooted in the recognition that economic freedom is no less important than freedoms of other kinds. Although all policy questions cannot be resolved in this way, many current restrictions on competition in agriculture would be illegal if economic freedoms were given constitutional protection.

Market failure and income redistribution are alternative explanations for government intervention in agriculture. The conventional market-failure view supported by agricultural interests has long been that U.S. farm programs are rooted in the public interest. A great deal of evidence is presented throughout this book, however, showing that current farm programs are better explained by the success of agricultural groups in using governmental power to increase their own wealth.

3

Government and the Economy
Private versus Collective Choice

There are basically only two ways to coordinate economic activity: the free market and central direction. A major issue in agriculture (as in all other sectors of the economy) involves deciding which activities should take place in the private sector and which should be conducted through the collective-choice or political process. For this decision to be made intelligently, it is necessary to understand how the private-choice and collective-choice mechanisms operate.

PRIVATE CHOICE

Private choice relies to a great extent on market exchange. Although much of the coursework in economics deals with markets, the concept of a market is not easily defined. A market is not always a *place* where goods are sold, but rather is a set of interrelationships involving supply and demand—a process of competing bids and offers.[1] The *market process* is fueled by the expectation of gains on the part of both producers and consumers. Market choices serve to increase wealth because exchange is mutually beneficial. A key feature of market exchange is the lack of force or coercion. Because market exchange, by its very nature, represents a voluntary *unanimous agreement* by the parties involved in the transaction, informed exchange between individuals is a Pareto-preferred outcome. A purchase of a loaf of bread, for example, increases the expected wealth of both the purchaser and the seller.

PROBLEMS ARISING FROM PRIVATE CHOICE

Despite the ostensible advantages of the voluntary nature of private choice, it is generally held to be beneficial to make some economic decisions through the collective-choice (or political) process. In several situations, often described as examples of "market failure," government action may be considered desirable in coordinating economic activity. Spillovers, public goods, "unsatisfactory" income distribution, monopoly, market instability, lack of information, and high transaction costs are commonly cited examples.[2]

Problems of Private-Property Rights

In some situations, it may be difficult to define property rights clearly and to enforce them adequately. *Spillovers*, or *externalities*, occur whenever the actions people take impose costs on others that the decision makers do not take into account.[3] If an action by one person infringes on the other person's rights—that is, imposes a cost on them without their consent—then a spillover problem or "externality" exists. The use of fertilizers or pesticides, for example, may create an externality insofar as a portion of these chemicals contaminate ground or surface water used by individuals other than the party who applied the chemicals. The spillover problem is analyzed in more detail in chapter 17.

Public goods involve another type of property-rights problem. Public goods, by definition, are characterized by *nonrivalness* and *nonexcludability* in consumption. There is nonrivalness in the sense that any satisfaction received by one consumer from a given amount of a public good does not detract from the enjoyment obtained from the good by other consumers. There is nonexcludability if, when a good is provided to a particular individual, other individuals cannot be excluded from the benefits of the good. National defense, for example, may be considered a public good insofar as it is impossible to protect one person from a foreign threat without at the same time protecting all other individuals.[4] If nonpayers cannot be excluded, however, individuals have an incentive to "free ride"—that is, to obtain the benefits of a good or service without contributing to its cost. The incentive for any one person to be a free rider is greater in large groups because each person may reason that the other beneficiaries will contribute enough to finance the good.[5] If all members of the community choose the free-rider strategy, however, there will be no production by the private sector. Consequently, in a case where there are strong incentives to "free ride," private production may not be feasible. The relevance of externality and public-goods ideas to current agricultural programs is discussed at various points later in the book, especially in chapters 17 and 18.

Distribution of Income

It is sometimes contended that the market system is unsatisfactory because the distribution of income (or resource ownership) may be very unequal. The "Edgeworth box" diagram is often used to show how exchange improves the allocation of consumption goods.[6] Consider the situation depicted in figure 3.1. In this diagram, assume that the initial distribution of the two goods (X and Y) between the two individuals (A and B) is such that A has all of both X and Y. Point Z indicates the initial distribution. Although individual B has none of either good, the situation is Pareto optimal because any move to another point on the contract curve (AB) will represent a decrease in welfare for individual A. That is, individual B cannot be made better off without reducing the welfare of individual A. The implication is that economic tools cannot be used to say how income should be divided. Even in the case of the stark distribution of income depicted by point Z in figure 3.1, economic theory cannot be used to justify redistribution.

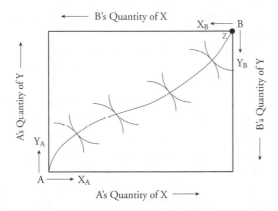

FIGURE 3.1 Economic theory and the distribution of income: The Edgeworth Box.

Can the government determine the distribution of incomes in a market system where each individual is allowed to use the diverse and specialized knowledge he or she possesses for his or her own purposes? The output of goods and services depends on how successfully market participants use this knowledge. The role of government in a market system is to provide a legal framework that assists individuals in the pursuit of their individual purposes. So long as people are allowed to make their own choices, government authorities cannot assure any particular distribution of income because actions taken by individuals are unpredictable. Thus, the idea that government can determine economic opportunities and ensure that they are the same for all members of society conflicts with the conditions and, indeed, the very rationale of a free society.[7] In short, the distribution of individual incomes in a market system is unlikely to conform to any predetermined pattern.

The preceding discussion does not mean that the distribution of incomes cannot be changed through the political process. As shown throughout this book, however, government programs designed to redistribute income are likely to be counterproductive both in determining overall economic output and in improving the economic opportunities of those at the lower end of the income scale.

Because many people are likely to be dissatisfied with the market-determined pattern of incomes, both public and private measures are used to alter it. In the case of voluntary transfers (charity), the redistribution of income presumably improves the welfare of both givers and recipients. Moreover, a gift by one person to those considered to be "needy" also makes other people feel good. Thus, it is argued, charity is a public good involving a consumption externality and results in too little redistribution. A gift to the poor by one person makes others feel better, but causes these others to act as "free riders," thereby reducing their charitable contributions. The implication is that we as individual citizens will not contribute enough to charitable causes unless others are also forced to contribute. Hence, it is alleged, private charity results in less than the Pareto optimal amount of redistribution.[8]

In this view, public-goods theory provides a justification for government transfer programs. For at least two reasons, however, Pareto optimality and public-goods theory do not provide a rationale for governmental redistribution. First, the Pareto criterion provides no guidance on policies that harm some people while benefiting others. Thus, the argument that a particular government transfer program can result in a Pareto improvement is incorrect as long as there is at least one person who is harmed by the redistribution. Second, voluntary transfers do not necessarily fit the public-goods framework. The nonrivalness and nonexclusion features of a public good may not be met in the case of voluntary transfers. If exclusion is feasible in the sense that only the donor knows about a gift to the donee, the free-rider problem does not arise. This may, under some circumstances, be the situation for private charity, where charitable contributions can be made without others' knowledge. For example, if Mr. Jones gives money privately to the low-income Smith family, enabling them to eat meat instead of potatoes, the Smith family's welfare presumably increases. Jones benefits from the knowledge of his gift, but potential free riders likely will not know that an act of charity has occurred—because the Smith family's appearance following the change in diet will likely not be obvious. Thus, there are instances where public-goods theory cannot be used to justify redistribution.[9] This conclusion reinforces the underlying premise of chapter 2 that all redistributional recommendations involve judgments of value.

Monopoly

Monopoly power is typically regarded as an important reason for government intervention. The standard textbook analysis demonstrates that relative to the competitive benchmark, a monopolist produces a lower quantity and charges a higher price. The losses associated with this (supposed) misallocation of resources are the basis for government intervention.

In conventional economic theory, the monopolist is defined as a single seller of a good for which there is no close substitute. Yet, when subjected to close scrutiny, this definition of monopoly cannot be sustained. If a good or service is defined narrowly enough (e.g., key limes at Albertson's grocery in Bozeman, Montana), every seller is a monopolist because no other seller can precisely match the product and conditions under which the product is sold. If, however, any good or service is defined broadly enough (e.g., fruit instead of key lime), there are substitutes within that good or service, and no seller is a monopolist.[10]

If perfect competition is used as a norm, every price searcher (seller facing a demand less than perfectly elastic) is labeled a monopolist. This is not a realistic approach for identifying markets where government intervention is warranted, however, because even the ten-year-old lemonade stand entrepreneur can generally increase sales by lowering the price. Another possible alternative is to define monopoly on the basis of the elasticity of demand. If one attempts to define a monopolist on the basis of "market power" or the elasticity of demand, however, the classification must be arbitrary because market power defined in this way is a matter of degree.

Perhaps the most meaningful way to define monopoly is in terms of a grant of government power that restricts other sellers' ability to compete.[11] The major source of monopoly or cartel power in agriculture (and in other economic sectors) in the United States today arises from government-sanctioned and enforced restrictions on competition. The tobacco, peanut, milk, and sugar programs are examples of government-enforced cartels in U.S. agriculture.

Market Instability and Lack of Information

Information is crucial in a smoothly functioning market process. Whether market participants will benefit from additional information, however, hinges on the costs and benefits of obtaining the information. Moreover, the costs and returns of acquiring information vary from person to person. Even if it were possible to acquire complete information, it would be uneconomic to do so. In the words of Nobel laureate economist George Stigler, "information costs are the costs of transportation from ignorance to omniscience and seldom can a trader afford to take the entire trip."[12] It is economical for market participants and other decision makers to acquire more information only if the expected benefits exceed the costs. Thus, the fact that market participants are not fully informed does not imply that they have "too little" information. (Chapter 18 addresses the topic of possible market failure owing to information problems and discusses government programs in agriculture designed to provide information.)

A great deal of government intervention in agriculture has been justified on the basis of market stabilization. There is, however, no way to eliminate market instability in a world of uncertainty. If government is to stabilize individual markets, planners must somehow overcome the information and incentive problems inherent in the collective-choice decision-making process. Government stabilization policies, as emphasized in chapter 4, are controlled not by impartial and omniscient experts, but by elected and appointed governmental decision makers who, like the rest of us, make and implement policy in light of their own interests and in response to the incentives they face. It is stressed in chapter 4 that all governmental policies in a democratic society are significantly affected by the relatively short time horizons of governmental officials who face pressures to adopt policies that yield short-run benefits but incur long-run costs.[13]

The results of recent government attempts to stabilize the entire economy provide little basis for optimism that such attempts will succeed. In the early 1960s, the argument was made that the federal government should "fine-tune" the economy to achieve a high level of aggregate demand by manipulating government expenditures and taxes. Twenty years later the once high hopes for economic fine-tuning were dashed on the shoals of economic and political reality. The evidence convinced many people that the federal government's monetary and fiscal policies in the 1970s, rather than stabilizing the level of economic activity, actually had a major destabilizing effect.[14] If government is to stabilize agricultural markets, government officials must overcome the same kinds of problems faced in previous attempts to stabilize the entire economy.

Certain government actions, however, do contribute to economic stability in agriculture. The government can create a climate that facilitates rather than impedes the development of crop insurance, options markets, and other institutions that are helpful in dealing with weather and market risks, as discussed in chapter 15. There is, however, a strong a priori case in general for decentralized competitive markets as the most effective means of coping with changing economic conditions. It should also be stressed that noninflationary monetary and fiscal policies at the national level are likely to contribute substantially to the stability of agriculture markets (see chapter 15).

Transaction Costs

Transaction costs are those costs incurred in the process of voluntary exchange, including searching for, advertising, bargaining for, monitoring, and enforcing contracts. Those who advocate collective action point to high transaction costs as a major justification for such action. The relative merits of private versus collective choice as the means of coordinating economic activity are influenced by the magnitude of transaction costs. In the case of services provided collectively, quite often it is not that the service *cannot* be provided through voluntary means. It is rather that the transaction costs of doing so are deemed to be too high. Consider the problem of privatizing police protection. It is often argued that the transaction costs of contacting individuals, collecting payment for services, and so on may be quite high. There is also the problem alluded to earlier that individuals have an incentive to free ride on the protection paid for by their neighbors. It is argued that high transaction costs in such cases may make it impractical to exclude nonpayers from the benefits of police protection. In cases where the costs of excluding nonpayers are very high, collective action may work better than private endeavors. In publicly financed police protection, for example, free-rider problems are solved by government's supplying the service to everyone and paying for it with involuntary contributions (taxes). The preceding example of police protection is frequently cited as one in which free-rider problems prevent the private provision of services. It is thus interesting to note that a 1990 study by the U.S. Department of Justice indicated that $52 billion was spent annually in the United States for private security. This figure contrasts with annual public expenditures of $30 billion on police services.[15]

PRIVATE ACTION VERSUS COLLECTIVE ACTION

The alternative to private decisions coordinated through decentralized markets is collective action coordinated through the political process. That is, central direction is the only alternative if market price signals are not used to coordinate economic activity. Government is unique among social institutions in that it is the only legal entity that possesses the power legally to secure cooperation through coercion. In contrast, in matters involving private choice, cooperation is induced by offering people additional options.[16] The substitution of collective action for private action is often considered appropriate when there is "market failure" of the types discussed earlier. Collective action is no panacea, however, because there are also inherent problems in coordinating economic activity through the political process.

Undesirable Consequences of Collective Action

It is generally assumed that law and order and other traditional functions of government are necessary because of high transactions costs and the free-rider problems. There is no consensus, however, as to the necessity or desirability of such government intervention in the provision of information, the redistribution of income, or the regulation of the economy. Government provision of information and regulation of voluntary exchange is particularly relevant to agricultural policy because the development and dissemination of information to consumers and farmers have long been considered to be major rationales for government involvement in agriculture.

The regulation of voluntary exchange in the form of price supports, interest subsidies, marketing orders, and other restrictions on competition have for many years been at the heart of government efforts to increase incomes within agriculture. Collective action is, however, subject to problems similar to those described earlier in the case of private choice. To determine the appropriate role for government in agriculture, it is important to compare the operation of actual markets with real-world political institutions. This comparison can be accomplished only if the problems inherent in private choice *and* in collective choice are taken into account in weighing the relative merits of government action. This is true whether the issue is price supports, subsidized credit, soil conservation, or government-funded agricultural research.[17]

Information Problems

Information problems are endemic in the collective-choice process because of the *separation of power and knowledge.* Market prices, which reflect demand and supply conditions, coordinate and transmit information to consumers and producers. In this way, the market system uses the detailed information contained in millions of minds more completely than is possible by any other known process. Much of the information incorporated in market prices simply cannot be articulated and conveyed to a central authority in statistical form.

Government intervention leads to a decrease in the volume and quality of information embodied in market prices and distorts the market's coordination process.[18] Consider the supply-demand situation depicted in figure 3.2. When government raises the price of milk, sugar, or any other product above the competitive market-clearing level (P_C) to $\overline{P}_S$, the market begins to give out false or misleading signals. Producers are induced to produce "too much," ($\overline{Q}_S$) and consumers are induced to consume "too little" ($\overline{Q}_D$). The inevitable result, a surplus of quantity *a*, has been evidenced by market surpluses of milk, wheat, corn, tobacco, and other products in U.S. agriculture during the past fifty years. Market prices provide correct signals to producers and consumers, and they properly ration goods and services when they are free to change in response to constantly changing economic conditions.

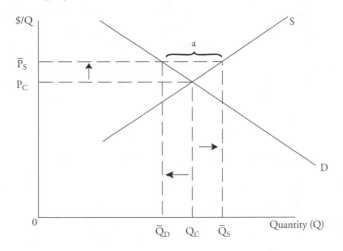

FIGURE 3.2 Upward-biased price signals create surpluses.

Incentive Problems

When decisions about resource use are made through the political process, problems also arise because of perverse incentives owing to the *separation of power and responsibility*. Profits and losses provide the driving force for change and progress in a market system. Entrepreneurial decisions are guided by perceptions of profit opportunities, and only those firms that best anticipate market conditions survive. In contrast, there is no "bottom line" in the case of government enterprise or collective choice where political decisions are substituted for the discipline of the market. This point is especially relevant to the case of subsidized credit in agriculture, discussed in chapter 16, where easy loan policies have spawned numerous hopeless economic ventures kept afloat by politically sensitive foreclosure policies.

The public-choice mechanism provides no reliable guidelines concerning the relative efficiency of various government agencies; there are no signals comparable to the profits and losses that drive the market process. Moreover, there is a tendency toward overconsumption of collectively provided goods and services because the goods generally are priced "too low." Whether the good is water, parks, schools, or USDA services, consumers usually do not pay the full cost of services provided by government.

Pricing collectively provided goods and services below "cost" is not accidental. Political incumbents and political employees obtain an advantage in keeping prices low because the law of demand applies to goods and services provided through government agencies just as it does to those goods and services produced in the private sector. Consequently, the lower the price of any government service, the larger the quantity of the service demanded and the larger the budget, number of jobs, and amount of political influence of the agency providing the service. Information provided by the Cooperative Extension Service to farmers, for example, typically is free. Thus, it is not surprising that there is usually a "shortage" of such services (and of many other underpriced collectively provided goods and services).[19]

Inability to Respond to Consumers with Different Tastes

The same level of any collectively provided good—such as national defense, education, the dairy program, and so on—is typically available to all citizens. Moreover, all taxpayers must contribute toward the provision of those goods whether or not they use them. This feature of collectively provided goods and services is fundamentally different from that of privately produced goods such as autos, clothing, and food, where the individual consumer has a choice, not only of whether to buy the good, but also of the quantity and quality of the good to consume.

Within the collective-choice process, there is also an inherent inability to respond to people with different tastes. Even if an individual fully agrees with the amount of public expenditures on agriculture, for example, he or she may disagree with how the budget is spent. One person, for example, may prefer more public expenditures on food assistance programs and less on price-support programs and income transfers to farmers; another person may hold exactly the opposite view.

Restrictions on Competition

Various groups frequently seek (and achieve) government programs to reduce competition as a means of increasing their own wealth. This practice is particularly important in the case of agricultural programs discussed in later chapters of this book. Effective price-support programs for milk, peanuts, tobacco, sugar and other products, for example, generally require restrictions or tariffs on imports to prevent consumers from substituting lower-priced imports for higher-priced domestic products. There is increasing interest from non-farm groups in commodity programs, import restrictions, and other governmental policies that have the effect of increasing the incomes of small groups at the expense of the public at large.

Rent-Seeking Activity

The reason why producer groups have an incentive to restrict competition through collusion is shown in figure 3.3. The output under competitive conditions is Q_C, which is sold at the competitive market price P_C. If the producers successfully form a cartel and restrict production to Q_m, the cartel price is P_m, and profits are increased by the amount of rectangle A. Each seller has an incentive to cheat on the agreement, however, because the price received (P_m) is higher than the marginal cost of production (MC). By charging a price slightly lower than P_m, any single firm can take sales away from other firms and increase profits. Thus, voluntary cartel arrangements are usually short-lived.[20]

One way to enforce cartel agreements is through the use of legal sanctions. If a producer group can get a cartel agreement enforced through government sanctions, the chances of success are greatly improved. In reality, most successful cartel agreements and other restrictions on competition are administered or enforced by government. In addition to agricultural programs, examples of government-enforced restrictions on competition include labor unions, import restrictions, the U.S. Postal Service, and occupational licensing.

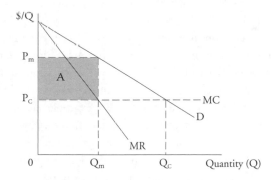

FIGURE 3.3 Cartels: Why producer groups have an incentive to collude.

The situation depicted in figure 3.3 provides an explanation for the widespread practice in which agricultural (and other) groups with narrowly focused interests attempt to use the power of the state to reduce competition and thereby to increase their own income. The concept of *rent seeking* is used to describe the resource-wasting activities that occur as individuals and groups compete for transfers of wealth under the aegis of the state.[21] Teachers, farmers, autoworkers, and other groups spend large amounts of time and money on lobbying activities, campaign contributions, and so on in attempts to influence the legislative process. Rent-seeking theory holds that the expected profits from legal restrictions on competition are likely to be competed away in rivalrous attempts initially to obtain and then to maintain governmental assistance and protection. It is possible for all of the potential gains (area A in figure 3.3) to be dissipated through rent-seeking activities. (In this situation, how would the marginal cost curve that includes rent-seeking costs be drawn in figure 3.3?) Rent seeking—or income redistribution—appears to be a useful concept in understanding, explaining, and predicting a great deal of government transfer activity in agriculture and other sectors of the economy.[22]

Despite the apparent importance of the rent-seeking phenomenon, the problem of identifying rent-seeking activities warrants more attention than it has received.[23] All of the resources used by individuals and groups in obtaining and maintaining government activities cannot legitimately be regarded as rent-seeking waste. Consider the most basic functions of government—law and order. The lobbying and other resource costs necessary to achieve, maintain, and improve these essential activities are predominantly associated with establishing the conditions necessary to produce wealth. The resources devoted to such efforts will appear to be rent-seeking waste, however, if one compares the real-world political process to the benchmark of a perfect, costless political system—an idealized polity where there are no information or incentive problems. But a perfect polity is no more helpful in evaluating the operation of real-world political processes than is perfect competition in evaluating real-world market activity. The operation of real-world political institutions and attempts to improve them, if measured against the benchmark of a perfect state, will always appear inefficient.

In reality, there is no clear-cut, objective procedure for distinguishing productive from wasteful government activities. For example, economists' opinions vary widely as to whether incomplete information, market power, price instability, and other so-called market failures provide a legitimate basis for government farm programs. Although agricultural price-support programs are frequently attacked in the press and by economists as prime examples of wasteful government activity, some agricultural economists justify the dairy, peanut, tobacco, and other programs on market-failure grounds. For example, an analysis of the milk price-support program, published in the *American Journal of Agricultural Economics*, concluded: "The relatively small implied consumer-to-producer transfers . . . resulting from classified pricing may be a small price to pay for the stabilizing aspect of classified pricing."[24] If the dairy program is considered to be a legitimate function of government, lobbying efforts to maintain the program will not necessarily be rent-seeking waste.

What are the implications of this discussion for the theory of rent seeking? Whether or not time and money spent to influence the political process is rent-seeking waste depends on whether or not the changes sought do indeed further the common good. The question of whether or not a particular governmental activity is thought to be beneficial, however, hinges largely on one's view of the state's proper role, a view that ultimately depends on ethical as well as economic considerations. In short, rent seeking is not a purely objective matter but depends inevitably on subjective valuations. Consequently, measurement of rent-seeking waste poses essentially the same problems posed by the identification and measurement of other types of economic inefficiency, as discussed in chapter 2.

The Public Interest

The *public interest* typically is identified with the general welfare or the interests of the public at large. It is usually not possible to say, however, if a particular collective-choice outcome is in the public interest.[25] Political decisions almost always create losers as well as winners. The problem of determining whether such a policy is in the public interest is the same as the problem discussed earlier in the context of policy evaluation: solving the problem requires making interpersonal utility comparisons. Moreover, although the term *public interest* is widely used to influence public opinion, the meaning of the concept is not clear because, as previously discussed, the satisfactions provided for different people cannot be meaningfully summed.

Assuming that the public interest is a meaningful concept, economists have devoted a great deal of effort to the question of whether such a thing as the public interest can exist.[26] Nobel laureate Kenneth Arrow investigated the effects of nonmarket decision making through democratic voting. His results challenged the traditional theory of democracy by showing that no voting rule leading to rule by the "will of the majority" is possible.[27]

The Arrow analysis can be seen as an extension of the economic calculation debate over the feasibility of socialism discussed in chapter 1.[28] The calculation debate demonstrated that the lack of information is central planners' Achilles heel. The Arrow result regarding the inherent problem of democracy in reflecting the public will is further evidence that the information incorporated in market prices in a private-property system cannot be duplicated.

The theoretical work as to whether it is possible to determine the public interest, however, has little practical relevance for public-policy analysis. Public officials, as shown in chapter 4, do not have enough information about preference functions, production functions, and available resources to determine which policies will best serve the public at large. Furthermore, even if government decision makers were able to determine what actions are broadly in the "public interest," they would be unlikely to execute these policies because of perverse incentives in the political process.

Although the concept of the "public interest" provides little guidance, decisions must be made about the role of government versus the market in coordinating economic activity. With regard to choices between alternative methods of organizing economic activity, it is important to avoid what Harold Demsetz calls the "nirvana approach"—the view that the relevant policy choice is between an ideal norm and an existing imperfect institutional arrangement.[29] Those who argue for intervention into an existing market because it does not conform to the norm of "perfect competition" are guilty of committing the nirvana fallacy. The relevant policy choice is always among real-world institutions—all of which are imperfect relative to unattainable ideals.[30]

SUMMARY

Goods and services may be provided through either the market or the collective-choice process. When property rights are not clearly defined, problems concerning externalities and public goods may arise in the market process. Other alleged problems associated with the provision of goods and services through private choice include an unsatisfactory distribution of income, monopoly, market instability, and insufficient information.

Provision of goods and services through collective action, however, is no panacea. There are also shortcomings and undesirable consequences in collective action, including information problems, incentive problems, the inability to respond to consumers with different tastes, a tendency to restrict competition, and decision makers' inability in the collective-choice process to determine which actions are in the "public interest."

The fact that market outcomes do not conform to the ideal of perfect competition does not imply that government intervention is warranted. Imperfections are as important in the political arena as in the market sector. A realistic choice concerning the extent of government intervention in agriculture (or in other sectors) must be based on a comparison of the real-world market process with the real-world political process.

4

Public Choice
The Economics of the Political Process

Public-choice theory involves the application and extension of economic theory to the realm of political or governmental choices.[1] This economic theory of politics emphasizes the actions and choices of *individual* decision makers in the political process. Political events, in this approach, are explained by focusing on the actions of individual participants rather than on the actions of groups because groups, *as groups*, do not act. Any agricultural legislation, for example, occurs as the result of individuals acting in the political process. "In sum, groups do not live, cannot choose, and are unable to act apart from the lives, choices, and actions of the individual members who make them up."[2] Moreover, individual action is assumed to be purposeful, and the decision maker is assumed to be the best judge of his or her own welfare. How is the merit of a specific public policy evaluated if social welfare cannot be measured because different individuals' utilities are not comparable? In this individualist approach, social utility is not regarded as some imagined entity standing on its own. Rather, it is viewed as an aggregate of individual welfares that lack a common basis of comparison.

The following analysis recognizes that individual participants in the political process are not motivated solely by pecuniary considerations. Moreover, it makes no claim that public-choice theory can fully explain either political activity or how individual members of the political process will act in any specific situation. The theory is useful, however, in helping to explain collective-choice decisions at each level of government. The analysis demonstrates how changes in costs and benefits can affect actions at different stages of the collective decision-making process.

The three branches in the U.S. system of government—the legislative, executive, and judicial—were designed to provide a system of checks and balances so that no branch would become dominant. Moreover, it is through the interaction of these branches of government and the bureaucracy that public policies in agriculture and other areas are proposed, developed, adopted, and carried out.[3]

Decision making occurs at each level in the political process. Voters elect members of the legislature. The legislature enacts laws that the executive branch administers. Legislation is actually implemented by the bureaucracy—that is, government workers who staff the various public agencies but who are not elected by voters. Judicial procedures and decisions can also be analyzed using the theory of rational choice, but they are taken as given throughout the following discussion.[4]

INDIVIDUAL PARTICIPATION

The individual voter is confronted with a number of decisions about participation in the political process, including such questions as: (1) Should I vote? (2) How active should I be in political activities (including campaign contributions)? and (3) If active, should I run for office?

The act of voting itself cannot be explained on the basis of narrowly defined self-interest. The probability that an individual's vote will be decisive in any given election is minuscule. It is notable, however, that Adolf Hitler was first elected head of the Nazi Party by a difference of only one vote.[5] Because voting involves a cost (mainly of time), the individual voter almost surely will choose not to vote on the basis of the costs she incurs and the benefits she expects to receive. Consequently, voting must be explained on other grounds; the individual may take an enlarged view of self-interest; she may receive satisfaction from participation in the political process; she may vote to avoid the social pressures against nonvoters who free ride in the democratic process, and so on.

Who are the activists in political activity? Both amateurs and professionals are active in the political arena.[6] Amateur activists do not depend on politics for their economic livelihood. They may be active in party activities at the "grassroots" level, or they may run for political office. Amateur politicians prefer campaigns based on a set of principles or goals and want to win elections to promote these preferences. For amateurs, the cost of returning to private life is usually quite low because their economic livelihood is not at stake. Professional politicians, in contrast, come from many occupations, but their bread and butter typically depend on political success. Consequently, when compared with amateurs, professional politicians are likely to be much more concerned with winning elections than with adhering to ideological principles. An amateur politician is willing to support positions that may be politically unpopular because the outcome of the election has less effect on her economic interests. Even if an amateur and a professional hold similar views, the professional politicians' actions and positions are more likely to be tempered by the general electorate's views because of economic considerations.

Costs and benefits are also important in determining who runs for office. Although campaign funding is highly important to political success, the purpose of campaign contributions is not the same for all donors. Campaign contributions can carry three different but not necessarily mutually exclusive interpretations—the civics book view, extortion, and bribery.[7] The civics book view is that political contributions resemble contributions to charitable organizations where the donor expects nothing in return. There undoubtedly are many small contributors who are motivated by ideology and altruism rather than by narrow self-interest.

There is a great deal of evidence, however, that the pecuniary motive is often important in political contributions.[8] Contributions may represent "extortion" in that they may provide protection money or insurance against unfavorable legislation or from legislation that would take away current benefits. Dairy co-ops, for example, donated $1.3 million to 293 members of the U.S. House of Representatives from 1981 until the 1983 Dairy and Tobacco Adjustment Act was passed. This legislation not only maintained but expanded the financial benefits of the dairy program by instituting payments to farmers to reduce milk production. Thus, contributions might also be viewed as "bribery"—payoffs to achieve specific public-policy concessions. In the case of the dairy legislation, the outcome was a costly act resulting in some individual dairy producers receiving more than $1 million. As another example, the establishment of the Department of Education during the Carter administration was widely viewed as a payoff for support given by the National Education Association during the 1976 presidential campaign.

In reality, the motives of those making campaign contributions are likely to be mixed. Only the individual, for example, knows whether his or her contribution can be more aptly characterized as bribery or as extortion—whether he or she was concerned more with obtaining new benefits or with losing existing benefits. The view of campaign contributions as bribery or extortion is most forcefully argued by those who wish to reform the political process through stricter limits on campaign contributions or through public financing of political campaigns or both.[9]

The potential benefits of elective office at the local level are likely to be highest for lawyers, real-estate brokers, and Chamber of Commerce members whose political exposure can serve as self-advertising for their vocation or business. At the national level, political experience often pays off for former congressional representatives and high-level political appointees in the form of lucrative employment opportunities with business firms interested in gaining Washington contacts and acquiring knowledge of the political process as it affects their own businesses. At the local level, the ability to influence land-use zoning decisions, the location and timing of public works, property tax rates, and so on can provide immediate economic benefits.

POLITICAL PARTIES

Economic theory is also important in explaining the existence of political parties. Different parties have ideologies that provide low-cost information to voters. Party labels are analogous in some ways to product brand names such as GE, GM, and Toyota that provide valuable information to consumers. The party labels Democrat, Republican, Libertarian, and Socialist reduce the cost to individual voters of obtaining information about the various candidates. The individual voter cannot expect to become well informed about all candidates from which he or she must choose. Because most candidates run on party platforms, however, the voter is likely to be able to determine a candidate's position on many issues solely on the basis of party affiliation.

William Maddox and Stuart Lilie separate questions of government intervention in the economy from issues involving civil liberties, and they propose a classification consisting of four ideological groups: liberal, conservative, libertarian, and populist (table 4.1).[10] The traditional liberal-conservative dimension, as depicted in table 4.1, is increasingly inadequate in characterizing the ideological views of U.S. voters and politicians. As shown in chapter 2, there is a growing awareness that economic freedom is no less important than personal freedom. Thus, both the conservative and liberal positions are inconsistent with this insight—conservatives discount the importance of personal freedom, and liberals devalue the importance of economic freedom.

TABLE 4.1 The Relationship of Economic and Personal Freedoms to Liberal, Conservative, Libertarian, and Populist Ideologies.

| | | Increased Economic Freedom | |
		For	Against
Increased Personal	For	Libertarian	Liberal
Freedom	Against	Conservative	Populist

LEGISLATIVE BRANCH

House and Senate members engage in three kinds of activities: advertising, credit claiming, and position taking.[11] Advertising is an attempt to give legislators public recognition by placing their names and persons before the electorate through press releases, public appearances, radio and television ads, billboards, and so on. In advertising, one key issue for any officeholder or political candidate is how much to spend. In theory, the answer is clear if only monetary costs and benefits are taken into account. The politician can afford to spend up to the present value of the sum of the expected stream of discounted future returns. The uncertainties of the political process, however, mean that such standard probability theory may be of little value in understanding such choices. Both the chance of winning and the returns if elected are highly uncertain. Moreover, most candidates are not motivated solely by financial considerations. Indeed, some candidates—such as Harold Stassen, a perennial candidate for president of the United States—run even when the expectation of winning is nil.

In addition to advertising, members of Congress also curry favor through credit claiming and position taking. A legislator may claim credit for the passage of specific legislation with benefits that flow principally to a particular constituency. Position-taking activities in Congress range from making speeches on issues to voting. Credit claiming and position taking may be motivated to some extent by ideology, but the desire to stay in office usually is the dominant influence. It is not unusual, for example, for a politician who is generally a staunch supporter of free enterprise, but who is also from a state with a strong agricultural constituency to promote restrictions on competition for milk, tobacco, wheat, and other products. In fact, it is much more uncommon for the serious political candidate to place ideology over short-run political considerations. One instance in which ideology may play a greater role is when a politician does not intend to run for reelection.

Legislative activity is heavily influenced by the committee and seniority system of Congress.[12] Agriculture is just one of the standing committees in the House and Senate (currently, the Senate has sixteen committees, and the House has twenty-four committees, although these numbers change from year to year). Congressional committees are centers of power in determining the fate of particular items of legislation. For example, the Agriculture Committee has jurisdiction over domestic price-support legislation, and all measures affecting that area are referred to the Agriculture Committee.

Members of Congress usually seek membership on a committee that has jurisdiction in an area most relevant to their constituents. A House member from a rural area, for example, might be expected to seek membership on the

Agriculture Committee. The committees still operate largely by the seniority system, and the person from the majority party who has served the longest on the committee usually is committee chairman—a position of great political clout and prestige. Seniority is determined by when the member was appointed to the committee. Thus, the chairman of the Agriculture Committee in the House or Senate is likely to be from a state where agriculture is an important industry.

For many years, committee chairs tended to be southerners because of the dominance of the Democratic Party in the South. Often reelected term after term, southern congressmen frequently attained seniority on congressional committees. In recent years, southern representatives have lost a great deal of influence on congressional committees because the South is no longer a one-party region and because of changes in congressional procedures.

Much of the power in Congress now resides in congressional subcommittees that tend to be organized mainly along functional lines in both the House and the Senate. The five subcommittees of the House Agriculture Committee in the 107th Congress are: Department Operations, Oversight, Nutrition, and Forestry; General Farm Commodities and Risk Management; Livestock and Horticulture; Specialty Crops and Foreign Agriculture Programs; and Conservation, Credit, Rural Development, and Research. The four subcommittees of the Senate Agriculture, Nutrition, and Forestry Committee are Forestry, Conservation, and Rural Revitalization; Marketing, Inspection, and Product Promotion; Production and Price Competitiveness; and Research, Nutrition, and General Legislation. In addition, there is an agricultural subcommittee of the Appropriations Committee in both the House and Senate.

It is no accident, as described earlier, that chairs and the general membership of committees and subcommittees in Congress tend to be from states where committee actions are particularly important. For example, the chairmen of the House and Senate Agriculture Committees in the 106th Congress were from Texas and Indiana, respectively. Interest in agricultural legislation by urban members of Congress has increased greatly since the 1960s, however, following an increase in the scope of USDA-administered food assistance programs.

Bureaucratic decision makers' actions in government agencies are influenced by the congressional electoral process. Reelection-minded representatives and senators have strong incentives to ensure that government agencies provide benefits to their constituents. The congressional-bureaucratic system is a means to this end.[13] In return for electoral support from tobacco or dairy farmers, for example, a representative from a tobacco or dairy state who is a member of the committee with jurisdiction over these USDA activities may work hard to provide a flow of benefits to his or her constituents. Moreover, a congressional member of the relevant committee has an incentive to use a farm program for political purposes. This phenomenon is no less important, of course, in non-agricultural areas. Thus, representatives and senators often play a key role in agency decisions, and sanctions are likely to be imposed on those government bureaus that fail to provide the benefits demanded by Congress. The conclusion is that the congressional-bureaucratic system confronts government agencies such as the USDA with strong incentives to serve the interests of members of the affected congressional committees.[14]

Members of Congress from districts with different types of constituents often engage in log rolling (vote trading). For example, rural representative X may vote for the food stamp bill of urban representative Y if Y will vote for the agricultural subsidy bill favored by representative X. This practice has become more important in agriculture with the growing number of food assistance, environmental, and other transfer programs favored by urban interests. Although vote trading is important and widespread, legal scholars disagree on its merits. Whenever log rolling results in legislation considered to be broadly beneficial, however, vote trading creates little controversy.

Lobbies or interest groups provide a way to bring together people of similar interests, to express their views to legislators, and to attain legislation beneficial to particular groups. Farm organizations and commodity groups, for example, often lobby for or against legislation affecting agriculture. Lobbying groups provide information and financial support to legislators. Depending on the nature of their activities, lobbying groups are sometimes referred to as "pressure groups."

THE EXECUTIVE BRANCH AND THE BUREAUCRACY

The executive branch is charged with carrying out the laws enacted by Congress. The president influences legislation through his proposals made to Congress, support or opposition to bills, and use of the veto. Various cabinet departments—the USDA, Department of Defense, and so on—are charged with specific areas of responsibility. The president appoints the top administrators in the departments and other agencies or bureaus, but the programs are administered by the bureaucracy. Although the top administrators change with a change in political administration, most of the government employees (e.g., more than 112,000 USDA employees as of 2002) do not.

The key decision maker in the implementation of legislation and in economic regulation generally is the "professional public servant"—the bureaucrat. Bureaucrats are government workers not responsible for making public policy, but rather for implementing policy decisions. The individual citizen's most frequent contact with government at all levels remains with bureaucrats. The ostensible functions of federal bureaus include supplying public goods, suppressing public ills, redistributing resources, controlling monopolies, and establishing property rights. Today in the United States, approximately one in seven members of the workforce is employed by some level of government.[15] Government bureaus confront decision-making problems unlike those faced by private firms. Most of these problems can be traced to the fact that there are no residual claimants in government bureaus. That is, no one in a government agency personally gains when resources are used in ways considered most beneficial to the public at large.

It is sometimes suggested that employees who staff government agencies act to maximize social welfare without regard to their own utility, power, prestige, income, or vote appeal. In view of the large size of the government sector and the fact that individuals frequently move between the private and public sectors, there is little reason to assume that government employees are significantly different from an average cross-section of the population having the educational qualifications required for that work.

Bureau employees are similar to other interest groups. It is to be expected, for example, that USDA personnel will actively defend and seek to expand government programs in agriculture. Research and extension workers who provide subsidized information and county workers who administer the various farm subsidy, food assistance, and other programs publicize the benefits and seek additional support for these programs through personal contacts, press releases, and legislative lobbying. Bureau personnel are active in the electoral process, although the Hatch Act restricts federal employees from public campaigning. They are also important sources of information in congressional hearings and for individual legislators.

What goals do decision makers in government bureaus pursue? Carrying out the "goals of Congress" is difficult because the goals are seldom clearly defined. Achieving the "public interest" is not feasible because the individual bureaucrat does not have the required information on consumer preferences, production possibilities, and available resources.[16] Moreover, even if decision makers in the collective-choice process can determine what actions are in the public interest, the incentive structure of the bureaucracy is not conducive to their following those actions.

What, then, are the bureaucrat's goals? The bureaucrat, like other members of the political process, has a vested interest in power and influence. One means of achieving such objectives is through maintaining and expanding agency growth. Bureaucrats may also tend to be highly adverse to risk and, as a result, may take actions that tend to minimize bureaucratic strain and to increase the odds of staying in power. There is an incentive to institute policies yielding immediate benefits and to forgo policies involving potentially higher returns that involve more risk and a longer time horizon.

Consider the example of Food and Drug Administration (FDA) testing of new drugs. Two costs are associated with the introduction of a new drug: *(a)* lives lost (or damaged) through premature introduction and *(b)* lives lost through excessive delay in introducing new drugs. The first cost is highly visible; the second cost is difficult to detect. Few people will condemn the FDA for lives lost because of the second cost, but sickness or death resulting from the use of a new drug will predictably evoke a public outcry. The result is that the FDA is likely to test drugs too much, if judged by a standard based on a realistic comparison of costs and benefits. In drug testing and in other areas, the political decision maker desiring to maintain power is well advised to minimize the probability of making detectable errors.

It is also helpful for a bureau head to maximize agency output that can be readily monitored—such as contacts made. One way to increase the demand for an agency's output is to offer the service to the public below the cost necessary to provide it. For example, USDA services such as those of the Cooperative Extension Service typically are heavily subsidized and priced below the actual cost of providing them to farmers, homemakers, and other users of these services. This pricing bias in the collective-choice process is likely to lead to a higher level of output than would be provided through private choice.

Members of government bureaus also benefit from agency growth. For the bureaucrat, salary, perquisites, public reputation, and patronage all increase with the size of agency budget.[17] One way to increase the budget is to charge below-cost prices (as indicated in the previous paragraph) to justify increased appropriations. Bureau officials also have an incentive to resist reductions in agency size. In responding to impending budget cuts, government officials are likely to sacrifice the services most highly valued by consumers rather than to make cuts that affect their own welfare. As James T. Bennett and T. J. DiLorenzo point out, "Typically the immediate response of a public agency to proposed budget cuts is some variant of . . . the 'Washington Monument syndrome.' When faced with a budget reduction, the National Park Service immediately announced that such cuts could only be accommodated by closing the Washington Monument, the most popular tourist attraction in the nation's capital."[18] Another closely related strategy employed by bureau officials is to make sure that no money remains in agency budgets at the end of the fiscal year. Even in periods of financial austerity, it is not uncommon to observe administrators in public agencies remodeling offices, adding new furniture, replacing carpets, and so on in order to use up their fiscal year budgets.

Another way to maintain agency growth is to expand the bureau's jurisdiction or to maintain a service after the original justification for government provision of the service is reduced or no longer exists. The Cooperative Extension Service, for example, was set up to provide information to farm families. As numbers of farmers decreased, Extension Service clientele was expanded, for example, by providing nutrition information to low-income urban households. Thus, there tends to be a ratchet effect that leads to growth of government agencies regardless of changes in economic conditions. It is predictable that decision makers with vested interests in the political-bureaucratic arena will not passively accept measures that increase competition or reduce the scope for collective choice. Consider George Bush's famous pledge made while running for president in 1988—"Read my lips, no new taxes." Bush, as president, eventually reneged on his campaign promise because of political pressures to maintain and increase government spending. A vast group of politicians, administrators, and employees have a vested interest in maintaining and increasing the scope of activities of existing agencies.

It should be noted that agency decision making operates within the congressional-bureaucratic system discussed earlier. Consequently, agency bureaucrats are beholden, at least to some extent, to a small number of representatives and senators sitting on the relevant oversight committees. Because congressional committee members evaluate an agency's performance and determine future budgets, there are pressures for agencies to serve congressional interests.[19]

GOVERNMENT FAILURE

A number of general shortcomings of the political process have already been discussed in contrasting private and collective choice (chapter 3). Consider now other things that can go wrong in the operation of the political process. There is "government failure" at each stage of the collective-choice process.

Voting

A problem arises in delegating choice. Citizens do not usually vote directly on government policies. Instead, they vote for delegates who make policy choices and who are elected on an infrequent basis—every two years in the House and every six years in the Senate. Thus, limited voting options erode citizens' control over delegates.

Because the same representative takes positions on many different issues in the electoral process, a bundling of issues poses a problem for the voter. A particular citizen, for example, may prefer the Republican candidate's position on national defense but the Democratic candidate's position on agriculture.

Political competition is highly imperfect. Candidates are tied to political parties and face pressures to run on the party platform. The situation with two major parties is analogous to duopoly in a market, where there are only two sellers of a product. In contrast, the ideal political democracy would be perfectly responsive to the "will of the people." That is, there would be no problems because of lack of information, uncertainty, delegation of choice, lags in responsiveness, and so on.

Problems also arise because democratic systems operate on the basis of majority rule. Political decisions are not consistent with the Pareto criterion because they always leave a minority of the electorate dissatisfied. Moreover, once a political decision is made, the same amount of the good or service often is available to everyone regardless of differences in individual preferences. If everyone is provided with or is taxed to provide a given amount of a specific good or service such as national defense or public education, many people will be frustrated. Log rolling, which is one way to take into account the intensity of minority preferences, is a very imprecise means to express the intensities of voter preferences. It should again be noted that the collective-choice process is fundamentally different from the market process in the ability to cater to minority tastes. In private choice, an individual is generally able to satisfy his preferences insofar as his budget permits, even though his tastes might be markedly different from those of the average person.

Responsible Participation

The political arena also provides fewer incentives for responsible behavior. We, as individuals, tend to act most responsibly when acting on our own behalf within a system of well-defined property rights and liability rules. As a result, we are likely to spend more time in the process of purchasing an automobile than in investigating candidates before voting in a legislative, congressional, or presidential race. There is a good reason for doing so. The effort spent in investigating cars will likely make more difference to our own welfare than the time spent in finding out about various political candidates. Whereas a voter may rationally choose to remain ignorant of political issues, equivalent ignorance in market decisions is much more likely to impose severe penalties.

A comparison of private choice with the collective-choice process suggests that responsible behavior is closely related to the existence and enforcement of property rights. Nothing invites irresponsible conduct as much as resources "owned" by everyone—the common-property resource problem. This problem is inherent in government spending decisions. Because voters, politicians, and bureaucrats are engaged in spending other people's money, with no claim to any residual profits, they have little incentive to economize. This problem is illuminated by the following principle: *nobody spends somebody else's money as carefully as he spends his own.*[20] This principle suggests that there may be substantial gains from extending well-defined private property rights into areas that are now publicly financed or treated as communal property or both.[21]

Short-Run Focus of the Political Process

The long run for the politician (and for many bureaucrats) is the next election. Herman Talmadge, who served for ten years as chairman of the Senate Agriculture Committee, incisively describes the short-run nature of the political process: "Most politicians live and breathe 24 hours a day in the hope of getting re-elected. They're politically motivated. Re-election means more to them than anything on the face of the earth except a death in their immediate families. And sometimes I think that if the family's not too close, the family would be secondary."[22]

The short-run nature of the political process explains politicians' preference for programs where the benefits are immediate and the costs are deferred. As vividly demonstrated in 1995, it is politically unpopular, for example, to enact policies that will balance the federal budget.[23] The costs of doing so are immediate, whereas the benefits occur in the long run when current incumbents may be out of office. Similarly, policies to reduce benefit levels of Social Security, agricultural subsidies, or other programs typically are considered to be politically infeasible, especially in an election year. Indeed, as shown later, it is much more likely that incumbent politicians will attempt to manipulate government policies for short-run political purposes. The conclusion is that the quest for votes encourages politicians to take a short-run perspective. Consequently, there is no assurance that any nonoptimal provision of public goods owing to "market failure" will be solved through collective action.

There is also evidence that the short-run focus of the political process creates economic instability. After analyzing elections from 1947 to 1976, Edward Tufte found a two-year political business cycle during which real income growth increased in eight of eleven election years as a result of increases in transfer payments. Tufte concluded that incumbent administrations manipulate short-run government policies affecting Social Security, veterans benefits, and so on in attempts to influence upcoming elections.[24] As shown in later chapters, short-run political considerations also loom large in the administration of agricultural programs.

Although the incentive structure of the political process quite often works against politicians and bureaucrats' taking actions in the best interest of the public at large, there is another reason why such public officials do not act in the "public interest." It is impossible for them to do so, as previously indicated, because of limits on information, conflicting interests, and the inherent difficulties in even defining the concept. This problem leads even the most selfless decision maker in the political process to choose some other goal, such as budget maximization.

Rationale for Economic Regulation

The problem of meaningfully defining the public interest is closely related to that of determining the rationale for government intervention. There is no consensus concerning the justifications for economic regulation by government. The conventional view has been that economic regulation in agriculture and other areas is instituted to protect the public interest. This explanation does not appear to be valid, either for many programs in agriculture, or for other areas that benefit the few at the expense of the many.

The *capture theory* is a distinctly different theory of economic regulation.[25] This theory holds that economic regulation is sought and initiated by the industry being regulated as a way to restrict competition and increase income. The capture theory appears to have relevance for much of the economic regulation of the USDA and other agencies initiated during the New Deal era. When applied to agriculture, the theory is consistent with the thesis of this book—that many USDA activities are better explained by rent seeking than by market failure. These regulations were initially sought by farmers, and many of them continue to be supported largely by agricultural interests.

The capture theory does not, however, appear to be very helpful in explaining the spate of safety and environmental regulations and agencies instituted during the 1970s, including the Occupational Safety and Health Administration (OSHA) and the Environmental Protection Agency (EPA). Support for these activities and environmental provisions in recent farm bills came largely from outside interests rather than from the firms subject to the regulations.

All of the preceding factors responsible for "government failure" can be traced to the two previously mentioned general problems inherent in the collective-choice process (see chapter 3). These problems warrant more emphasis. First, there are *incentive problems* caused by the *separation of power* and *responsibility*. Public officials are unlikely to economize because they neither bear the full costs nor reap the full benefits of their decisions. Cost saving that leaves unspent budgetary funds, for example, is likely to affect the public-agency deci-

sion maker's income and power adversely. Thus, there is no incentive to economize as there is with private ownership, where cost-saving innovations increase
the innovator's income. Another frequently observed action resulting from perverse incentives is the mad scramble to exhaust the budget of a public agency
near the end of the fiscal year. The budget in this case is treated as a common-
pool resource. "A common pool resembles one soda being consumed by several
small boys each with a straw. The 'rule of capture' is in effect: ownership of the
liquid is not established until it is in one's possession."[26] The discussion so far
is restricted to public officials' legal responses to economic incentives. As government grows, however, the opportunities and incentives for corruption also
increase.[27]

Second, there are also *information problems* owing to the *separation of power*
and *knowledge*. Even if government agencies were run by selfless public servants
dedicated to serving the public interest, they would be unable to do so. The secretary of agriculture, for example, has no objective way to determine the correct price-support level for milk or the optimal amount of subsidized credit to
extend to farmers. These programs are income-redistribution programs, and,
consequently, there is no value-free means to determine how much income, if
any, should be redistributed; that is, how extensive and costly these and similar
programs should be inevitably involves value judgments.

IMPROVING THE COLLECTIVE-CHOICE PROCESS

Recent presidents have attempted to make the federal bureaucracy more responsive to their policy agendas but have had little success.[28] Many programs are
mandated by Congress and are beyond the president's immediate control.
Further, a president does not have the time to monitor the actions of the vast
federal bureaucracy, which comprises more than two thousand agencies. Thus,
as long as bureaucrats do not draw too much attention, they are usually left
largely on their own. Although no reform can eliminate the incentive and information problems inherent in government bureaus, there is increasing interest
in possible measures to reduce the magnitude of these problems. *Privatization*
refers to a range of measures designed to increase the role of market forces in
the delivery of goods and services currently financed, produced, or regulated by
government.[29] The most common types of privatization involve contracting out
or franchise arrangements, user charges, and so-called load shedding in which
government bows out and allows private producers to produce and offer goods
and services directly to consumers. There is evidence that user fees, franchises,

contracting out, and other privatization measures can improve current methods of financing and producing collectively provided goods and services.[30] None of these limited privatization procedures, however, provides the incentive and informational advantages of production under decentralized competitive conditions.

The potential for cost reduction through various types of privatization is affecting the mix of publicly and privately funded activities in countries throughout the world. In the United States, for example, some state and local governments have contracted out such services as garbage collection, janitorial services of publicly owned buildings, and even the operation of prisons. Privatization also is affecting agricultural policy. In an economywide restructuring that began in 1984, the New Zealand government eliminated output subsidies for farm products and fully privatized extension-type farmer advisory services. Moreover, Ministry of Agriculture activities such as meat and food inspection now operate on a self-sustaining basis.[31]

SUMMARY

Public-choice theory involves the use of economic principles to explain political decisions. Economic costs and benefits are important in decisions by the individual voter, by political candidates, by legislators, by the executive, and by the bureaucracy that administers and implements the laws enacted by the legislature. Just as markets work imperfectly compared to the ideal of perfect competition, the political process also "fails" when compared to the perfect polity.

Public-choice theory demonstrates why majority rule in a democracy does not guarantee results consistent with individual preferences. In voting, political competition is highly imperfect because of information problems, uncertainty, and delegation of choice. There is a short-run bias in the political process in favor of programs where benefits are immediate and costs are deferred. Finally, there are inherent information and incentive problems in the collective-choice process. Whereas price and profit signals induce economizing behavior by consumers and producers in decentralized markets, there are no comparable signals in public agencies. Votes and bureaucratic inducements provide no reliable signals concerning how much to produce or whether production is beneficial. The conclusion is that the presence of "market imperfections" such as externalities, monopoly, lack of information, and public goods does not necessarily warrant government intervention. The relevant choice is always between imperfect institutional arrangements.

The theory of public choice emphasizes that problems similar to those affecting private choice are no less important in the collective-choice process. Furthermore, in the public sector, no one in authority personally gains by using resources in ways that are most beneficial to the public at large. The absence of residual claimants in government and the presence of the incentive to cater to special-interest groups give rise to rent-seeking activities by individuals and groups with narrowly focused interests. There is increasing interest in contracting out, user charges, and other privatization measures as a means of reducing the magnitude of problems associated with the production and financing of goods and services provided through the collective-choice process.

5

Implications of Public-Choice
Theory for Agricultural Policy

Government policy in U.S. agriculture has changed dramatically over time. During the first 150 years of our country's independence, the federal government had relatively little influence on the production and marketing of goods and services. During the Great Depression of the 1930s, however, a dramatic increase occurred in government economic regulation and income support to farmers. And there was another significant change in the method used to redistribute income to farmers in 1996. This change was undone, to some extent, by the 2002 farm bill.

Why has government provided so much financial assistance over the years to the farm sector? An understanding of the operation of the political process is helpful in answering this question. It is assumed throughout this book that the public-policy process in agriculture is not fundamentally different from that in other areas. In this chapter, public-choice theory is applied specifically to the development of U.S. agricultural policy, and it is shown why similar pressures exist to overspend on agricultural programs as on programs in other sectors of the economy.

THE CHANGING AGRICULTURAL AGENDA

Productivity was the dominant theme of public policies directly affecting agriculture during the latter half of the nineteenth century when several important pieces of legislation affecting agriculture were enacted. The creation of the USDA in 1862 raised agriculture to cabinet status at the federal level. The

Morrill Act of 1862 created the land-grant college complex. The Hatch Act of 1887 provided funds to each state for agricultural research leading to the system of state agricultural experiment stations. The Smith-Lever Act of 1914 created the cooperative federal-state Agricultural Extension Service, and the Smith-Hughes Act of 1917 provided federal support for the teaching of vocational agriculture in high schools.

Prior to the Roosevelt administration in the 1930s, government programs in agriculture were small and seldom directly affected the individual farmer. Federal intervention in agriculture, however, increased dramatically during the Great Depression as President Roosevelt launched a host of "action programs" in agriculture, many of which are still in existence. The nature and effects of the various price-support, production-control, credit subsidy, crop insurance, conservation, and other farm programs initiated at that time are the major focus of later chapters of this book.

What brings about changes in the agricultural public-policy agenda? A dramatic change in public policy is typically associated with an economic crisis. The "emergency" label was attached to almost every piece of early New Deal legislation enacted during the economic chaos of the Great Depression.[1]

New groups also arise periodically to challenge the status quo. The challenge is often in the form of some attention-getting event or action. The modern environmental movement, for example, can be traced to the publication of Rachel Carson's book *Silent Spring* in the early 1960s. Similarly, the "hunger lobby" in the 1960s was important in increasing funds for food stamp and other food assistance programs.

Prior to the 1960s, the agricultural policy agenda was dominated by commercial agricultural interests. Since that time, many groups—including rural nonfarm residents, the poverty lobby, hired farmworkers, minority groups, consumers, safety advocates, and environmentalists—have challenged traditional farm programs. The large increase in government expenditures for food stamp and other transfer programs and for safety, environmental, and civil rights legislation since the mid-1960s is a reflection of these various groups' effectiveness in the public-policy process. During this period, many new programs affecting agriculture were enacted outside the usual agricultural policy process. Regulation of pesticides, for example, was assigned to the newly created EPA in 1970. Agricultural safety became the concern of OSHA. In addition, the interest of urban groups in agricultural programs increased as the food assistance portion of the USDA budget increased dramatically.

A model of the agricultural policy-making process is shown in figure 5.1.[2] It emphasizes the fact that interest groups play an integral role in agricultural legislation. Numerous interest groups are now heavily involved in determining the agenda for agricultural legislation.[3] First, the research and education movement goes back to the pre–New Deal era. The USDA and the state experiment stations associated with the land-grant universities play a key role in maintaining public support for agricultural research. This public research establishment measures and publicizes the benefits of agricultural research and lobbies to maintain and increase public funding for this activity. The network of extension workers in every state associated with the land-grant colleges is also important in maintaining support for the continuation and increase of government research, education, and extension efforts in agriculture.

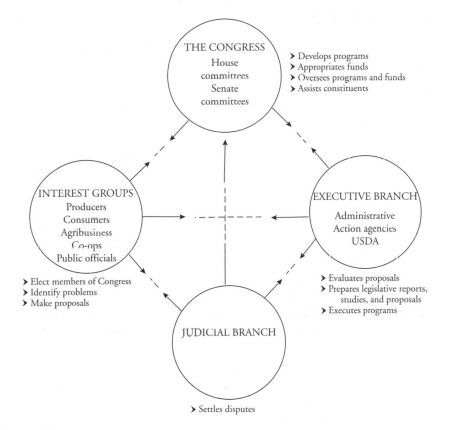

FIGURE 5.1 Model of the agricultural policy-making process.

Second, certain groups support the income-support, price-support, production-control, and other farm programs inherited from the New Deal era. In this movement, individual commodity groups (e.g., the American Soybean Association) and farm organizations (e.g., the American Farm Bureau

Federation) continue to play important roles. Numerous political action committees (PACs) augment efforts by these professional farm groups, which frequently engage in lobbying activities.

Third, agribusiness groups, including farm supply and marketing cooperatives, are important political forces in maintaining government programs that stimulate farm production, which thereby increases the demand for their products and services.

Fourth, the network made up of county Farm Service Agency (FSA), Natural Resources Conservation Service, and Rural Development offices that administer the price-support, credit, rural development, conservation, and other programs is also important in ensuring grassroots support for government intervention in agriculture.

A fifth group, consisting of individuals interested in food stamps, environmental controls, and other consumer issues, is also increasingly important in the legislative process affecting farm policies. Don Paarlberg coined the term *new agenda* to indicate this relatively new influence of small farmers, farmworkers, the poor, racial minorities, consumers, and environmentalists, an influence he attributed to various "public-interest" advocates.[4] This group has a vast clientele and significant political clout, as evidenced by the large increases in public expenditures on consumer, environmental, and poverty programs during the past several decades. The impact of this group on the USDA agenda has grown greater at the expense of commercial agriculture. As one example, USDA expenditures for subsidized food programs have increased dramatically since the mid-1960s relative to outlays on price supports and other programs that more directly benefit commercial agriculture.

Finally, consumer and other groups that some might argue represent the public at large are becoming more vocal. There is an increasing recognition that farm programs affecting wheat, corn, milk, peanuts, oranges, sugar, and other commodities benefit producer groups at the expense of consumers and taxpayers. Price-support programs, as shown later, raise domestic prices of farm products and often require import controls to prevent U.S. consumers from purchasing lower-priced imports. Domestic manufacturers who use price-supported products such as peanuts, sugar, tobacco, and so on as inputs in production also frequently are critical of farm programs.

In recent farm bills, vote trading between agricultural and urban interests has become more important. Agricultural interests have supported food stamps, minimum wages, solar energy development in agriculture, and other projects in exchange for urban backing for price supports and other farm programs. Despite the decrease in numbers of farms, commercial agricultural interests continue to get government programs enacted that transfer income to them through such means as direct government payments or through higher product prices to consumers. The farm sector's current political clout is surprising when it is realized that only approximately 3 percent of the population lives on farms. Moreover, the dairy, tobacco, sugar, and several other price-support programs apply only to a small section of the total farm population. How are these relatively small groups of farmers able to use government for their own ends?

THE BIAS OF THE COLLECTIVE-CHOICE PROCESS IN AGRICULTURE

In the previous chapter, it was shown why there is generally a systematic bias toward expansion of the role of government. The political process is oriented toward the short run, and each government official has an incentive to maintain and increase the scope of his or her own agency. Moreover, the political process is biased in favor of activities that confer concentrated benefits on the few but impose widely dispersed and (often delayed) costs on the many. This description of the collective-choice process appears to be consistent with current agricultural programs.

Agribusiness

Consider the farmers and agribusiness groups who benefit from government programs affecting sugar, dairy, wheat, feed grains, tobacco, and other products.[5] When economic benefits to a small group can be achieved through political action at relatively low cost, that group has an economic incentive to use the political process to obtain wealth transfers. For example, prior to consideration of the much criticized sugar program in the 1990 farm bill, sugar PACs contributed almost $340,000 to congressional candidates in the 1988 election cycle.[6] More recently, between 1995 and 1999, supporters of the troubled sugar program contributed $7.2 million by means of PACs, soft money, and individual donations.[7] Regardless of whether these contributions were a key factor in the reauthorization of the sugar program in recent farm bills, there is no doubt about the effectiveness of sugar, tobacco, peanut, cotton, and wheat and feed grain interest groups in maintaining and often expanding the role of government in agriculture.[8]

The assistance provided by government to well-organized groups may occur in a number of different ways, including price supports, subsidies, tax relief, and protection from competition. The major types of government farm programs are described in later chapters. Product price supports through the years prior to 1996 were the most costly farm program in terms of government Treasury outlays. The 1996 farm bill partially removed the link between income-support payments and market prices for a number of commodities by providing seven annual fixed (but declining) payments to producers that were independent of farm prices. The link was not completely severed, however, and with the passage of the 2002 farm bill, the link between government payments and market prices was firmly reestablished.[9]

It should be noted that in a significant sector of agriculture, including many fruits and vegetables, poultry, and livestock, there have been no effective price-support programs. This largely unregulated sector of agriculture accounts for approximately one-half to two-thirds of U.S. farm production. Public-choice theory has been quite successful in explaining how small groups of agricultural producers are able to use the political process to increase their own wealth. This theory has been less successful in explaining why a sizable proportion of U.S. farmers and commodity groups either have made little effort or have had limited success in restricting competition through political action. Published research examining the issue of why there is variation in government support for commodity groups over time and across commodities, however, has provided some insights into this issue. Bruce Gardner, for example, finds that producer groups with high costs of generating political influence receive less support and that an increase in the social cost (deadweight loss) of transferring income to producer groups reduces government support.[10]

The USDA

The USDA, a component of the executive branch of government, is a second important interest group directly involved in the policy process. Consistent with earlier discussions of producers', politicians', and bureaucrats' incentives, the USDA until fairly recently was generally viewed as representing farmers instead of the public at large. Indeed, the USDA mainly represented commercial farmers before and after World War II until the late 1960s. Since that time, the influence of consumer, environmental, and other groups on USDA policy has increased at the expense of commercial agriculture. In the Carter administration (1977–80), the USDA actively cultivated the support of groups "favoring better nutrition, environmental protection and rural community development."[11] Regardless of the relative strength of the different groups influencing USDA activities, decision makers in the USDA have an incentive to expand the agency's role because power and perquisites tend to be positively correlated with agency size. Consequently, USDA officials predictably seek to expand the range and scope of the agency's activities.

Congressional Committees

The legislative committees of Congress are a third interest group directly involved in the agricultural policy process. Legislators from farm states tend to dominate the agricultural committees and subcommittees. Members of these committees tend to favor expanded government programs, both because they typically represent districts where the commodities affected are important and because expanded programs increase their power and influence. This is not merely a matter of conscious wealth seeking or aggrandizement of power. Members of special-interest groups generally have the ability to rationalize that whatever is in their own interest is also in the "public interest." Thus, program proponents in tobacco and dairy production areas come to view the tobacco program or the dairy program as beneficial to a legislator's own district and, indeed, to the entire nation. In addition to farm groups, the USDA, and congressional committees, various consumer and environmental groups also actively participate in the legislative process when proposed agricultural legislation is related to food stamp benefits, environmental issues, or other areas of concern.

THE PROBLEM OF BUDGET DISCIPLINE

To put the growth of federal agricultural programs in perspective, it is useful to discuss some reasons why government spending in general has increased. Such a perspective is particularly appropriate given both the recent change from surplus to deficit status of the federal budget and the large increase in expected spending in the 2002 farm bill.

After the federal budget operated in the red continuously for twenty-nine years (1970–97), surpluses emerged in 1998 and continued through 2001 (table 5.1). Chronic federal budget deficits (and increasing federal debt) intensified a long-standing public concern about lack of federal budget discipline. The annual budget deficit exceeded $100 billion each year from 1982 to 1996, ranging between $107 billion and $290 billion. Larger nominal deficits, however, did not necessarily mean larger real deficits because of inflation. The largest real deficit, $207.8 billion, occurred in 1983, amounting to 6.1 percent of gross domestic product (GDP) (table 5.1).

Did the emergence of a budget surplus in 1998 portend the end of the chronic tendency for federal budget deficits? Why did a surplus occur after twenty-eight years of continuous deficits? Was there a change in the underlying political economy that gave rise to deficits for almost three decades? Or were the surpluses at the end of the century owing to unique economic conditions prevailing at that time? There appears to be a great deal of evidence to support political economist Paul Heyne's conclusion that "The surplus that finally emerged in 1998 after almost three decades of unrelenting deficits was not produced by any turn toward virtue on Capitol Hill or in the White House but by the greatly increased tax revenues that a sustained economic expansion generated."[12]

Deficits exceeding $200 billion annually from 1990 to 1994 fell steadily and finally turned into a surplus in 1998 mostly because of healthy increases in government receipts during the longest peacetime expansion in economic activity in U.S. history.[13] The federal government relies heavily on income taxes for revenue, and corporate and personal income tax receipts increase automatically in periods of economic expansion and fall during economic recessions. The budget deficits in 2002 and 2003 support the position in the preceding quote that recent surpluses were not caused by any "turn toward virtue" in political arenas.

Why did the federal government run chronic budget deficits for almost thirty years? The long string of budget deficits prior to 1998 occurred despite the adoption of a new budget process in 1974 and other futile congressional attempts to control the deficit. The 1974 budget process consisted of a budget resolution that sets the annual spending level based on revenue estimates and "budget reconciliation," the process by which Congress presumably stays under the spending ceiling. This attempt was followed by the Deficit Reduction Act of 1985, which established a procedure to reduce the deficit year by year so that the deficit would be eliminated by 1991. The budget deficit, in fact, was more than $250 billion in 1991, and the Deficit Reduction Act was effectively discarded.

Attempts by both Democratic and Republican administrations to eliminate the deficit were unsuccessful until the prolonged economic expansion of the 1990s yielded a cornucopia of federal revenue. However, the federal government operated in the red even in times of economic boom as well as during recessions. During the 1980s and 1990s, for example, federal tax receipts were around 18–20 percent of GDP—higher than they were during most post–World War II years before budget deficits became a chronic problem in the early 1970s. The deficit problem emerged and persisted because government outlays were 20–23 percent of GDP—significantly higher than government receipts.[14] Thus, the evidence suggests that the chronic federal budget deficits from the early 1970s until 1998 were rooted in increases in spending rather than in reductions in tax receipts.

TABLE 5.1 Federal Budget Deficits as a Percentage of GDP, Fiscal Years 1969–2003.

Fiscal Year	Surplus or Deficit	
	Billions of Dollars	Percent of GDP
1969	3.2	.3
1970	-2.8	-.3
1971	-23.0	-2.1
1972	-23.4	-2.0
1973	-14.9	-1.1
1974	-6.1	-.4
1975	-53.2	-3.4
1976	-73.7	-4.2
1977	-53.7	-2.7
1978	-59.2	-2.7
1979	-40.7	-1.6
1980	-73.8	-2.7
1981	-79.0	-2.6
1982	-128.0	-4.0
1983	-207.8	-6.0
1984	-185.4	-4.8
1985	-212.3	-5.1
1986	-221.2	-5.0
1987	-149.8	-3.2
1988	-155.2	-3.1
1989	-152.5	-2.8
1990	-221.2	-3.9
1991	-269.4	-4.5
1992	-290.4	-4.7
1993	-255.1	-3.9
1994	-203.3	-2.9
1995	-164.0	-2.2
1996	-107.5	-1.4
1997	-22.0	-0.3
1998	69.2	0.8
1999	124.6	1.4
2000	236.4	2.4
2001	127.0	1.3
2002[a]	-46.0	–
2003[a]	-40.0	–

[a] CBO Baseline Projections.
Sources: For 1969–2000, *Budget of the United State Government, FY2002* at:
http://www.gpoaccess.gov/usbudget/fy02/browse.html. Historical Tables 1.1 and 1.2; for
2001–2003 at: http://www.cbo.gov/showdoc.cfm?index=1944&sequence=0&from=7.

The budget deficits occurred in part because government transfers have become increasingly important. During the past fifty years, efforts by individuals and groups to obtain and maintain wealth transfers under the aegis of the state have dramatically increased.[15] On the other hand, there has been a relative decrease in efforts devoted to production. This phenomenon is not restricted to agriculture. The sugar program, for example, is similar in this respect to a host of other programs, including education subsidies, steel tariffs, auto import quotas, and food assistance programs.

In achieving their objectives, groups use their lobbying power to influence governmental policy, thereby bringing about an increase in the scope and complexity of government. The implementation of a government program requires highly detailed rules and regulations, which both increases administrative cost and reduces entrepreneurial flexibility. Mancur Olson argues that the effect of the increase in transfer-seeking activities by specialized pressure groups is gradual strangulation of the economy.[16] Moreover, as special-interest groups become more important and distributional issues more significant, political issues become more divisive. Efforts by specialized pressure groups to achieve wealth transfers have intensified since the mid-1960s. F. A. Hayek graphically describes the effect of these efforts on the political system: "So long as it is legitimate for government to use force to effect a redistribution of material benefits . . . there can be no curb on the rapacious instincts of all groups who want more for themselves. Once politics becomes a tug-of-war for shares of the income pie, decent government is impossible."[17] As shown later, such rent-seeking behavior poses a social dilemma both for voters and their congressional representatives.

Rent Seeking—a Social Dilemma

A prisoners' dilemma incentive problem must be overcome in establishing and maintaining the appropriate institutional framework or set of rules that govern political relationships in a democratic system.[18] The prisoners' dilemma is a negative-sum game that often results in an outcome that participants jointly prefer less than another pair of outcomes. In the anecdote first used to illustrate this breakdown of the invisible hand, two prisoners in isolated cells face interrogation after they are arrested for a crime.[19] The prisoners jointly do worse when each prisoner's response is based on narrow self-interest than when each shows restraint. Similarly, as shown later, individuals and groups have incentives to engage in rent-seeking activities to the extent that opportunities for individual gains exist within the prevailing institutional framework. These incentives create a social dilemma. The prisoners' dilemma model demonstrates that the invisible hand of self-interest in the political process often leads individuals to make socially harmful choices.

A social dilemma arises for the electorate in a democratic society because rent seekers, in striving to increase their income, face problems related to the prisoners' dilemma.[20] In the hypothetical situation depicted in table 5.2, the economy is aggregated into two sectors—agriculture and all other sectors combined. Participants in each sector may engage in two types of activity in their attempts to increase wealth—market activity and rent-seeking political activity. If participants restrict their activities to production and exchange, market activity is the sole source of income. If individuals and groups are successful in rent seeking political activity, however, income is augmented by government programs that restrict competition, such as subsidies, price supports, trade restrictions, and so on.

TABLE 5.2 Rent Seeking and the Prisoners' Dilemma.

		Other Sectors	
		Production and Exchange	Rent Seeking
Agricultural Sector	Production and Exchange	200, 800	100, 850
	Rent Seeking	250, 500	125, 600

Consider the hypothetical situation depicted in table 5.2, where the numbers in each cell represent GDP in the agricultural and "other" sectors, respectively. If activity in each sector is limited to production and trade, the combined GDP is 1,000: 200 for agriculture and 800 for the rest of the economy. If, however, both sectors engage in rent-seeking activity, there is a significant decline in income in each sector and in combined income (from 1,000 to 725: 125 for agriculture and 600 for the rest of the economy).

The social dilemma is that an outcome that all would prefer to avoid occurs if decision makers in each sector cannot make binding agreements and instead act on the basis of narrowly defined self-interest. For example, as shown in table 5.2, if individuals in agriculture engage in rent seeking, but those in other sectors refrain, income in the agricultural sector increases to 250, an amount larger than that from production and exchange alone (250 versus 200). Moreover, if groups in other sectors engage in rent-seeking activity, agricultural income is higher with rent seeking than if individuals in agriculture restricted their activities to production and exchange (125 versus 100). Thus, when the dominant strategy for each sector is to engage in rent seeking—regardless of what the other sector does—the result is a significant reduction in income to both sectors!

In general, individuals and groups have incentives to expend time and money on the political process to secure economic gains, no matter what others do, although the effect is to reduce total output. In short, there is a social dilemma because the dominant strategy is to engage in rent-seeking activity even though income would be higher for each group if all groups refrained from rent seeking. The relevance of this model in explaining why it is difficult to reduce rent seeking by dairy, sugar, corn, peanut, and other agricultural interest groups in agriculture is described later in this chapter.

A similar social dilemma also manifests itself in the behavior of elected public officials. Political decision makers have an incentive to treat the budget as a common-pool resource, with everybody racing to get their share before the resource is exhausted—even if they prefer that the government expenditure not be made at all. This attitude creates fiscal irresponsibility. A comparison of the federal budget to a dinner check demonstrates the overspending bias inherent in the collective-choice process.[21]

The Federal Budget as a Common-Pool Resource

Suppose one hundred people go out to eat. Compare each individual's likely behavior under two different situations. In the first, each person pays his own bill; in the second, the bill is divided evenly. Each individual has an incentive to spend more in the latter case because eating a one-dollar dessert under the check-splitting arrangement, for example, would cost the individual only one cent (rather than one dollar). Incentives in the political process, where the costs of increased benefits for one interest group are split among all taxpayers, parallel the incentives in the check-splitting arrangement. Thus, the collective-choice process leads to "pork-barrel" legislation in agriculture and other areas. Because the amount a legislative district will pay toward, for example, a dairy price-support program is very small relative to its total cost, every representative in Congress has an incentive to obtain income transfers for farmers (and other special-interest groups) in his or her legislative district.

The analogy of the federal budget to a dinner check can be carried one step further. Suppose the check is to be divided evenly among the large group, but the ordering will be done by committee so there will be separate committees for drinks, appetizers, entrees, salads, and desserts. Because each person is able to serve on the committee of his (or her) choice, lushes end up on the drinks committee, vegetarians on the salad committee, sweet tooths on the dessert committee, and so on. This arrangement further exacerbates the tendency toward overordering and overspending. The arrangement just described closely resembles the committee structure of the U.S. Congress.

The dinner check analogy is even more telling if one assumes that the diner can use a special type of credit card in which the bill does not have to be paid if the diner loses his job or retires. "Buy now—pay later" is very appealing to the representative primarily concerned with getting reelected. The conclusion is that spreading the costs in small shares while concentrating benefits creates incentives for the continued expansion of government activity. As suggested earlier, the collective-choice process necessarily produces majorities and minorities, winners and losers, and a separation of cost and benefit calculations.

The congressional reforms of the 1970s, which increased the powers of narrowly focused congressional subcommittees, have contributed greatly to the problem of overspending. The powerful subcommittees in agriculture (and other areas) encourage lobbying by commodity groups.

REDUCING THE OVERSPENDING BIAS

Governments that respond to popular opinion are tempted to spend more than they collect in taxes.[22] The problem of overspending has created interest in ways to offset both the inherent bias toward overspending in a democratic system and the increase in government that tends to accompany such overspending.[23] What is the solution to this systematic bias toward expansion of the federal government's role in agriculture and other areas? Some political analysts view basic institutional and constitutional change as the only appropriate avenue for constructive reform and improvement.[24] Others deny that institutional and constitutional changes will be effective, contending instead that the problem is political.[25]

The Overspending Bias and Institutional Reform

The prisoners' dilemma model also helps explain the actions of both voters and elected officials. It demonstrates why rent seeking is likely to be substituted for production and exchange in a democratic society unless the potential benefits from rent seeking are restrained by constitutional rules that affect all. Unless there is a general agreement that prevents rent seeking by all groups, every group will have an incentive to use the political process to further its own economic interests. Moreover, each group's congressional representatives have an incentive to respond to the group's desires. Each group and its political representatives, even if fully aware of the harmful effects of "special-interest" legislation, has an incentive to maintain the group's special advantage and to free ride on attempts to restrict similar opportunities for others.[26] In short, without an agreement that simultaneously affects all groups, the pursuit of self-interest through the political process is likely to be self-defeating both for the individual and for society.

If political decision makers were motivated solely by narrowly defined self-interest, efforts to restrain rent seeking through institutional reform, a "public good," would appear to be doomed. A member of Congress cannot expect to benefit personally from efforts devoted to improving the political system. The potential benefits from institutional reforms to balance the budget or to achieve other generally agreed upon desirable goals are uncertain, will occur in the future, and will benefit the public at large, whereas the costs are highly concentrated and occur immediately.[27]

Constitutional Political Economy

Public-choice theory emphasizes the lack of effective incentives for members of Congress who might like to alter the institutional framework to achieve long-run goals. This lack of incentives suggests, in turn, that good government is much more a matter of having institutions that channel self-interest in valuable directions than it is of electing "better people" or of exhorting people to act in the "public interest."[28] That is, success in coping with rent seeking, special-interest legislation, and bureaucratic inefficiency and waste hinges much more on the ability to develop, institute, and maintain sound rules and procedures than on the characteristics of individuals who occupy positions of political power.

A new subfield of public-choice theory, *constitutional political economy*, emphasizes the importance of the institutional framework and focuses on the importance of considering the economic, political, and social effects of alternative institutional arrangements in public-policy analysis.[29] Recent attempts to amend the Constitution to control federal spending indicate the acknowledged importance of institutional arrangements on actions of the executive and legislative branches of government. In traditional approaches, policy analysts in agriculture and in other areas have largely taken the institutional framework as given in considering ways to balance the budget and in evaluating various public-policy alternatives.

James Buchanan, a leading proponent of the constitutional approach, argues that the rules of politics matter and that these rules determine the pattern of outcomes "almost independently of whom we may elect and who writes position papers offering policy advice."[30] In the constitutional approach, a necessary prerequisite to reform is the development of a wider recognition of the effects of organized groups that use governmental power to enhance their own wealth. As things stand now, the failure of a specific farm program, for example, will only rarely lead to its abandonment because it will almost always be supported by at least one vociferous interest group that benefits from the program. Hayek graphically argues that the eventual outcome of these redistributive activities (and the resulting overspending bias) will be a continuing increase in the share of income controlled by government, which "if allowed to continue, would before long swallow up the whole of society in the organization of government."[31]

Hayek's analysis is consistent with Olson's hypothesis that the redistribution costs associated with the increase in specialized pressure groups as they expend resources to obtain and maintain government transfers is a key factor in nations' declining growth rates.[32] Consequently, it might be argued that educating the public on the incentives inherent in the political process is a necessary and sufficient condition to achieve meaningful reductions in government spending. Indeed, some analysts argue that public recognition of the problem and public pressure for action would be enough to reduce rent seeking significantly and to offset the bias toward increased government spending.[33]

Even if the harmful long-run effects of individuals and groups' efforts to achieve income transfers are fully recognized, however, there is a "you-first" problem in limiting government activity. The dairy farmer, for example, is generally reluctant to start the process, even if he or she recognizes the desirability of limiting transfer activity. As is the case for all other recipients of government largesse, the dairy farmer has an incentive to take the following position: "I will give up my government aid if the aid to other groups also stops." But no one has an incentive to be first.[34] Indeed, the dairy farmer has an economic incentive to attempt to maintain the dairy program while favoring a reduction in the transfers received by steelworkers, textile workers, schoolteachers, and other groups. The federal budget problem may eventually become so great, however, that dairy farmers and other transfer recipients will have to agree to constitutional limits on their program benefits if others will also agree to do so.[35]

An analysis of different methods of limiting the harmful effects of narrowly focused interest groups in agriculture (and other areas) is beyond the scope of this book. Various constitutional measures, including balanced-budget and line item veto amendments, have been proposed to reduce the bias toward overspending by the federal government.[36] Constitutional restrictions affecting government spending might have an important psychological impact on members of Congress. Such measures, however, are no panacea because legislators are likely to find ways, such as off-budget spending, to circumvent statutory and constitutional roadblocks. As one skeptical observer noted, "The proposed statutes setting limits on expenditures . . . have a glaring political weakness. Congress can, if it wishes, waive or override them."[37]

It is also possible that institutional changes in the congressional committee system might be helpful in reducing the current bias that favors the interests of highly organized small groups at the expense of the public at large. A system of random or rotating committee assignments in Congress, for example, is one possible change. Under a system of rotating committee assignments it would be less likely that dairy, tobacco, or other narrow interests would be able to use the political process to obtain programs that benefit the few at the expense of the many. A problem, as in the case of an urban representative serving on an agriculture committee, however, would be that members of such committees are likely to have little knowledge of the issues or industries affected by their actions.

Granting the president line item veto power is another possible means of decreasing the role of government by reducing vote trading and pork-barrel legislation. No one knows, however, how the new presidential power would work in practice. By strengthening the executive branch, a line item veto might result in increased spending if the president were able to use threats to veto congressional priorities as leverage to press for increased spending on his own programs.[38] In sum, there is no consensus concerning the extent to which the spending and deficit problem is institutional and constitutional as opposed to political and educational. As a result, there is no consensus concerning the appropriate approach for correcting these problems.

Ideas Have Consequences

It is conceivable, however, that a change in public attitudes might make it possible to bring about fundamental institutional reform, despite the inherent obstacles in changing the political system to reduce rent-seeking opportunities. The evidence is strong that "ideas have consequences."[39] The New Zealand deregulation episode of the 1980s is a case in point.[40] Despite people's economic incentives to act in their own narrowly defined self-interest, there was a dramatic restructuring of the New Zealand economy in 1984, including the elimination of most agricultural subsidies. Knowledge by key public officials about the harmful effects of protectionist policies increased public awareness of the benefits of competition and of the fact that statist policies had reduced the standard of living. Decreased public support for the status quo helped create a political climate conducive to institutional reform.[41] The success of the New Zealand economic reforms affecting agriculture reflects an important insight of constitutional political economy. The political consensus that largely eliminated protectionist agricultural policies in New Zealand was made much easier both because of the existing economic crisis and because it was part of a general agreement that simultaneously deregulated other sectors of the economy.

SUMMARY

Although U.S. agricultural policies have always arisen through the interaction of the three branches of government, these policies have changed dramatically over time. From 1862 until the 1930s, the major goal of government efforts in agriculture was to increase productivity. During the Great Depression of the 1930s, a host of "action programs" was instituted in the midst of economic chaos. From the USDA's inception in 1862 until the mid-1960s, commercial agriculture dominated the agenda in federal agricultural policy. Since the mid-1960s, the influence of groups concerned about poverty, environmental, and safety issues has increased at the expense of farmer and agribusiness interests.

A systematic bias toward expansion of the role of government exists in agriculture as in other areas. The interaction of interests from commercial agriculture, the USDA, and the legislative committees in Congress tend to advance the interests of narrowly focused groups at the expense of the public at large. The impact of a growing environmental lobby also has increased government regulation, further expanding the role of government in agriculture as in other sectors of the economy. The result has been a dramatic increase both in the growth of government and in government spending during the last quarter of the twentieth century.[42]

Some political analysts contend that the solution to the overspending problem is institutional, whereas others contend that educating the public is the key. Even if the public understands the problem, however, the incentive to overspend remains. A number of institutional and constitutional remedies have been proposed to offset the overspending bias at the federal level. At the legislative level, random or rotating committee assignments might be one way to reduce the influence of commodity groups on agricultural legislation. At the executive level, giving the president the power of line item veto might reduce the amount of pork-barrel and other spending that is not broadly beneficial. Finally, a constitutional limit on government spending, such as through the widely discussed balanced-budget amendment, has been proposed as a way of limiting government expenditures.

It is not clear how effective any of these measures might be in limiting overall spending or what the effect on specific programs might be. Indeed, it has been argued that representative democracy under majority rule is not likely to produce what the majority wants.[43] Rather, it tends to produce what each interest group making up the majority must concede to other groups to get their support for what it wants. Despite the lack of consensus about the nature of the problem, attention is likely to remain high concerning possible ways of reducing the effects of narrowly focused special interests on the democratic process.

6

The Farm Problem and
Economic Justice

The farm problem has historically been considered to be one of relatively low incomes and farm product prices. In large measure, the farm problem can be traced to the destabilizing effects of economic growth. During most of the past two hundred years, the manufacturing and service sectors of the U.S. economy have been growing relative to agriculture. Because agricultural wage rates increased less rapidly than wage rates in the nonfarm sector, it is not surprising that agricultural interests perceived this difference as a "farm problem." Indeed, over the years, many people have challenged the economic growth explanation of the farm problem, arguing that farm incomes are low because of a lack of "bargaining power."

There is also a great deal of interest in the concept of economic justice. The topic is ancient, but a number of economists and philosophers continue to work on the issue of how the economic pie *should* be divided. Some economists, recognizing that consumers are the main beneficiaries of agricultural progress, have argued for a general policy that would compensate farmers for losses associated with economic growth in the economy.[1] Before further consideration of problems relating to farm versus nonfarm income comparisons and economic justice, let us first consider two quite different explanations of the so-called farm problem.

ECONOMIC GROWTH VERSUS MARKET POWER

A great deal of evidence indicates that the farm problem is due primarily to economic growth.[2] Economic growth requires a shift of labor and other resources from farming to other sectors of the economy. In a market system, expected income is the primary means by which labor resources are allocated both within agriculture and between agriculture and other sectors. For resources to be bid away from agriculture in a decentralized market economy, it is necessary for incomes to be higher in nonagricultural sectors than in agriculture.

In U.S. agricultural programs, a great deal of effort has been devoted to raising prices of farm products as a means of increasing farm incomes. With or without farm programs, there has been chronic downward pressure on prices of farm products because supply tends to increase more rapidly than demand as economic growth occurs (figure 6.1). Mechanization, improved seeds, and the development of new pesticides and herbicides have increased supply through dramatic increases in agricultural technology. In 1950, farm employment was 9.9 million in a population of 152 million. By 1997, there were only 3.4 million farmworkers in a population of 268 million.[3] The change in numbers of workers in nonfarm agribusiness firms providing inputs to agriculture and marketing farm products has been much less than the decrease in the number of farmworkers, but data on nonfarm agribusiness employment are not available. During the period from 1950 to 1997, numbers of farmworkers decreased from 5.4 million to 2.1 million, but average farm size increased from 215 to 471 acres per farm.

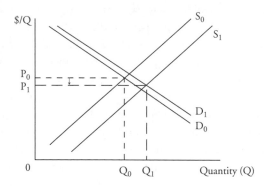

FIGURE 6.1 Why farm product prices tend to decrease with economic growth.

The demand for farm products, which increases mainly owing to increases in population and increases in consumer income, has not increased to the same extent as the supply of farm products. Demand increases resulting from population growth are gradual. Demand shifts owing to increases in consumer income hinge on economic growth and the income elasticity of demand for farm products, which is low relative to that for nonfarm products. This suggests that a smaller and smaller part of the household budget will be spent on food as economic growth occurs.

The demand for farm products faced by farmers in the aggregate is also generally considered to be quite inelastic with respect to price, although the demand for a number of farm products is becoming more elastic as the export market for farm products increases in importance. The implications of this increase in elasticity of demand for domestic price-support programs are discussed in chapter 14. Recall that the more inelastic demand is, the larger is the price decrease when the supply of a product increases relative to demand. The combination of an inelastic demand for farm products and supply increasing faster than demand is important in any historical explanation of the U.S. farm problem. As shown later, however, despite lower product prices, incomes of farm households have increased over time because of increased output per acre, increased farm size, and increases in off-farm earnings.

Market power has been suggested as an alternative explanation of the farm problem. The New Deal action programs of the 1930s were based on the idea that farmers are dispersed and weak, whereas the rest of the economy either is monopolized or has the ability to "administer" prices without regard to the basic underlying supply and demand conditions. It is sometimes held that farmers are at a disadvantage in terms of bargaining power within the agricultural sector, both in buying inputs and in selling farm products. Instead of attempting to increase competition among the allegedly monopolistic agribusiness firms, however, there was (and continues to be) a deliberate government policy of restricting competition in agricultural product markets. That is, government-organized producer cartels were formed to raise prices of cotton, tobacco, milk, peanuts, and other products above their competitive market-clearing levels.

Market power is a relevant concept because sellers often do not face perfectly elastic demands. Government intervention in agriculture during the Great Depression, however, did not occur because agriculture operated as an island of competition surrounded by a sea of monopolistic firms selling farm inputs and buying farm products. As shown in chapter 7, the New Deal instituted measures to restrict competition throughout the economy.

Whatever the relevance of market power during the New Deal era, the level of farm product prices today has little if anything to do with lack of either market power (bargaining power) by farmers or "administered prices" by sellers. The free-rider incentive is typically strong enough to reduce the viability of voluntary cartels greatly because each firm has a strong incentive to cheat on any voluntary agreement to restrict output for the purpose of increasing price.[4]

Moreover, even if a group of sellers were able to effectively restrict sales, consumers would not be completely at the their mercy. Product price cannot be set independently of market demand—the higher the price, the smaller the amount that can be sold. Moreover, close substitutes exist for most goods and services.

For example, even in the highly concentrated U.S. automobile industry, in the absence of government assistance to restrict imports, colluding domestic auto companies would be able to do little to raise auto prices. In short, farmers and the public at large in the United States today are likely affected more by restrictions on competition obtained by rent seeking than from voluntary business cartels. In summary, the evidence does not support the market power explanation of the farm problem.

FARM VERSUS NONFARM INCOMES

The argument has been made that the government should intervene to equalize wages between different economic sectors. Such equalization would undermine the role played by price signals in a competitive market economy. As explained in chapter 1, wages and other prices play a central role in allocating resources. If public policies were instituted to equalize wages in each sector for comparable units of labor, there would be little incentive for labor to adjust in response to changing economic conditions. The resulting misallocation of resources would hinder economic growth.

Despite these problems, there has been, and continues to be, considerable interest in comparisons of farm and nonfarm incomes. The initial justifications for redistributing incomes with government programs in the 1930s were based in part on farmers having lower incomes, on average, than nonfarmers. We discuss later a number of important issues related to such income comparisons, but first we look at general factors that affect incomes. In particular, we consider how individuals' incomes vary over the course of their lives, and some dynamic considerations important for understanding income data. We then critically examine the relationship between farm and nonfarm incomes by discussing factors that must be considered to make sensible comparisons. Finally, we look at how these groups' relative incomes have changed over time. The discussion shows that although it is easy enough to compare farm and nonfarm incomes when the data are available, it is extremely difficult to make such comparisons meaningful.[5]

Why Do Incomes Vary?

In general, incomes vary between individuals because of differences in the quantity and quality of resources owned. Indeed, much of the observed variation in incomes can be explained by a life-cycle theory of education and job experience (figure 6.2). Individuals who invest in post–high school education expect to have a different time profile of income than individuals who begin working immediately after high school. Income is lower (or negative) during the educational period between ages eighteen and twenty-two and then, on average, rises faster than the income of individuals not acquiring additional education and training. Thus, there will always be a "natural" amount of income inequality owing to differences in age, education, and training.

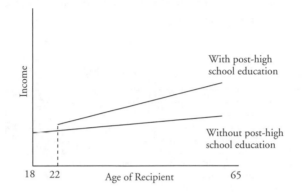

FIGURE 6.2 Incomes vary because of differences in education and experience.

Studies have shown that a great deal of the variation in incomes between individuals can be explained by the life-cycle model of income. Although cross-sectional studies show incomes to be highly unequal between individuals, these differences, to a considerable extent, reflect individuals' different positions in their lifetime income-earning profile. The income of a recent college or university graduate, for example, is likely to be considerably less than the income of an individual with similar education who also has (say) twenty years experience (figure 6.2). Similarly, the income of the high school graduate at age forty-five is expected to be less, on average, than that of the college graduate. The observed income differences, however, tend to disappear when one takes into account the costs of education and the value of experience. Stated differently, much of the observed inequality in incomes that shows up at any given moment in time disappears when adjustments are made for differences in education, training, and experience.

Most income distribution data fail to take account of the dynamics that affect individual incomes over time. When these factors are taken into account, there is a remarkable degree of movement, largely upward, by individuals and families within the American income distribution, even among the poorest segments of the population. The upward mobility is shown by a University of Michigan survey that tracked incomes of a group of individuals from 1975 to 1991.[6]

Income earners were grouped by quintile. Of individuals who were in the lowest income quintile in 1975, only 5.1 percent were still there in 1991; 14.6 percent had moved up to the second quintile, 21 percent to the middle quintile, 30.3 percent to the fourth quintile, and 29 percent to the highest income level (table 6.1). The rise in income can be swift, especially for those with education and skills—more than half of those in the lowest quintile in 1975 had moved into the middle class (top three tiers) within four years, and three-fourths of them had moved in nine years.[7]

TABLE 6.1 Income Mobility.

Income Quintile in 1975	Percentage in Each Quintile in 1991				
	1st	*2d*	*3rd*	*4th*	*5th*
5th (highest)	.9	2.8	10.2	23.6	62.5
4th	1.9	9.3	18.8	32.6	37.4
3rd	3.3	19.3	28.3	30.1	19.0
2d	4.2	23.5	20.3	25.2	26.8
1st (lowest)	5.1	14.6	21.0	30.3	29.0

Source: W. Michael Cox and Richard Alm, "By Our Bootstraps: Economic Opportunity and the Dynamics of Income Distribution," in *Federal Reserve Bank of Dallas Annual Report*, 2–24 (Dallas: Federal Reserve Bank of Dallas, 1995).

What happened to the "rich" of 1975—those in the highest income category? Nearly two-thirds were still at the top in 1991, and almost all others remained in the "middle class"—fewer than 4 percent had dropped to the bottom two income classes (table 6.1).

The upward mobility shown by these data strongly contradicts the idea of a society settled into stagnant income classes. The income streams of many, if not most, people are, however, characterized by years of low and high earnings and sudden changes in family size. Indeed, an earlier study found that most significant income changes follow some major change in family situation such as divorce, death, marriage, children leaving home, and so on.[8] The conclusion is that any snapshot of the income distribution at a point in time that does not take such factors into account is likely to be highly misleading.

Comparing Farm and Nonfarm Incomes

Farm incomes in the United States historically were lower than nonfarm incomes. In 1945 farm incomes were only about half as large as nonfarm incomes. This difference has frequently been offered as a justification for federal agricultural programs. Although farm incomes relative to nonfarm incomes vary from year to year, the income gap now has disappeared (table 6.2). That is, incomes of farm households, on average, are roughly on par with incomes of all

U.S. households. A number of issues must be considered, however, in making income comparisons of this type.

TABLE 6.2 Average Household Income, Farm Operators and All U.S. Households, Selected Years, 1960–1997.

Year	Farm Households ($)	U.S. Households ($)	Farm as % of U.S.
1960	4,054	6,227	65
1965	6,344	7,704	82
1970	9,472	10,001	95
1975	15,692	13,779	114
1980	18,504	21,063	88
1985	35,473	29,066	122
1990	38,237	37,403	102
1995	44,392	44,938	99
1997	52,347	49,692	105

Source: USDA Web site:
http://www.ers.usda.gov/briefing/FarmStructure/QA/Tables/historic.html.

First, the concept of "average farm income" has little meaning because income per farm family varies widely depending on farm size. The smallest size class (less than $20,000 in annual production), representing 58 percent of farms, generated only 4.6 percent of the value of the farm sector's final output (table 6.3). In contrast, the largest farms (those with more than $1,000,000 in annual production) represented only 1.4 percent of farms but accounted for 42.3 percent of the value of production.

TABLE 6.3 Farm Production by Size Class of Farms, 2001.

Type Farm	Production Class	Farms No.	Percentage	Percentage of Production
Rural Residences	Less than $20,000	1,251,944	58.0	4.6
Small Family Farms	$20,000–49,999	336,812	15.6	4.7
Family Farms	$50,000–99,999	201,968	9.4	6.1
	$100,000–249,999	199,163	9.2	13.9
Large Family Farms	$250,000–499,999	88,901	4.1	13.6
Very Large Farms	$500,000–999,999	48,766	2.3	14.8
	$1,000,000 or more	30,856	1.4	42.3

Source: USDA Web site: http://www.ers.usda.gov/data/farmincome/finfidmu.htm.

Moreover, farm earnings over time have become less and less reliable as a measure of farmers' household income. Farmers now are highly dependent on off-farm earnings. In the 1990s, for example, farm households on average derived almost 90 percent of total household income from off-farm earnings.[9] Indeed, during the 1990s, small farms on average have been completely dependent on off-farm earnings; net farm earnings for farm operator households on farms with sales of less than $50,000 per year have been negative.[10] That is, *all* of the disposable income for these farms came from off-farm sources. The conclusion is that discussions of "average farm income" are generally highly misleading because the farm is not the primary source of income for many farmers. This is particularly true for small farms.

Second, any meaningful comparison of farm and nonfarm incomes must take into account differences in worker productivity that result from differences in capital investment, education, training, and experience. If these differences are not accounted for, observed income differences have little economic meaning. Income comparisons such as those presented in table 6.2 make no adjustments for these factors. The productivity of farm labor, of course, hinges largely on capital investment per worker. Increases in agricultural technology related to mechanization, chemical pest control, improved varieties, and so on have dramatically increased output per farmworker. At the same time, the increased capital investment per farmworker has eliminated much of the low-skill, low-wage hand labor in agriculture. Thus, it may be that much of the closing of the farm/nonfarm income gap over time is due to a relative increase in farmworkers' productivity.

Third, farming is land and capital intensive, and returns to farmers' land and business capital comprise a higher share of their "income" than the capital returns' share of income for most of the nonfarm population. Much of this income is not included in USDA income statistics for the farm sector. During the inflationary period of the late 1970s, for example, owners of farm assets received huge increases in wealth as prices of land and other farm assets increased. Farm real estate values in the United States, on average, increased 245 percent from 1970 to 1980—much more than the 112 percent increase in the overall price level. During the 1980s, in contrast, owners of farm assets incurred huge losses in wealth as prices of farm real estate plunged. During the period from 1981 to 1987, U.S. farm real estate values decreased by 35 percent, on average, and by more than 50 percent in some states (e.g., Indiana). The overall price level increased by 25 percent during this time. Inflation further eroded the real wealth of owners of farm assets during this period of falling land prices. A meaningful comparison of farm versus nonfarm well-being must take into account such changes in real wealth.

Fourth, cost of living and tax differences must be taken into account. Money incomes must be adjusted for differences in cost of living, capital gains, and taxes in making comparisons of real incomes for farmers versus nonfarmers. In general, the real income level for a given money income is somewhat higher in rural areas because of cost of living and income tax advantages, including consumption of home-produced products. Although differences in cost of living between rural and urban areas are still important in assessing the well-being of farm versus nonfarm families, the consumption of home-produced products over time has become a much less important consideration, particularly for commercial farmers.

Finally, nonpecuniary aspects of employment play an important role in the decision to enter farming or to continue farming. The satisfaction gained from working in the outdoors and of being one's own boss may be high enough to substitute for a substantial amount of money income. Of course, nonpecuniary considerations also may influence individuals' decisions to enter and stay in other occupations. Nonpecuniary considerations, however, arguably play a larger role in occupational choice in farming than in most other occupations. Regardless of whether this is correct, real incomes or well-being of farmers cannot legitimately be compared to real incomes of individuals in other occupations without taking into account the nonpecuniary factors that influence occupational choice.

When all of these factors are taken into account, there is no persuasive evidence either that incomes are now lower in agriculture or that the overall well-being of farmers is less than that of nonfarmers. Regardless of the relative position of incomes in agriculture currently, attempts both now and in the past have been made to increase agricultural incomes by increasing farm product prices. The result of increasing incomes by agricultural price supports is predictable. When product prices are increased, small farmers are affected relatively little because the benefits of higher prices vary with sales. The same holds for direct government payments to farmers. For example, in 2001, the largest one-fourth of all farms (in table 6.4 those farms with annual sales exceeding $50,000), received more than 80 percent of all direct government payments. Although the effects of various government programs vary widely (even for farms of a given size) depending on crops produced, the conclusion holds that large farms receive most of the short-run benefits.

INCOME INEQUALITY AND ECONOMIC JUSTICE

The preceding discussion illustrates some of the issues a careful analyst must consider when trying to interpret and understand income data. Given these caveats, we now discuss two tools commonly used in analyses of income distributions: the Lorenz curve and the Gini coefficient. We then use these tools to illustrate some systematic characteristics of direct government payments to farmers.

The Lorenz Curve

The Lorenz curve is a tool developed to provide information on the distribution of incomes. Along this curve (figure 6.3), income recipients are ranked from lowest to highest (with no adjustments made for the productivity differences discussed earlier), and against their cumulative number the cumulative percentage of income received is plotted.[11] The straight line from the southwest corner to the northeast corner of the rectangle represents a perfectly uniform distribution of income in which every individual (or household) has the same income. At point A, for example, 50 percent of the individuals get 50 percent of the income. This, of course, is not what one expects to find in the real world. The actual distribution of incomes is consistent with a convex Lorenz curve. In the unequal distribution of incomes depicted in figure 6.3, the lower 50 percent of individual income recipients get less than half of the income (point B).

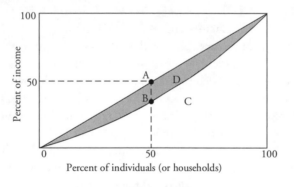

FIGURE 6.3 The Lorenz Curve

The Gini coefficient (G) for a Lorenz curve is a measure of degree of inequality of income distribution and is calculated as

$$G = \frac{Area\ D}{Area\ C + Area\ D}$$

The straighter the Lorenz curve, the closer G is to zero and the more equal are incomes. Conversely, the more convex the curve, the closer G is to one, and the more unequal are incomes. Thus, where the necessary information is available to compute it, the Gini coefficient provides a measure of the equality of incomes.

An important component of income for many farmers is direct government payments. Policymakers, industry observers and participants, and the news media commonly raise issues related to the distribution of these payments among farmers. This was especially true during the debate over the 2002 farm bill. An Environmental Working Group (EWG) Web site was created in 2001 to show the amounts of government farm payments received by individual farmers throughout the United States in recent years. These data were widely cited in the news media and in Congress during 2001 and 2002 before enactment of the farm bill.[12] For purposes of illustration, we use a Lorenz curve approach to analyze the distribution of direct government payments to farmers in 1998. As expected, under farm policies where payments increase with output, benefits accrued disproportionately to larger producers (table 6.4). (Readers may find it useful to sketch the convex Lorenz curve and calculate the value of the Gini coefficient implied by the data in table 6.4 to verify the heavy concentration of government payments received by larger producers.)

TABLE 6.4 Size of Farm and Government Payments, 2001: An Example of a Convex Lorenz Curve.

Value of Sales Category	Farms		Direct Government Payments Received	
	Number (thousands)	Percentage	Millions dollars	Percentage
$1,000,000 and more	31	1.4	2,029	9.8
$500,000–999,999	49	2.3	3,252	15.7
$250,000–499,999	89	4.1	4,492	21.7
$100,000–249,999	199	9.2	5,213	25.2
$50,000–99,999	202	9.4	2,224	10.7
$20,000–49,999	336	15.6	1,436	6.9
Less than $20,000	1,252	58.0	2,081	10.0
All farms	2,158	100.0	20,727	100.0

Source: USDA, Economic Research Service, "U.S. and State Farm Income Data, Value Added by Size Class," available at:
http://www.ers.usda.gov/data/farmincome/finfidmu.htm.

An argument might be made for focusing government payments on farms having financial difficulty—that is, farms with low or negative net incomes. The data in table 6.4 relate to gross sales revenues, which, of course, are not the same as net income. A large farm may have a lower *net* income than a smaller farm. Unfortunately, net income data for farms in different size categories are not available. In reality, much debate over the 2002 farm bill focused on the fact that small farms (those with low gross sales revenues) received a small proportion of all government payments, as indicated in table 6.4.

It should be emphasized that the Lorenz curve and the Gini coefficient provide *no* information as to whether the distributions of incomes or farm income payments are different from what they *should* be. The problem of determining what incomes "should be" is essentially the same as that of describing the distribution of incomes consistent with *economic justice*.

Economic Justice

A primary problem associated with the concept of "economic justice" is related to the difficulties in determining what is meant by a "just" distribution of incomes. Much of the discussion about the distribution of incomes implicitly assumes that a more equal income distribution is more "just." If this were the case, the ideal would be a perfectly equal distribution of incomes. Such an ideal might be defensible in a world where goods and services did not have to be produced and the only economic problem was the distribution of existing goods and services. Indeed, much of the discussion of economic justice implicitly assumes that production and distribution are distinct economic activities so that income distribution has no influence on the production of goods and services. In reality, of course, production and distribution are not distinct activities, but are instead integral parts of the same economic process.

The way the economic pie is divided (the size of factor shares) has a crucial influence on the size of the economic pie (the amount of goods and services produced). What would happen to output, for example, if there were no connection between work and financial reward so that every worker received the same income regardless of the amount of work done? The effect on output of goods and services is obvious. (If the instructor announced on the first day of class that everyone would get the same grade regardless of class performance, how would the students' effort and incentives be affected?) Few people would contend that a system where there is no connection between work and reward is just. Indeed, most people think that as the amount of goods and services an individual produces increases, the income received by that person should also increase. This link between economic output and anticipated financial reward is necessary for maintaining a productive economy; it is also desirable from the standpoint of fairness. As shown later, however, the fairness of individual incomes cannot be determined independently of the operation of the market process that generates those incomes.

Although the term *economic justice* is widely used, F. A. Hayek concludes that the phrase has no meaning in a free society.[13] Although it is certainly true that returns to labor and other resources tend to be based on their contributions to output of goods and services, incomes are also affected by luck (both good and bad!) as well as by entrepreneurial foresight and skill. Furthermore, incomes of different individuals under similar circumstances may vary widely, and often there is no way to distinguish between the income due to skill and foresight and income obtained through mere luck. Consequently, the pattern of incomes that results from the competitive market process in a world of risk and uncertainty is likely to appear "unfair" and to give rise to political efforts to redistribute income in order to further economic justice.

In a decentralized system where individuals are allowed to use their own highly specialized knowledge for their own purposes, however, economic (or social) justice is an empty concept. In a free society, nobody's will can determine relative incomes or prevent them from being determined in part by accident. Moreover, any attempt to impose anyone's concept of economic justice through the political system must conflict with economic freedom—individuals' right to engage in mutually beneficial exchange. Thus, it is not possible to preserve the voluntary nature of the competitive system while also imposing on it some "socially just" pattern of remuneration determined by an authority with power to enforce it. The belief that a just distribution of incomes can be objectively determined through the political process not only ignores government-failure problems, but also minimizes the importance of the coordination and informational roles of competitive price signals. In short, an appeal to economic justice provides no guide to determining what the relative remunerations of a farmer, a lawyer, or the inventor of a life-saving drug *should be*.[14]

The issue of economic justice is essentially the same as that of the "just" wage. Philosophers have struggled for centuries with the meaning of the concept of a "just" wage or income. The analogy between the market process and athletic competitions is helpful in thinking about "just" or "fair" incomes (or wages). Fairness in either case is most appropriately evaluated in terms of the fairness of the underlying process that generates the outcomes. The fairness of an athletic contest or any other game involving skill, for example, typically is evaluated on the basis of the appropriateness of the rules. If the rules of a game are clearly stated, known and accepted in advance, and impartially enforced, the outcome of the game is not used as a test of the game's fairness. The fact that the Oklahoma football team typically defeats most of its opponents by huge margins, for example, does not suggest that the games played are unfair.

Similarly, in the economic arena, justice or fairness should be based on the fairness of the underlying institutional framework—not on the basis of the economic outcomes generated. Thus, wages and prices in decentralized competitive markets are "just" in the same sense that outcomes of fair games are just.[15] In contrast, a pattern of incomes influenced by widespread redistribution might be considered unfair because the institutional framework that permits rent-seeking groups to increase their incomes through the power of government is unfair. There is increasing interest among political economists and philosophers concerning the significance of "competitive" prices and the decentralized market system, both in the production of goods and services and in the maintenance of individual and political freedom.[16]

SUMMARY

Two competing explanations for the "farm problem" are economic progress and a lack of bargaining power by farmers. The weight of the evidence suggests that the farm problem in the United States can be traced to economic growth. As economic growth occurs, agriculture decreases in importance relative to other sectors of the economy. Higher incomes have historically been the means by which labor resources were bid away from agriculture in a developing economy. Advancements in technology over time have also increased the supply of farm products more rapidly than demand, exerting chronic downward pressure on farm product prices. Farm incomes in the United States have increased, though, despite lower prices of farm products, for several reasons. Higher yields per acre and increased acreage tended have been important factors in maintaining farm earnings. However, the dominant factor in the increase in total household income, particularly for smaller farms, has been the increase in the nonfarm portion of family income.

Farm incomes were low relative to nonfarm incomes a generation ago. Today, average income of farm households is comparable to the income of nonfarm households. Meaningful farm versus nonfarm income comparisons are difficult to make, however, because of differences in farm size, worker productivity, cost of living and tax differences, and nonpecuniary aspects of employment. Income equality does not imply "economic justice." Although it is easy to determine that individuals' incomes vary widely, income differences do not necessarily imply that incomes are "unjust." Indeed, the concept of economic justice has no clear meaning in a free society where individuals are able to use their resources for their own purposes. Moreover, it is not possible to preserve free markets while imposing on a society any "socially just" pattern of remuneration.

Much of the discussion related to differences in individual incomes assumes that production and distribution are separate and distinct economic activities. In reality, incomes are received by resource owners in the operation of the market process. Consequently, the remuneration received by resource owners affects resource use and therefore the level of production.

7

The Role of Government in U.S. Agriculture

This chapter examines the roots of current farm programs, the initiation of these programs, growth in farm programs over time, and possible explanations for the growth of government in the United States.

ROOTS OF CURRENT FARM PROGRAMS

Governmental efforts were made to intervene extensively in agriculture for most of the twentieth century. Although many aspects of current farm programs are firmly rooted in legislation enacted during the Great Depression or the New Deal era, the basic approach can be traced to earlier years.[1] The McNary-Haugen two-price plan of the mid-1920s, for example, had the goal of raising farm product prices in the domestic market above those of the world market through the use of export subsidies. The subsidies were to be financed through assessment of a tax on processors or handlers of particular farm commodities. Under the McNary-Haugen plan, a government export corporation would buy wheat and other products as a way of increasing domestic farm prices. These surplus farm products were then to be "dumped" in international markets, and reimports were to be restricted by tariffs. Five McNary-Haugen bills were introduced from 1924 to 1928, but none of them was enacted into law. The principal features of these bills were adopted, however, in the New Deal legislation of the following decade, which provided for the financing of export subsidies out of tariff receipts.

The Capper-Volstead Act of 1922 was another important early piece of legislation that marked the beginning of the modern cooperative movement. The act gives producers the legal right to work together in jointly marketing their products. Thus, members of agricultural co-ops enjoy a favored status when contrasted with other business firms, which are legally prohibited from such collusive activity by antitrust laws. Without the act, many of the marketing activities currently engaged in by agricultural co-ops would be violations of one or both of the two primary statutes that govern antitrust policy in the United States—the Sherman Antitrust Act and the Clayton Act. Co-ops presumably do not maintain their exemption when they engage in predatory market activities to achieve "undue price enhancement." Enforcement, however, is entrusted to the secretary of agriculture rather than to the Department of Justice.[2] It is not clear what activities are forbidden, and no secretary of agriculture has found an example of undue price enhancement by agricultural marketing co-ops. During the 1980s, however, milk, navel orange, and other co-ops came under increasing pressure from both consumer interests and government watchdog agencies, such as the Federal Trade Commission, for their use of marketing orders to raise prices of farm products above competitive levels to the detriment of consumers. Marketing orders and other co-op activities are described in more detail in later chapters.

The Federal Farm Board was the most immediate forerunner of New Deal action programs in agriculture. The board was created in 1929 by President Herbert Hoover, who envisioned the farm problem as one of temporary overproduction and low prices. The basic idea was to raise prices of wheat, cotton, and other "surplus" products through government purchase and storage of the products until some future period of production shortfalls. The board first attempted to support farm prices through a government-sponsored grain-storage program. No shortfalls occurred, however, and the board's budget was soon exhausted. President Roosevelt abolished the Federal Farm Board in 1933.

THE AGRICULTURAL ADJUSTMENT ACT OF 1933 AND THE GREAT DEPRESSION

Governmental activism in U.S. agriculture, as in the case of the Federal Farm Board, was an aberration prior to 1933. The agricultural policy agenda historically focused mainly on agricultural research and extension programs to increase productivity and to maintain competitive markets. Federal intervention on a massive scale was initiated during the Roosevelt New Deal, and there was a pronounced change in program goals as the USDA under Secretary of Agriculture Henry Wallace developed a host of new action programs. Instead of increased production and competitive markets, the Agricultural Adjustment Act (AAA) of 1933 established the goals of "parity" prices and incomes in agriculture to raise farm product prices (and farm incomes) above the free-market level. The specific goal of the parity price approach was to raise product prices so that a physical unit of a particular product (pound, bushel, and so on) had the same buying power that prevailed during the base period from 1910 to 1914.

Enacted during the depths of the Great Depression, the 1933 AAA signaled a huge increase in government involvement in agriculture in the United States. To understand this fundamental shift in policy, it is useful to put the events of the Great Depression in perspective by considering conditions in the agricultural sector for the two decades preceding the Great Depression. The decade from 1910 to 1920 was a period of relative prosperity for U.S. agriculture. An important source of this prosperity was the war in Europe during the second half of the decade, which drastically reduced the productive capacity of Europe, thereby increasing the demand for U.S. products. Prices and farm incomes rose accordingly. After the war ended late in 1918, European productive capacity recovered slowly, and prosperity in U.S. agriculture continued for a period as commodity prices and net incomes remained at high levels. The fact that land prices and farm mortgage debt continued to increase immediately after the end of the war suggests that U.S. farmers expected prosperity to continue.

During 1920 and 1921, U.S. farm prices plummeted as European production recovered more quickly than expected. Declining production costs during this period only partly offset the effects of falling output prices. Aggregate net farm income fell by 50 percent, and land values fell by almost 20 percent during these two years. Between June 1920 and December 1921, corn prices fell from $1.85 to $0.41 per bushel; wheat prices fell from $2.58 to $0.92 per bushel; hog prices fell from $0.19 to $0.065 per pound; and the index of prices received by farmers fell by 41 percent.

From 1923 to 1929, U.S. agricultural prices and net farm incomes were relatively stable, and although land prices continued to decline, the rate of decline was relatively low. Then came the Great Depression, which held the U.S. economy in its grip throughout the decade from 1929 to 1939. The Great Depression was a period of economic chaos and massive economic contraction. During the three-year period from 1929 to 1932, stock (equity) prices lost nine-tenths of their value; real gross national product (GNP) decreased by one-third; industrial production was reduced by one- half; and unemployment reached 25 percent of the labor force. The overall level of prices fell by 9 percent in 1931 and by 11 percent in 1932.

Conditions in the U.S. farm sector were severe during the Great Depression. The index of prices received by farmers fell by 55 percent between 1929 and 1933. Grain, cotton, and livestock producers were particularly hard hit during this period, but changes in dairy, fruit, and poultry prices were somewhat less dramatic. Net farm revenues fell by 69 percent between 1929 and 1933, and an index of land values fell by 37 percent.

A useful indicator of the extent of the distress in agricultural sector is the rate of farm failures. Failure rates were less than five per thousand per year until the early 1920s, at which time they increased to approximately fifteen per thousand. In 1932, farm failure rates skyrocketed to approximately thirty-eight per thousand! In other words, almost 4 percent of all farms in the United States failed in 1932. Failure rates gradually declined, and by the early 1940s had fallen back to less than five per thousand. From that time until the mid-1980s, when collection of data for this particular data series was discontinued, the rate of farm failures never again approached five per thousand. To evaluate the appropriateness of the government policies instituted in the 1930s, it is helpful to understand why the Great Depression occurred.

CAUSES OF THE GREAT DEPRESSION

The conventional wisdom has been that the market economy is inherently unstable and that the Great Depression was merely a severe manifestation of this instability.[3] Thus, it is frequently argued, the government must intervene in agriculture and other areas to regulate and stabilize the economy. There are, however, strong reasons for doubting this conventional explanation of the beneficial effects of government intervention during the Great Depression.[4] Contrary to what has been taught to generations of students and future policymakers, a great deal of evidence demonstrates that government intervention in the form of high tariffs, high taxes, restrictive monetary policies, and policies to maintain wages and prices either caused or greatly exacerbated the economic chaos prevailing at that time.[5] The Smoot-Hawley Tariff Act enacted in 1930, for example, raised import tariffs to the highest levels in the twentieth century—52.8 percent on an ad valorem basis. Restrictions on imports by the United States led to retaliatory measures by foreign trading partners, and protectionism ran wild as countries worldwide raised tariffs and erected other trade barriers, including quotas. Prices of export commodities, notably U.S. farm products, dropped with "ominous rapidity" following the passage of the tariff bill.[6] It was to a large extent because of retaliatory protectionist measures by foreign trading countries that exports of U.S. farm products were reduced by two-thirds from 1929 to 1933. Agriculture was hit especially hard by the protectionist trade policies because of its heavy dependence on the exporting of its products. The result was that farm prices plunged, many farm loans turned bad, and farm foreclosures skyrocketed.

A purchasing-power theory of wages during the Great Depression had a profound effect on public policy. Under this mistaken theory, depressions occur when the share of income received by workers is too small. Because low wages lead to underconsumption, maintaining wages was seen as the appropriate policy during the Great Depression.[7] Thus, the U.S. government actively resisted the market forces that were working to reduce wages and prices at a time of critically decreasing demand and high unemployment. Whereas President Hoover merely "jawboned" to keep wages up, President Roosevelt enacted the National Industrial Recovery Act (NIRA). The general thrust of the act was to suppress competition in whatever form it might take. The NIRA, for example, empowered the president to approve "codes of fair competition" that applied cartel-type codes on an industry basis and legally prevented wages and prices from falling.[8] At the bottom of the severe depression, a spate of wage increases followed as a result of these policies. Such increases, of course, only exacerbated unemployment problems. Thus, the price-support policies in agriculture (described in detail in later chapters) were consistent with the NIRA and other government attempts to suppress competition and to maintain high prices.[9] The theory that falling prices were causing the depression and that government-enforced cartels would hasten recovery by halting price declines was as mistaken in agriculture as in other sectors.

Fiscal and monetary policies also contributed to the economic chaos. The prevailing view of fiscal policy at the time was that the federal budget should be balanced. Thus, as economic activity declined, tax revenues fell, and the deficit increased. The response was to increase taxes, which only acted to decrease disposable incomes and aggregate demand further. Accordingly, the Hoover administration enacted the biggest percentage increase in taxes in peacetime history in 1932, and President Roosevelt hiked taxes in 1935 and routinely thereafter. By 1938, the corporate tax rate had gone from 11 to 19 percent, and the top income tax rate had increased from 24 to 79 percent.

During the 1920s, a slow but steady increase in the supply of money occurred. When banks failed in the early 1930s, the Federal Reserve failed to act as a lender of last resort, and the supply of money fell by one-third from 1929 to 1933.[10] Increased taxes and the reduction in the supply of money acted to reduce the aggregate demand for goods and services further, thereby worsening the already serious condition of the economy.

In summary, the government policies during the Great Depression—high tariffs, high taxes, monetary mismanagement, and political manipulation of wage rates and prices—probably could not have been better designed had policymakers *wanted* to bring about economic stagnation or to prevent economic recovery. The programs instituted to restrict competition in agricultural markets were consistent with the collectivist thrust of the NIRA and of other New

Deal initiatives instituted to remedy supposed market failures. "The incredible aspect of these actions is that they were justified by the belief that the private sector was responsible for the Great Depression."[11]

NEW DEAL MEASURES IN AGRICULTURE

A broad range of New Deal programs was instituted to deal with the farm problem. Included were programs providing for:

- Production controls and price supports
- Subsidized food distribution
- Export subsidies
- Subsidized farm credit
- Conservation of land and water resources
- Crop insurance and disaster payments
- Expanded agricultural research and extension services

Programs in all of these areas are still in effect, although many changes have been made since the programs began. The remainder of this book is devoted to an analysis of such programs and policies, including a description of major changes in the programs over time. The programs listed here have inconsistencies both in their objectives and in their effects. Agricultural research, for example, is designed to improve technology, which tends to increase supply and decrease product prices. Price-support programs, in contrast, are designed to increase product prices. The more effective the research and extension programs, the more costly it is for taxpayers to support product prices at any given level. Other examples of inconsistent policies are discussed in later chapters.

THE GROWTH OF GOVERNMENT INVOLVEMENT IN U.S. AGRICULTURE

Evidence of Growth

A dramatic increase in government involvement in U.S. agriculture took place during the Roosevelt New Deal era. USDA expenditures increased from less than $200 million in 1929 prior to the New Deal to $1.2 billion in fiscal year 1935 (table 7.1). The USDA outlays as a percentage of the total federal budget increased markedly in the 1930s, declined during World War II, rose again following the end of the war, slowly declined until 1970, increased again in the 1980s, and decreased in the 1990s. The USDA budget as a percentage of the total federal budget increased from 4.3 percent in 1970 to approximately 6 percent in the early to mid-1980s, even as the total U.S. budget was rising at an unprecedented peacetime rate. As shown in chapter 20 (see table 20.1 in chapter 20), increases in food and nutrition programs were responsible for much of the USDA budget growth from 1970 to 1980. Price-support program payments accounted for most of the large increase in USDA outlays during the 1980s, but food and nutrition programs again were responsible for most of the increase in government support to agriculture in the 1990s.

The growth in USDA expenditures since World War II has been dramatic, measured on either a per farm or a per farmworker basis. As indicated in table 7.1, on a per farm basis expenditures increased from $549 in 1950 to almost $25,000 in fiscal year 1998—which is equivalent to $3,700 in 1950 prices. A large proportion of this increase was not, of course, paid directly to farmers because there was a pronounced increase in the food stamp and other food assistance programs during this period. These programs, although not directly benefiting farmers, do benefit them indirectly, at least to some extent (see chapter 13).

USDA employment increased continually from 1929 to 1980, even as the number of farms and farmers decreased. USDA employment rose most rapidly during the New Deal era, more than tripling from 1929 to 1935. Employment increased continuously following World War II until 1980, but since then has trended downward.

The growth of the USDA classified by general purpose of expenditure is presented in chapter 20, following our discussion in ensuing chapters of the various individual programs. Outlays for stabilization of farm prices and incomes increased dramatically in the early 1980s, peaking in 1986. Since then, outlays have varied widely, depending on product prices, price-support levels, weather, export sales of farm products, and so on. Although payments to farmers were significantly lower in the 1990s than in the 1980s, additional "disaster" or "emergency" assistance dramatically increased stabilization outlays in 1998, 1999, and 2000 above levels authorized under the 1996 farm bill.

Reduced outlays for stabilization of farm prices and incomes over the past decade also have been compensated for to some extent by increased outlays for other farm programs—most notably food and nutrition programs. Outlays on food and nutrition programs more than doubled from the mid-1980s to the mid-1990s and now constitute two-thirds of the total USDA budget. This pattern of USDA activities is consistent with public-choice theory. In the classic expansion pattern of a bureaucracy, the USDA, having outgrown the area it was originally

TABLE 7.1 USDA Expenditures and Employment, 1929–1998.

Year	USDA Expenditures					USDA Employment		
	Total outlays ($ billions)	% of total budget	% of net farm income	Per farm ($)	Per farm worker ($)	Total (thousands)	Per thousand farm workers	Per thousand farms
1929	0.2[a]	5.2	2.5	27	13	24.4	2	4
1935	1.2	16.2	21.4	175	94	85.1	7	12
1940	1.6	22.3	29.7	259	144	81.9	7	13
1945	2.3	2.3	16.9	386	226	82.0	8	14
1950	3.0	7.4	18.8	549	298	84.1	8	16
1955	4.6	7.2	34.3	996	553	85.5	10	18
1960	5.4	7.1	47.0	1,368	768	98.7	14	25
1965	6.9	5.9	54.0	2,068	1,237	113.0	20	34
1970	8.4	4.3	61.0	2,847	1,860	116.0	26	39
1975	15.6	4.7	61.0	6,170	3,583	121.0	28	48
1980	34.8	5.9	214.7	14,259	9,388	129.1	35	53
1985	55.5	5.9	192.8	24,219	17,819	117.8	38	51
1990	46.0	3.7	102.7	21,443	15,916	122.6	42	57
1995	56.7	3.7	157.4	25,799[b]	16,473	103.8	30	47
1998	53.9	3.2[b]	122.3	24,628[b]	15,970[b]	107.1	32	49[b]

[a] More than 50 percent of expenditure was for road construction, an item not reported in later USDA budgets.
[b] Preliminary.
Sources: USDA and total budget outlays for years 1929–1960 from U.S. Department of Commerce, *Statistical Abstract of the United States* (Washington, D.C.: U.S. Government Printing Office, various issues); later years from Office of Management and Budget, *Historical Tables, Budget of the U.S. Government* (Washington, D.C.: U.S. Government Printing Office, various issues). Agricultural employment and net farm income from *Economic Report of the President* (Washington, D.C.: U.S. Government Printing Office, various issues). Number of farms from various issues of USDA, *Agricultural Statistics.* USDA employment from *Statistical Abstract* and USDA Office of Budget and Program Analysis, *Budgetary Tables* (Washington, D.C.: U.S. Government Printing Office, various issues).

designed to aid, has nevertheless maintained and even increased its constituency by moving into tangential areas such as rural recreation, community facilities, urban nutrition, and so on. (The growth in the USDA classified by general purpose of expenditure is presented in chapter 20, following our discussion of the various individual programs in the intervening chapters.)

Total USDA outlays decreased substantially after 1986, but nominal outlays by the mid-1990s had again increased to mid-1980s levels. However, the USDA budget in 1995, adjusted for inflation, was some 40 percent lower than it was a decade earlier. The reduction in real outlays can be attributed in part to increased pressure on farm programs because of heightened congressional concerns and because of actions taken to reduce federal budget deficits.

Changes in the relative importance of farm program expenditures also reflect the changing pressures exerted by various groups on the USDA over the years. The main thrust of the action programs instituted during the New Deal era was income support to commercial agriculture. The USDA was influenced primarily by the demands of commercial agriculture until the 1960s (as described in chapter 6), at which time the influence of nonfarm groups became much more important. During the Carter administration (1977–80), the influence of various consumer and environmental groups on the USDA agenda increased at the expense of commercial agricultural interests. Although the pendulum swung back toward commercial agriculture to some extent during the Reagan administration (1981–88), the influence of commercial agriculture on USDA activities is unlikely to be restored to its previous position of dominance.

So long as government expenditures on agricultural programs were viewed as being in the "public interest," these programs were subject to relatively little criticism. More and more, however, consumer groups are challenging marketing orders for milk, oranges, and other products; the sugar program; the tobacco and peanut programs; and other farm programs that benefit only a relatively small number of agricultural producers at the expense of the public at large. Agricultural programs are increasingly being viewed as income-redistribution programs rather than as "public-interest" activities.

Reasons for Growth of Government Farm Programs

A number of factors are important in the growth of government farm programs. The fact that benefits are highly concentrated and costs are widely diffused is important in understanding increases in wealth by various groups achieved through the political process. Opportunities to achieve wealth transfers through the political process are not new, however. Why have groups of farm producers and other narrowly focused special interests chosen to rely more and more on the political process over time rather than on market opportunities as a means of enhancing their wealth? Why did aggregate federal expenditures as a share of GDP increase from 2.5 percent in 1929 to approximately 22 percent in 1995?

A number of alternative explanations for the growth of government have been offered. First, there is the notion that a modern industrial economy must have an expanding government sector to deal with public-health and environmental problems that accompany the increased complexities of modern life.[12] This factor, although seemingly plausible, has limited explanatory power because regulation of public-health and environmental externalities accounts for only a small part of what the government actually does. In agriculture, for example, price and income supports, credit subsidies, and most of the other activities in which government is engaged have little or no connection with the increased complexity of the economy.

The "public-goods" model is a second and closely related justification for the growth of government. In the case of public goods, it is argued, government coercion is required to overcome the free-rider problem. This explanation, however, has little relevance for most expenditures on agricultural programs. Although a public-goods argument may justify agricultural research and educational programs (chapter 18), it does not explain the outlays for farm price and income supports, agricultural credit subsidies, and food assistance. Indeed, in the case of marketing orders and other government-enforced cartel-type activities, producer groups use government to discourage free-rider activities that would, in the absence of government sanctions, result in competitive market conditions.

Third, it is suggested that a change in ideology has occurred over time—in the public perception of the appropriate role of government. Prior to the New Deal era, there was a consensus that the role of government should be limited mainly to its protective functions. This attitude is evident in the view expressed by President Grover Cleveland concerning a congressional appropriation in 1887 of $10,000 for seed grain to assist drought-stricken farmers in Texas. Cleveland considered it wrong to use public funds to indulge a benevolent and charitable sentiment. He vetoed the appropriation with the message that "the lesson should constantly be enforced that though the people support the Government the Government should not support the people."[13]

During the past fifty years, constitutional restraints on the exercise of government power have broken down as individuals and groups have come to feel that government should play the role of problem solver. Government has increasingly become a vehicle for accommodating the demands of narrowly focused special interests rather than for protecting the interests of the general public.

Fourth, emergency or economic crisis is another explanation for the growth of government in agriculture and other sectors of the economy. In U.S. history, the most significant crises have taken two forms: war and business depression.[14] As mentioned earlier, the New Deal's AAA represented a large increase in the government's role in U.S. agriculture. In 1933, it was argued that the individualistic approach of the market was unable to cope with the current economic crisis and that government planning was required to stabilize and enhance conditions in agriculture and in other sectors of the economy. Thus, the AAA and other New Deal measures were justified on the basis of economic crisis, and Congress attached the emergency label to almost every bill it enacted.[15] It is significant that expansions of state power justified on the basis of emergency conditions often do not disappear when the crisis is over. Many of the New Deal measures enacted to deal with the economic crisis in agriculture, for example, remain largely intact sixty-five years later.

There is no simple answer to the question of why government intervention has increased in U.S. agriculture. It is likely, as in many other areas of economic activity, that there is no single reason for the dramatic growth of farm programs during the past sixty-five years. The growth of government in general, however, appears to be related much more to the erosion over time of constraints on the powers of the federal government than to which political party is in power.

A study in the mid-1980s investigated the effect of political party on total federal spending in the United States since World War II—a period in which the role of government was greatly expanded. During the period analyzed, the Democrats and Republicans alternated in sharing control of the White House, but the Democrats had control of Congress for virtually the entire period. The study found that the rate of growth in real total federal spending in the United States bore no significant relationship to which party had control of the presidency.[16] Indeed, real domestic spending increased more rapidly under Republican presidents and included some major expansions in the role of the federal government. The EPA, for example, was an initiative of the Republican Nixon presidency.

Political party also has had little effect on spending for farm programs—although the Republican-crafted 1996 farm bill did affect the role of government in agriculture. The "Freedom to Farm" approach in the 1996 farm bill was enacted following the election of Republican majorities in both the House and Senate in 1994. It eliminated most planting restrictions for affected crops, including wheat, feed grains, cotton, and rice. In addition, at the time of passage of the 1996 farm bill, it generally was thought (mistakenly, in retrospect) that loan rates were established at levels low enough to be nonbinding. Although the 1996 farm bill represented a significant reduction in government intervention in the farm sector, there was in fact little change in the amount of income support to farmers.

SUMMARY

During the Great Depression, a host of action programs involving price supports, credit subsidies, export subsidies, subsidized food distribution, crop insurance, and conservation were launched to deal with the economic chaos in U.S. agriculture. Although government programs in agriculture today have roots in pre-1933 farm programs and proposals such as the McNary-Haugen two-price plan, the Capper-Volstead Act, and the Federal Farm Board, almost all current farm programs have a direct link to the New Deal era. Market transition payments in the 1996 farm bill, which enable participating producers of wheat, feed grains, cotton, and rice to receive government payments that are largely independent of farm output and prices, is a significant exception.

The conventional wisdom has been that the Great Depression resulted from a failure of the market process and that massive government intervention was necessary to stabilize agriculture and the rest of the economy. A considerable amount of evidence, however, demonstrates that government policies of high tariffs, high taxes, monetary mismanagement, and political attempts to maintain high wages and prices either caused or greatly exacerbated the chaotic economic conditions of that era.

The record of government programs in agriculture since the New Deal era is consistent with the predictions of public-choice theory. The programs instituted at that time to deal with emergency conditions have been maintained and increased over time, seemingly regardless of economic conditions. USDA employment and expenditures have increased dramatically since the 1930s even as the number of farms and number of farmers were decreasing and farm income was increasing relative to nonfarm income. For more than a century after its founding in 1862, the USDA primarily represented commercial agriculture. Since the mid-1970s, however, the influence of environmental and consumer groups in agency decisions has increased greatly. More and more, consumer groups and the general public recognize that income redistribution is a major impetus behind U.S. farm programs. Other factors, however, including a change in public opinion as to the appropriate role of the state, may also be important in the growth of government in agriculture (as well as in other sectors).

8

Price Supports, Parity, and Cost of Production

The basic idea of the farm price-support programs launched during the 1930s, as explained in the previous chapter, was that wages and prices should be kept high in a period of falling prices. In agriculture, farm product prices were deliberately supported at levels above the market-clearing price. The problem of how high to set prices of wheat, cotton, tobacco, and other farm products then arose: Should product price be set 10 percent above the market level, 20 percent above the market level, or at some other level? This chapter describes the parity-price and cost-of-production approaches to setting price supports. It also analyzes price setting to increase market stability and emphasizes why there is no economically defensible means of determining correct levels for price supports.

PARITY PRICE

The parity-price concept was an objective and widely accepted basis for determining price-support levels for farm products. *Parity* was defined as the price that gives a unit of the commodity the same purchasing power in the current period that it had in the period 1910–14. As one might predict from public-choice theory, this base period in the computation of parity prices for farm products was not arbitrarily chosen. The period 1910–14 is known as a "golden period" of agriculture because prices received, when compared with prices paid by farmers, were highly favorable during that era (figure 8.1). Indeed, the 1910–14 base period used during the 1930s to define a "fair price" was the most favorable peacetime period for agriculture since the Civil War.[1]

FIGURE 8.1 Ratio: Prices received to prices paid.
Source: *Agricultural Statistics*, various issues

The objective of the parity-price approach for farm products is quite simple. For example, if a bushel of wheat would buy, say, a shirt in the period from 1910 to 1914, then to be at parity a bushel of wheat should be priced so as to buy a shirt today. (This example assumes that the price of shirts has increased at the same rate as the price of goods and services generally.) In the computation of the parity price with this original formula, the price of wheat in the base period was multiplied by the "parity index," the current index of prices paid by farmers for commodities, interest, taxes, and wage rates expressed on the 1910–14 = 1.00 base. For example, the price of wheat in the period 1910–14 was $.88 per bushel. In 2001, the annual average prices paid index (as computed by the USDA) was 16.46.[2] Thus, the 2001 parity price for wheat computed by the original parity formula would be 16.46($.88) = $14.48 per bushel. The actual price of wheat averaged only $2.80 per bushel during the 2001 crop year.[3] During the period since the 1930s, farm product prices generally have been considerably below the parity level.

Farm product prices have seldom been supported at 100 percent of parity, even when price supports were based on the parity concept. Indeed, a great deal of debate over farm policy during the 1940s and 1950s was concerned with the appropriate "level of parity." That is, the agricultural policy debate quite often was concerned with whether the price of wheat, milk, or another price-supported product should be supported at 75 percent, 80 percent, 90 percent, or some other proportion of parity.

It is fully predictable that an effective price support based on parity, or on any other standard, will inevitably create surplus problems. Thus, a watering-down of the parity approach occurred because of problems created by surplus production.

In addition to supporting prices at less than 100 percent of parity (based on the original definition of parity), the parity formula itself has been changed over time. Most notably, the parity formula was "modernized" in 1948.[4] The important change made was to introduce a ten-year moving average of prices into the formula. The moving average in the new parity formula effectively lowered parity prices for commodities that had been trending downward more rapidly than farm prices generally and raised the parity price for products whose recent prices were stronger than the aggregate (as measured by the prices-received index). Consequently, with this change, parity prices more accurately reflected recent market conditions. This approach also permitted parity prices to be calculated for commodities that were not widely grown in the 1910–14 period (e.g., soybeans).[5]

The relevance of parity in farm programs over time has been greatly reduced—but not completely eliminated. Neither the 1996 nor the 2002 farm bill mentions the term. However, the USDA still regularly calculates parity prices for more than one hundred commodities.[6] Moreover, the Agricultural Act of 1949, the last farm bill enacted without an expiration date, requires the USDA to base price supports on parity prices for dairy, wheat, and other "basic commodities." All subsequent farm bills have been amendments to the 1949 law and have been temporary.[7] If a new farm bill had not been enacted before the 1996 farm bill (which was temporary farm legislation) expired, for example, the parity provisions of the 1949 law would have gone into effect. Parity prices are also used in administering marketing orders for agricultural commodities.[8]

Shortcomings of the Parity-Price Approach

A number of problems are associated with the use of the parity concept. First, the use of parity prices hinders the functioning of the market process. An assumption in its use is that farm product prices and input prices were in the proper relationship in the 1910–14 base period and that this relationship remains the same over time. There is no logical reason, however, for tying current price relationships to any particular historic time period. Market price at any point in time is determined by the interrelationship of supply and demand, and there is no reason to expect the supply and demand for any particular product today to bear the same relationship to other goods and services that it did from 1910 to 1914 (or in any other historical time period). Indeed, relative prices in a market system are constantly changing in response to changing demand and supply conditions. By adopting a historical base period, the parity formula freezes an otherwise self-adjusting price mechanism.

Second, in tying price relationships to a base period, parity fails to allow for differences in changes in productivity over time. For example, increases in output per hour of labor since 1965 have been greater in poultry than in vegetable production. Thus, there has been more downward pressure over time on poultry prices because of increasing supply. Consequently, a price-support program based on parity prices during this period, other factors being constant, would have created larger surplus problems for poultry than for vegetables. Similarly, parity fails to allow for differences in changes in demand over time. If the demand for chicken increases relative to pork, other factors being constant, the price of chicken will increase. If prices of these products were supported at parity on the basis of 1910–14 relationships, the surplus problem would be more acute for pork.

Third, and closely related, the use of parity prices reduces the competitiveness of domestic products in both foreign and domestic markets, resulting in either surpluses or the imposition of production controls or restrictions on input usage. Thus, parity prices are inconsistent with free trade, domestically and internationally.

Fourth, because incomes are determined by both quantity produced and price, parity prices likely will have only a small effect on many farmers' income. A parity price for wheat, for example, will have little effect on the producer who has few bushels of wheat to sell. Thus, even if all farm products were supported at 100 percent of parity, many small farmers would continue to have relatively low net farm incomes.

Finally, the problem of selecting the appropriate level of parity price is similar to that of determining the long-discredited "just price." When price is raised above the market-clearing level, there is no objective procedure for determining what the price *should* be. That is, when market price signals are consciously ignored through the use of price supports, credit subsidies, and so on, setting prices involves judgments of value, which are necessarily subjective. In the parity-price approach, there is no objective basis for selecting any particular base period or, once the base period is selected, for setting prices at 70, 80, 90, 100 (or any other) percent of parity. The problem of determining the level of price supports is the same as for all other income-redistribution policies that benefit some people at the expense of other people—there is no objective basis for determining the effect of the redistribution or, even more basic, whether it should occur at all.

COST OF PRODUCTION

Beginning in the late 1970s, another method was used in determining the level of price supports. The Food and Agriculture Act of 1977 embraced cost of production as the primary guide in determining the level of farm product price supports. Cost of production, however, is no more defensible than parity as a procedure for determining what the level of product prices *should* be.

To understand why, consider first the problems in measuring cost as it influences entrepreneurial choice. Choice is influenced by opportunity cost, the value of the highest sacrificed alternative associated with any action. For example, the cost to a farmer of using land to produce corn is the value of the land if used in the best alternative use—say, growing soybeans. The expected return to land in soybeans, however, depends on soybean price, yield, and production expenses. Different producers will make different estimates of costs and returns and of the return to land in soybeans. Jones, for example, may anticipate a net return to land of $75 per acre when using land in soybeans. Smith, being more optimistic about future soybean yields, may anticipate a net return of $100 per acre to land in soybeans. Under these conditions, the opportunity cost per acre of land to produce corn is $75 for Jones and $100 for Smith. These costs are the relevant costs to Smith and Jones for using land to produce corn, whether the land in question is owned or rented.

Land is not unique in this respect. Different farm operators also will make different estimates of the value of machinery, buildings, and other durable resources in alternative uses. Thus, the opportunity costs of these resources will vary widely from farm to farm.

The preceding discussion illustrates a basic principle. Opportunity cost is subjective, and there is no reason to expect the opportunity cost of resources for Farmer Jones to be the same as for Farmer Smith.[9] Moreover, the outside observer has no way to determine or measure the opportunity cost that influences the producer's decision.

Consider next that, based on accounting records, different producers will generally appear to have different costs. In the North Carolina Farm Business Management System, a farm record-keeping program initiated to help farmers improve their business-management practices, for example, the total expense of producing one hundred pounds of milk in 1996 was more than 40 percent higher on the highest-cost dairy farm than on the lowest-cost dairy farm.[10] Hence, any effective level of price support selected for a farm product quite likely will be above the costs reported by some farmers and below the costs reported for others.[11]

This observed variation in accounting costs between farms is not necessarily caused by differences in opportunity costs, but may simply be the result of differences in the accuracy of the reported data or to lags in input markets in revaluing specialized resources. Competition in input markets tends to force expected costs at the farm level toward expected product price.[12] If product price is supported above the market level, competition for the resulting profits will cause costs to rise to equal product price. Thus, an additional shortcoming of using cost of production as a basis for price supports is the capitalization problem—competition will cause cost to increase with the level of the support price.

When product price is increased above the market level to Ps, prices of land, rights to produce, skilled workers, and other specialized resources are bid up so that production outlays tend to equal product price. In this way, the income-earning potential of land, allotments, marketing quota, and so on is converted into increased prices of these resources. The process by which the income-earning potential of an asset is converted into the value of the asset is described as capitalization. The capitalization process ensures that a price-support program that increases price will tend to cause costs to rise to equal price—and supply to shift to the left.

Moreover, despite the fact that firms differ because of specialized resources such as land, labor, and allotments, the average cost of production will tend to be the same for different firms and equal to product price. To understand why this is so, consider, as an example, wheat production where land is the only specialized resource and is either typical or superior in terms of productivity. In each panel of figure 8.2, E(P) is expected product price, and the average variable cost of production, AC_0 in the first panel and AC in the second panel, includes the rental cost of typical land. Suppose there is initially an additional return ("rent") to the superior land indicated by the shaded rectangle in figure 8.2. The fact that the land is more productive does not necessarily mean that its use will be more profitable (in the sense that the rate of return on investment will be higher). Any expectation of greater income earning potential on the more productive land is likely to lead quickly to higher land prices. That is, the lure of greater expected profits provides the impetus for the price of more productive land to be bid up. How much will the market price of the superior land increase? Competition will lead profit-seeking investors to bid up the price high enough so that the expected rate of return from its use is no higher than from other investments of similar risk. In this way, the added yield from more productive land is capitalized or converted into increased land values—which also means higher opportunity costs of using the land—whether it is owned or rented out. The result is that when rents are properly assigned, production costs per unit of output will tend to be as high on superior land as on the less-productive land. In each case (figure 8.2), average cost of production will tend to equal product price.

In the standard neoclassical model of a competitive industry with homogeneous inputs, demand and cost of production are independent of each other. When there are specialized inputs such as land, however, costs cannot be determined independently of demand or product price. In the example depicted in figure 8.2, if there were an increase in demand for wheat and the price of wheat [E(P)] increased, expected returns to all land would increase. The anticipated increase in returns to land would quickly be converted into higher land prices and cost of production would rise enough so that wheat price would again tend to equal cost of production—on superior land as well as on typical land.

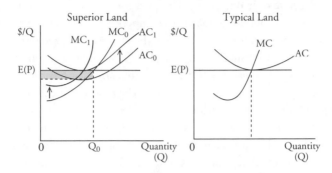

FIGURE 8.2 The advantage of superior land is capitalized into higher costs.

The fact that cost cannot be determined independently of demand or product price when there are specialized resources is highly important for U.S. agricultural policy. Consider the economic effects of a policy to increase dramatically the price of corn to, say, $10 per bushel. The previous analysis suggests that the price of land and other specialized corn-growing resources would be bid up so that costs would also tend to equal $10 per bushel. In figure 8.3, this relationship is shown by the shifts in cost curves from AC_0 and MC_0 to AC_1 and MC_1. That is, the prices of land and other specialized resources vary with corn price, and competition results in the price of these resources being bid up high enough to make price equal to average cost regardless of how high the price is set.

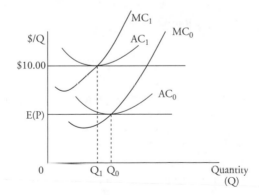

FIGURE 8.3 When product price is increased, costs rise to equal expected price.

The conclusion is that cost of production is not a defensible basis for agricultural price supports.[13] Any effective price support will affect the cost of production. A price support will bring about an increase in the price of specialized resources even if the price support is effective only some of the time. If a price support is effective only one year out of five, for example, it will still increase expected profits, which leads to increased competition and increased costs of production. Furthermore, under real-world conditions of specialized resources, there is a ratchet effect if price supports are based on costs of production. An effective increase in the support price will inevitably increase cost of production. If, in turn, price-support levels are based on costs, the increase in cost will cause the price-support level to increase, which will then lead to higher costs, and so on.

The preceding analysis suggests that regardless of the method used to increase product price, price supports affect resource allocation and result in higher prices of land, allotments, and other specialized resources. Thus, if price supports are set high enough to be effective, the allocation of resources will be affected. There is no way to devise a system of effective price supports that does not distort the pattern of resource use. Furthermore, when price is arbitrarily raised above the competitive market-clearing level, there is no defensible procedure for determining the appropriate level of price support.

Cost of production as a basis for setting price supports was deemphasized in the 1981 farm bill, but the National Agricultural Cost of Production Standards Review Board was established to review annually the cost of production procedures used by the USDA in administering price-support programs.[14] Cost of production is no longer used in establishing or adjusting levels of price supports under the 1996 or 2002 farm bills. However, legislation mandating that the secretary of agriculture make annual cost-of-production estimates is still in place, and the USDA continues to make and publish cost-of-production estimates for various crop and livestock enterprises.

PRICE SETTING TO INCREASE MARKET STABILITY

Increased market stability is often cited as a rationale for agricultural price supports. The argument is made that operation of markets for farm products might be improved if price supports were set at or below expected equilibrium price levels as a means of decreasing market instability. If the price-support level were set at the expected competitive market-clearing price level, for example, risks associated with downside price movements would be decreased. Recognizing that government officials in the real world seldom attempt to set agricultural price supports in this way, let us consider the potential of such price setting to increase market stability.

If price setting is to increase market stability, government officials must cope with the information and incentive problems inherent in the collective decision-making process in general, as discussed in chapter 3. The information problem in setting prices to increase market stability is that there is no way to know before a crop is planted what the actual market-clearing price will be. Indeed, as markets throughout the world for farm products become more interdependent, market prices for U.S. farm products are influenced more and more by supply and demand factors in other countries. And, in light of the perverse incentive problems endemic to the political process, there is no reason to think that information about supply and demand conditions will be more accurately assessed by government officials than by market participants. In other words, it is unlikely that government-generated forecasts will be as accurate as, say, market-generated futures prices for farm products.

Moreover, setting prices to increase market stability without distorting resource use is not an attainable goal. If product prices were set above the market-clearing level, any increase in market stability would be at the expense of increased cost of production as the benefits of higher prices are incorporated into higher resource prices, as described earlier. And the price support need not be set high enough to be effective each year for capitalization effects to increase prices of land and other specialized resources. Indeed, a price support set at or below the expected market-clearing price will distort resource use so long as the price is set above the *minimum price* in the distribution of expected prices.

If, as suggested earlier, price were set at or below expected market price, market instability might be reduced. However, such stabilization schemes, though interesting intellectual exercises, are of little practical significance for U.S. farm policy. Assume that government officials *can* determine and set a minimum price at the market-clearing level. It would reduce producer uncertainty and thereby increase market stability. The incentives are such, however, that political decision makers with a strong vested interest in the agricultural sector would be highly unlikely to do so. And even if they were to do it, political pressures would quickly mount on them to raise the price. Thus, the information and incentive problems endemic in such a policy would inevitably create a great deal of policy uncertainty—uncertainty about both the effectiveness and the future of the policy itself.

The conclusion is that price setting to increase market stability in a way that does not distort resource use is a chimera—market stability is no more defensible than parity or cost of production as a rationale for government price setting. Indeed, as shown in chapter 15, government farm programs in reality not only distort resource use, but also often decrease rather than increase market stability.

SUMMARY

The agricultural price-support programs initiated during the 1930s deliberately raised product prices above market-clearing levels. The parity price for a product was designed to give the product the same purchasing power on a per unit basis that it had during the base period 1910–1914. Although the parity formula was later modified, the inherent problems of this approach have not been resolved. Parity prices hinder the operation of the price mechanism in the market system. Product prices are determined by supply and demand conditions, and relative prices constantly change over time as economic conditions change. As a result, there is no reason to expect the price of any product today to bear the same relationship to the prices of other products that it had in some historical time period. Although still used as a rallying cry by some farm groups, parity is no longer used in setting price-support levels for farm products; it continues to be used, however, in administering marketing orders for agricultural commodities.

In the Food and Agricultural Act of 1977, cost of production was adopted as a guide in determining the level of price supports. This approach has two major shortcomings. First, cost as it influences choice is subjective, and there is no way for the outside observer to measure the costs that influence individual decisions. Second, in a world of specialized resources, cost cannot be determined independently of demand or product price. If product price is supported above the market-clearing level, competitive forces will cause prices of land, allotments, and other specialized resources to be bid up so that there is a tendency for cost to rise to the level of product price, regardless of how high price is set. That is, the benefits of price-support programs are largely capitalized into higher prices of land and other specialized resources. Under recent farm bills, cost of production is no longer the key factor in determining the level of price supports.

The search for an economically defensible basis for setting the level of price supports will predictably fail. The problem of how high to set the level of price support is essentially the same as the problem of other measures used to redistribute income. Redistribution through legislated price supports can no more be justified on the basis of economic theory than can any other income transfer. Any attempt to justify the setting of agricultural prices above the competitive market level involves interpersonal utility comparisons and value judgments, which are "essentially incapable of scientific proof."[15] Moreover, price setting to increase market stability is not feasible because of information and incentive problems inherent in the political process.

9

History and Overview of Production
Controls and Marketing Quotas

Three main types of government policy tools have been used to support (raise) agricultural product prices since the New Deal action programs were instituted in the 1930s: (1) price supports, which support selected commodity prices directly; (2) restrictions on output or input use (typically land); and (3) compensatory payments. Many former U.S. commodity price-support programs and those currently in effect use one or more of these policy tools. We begin by describing these primary policy tools and discussing their economic effects. Next we briefly review the overall historical development of U.S. commodity programs. We then describe several notable former individual commodity programs and discuss their economic effects.

PRICE SUPPORTS ALONE

The simplest type of price-support program is one where the government merely sets price (on the basis of parity, cost of production, or some other criterion) above the market-clearing level. If the price is set at P_s as in figure 9.1, there will be surplus production. In a pure price-support program of this type, the government presumably acquires the surplus produced at the policy-determined price. The acquisition cost to taxpayers is the amount of surplus (A in figure 9.1) times the support price P_s. The net cost to taxpayers, which does not include the deadweight and other opportunity costs from overproduction and taxes required to operate the program, is the acquisition cost plus storage cost less whatever the government receives from selling the stocks.

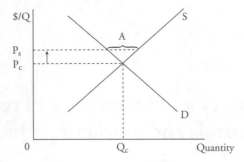

FIGURE 9.1 Price supports without quantity restrictions.

Government commodity programs are much more complex than the program illustrated in figure 9.1. Nonetheless, that simple model can provide useful insights into the impacts of commodity programs. Consider the current U.S. dairy program, in which Congress has for many years set the level of price support (see chapter 11 for more detail on this program).[1] Milk price is then supported by a standing offer from the government to buy enough milk products (dry milk, butter, and cheese) to raise milk price to the support level.[2]

Surpluses are inevitable and fully predictable when government uses price supports to raise farm product prices above competitive levels. For example, the U.S. government has at various times acquired huge stocks of dairy products under the dairy program. Between 1984 and 1986, government inventories of butter, cheese, and dry milk averaged almost 2.5 billion pounds—more than 8 pounds for every person in the United States.[3] More recently, government-owned stocks of butter and cheese have fallen to zero. In 1997, government-owned stocks of dry milk decreased to 30 million pounds, but by 2000 these stocks increased to more than 600 million pounds. The U.S. government also has purchased large amounts of wheat, feed grains, cotton, and other products at various times during the past sixty years in the operation of other price-support programs.

PRICE SUPPORTS WITH RESTRICTIONS ON OUTPUT LEVELS OR INPUT USE

Price supports inevitably lead to increased production, which, as indicated earlier, leads to surpluses and Treasury costs, thereby creating an incentive for further government involvement through programs to control production. A price-support program that involves government acquisition of surpluses will be costly to taxpayers, but the magnitude of the Treasury cost will hinge on how high the price support is set above the market-clearing price. One way for the government to reduce the cost to taxpayers is to restrict the quantity of the product produced or marketed. If production were restricted to Q_s as in figure 9.2, the support price P_s would be achieved without any surplus production. As shown later, however, resource use is distorted, regardless of whether production is reduced by restricting the use of inputs or by limiting output.

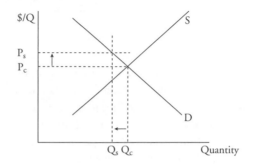

FIGURE 9.2 Price supports with quantity restrictions.

Restrictions on Input Use—Acreage Allotments

Although it is conceivable to reduce output through restrictions on the use of labor or capital, land is the input most commonly restricted in production-control programs. At various times since the 1930s, restrictions on acreage, which may take various forms, including both mandatory allotments and voluntary set asides, have been used in price-support programs for cotton, corn, wheat, tobacco, peanuts, and other products. Restricting the use of land by legal means, however, alters the productive pattern of resource use that would occur in an unhampered market, thereby distorting input use and increasing production costs. Suppose, as in figure 9.3, that a price support increases product price above the competitive level, from P_c to P_s, and that government costs are reduced through the use of mandatory acreage restrictions. The increase in price due to the price support provides each farmer with the incentive to produce more output per acre on his restricted number of acres. Farmers will accomplish this by substituting other inputs, including fertilizer and pesticides, for land. When input use is distorted in this way, marginal cost per unit of output is higher than it would be in the absence of the constraint on resource use—as illustrated by the shift from MC_0 to MC_1 in figure 9.3.

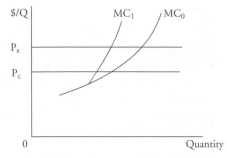

FIGURE 9.3 Production cost is increased when land use is restricted.

The effectiveness of acreage allotments in restricting production is undermined both by advances in production technology and by the substitutability of other inputs for land. In the tobacco program, for example, as technology increased and other inputs were substituted for land, tobacco yields under acreage allotments increased from 1,083 pounds per acre in 1944 to 2,208 pounds in 1964. Thus, acreage allotments had to be reduced again and again during this period to restrict production to the desired level.[4]

Voluntary Diversion of Land

A number of farm programs over the years have been voluntary—providing financial incentives for farmers to reduce the amount of cropland in use. In the Soil Bank program, which was instituted in the Agricultural Act of 1956, for example, farmers were paid to take land out of production. The diversion of cropland also was an important feature of the cotton, wheat, and feed grains programs prior to the 1996 farm bill.

The overall objective of farm programs involving the voluntary diversion of land is the same as for mandatory acreage-allotment programs: to increase product price by reducing production. The basic difference is that in voluntary diversion programs the individual producer's choice of whether to participate is based on economic incentives rather than on legal coercion. Prior to the 1996 farm bill, participation in the cotton, wheat, and feed grain programs was optional. Farmers who chose to participate were required to set aside specified amounts of land for conservation uses to qualify for support payments.

The effect of such land-diversion or acreage-restriction programs on product supply at the market level is depicted in figure 9.4. At low price levels, the restriction on acreage is not binding and so has no effect on the supply function. At the quantity-price combination (Q_0, P_0), however, the acreage restriction becomes binding. As price increases above P_0, producers have incentives to increase production, but must now do so by combining inputs in less-productive ways than without the acreage restriction. Costs increase with the acreage restriction because now output is increased by, for example, using more fertilizers and pesticides and by planting more intensively than without the acreage restrictions. In essence, for output levels greater than Q_0, the cost of production is increased by the acreage restriction, as indicated by the change in the supply function from S_0S_0 to S_0AS_1. In figure 9.4, the acreage restriction reduces the surplus from CB (the amount of the surplus at the support price without a restriction on land use) to CE. The less substitutability there is between land and other inputs, the steeper will be the supply curve beyond Q_0, and the greater will be the reduction in the surplus.

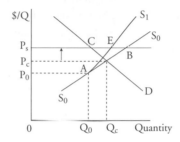

FIGURE 9.4 The effect of land diversion programs on product supply, output, and price.

Restrictions on Output

For some commodities, problems associated with mandatory acreage allotments have resulted in legal restrictions on the amount of output each producer can legally produce and sell. For example, in 1965 the tobacco price-support program was changed so that production was restricted by a marketing poundage quota.[5] The marketing quota specified the number of pounds of tobacco that a producer can sell in a given year. From 1978 until the passage of the 2002 farm bill, the peanut price-support program also involved the use of marketing quotas.[6] Marketing quotas typically are a much more effective means of restricting production (or sales into particular markets) than are restrictions on input use. When operating under acreage restrictions, farmers can continue to increase output, at least to some extent, by substituting other inputs for land, but they cannot legally circumvent mandated restrictions on the number of units of products that they may produce and sell. As shown later in this chapter (and in chapter 10), however, marketing quotas also distort the pattern of production and resource use—thereby increasing the cost of production.

Market Value of Allotments and Quotas

Acreage allotments and production (or marketing) quotas are in a sense artificial factors of production. When quantity restrictions are placed on the production or marketing of a product and the profits associated with those activities increase as a result, the *right* to produce or sell that commodity acquires a value. In general, the demand for any productive input is derived from the demand for the final product that it produces.[7] There is a derived demand for acreage allotments or marketing quotas just as there is for other inputs. (Because the economic effects of acreage allotments and output quotas are similar in many ways, the following analysis is limited to production or marketing quotas.) If the government specifies the number of units that may be sold and hence produced, production rights can be viewed as a factor that is perfectly inelastic in supply. In panel *(b)* of figure 9.5, for example, the supply of quota is vertical at the government-determined level Q_s.

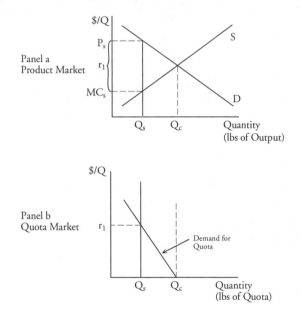

FIGURE 9.5 Rental value of production quota is derived from the product market.

The demand for quota and the price producers are willing to pay to rent or purchase quota are determined by conditions in the product market. Assuming free trade in quota, competition will cause the annual rental value of the quota to equal the difference (at the level of the quota) between product price and the marginal cost of production (excluding the quota cost). Thus, in figure 9.5, the annual rental price of quota is r_1. Moreover, when there is a change in the amount of quota, rents to other factors are affected. If a reduction in the amount of quota were to occur, for example, some of the previous rent to land and other specialized factors would be absorbed in higher quota rental prices.

The market value of the government-determined right to produce and sell a product is the present value of the stream of expected annual quota rents. Moreover, the higher the product price is above nonquota marginal production costs (supply) at the mandated level of output, the more valuable the right to produce and the greater the rental rate for quota.

The value of the right to produce, as described earlier, is capitalized into the market price of quota. Consequently, price-support programs that restrict production through quotas and allotments *increase* production costs for producers, regardless of whether they own or rent quota. If a nonquota owner rents (or buys) quota to obtain the right to produce, production outlays are increased. If the quota owner produces the product himself, use of the quota still has an opportunity cost. Moreover, the more production is restricted, the higher will be the quota or allotment price. The difference between product price and nonquota marginal cost is greater in low-cost production regions and so is quota value. Stated differently, the lower nonquota production costs are, the higher the derived demand for quota and the higher the quota price for any given level of marketing quota. During the heyday of the flue-cured tobacco program in low-cost production regions, for example, the annual rental value of marketing quota on a per acre basis often exceeded $1,000 per year. The issues in the preceding paragraphs are more fully discussed in chapter 10 in connection with the tobacco program.

COMPENSATORY PAYMENTS

An early proposal to adopt price supports that involved the use of compensatory payments was contained in the Brannan Plan of the late 1940s, which was named after Charles Brannan, the secretary of agriculture in the Truman administration (1945–53). The compensatory-payments approach is illustrated in figure 9.6. Product price is supported at the level P_s. At this price, producers are willing to produce the amount Q_s.

In the compensatory-payment approach, the government does not purchase the amount that consumers do not buy at the price-support level, P_s, as is done in the simplest type of price-support program. Instead, the amount produced (Q_s) is sold by producers at whatever price will clear the market (P_m). A government subsidy of P_s–P_m per unit of product produced is then paid to producers. The total subsidy is $(P_s$–$P_m)\cdot Q_s$. Producers know in advance what price they will get but not how much of this price will be received through the market and how much through government payments.

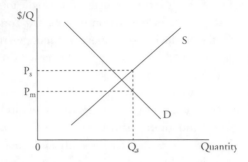

FIGURE 9.6 Price supports with compensatory payments.

Prior to the 1996 farm bill, the compensatory-payment approach was a major component of the cotton, rice, wheat, and feed grain programs, where a "target price" was guaranteed by paying producers the difference between the target price and the market price (or the loan rate). These government outlays were referred to as "deficiency payments." Although target prices were reintroduced in the 2002 farm bill, deficiency payments per se no longer exist, having been replaced by direct payments with new names. The resource-allocation and income-redistribution effects of the target-price approach, as well as its effects on domestic and international markets for farm products, are further described in chapters 10 and 14.

HISTORY AND OPERATION OF PRODUCTION-CONTROL PROGRAMS

The Agricultural Adjustment Administration, which was created in the AAA of 1933 quickly initiated a program of production controls and price supports for the "basic crops" listed in the AAA, including wheat, cotton, corn, tobacco, milk, and dairy products.[8] As indicated previously, the AAA of 1933 was one of many New Deal measures that restricted production, set prices, restricted imports, and so on. The implementation of these programs marked the turning point from a largely free to a highly controlled U.S. farm economy. The effectiveness of initial attempts to increase product prices by controlling production, for example, was undercut by three factors: (1) farmer ingenuity in circumventing planting restrictions; (2) incentives for farmers to increase production in response to high price supports; and (3) the production-increasing effects of other government programs such as soil conservation payments and low-cost credit.[9] The operation of the programs led to a number of changes over time to cope with unforeseen consequences—notably mounting surpluses, increasing Treasury costs, and a lack of competitiveness of U.S. farm products in world markets—that necessitated major changes in the nature of the programs over time.

The First Phase: Supply Management

The emphasis on supply management to reduce output as a means of increasing product prices without unacceptably large Treasury costs lasted from 1933 to the mid-1950s. Under the AAA of 1933, acreage allotments restricted farmers to planting only a specific number of acres of particular crops such as rice, wheat, cotton, peanuts, and tobacco. A national acreage allotment for a crop was set at a level that would meet anticipated domestic and export consumption at the support price. The national allotment was then apportioned among individual farms based on historical plantings of the crop. Farmers also were paid to take land out of production voluntarily as a way of increasing prices of farm products. Other production-control measures received a great deal of criticism. For example, farmers were paid to plow up cotton, and the government, in a widely publicized and much criticized program, bought up pigs and killed them to reduce the supply of pork.

Prices to farmers for the basic crops were guaranteed by the U.S. government by granting producers "nonrecourse loans" on their commodities stored by the Commodity Credit Corporation (CCC). The CCC, a government agency, was created as a companion policy of the AAA in 1933 to provide for loans to farmers and storage when production was "too large."[10] The wheat farmer, for example, could store wheat and obtain a loan from the CCC using the wheat as the collateral. The loan rate per bushel was the support price of wheat. If the price of wheat fell below the predetermined support price, wheat farmers could satisfy their loan obligations by forfeiting their rights to the commodities held by the CCC. In such a situation, the CCC had no recourse other than to assume ownership of the commodity. CCC stock holdings of the various program crops indicated amounts not sold at market prices. Through the years, these stocks have provided a good measure of surplus production attributable to farm programs.

The AAA of 1933 was declared unconstitutional by the U.S. Supreme Court in 1936.[11] Although the Roosevelt administration (1933–45) lost this battle, Congress quickly enacted the Soil Conservation and Domestic Allotment Act of

1936, which combined conservation with production controls. This act, which was financed by direct appropriations from the Treasury, essentially accomplished the same purpose as the AAA of 1933. The Agricultural Marketing Agreement Act of 1937 provided for agricultural marketing orders, which were used and continue to be widely used for milk, oranges and other fruits, vegetables, and specialty crops. Finally, the AAA of 1938 became the blueprint for subsequent farm programs involving production controls. This act provided price supports and production controls for "basic crops"—wheat, corn, cotton, rice, peanuts, and tobacco—and mandated that price-support levels be set at the discretion of the secretary of agriculture, between 52 and 75 percent of parity.

In the early years, price-support programs generally involved mandatory controls for all producers if the program was approved in a producer referendum. Marketing quotas were binding on all producers if two-thirds of the producers holding production allotments voted in favor of quotas in a referendum. The 1949 farm bill, the last permanent farm legislation enacted into law (as explained in chapter 8), also provided for acreage allotments and marketing quotas if approved by two-thirds of the voting producers.

The initial production controls in the form of acreage allotments and unusually severe droughts in the mid-1930s resulted in lower output of most of the controlled crops during this period. Total acreage of crops grown, however, changed little as farmers substituted noncontrolled crops for controlled crops. Sharp increases occurred, for example, in acreage of soybeans, rice, and sorghum grain. Moreover, surpluses of corn and other controlled crops soon mounted because of sharp increases in yields as farmers intensified their farming practices on the restricted acreage. And to the extent that noncontrolled crops, such as sorghum grain, were good substitutes for corn as feed for livestock, increases in noncontrolled crops further exacerbated surplus problems in the corn market.[12]

The surplus stock problem, or the lack of balance between supply and demand, resulted from the government's setting prices above the market level. As a result, in part, of severe droughts, problems of overproduction and surplus stocks remained manageable from the initiation of the New Deal AAA farm programs in 1933 until World War II. Production controls were removed during the war as commodity prices increased and stocks were liquidated because of increased war demand. The postwar economic recovery of war-ravaged Europe and Asia and then the Korean War kept demand strong so that surpluses of U.S. farm products were not a major problem into the early 1950s. In the mid-1950s, however, high price supports led to mounting surplus problems. The pace of advancements in agricultural technology quickened following the Korean War, and accumulating surpluses led the Eisenhower administration (1953–61) to launch several new initiatives to cope with the overproduction.

Before consideration of the second phase of farm policies designed to cope with surplus problems while maintaining high farm prices and incomes, it is useful first to consider the two primary reasons why supply management failed to prevent overproduction.

Why Supply Management Failed

Supply management failed first because of farmer ingenuity in circumventing planting restrictions. Farmers minimized the effects of planting restrictions in a number of ways. In adhering to the acreage restriction, farmers took the less-productive land out of production. They further circumvented acreage restrictions by skip-row planting. By leaving half the rows in a field unplanted, skip-row planting enabled them to have only one acre counted against the allotment for every two acres in the field. Yields per row increased because the plants received more sunlight and water. In addition, yields per acre increased as higher product prices made it profitable for farmers to increase the use of nonland inputs, such as chemical fertilizers, lime, improved seed, and so on. Thus, as use of nonland inputs was intensified, acreage controls were even less effective in decreasing crop production than in reducing overall crop acreage. High price supports also undermined supply management because high product prices spurred the development of substitute products and alternative sources of supply, making U.S. farm products less competitive, both at home and abroad.[13]

Supply management also failed because other government farm programs increased the supply of farm products, working against the stated policy goal of decreasing farm output. Large subsidies, for example, in the form of government cost sharing for soil conservation and improvement were established. Payments of roughly 50 percent of the cost were made to farmers for use of commercial fertilizers, lime, cover crops, terracing, drainage, irrigation, and so on. Although often contingent on shifting more acres into grasses and legumes, the program also provided the incentive to use more fertilizer on crops under acreage allotments. Expanded subsidies for federal research and farmer education and the institution of new programs to subsidize farm credit also led to further increases in farm output.

The Second Phase: Surplus Problems and Export Subsidies

As surplus farm products mounted in the 1950s after the end of the Korean conflict, a political consensus emerged that farm programs should be modified because the cropland base was too large. Measures instituted at this time to alleviate overproduction included flexible and lower price supports, land retirement, and programs to increase the demand for farm products. Secretary of Agriculture Ezra Taft Benson in the Eisenhower administration, realizing that the surplus problem was rooted in prices being held above the market level, recommended that price supports be reduced below the existing level of 90 percent of parity. The Agricultural Act of 1949 gave the secretary of agriculture authority to lower price-support levels, and price supports were decreased somewhat from 1953 to 1960, despite heated opposition in Congress.

The concept of parity has a fundamental problem: there is little or no relationship between historically based parity prices and the contemporary market price, which is determined by existing supply and demand conditions. Consequently, a price support set at 90 percent, 80 percent, or even 50 percent of parity still may be above the market-clearing level. Moreover, the market price for wheat, corn, or any other farm product is reduced by an increase in supply. Thus, ongoing dramatic advances in agricultural technology, along with government subsidies for nonland inputs, research, farmer education, and so on, continued to lower the market-clearing price for farm products throughout the 1950s. The modest reductions in price supports during the mid- to late 1950s were not sufficient to eliminate surpluses in the face of increasing supplies.

Continuing surplus problems in this era led to the implementation of another approach to reducing the total capacity of U.S. agriculture. Under the 1956 Soil Bank program, farmers were paid to take cropland out of production. The Soil Bank, a response to the surplus production created by price supports, was viewed as an alternative to acreage allotments and marketing quotas. The basic idea was to take land out of production on a long-term basis as a way of reducing the output of farm products. Under this program, sections of farms and entire farms were removed from production for periods ranging from three to fifteen years. This program was designed both to reduce the output of crops then in greatest surplus and to shift land out of cultivation and into forage, trees, and so on. It also tightened compliance with crop-specific acreage allotments in an attempt to reduce the shift to secondary crops by limiting the *total* acreage of crops grown so that shifts into secondary, noncontrolled crops did not defeat the purpose of the controls. Although farmers retained the option of whether to participate in these new farm programs, the new measures tempered somewhat the rate of increase in farm output.

During the period from 1961 to 1972, an average of 12 percent of U.S. farmland was enrolled in the Soil Bank program.[14] The annual cost of the program reached a peak of almost $1 billion in 1971. Objections to the program, in addition to its cost, were based on its negative impacts on rural businesses and institutions in communities where farmers placed whole farms in the Soil Bank.

The Soil Bank program provides another example of how government programs often create pressure for additional government action to cope with the undesirable consequences of the original program. Although the Soil Bank program did decrease overproduction created by price supports, paying farmers to leave productive land idle is not consistent with efficient resource use. The program induced farmers to shift large amounts of land from more-productive to less-productive uses. The land was idled not because its use was inherently unprofitable, but rather because surplus production created by government price-support programs needed to be reduced. Large amounts of valuable output were foregone in idling millions of acres of productive farmland in this way.

In addition to these measures to reduce farm output, government initiatives were launched beginning in the 1950s to increase the consumption of farm products. A massive government-subsidized export plan, known initially as Public Law 480 (PL 480) and later as Food for Peace, was implemented to encourage the export of price-supported commodities to countries unable to make commercial purchases and to assist agricultural development in less-developed countries. Although this program did provide an additional outlet for U.S. farm products, it is not consistent with open markets, and it has had harmful effects on producers in the recipient countries.[15] In addition to this subsidized effort to increase foreign demand for farm products, domestic food subsidies—including the school lunch and food stamp programs—also were expanded. These measures to dispose of overproduction in a politically acceptable manner contributed substantially to the dramatic increase in the costs of government farm programs from the early 1950s to the early 1960s.

The Third Phase: Direct Payments

Despite the increasing costs of farm programs, it became apparent that the price-support and acreage-control programs were not solving the income problem in agriculture; net farm income, for example, was lower in the early 1960s than it had been a decade earlier. Direct payments to farmers jumped with the Soil Bank program in 1956 and increased under the 1961 farm bill, in which participating farmers received diverted acreage payments that affected corn and other feed grains. Direct payments to farmers remained important under succeeding farm bills in 1965 and 1970.

Direct payments from the government assumed even greater importance with the 1973 farm bill, which implemented for the first time an entirely new system of direct payments—target prices.[16] The target-price method of price supports for wheat, cotton, and feed grains remained in effect for more than twenty years, was discontinued under the 1996 farm bill, and was revived in a somewhat modified form in the 2002 farm bill. Under the target-price method of crop subsidy, participating farmers received a government-determined target price for their crops. The farmer either sold the product at the market price (the price at which the quantity supplied by farmers at the target price equals the quantity demanded) or placed it under CCC storage at a specified loan rate. The government then paid the farmer an amount—known as a *deficiency payment*—to ensure that she received the target price.[17] Direct payments to U.S. farmers reached a peak in the severe recession of the mid-1980s. The anticipated budgetary costs were $1–2 billion when the 1981 farm bill was enacted.[18] However, program costs increased sharply—totaling nearly $19 billion in 1983 as commodity markets weakened in the early 1980s and price supports remained high. Direct payments to farmers remained important in the 1996 farm bill, in which farmers who participated in the target-price programs were guaranteed "transition payments" for seven years (see chapter 10). Direct payments also are important in the 2002 farm bill (see the discussion in the appendix of direct decoupled and countercyclical payments).

OTHER NOTABLE PAST COMMODITY PROGRAMS

Payment-in-Kind Programs

A payment-in-kind program was initiated in 1983 to reduce government stock holdings, to avoid the budget outlays associated from forfeiture of large amounts of grain to the CCC, and to reduce production. In this program, the USDA used Payment-in-Kind (PIK) certificates, negotiable certificates redeemable for commodities held by the CCC, to retire land from production for one year and to avoid paying benefits in cash.[19] The certificates were generic in the sense that any commodity held by the CCC could be purchased with them. A farmer with commodities under a CCC loan who received PIK certificates could use certificates to pay off the loan or to buy corn (or other commodities) from the CCC. Alternatively, the farmer could sell the certificates to anyone else who wanted to buy them.

The payment rate on land not planted was highly attractive to cooperating farmers—80 percent of average production for feed grain and cotton and 95 percent for wheat. Thus, farmers who idled their wheat land received PIK certificates for 95 percent of their average yield without having to incur any production costs! As might be expected given these generous incentives, participation rates were high—more than one-third of the cropland (some 82 million acres) was idled in 1983 by the PIK programs, and farmers received PIK certificates for commodities with a book value of approximately $9 billion.[20] As a result, the PIK program was the most massive and costly acreage-reduction program in the history of U.S. farm policy.[21] And, as is generally true for price-support programs, large producers were the major gainers from the program. The $50,000 limit on price-support payments to any one farmer under previous programs was lifted, and some individual farmers received PIK payments of more than $1 million!

The PIK program provides yet another good example of government programs having effects that cannot be foreseen, which in turn create pressures for new programs to deal with these unanticipated consequences. By decreasing farm production activities, the PIK program reduced sale of farm equipment, fertilizer, and other agricultural inputs, disadvantaging firms that sold those inputs. Congress then made agribusiness firms eligible for subsidized Farmers Home Administration (FmHA) loans. A new program administered by the Small Business Administration was also initiated. This program offered low-interest loans to businesses in counties with heavy PIK participation that could prove PIK reduced their income by stipulated amounts.

The PIK program also adversely affected consumers and purchasers of affected farm products. Livestock and poultry producers, for example, were harmed by the PIK program because of sharply higher feed costs. By restricting production and increasing prices, the PIK program also reduced exports of U.S. farm products. Moreover, although PIK was effective in reducing government stocks of surplus commodities, it did nothing to reduce long run production incentives. The PIK program has not been in effect since the late 1980s. Whether it will be reinstituted remains to be seen; it was, for example, reauthorized under the 1999 emergency aid bill.

The Farmer-Owned Reserve

The Farmer-Owned Reserve (FOR) for wheat and feed grains was introduced in the late 1970s by the Carter administration. It allowed producers holding regular nine-month loans for wheat or feed grains to extend reduced interest loans beyond the regular term and to receive additional storage payments. The FOR was designed to stabilize prices and to provide increased supply assurance to domestic and foreign customers.[22] The loans were made for three years and could be extended "as warranted by market conditions."[23] They could be called in prior to the maturity date only if the secretary of agriculture determined that emergency conditions required that the commodities be made available.[24] Although the 1996 farm bill suspended authority for the FOR through the 2002 crop year, it is unlikely that the lure of government-controlled storage is a dead issue.

The operation of the FOR program faces the same questions as other government programs established to manage reserve stocks. First, why should the government subsidize the storage of stocks? Storage operations in the market will be undertaken to the extent that private entrepreneurs think storage will be profitable. When storage operations are subsidized, more of the product is stored than is warranted on the basis of market information available when the storage decision is made. Moreover, if the amount of farm products stored in the United States increases, storage of these products in importing countries is discouraged.

Second, is the government better able to make storage decisions than farmers (and other private entrepreneurs)? Storage decisions inevitably involve uncertainty, but public officials are unlikely to have more accurate information about current and future market conditions than are actual market participants. Furthermore, private entrepreneurs, with their own funds at stake, have a greater incentive to make the best use of available information. When storage decisions are made through the political process, short-run political considerations are likely to dominate economic considerations. In summary, when information and incentive problems are taken into account, there is no reason to think that storage decisions made through the collective-choice process will improve on storage decisions made by private entrepreneurs operating in decentralized markets.

MANDATORY VERSUS VOLUNTARY PRODUCTION CONTROLS

Over the years, the extent to which farmers have been free to choose to participate or not to participate in production-control programs has varied a great deal. In the early years, most production-control programs were voted on by farmers, and all were bound if two-thirds of farmers who voted were in favor of controls. A watershed in the freedom of individual farmers to participate in farm programs occurred during the Kennedy administration of the early 1960s. The Food and Agricultural Act of 1962 gave the president the authority to impose mandatory production controls following approval by two-thirds of the producers. The controls were not to be on acreage, but rather on the pounds or bushels sold. In a 1963 wheat referendum, mandatory controls were soundly defeated.[25] Most of the production-control programs developed since that time have been instituted on a voluntary basis, with farmers paid to participate. Prior to the 1996 farm bill, wheat, feed grain, and cotton price-support and production-control programs were operated on such a voluntary basis. The producer who did not sign up and comply with program provisions, however, was not eligible for price supports. Similarly, under the 1996 and 2002 farm bills, a farmer—though having much greater flexibility to make planting decisions than previously—still is required to sign up and comply with program provisions in order to receive the direct government payments in each year since 1996 (see chapter 10).

That a plebiscite (a vote by farmers) precedes compulsion in the case of production-control programs—such as the tobacco program, the pre-2002 peanut program, and some marketing orders—does not remove the coercive aspect of these nonvoluntary programs. The minority of producers who oppose a mandatory program are still required to participate.

Moreover, it should be emphasized that the distinction between voluntary and mandatory production-control programs is not always as clear-cut as implied by the preceding discussion. The *voluntary* versus *mandatory* distinction—as used in discussions of agricultural policy—typically refers only to decisions by farmers as producers of the product involved. Other individuals affected by the programs have no direct voice in their adoption. In fact, all price-support and production-control programs are inconsistent with the competitive market process. That is, a fundamental incompatibility exists between effective domestic agricultural price-support policies and free trade. When the domestic price of any product is raised above the world price, imports must be restricted to prevent domestic users from buying the lower-priced foreign product. The plebiscites conducted in the operation of farm programs do not include the much larger number of taxpayers and domestic and foreign consumers who bear the costs of the programs.

SUMMARY

Three different types of price-support programs have been used in U.S. agriculture. In the case of a price support alone, price is supported above the market level, and the government buys the surplus created by the support program. If the price support is effective, the government outlay required to operate the program is likely to create pressures to reduce supply through restrictions on production. Product output can be reduced either by restricting input use or by controlling output directly. Both acreage allotments and marketing quotas have been widely used in the operation of U.S. price-support programs. When output is restricted, the right to produce the limited quantity acquires a value. Increases in product prices resulting from price-support programs are capitalized into prices of land, allotments, and other specialized resources, thereby increasing production costs.

In the simplest compensatory-payments approach, producers are permitted to produce as much as they wish at the supported price. The quantity produced is sold at the price that will clear the market. Producers then receive a payment directly from the government for the difference between the market price and the support price. The target-price approach of recent farm bills (temporarily eliminated by the FAIR Act of 1996) is a compensatory-payment approach.

Price-support programs lead to government purchase and storage activities for agricultural products. The CCC is the government agency responsible for the financing of surplus removal. In a nonrecourse loan, the farmer obtains a loan from the CCC by pledging an eligible commodity as collateral. The farmer may either repay the loan within a specified period and regain control of the commodity or default on the loan, in which case ownership of the commodity passes to the CCC.

The long-run effect of price supports on product price will be different from the short-run effect. The initial effect of price-support programs is to increase prices of farm products. The raising of product prices, however, not only holds resources in agriculture, but also attracts new resources into production that would otherwise have been allocated to more productive uses. These excess resources increase supply, thereby placing downward pressure on product prices—or increased pressure on the federal Treasury to finance price-support programs.

The production-control programs operated in conjunction with price-support operations in the New Deal era were mainly mandatory for all producers once the programs were approved in a farmer referendum. Currently, the individual producer must comply if production controls are approved by two-thirds of the producers in the case of tobacco and marketing orders. After the early 1960s, producer participation in most other production-control programs was on a voluntary basis for domestic producers. The 1996 and 2002 farm bills no longer require cropland diversion on the part of participating producers of cotton, wheat, and feed grains. Since 1996, qualifying farmers who recently participated in price-support programs for these commodities have received direct annual income payments.

All effective price-support programs and programs that artificially reduce market prices below world levels are inconsistent with the competitive market process. As shown in upcoming chapters, such programs inevitably impede mutually voluntary exchange and distort markets through accompanying import quotas, export subsidies, and other restrictions on competition.

10

Production Controls, Price Supports, and Current Farm Programs

For some time after passage of the FAIR Act of 1996, commonly referred to as the 1996 farm bill, many felt it represented a sweeping change in direction for U.S. farm commodity programs. Price-support and income-support payments for wheat, feed grains, and cotton had been linked to a farm's production history and to current production from the initial AAA in 1933 until passage of the 1996 farm bill. Under the 1996 farm bill, annual lump sum payments known as *production flexibility contract payments*, or Agricultural Market Transition Act (AMTA) payments, were made to producers of these commodities.[1] These payments were linked to previous production, but were independent of a producer's production of these commodities in any given year. This decoupling of the link between government payments and production was viewed as a landmark change in commodity policy because of the reduced impact of government commodity payments on farmers' production decisions.

The FAIR Act also included loan rates for many commodities, including those designated to receive AMTA payments, although the legislated rates were considerably below market prices for a period after the bill was enacted. When market prices fell in recent years, however, the loan rates became effective. Because federal payments made on marketing loans and loan deficiency payments (LDPs) are based on current production, this component of government payments still influences farmers' planting decisions.

Various provisions of the 2002 farm bill are discussed in the appendix to this book. This farm bill generally increases the level of government expenditures on a wide variety of farm programs. Loan rates for most commodities have been increased, and marketing loans and LDPs are continued for wheat, feed grains, and cotton (as well as for a number of other commodities), with all production eligible for these payments. Annual lump sum payments are continued for these commodities, with the level of payment based on previous production levels. The fact that farmers are allowed to update their base acres and program yields using 1998–2001 acreage and yields, however, suggests that current production may influence future government payment levels. Further, as discussed in the appendix, target prices have been reinstituted in the 2002 farm bill.

Participation in price-support programs for cotton, rice, wheat, and feed grains was voluntary to the individual producer even before passage of the FAIR Act. In the case of the tobacco program (which was eliminated in October 2004), participation was mandatory, and production historically involved stringent poundage or acreage controls or both. Although the peanut and tobacco programs historically were quite similar, peanut producers (as explained later) historically had somewhat more flexibility in production. The operation of both optional and mandatory participation programs is discussed and contrasted in this chapter.

PROGRAMS WHERE PARTICIPATION IS OPTIONAL

In this section, we first discuss the target-price method of price supports for cotton, rice, wheat, and feed grains. This type of program has been in effect since 1973 except during the years covered by the 1996 farm bill when the target-price programs for these commodities were (temporarily) abolished. In these programs, support payments to farmers were linked to production history. It is important to know how these programs operated in order to understand better how the annual lump sum contract payments were determined under the 1996 farm bill and how payments operate in the 2002 farm bill. After discussing the target-price method of supporting prices, we then describe income-support programs for other commodities where benefits are determined primarily by current production and where producer participation also is optional. After that, we discuss the tobacco and peanut programs, where producer participation historically was mandatory.[2]

Target Prices, Loan Rates, and Deficiency Payments: Support Payments Linked to Current and Past Production

The concept of "target price" was first implemented on a large-scale basis in the Agriculture and Consumer Protection Act of 1973. In this compensatory-payment approach, the target price was the effective price-support level in implementing wheat, cotton, rice, and feed grain programs. When the market price fell below the target price, participating producers received direct government payments, referred to as *deficiency payments*. The amount of government payments increased with acreage used for production because payments were based on a farm's crop acreage base. A farm's production history was used to determine the crop acreage base for each of the commodities on the farm eligible for government payments.[3] The county Agricultural Stabilization and Conservation Service (now the FSA) office maintained records of crop bases for various commodities for each farm.

The deficiency payment rate per unit of product was equal to the difference between the target price and the higher of the loan rate or the market price. The total deficiency payment on a farm was determined by the deficiency payment rate (per unit of the commodity), program acreage, and payment yield (which was based on historical yields for the farm). This meant, of course, that local USDA officials had to maintain detailed records of each farmer's farming activities.

In the following sections, we first describe the nonrecourse loan program (which was an important component of target-price programs) and the role played by the CCC. We then describe the determination of deficiency payments and conclude with an analysis of the impacts of target-price programs on output and market price.

The CCC and the Nonrecourse Loan Program

The CCC, although created as a temporary agency, continues to serve as the government's arm for acquisition, storage, and sale of surplus commodities. Within the USDA, the CCC retains responsibility for providing the financial and storage functions related to price-support and income-support programs. The CCC has no operating personnel. Its activities are carried out through the staff and facilities of the USDA's FSA, and it borrows directly from the federal Treasury. The CCC employs two measures to increase prices: direct commodity purchases, as in the dairy program, and nonrecourse loans.

In a *nonrecourse loan*, a participating farmer obtains a loan from the CCC by pledging a specified quantity of a commodity as collateral. Loans are made at a fixed rate per unit called the loan rate, which varies from year to year according to current legislation and administration. A farmer may store the product in his own facilities or in commercial facilities. The farmer obtaining a loan may elect either to repay the loan within a specified period (usually nine or ten months) and regain control of the commodity or to default on the loan. If the loan rate is above the market price and the borrower defaults, the government has no recourse—hence, the name, *nonrecourse* loans—and ownership of the commodity passes to the CCC, thereby terminating the loan obligation. Commodities obtained by the CCC on defaulted loans become government property and are held in CCC storage until released on the market or disposed of in some other manner. The CCC and taxpayers lose on such transactions, unless bailed out by war or other exigencies, because the CCC must generally dispose of goods at market prices below loan rates.

The nonrecourse loan provides a ready source of capital that permits the producer to store the commodity and delay marketing, thus retaining the potential to obtain a higher price later in the marketing season if the price increases above the loan rate. If the loan is redeemed, the producer must repay the loan plus interest based on a subsidized interest rate (2.75 percent in October 2002). Because the subsidized interest rate has tended historically to make CCC loans a cheap source of credit when compared with funds from commercial sources, farmers have sometimes placed grain under loan even when harvest prices were above the loan rate.[4] Nonrecourse commodity loans were retained in the 1996 and 2002 farm bills. Loan rates continue to be based on averages of recent market prices.

The loan rate historically tended to establish a floor for the market price. The Food Security Act of 1985 changed the role of CCC loans through the introduction of marketing loans and generic PIK certificates.[5] With the marketing loan provision, a producer is allowed to repay a loan at less than the announced loan rate whenever the market price (more precisely, the CCC-determined value for repayment) is less than the commodity loan rate.[6] If, for example, the loan rate is $2.00 and the market price is $1.50, the farmer can repay the loan and sell the commodity for $1.50. The difference between the loan rate and the market price ($.50 in this example) is referred to as a *marketing loan payment*.[7] The marketing loan effectively divorces nonrecourse loans from their role as a market mechanism and is equivalent to an export subsidy.[8] The 1996 and 2002 farm bills continued marketing loan provisions for wheat, feed grains, cotton, soybeans and oilseeds, allowing repayment of loans at less than full principal plus interest when prices are below loan rates. The 2002 bill also implements marketing loan programs for several commodities, including peanuts, honey, wool, mohair, small chickpeas, lentils, and dry beans.

The Determination of Deficiency Payments

The deficiency payment rate under target-price programs varied, depending on how high the target price was in relationship to the loan rate and market price. If the market price, P_M, was above the target price, P_T, the price support was ineffective, and no deficiency payments were made (figure 10.1). Target-price levels, however, were usually set high enough to be effective. Consider the situation depicted in figure 10.2, where the market price is above the loan rate but below the target price. In this case, the target price P_T results in an output of Q_T, which clears the market at a price P_M.[9] Here the per unit "deficiency payment" would be the difference between the target price and the market price, and the total government deficiency payment would be $(P_T - P_M) \cdot Q_T$.

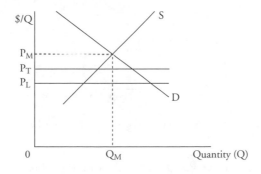

FIGURE 10.1 Target-price approach where price support is ineffective.

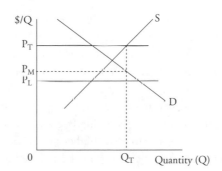

FIGURE 10.2 Target price approach where market price is above the loan rate.

Eligible producers under the 1996 and 2002 farm bills continue to have the option of obtaining a commodity loan from the CCC at the loan rate, which is the price per unit at which the CCC provides nonrecourse loans to farmers. Participating producers have an incentive to place a commodity under loan to the government if the market price of that commodity is expected to be below the loan rate. Prior to the 1996 farm bill, deficiency payments of $(P_T - P_L) \cdot Q_T$ were made to eligible producers when the market price was below the loan rate. Such a situation is shown in figure 10.3, where a portion of the quantity produced, $Q_T - Q_1$, is placed under loan. For participating producers who elected to place commodities in the nonrecourse loan program, the price received was the target price comprised of the loan rate plus the deficiency payment. Marketing loan gains have the potential to increase producer income further when the repayment rate for marketing loans is below the (contemporaneous or expected future) market price.

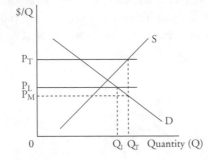

FIGURE 10.3 Target-price approach where market price is below the loan rate.

Effects of a Target-Price Program on Output and Market Price Acreage Reductions

Price-support programs for cotton, rice, wheat, and feed grains were tied to voluntary reductions in land use prior to the 1996 farm bill. The acreage-reduction feature of these programs was first introduced in 1970. It required that a certain percentage of a participating farmer's base acreage of cropland be taken out of production in return for the farmer's right to receive program benefits. The base acreage for a particular farmer in any year was determined by the average acreage devoted to the crop during the preceding five years. Because producer participation was optional, benefits from the higher prices had to be large enough to offset the farmer's foregone income from the reduced acreage required for program participation. The producer not only lost production from the acres taken out of production, but also incurred some of the cost of planting a cover crop in placing the land in a "conservation reserve."[10]

Input use was distorted in target-price programs because the acreage-reduction requirement diverted productive land to lower-valued uses. Thus, one effect of the target-price approach was to decrease product supply.[11] Observed output may not decrease even though supply decreases, however. The effect of a target price on market price and output depends on how high the target price is set above the competitive price and the extent to which supply decreases because of the acreage reduction requirements of the program. The possible effects or a target price on output and market price, when compared with free-market conditions, are shown in figure 10.4.

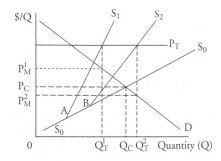

FIGURE 10.4 Effect of target-price and acreage-reduction program.

P_C and Q_C are the competitive price and output under free-market demand and supply conditions. If the supply curve under the target-price program (with acreage restrictions) is S_0AS_1 and the target price is P_T, the quantity of output is Q_T^1, and P_M^1 is the market-clearing price. In this situation, where there is a large decrease in supply and the target price is substantially above the competitive price level, output is less than the free-market level. Thus, output under a target-price system of price supports may be reduced below the free-market level if the decrease in supply due to the acreage-reduction requirement is large.

Output can increase, however, if the target price is well above the competitive price level or if the acreage-reduction requirement is not large. Such a situation is depicted by the supply curve S_0BS_2 in figure 10.4, where quantity produced with the target-price program is Q_T^2 and the market-clearing price is P_M^2. Target prices that bring about increases in production can be viewed as an indirect means of subsidizing exports (this issue is further discussed in chapter 14).[12]

The FAIR Approach: Support Payments Not Linked to Current Production

The 1996 farm bill (FAIR Act) was passed after a lengthy farm bill debate. This legislation implemented significant changes in the structure of farm programs and called for decreased federal spending on farm programs. Some of the changes under this bill were overturned or altered by the 2002 farm bill, however, and actual farm program expenditures under the 1996 bill (as shown later) were considerably greater than the contract payments specified in the legislation.

The most important break with the past was in Title I, the AMTA, which provided income support for eligible producers of wheat, feed grains, cotton, and rice for the seven-year period, 1996–2002. The legislation removed the link between income-support payments and farm prices by providing for annual *contract payments* for seven years. The contract payments for a particular farm, as explained later, were determined by the amount of crop acreage bases that would have been in effect under the 1990 farm bill. A participating farmer's crop acreage base for wheat and feed grains was a five-year moving average of acres planted plus land not planted because of the acreage-reduction requirement. A three-year average was used in determining the crop acreage base for cotton and rice.

The 1996 farm bill's income support for producers of the affected commodities had three main elements: a seven-year contract between the USDA and eligible producers, planting flexibility, and contract payments. A farmer was eligible to enter a contract if he had at least one crop acreage base and participated in any of the farm programs for wheat, feed grains, cotton, or rice in any of the crop years 1991 through 1995. Participation was restricted, however, to eligible producers who entered into a "production flexibility contract" with the USDA for the period 1996–2002 during the one-time sign-up period that ended August 1, 1996. The farmer could enroll all or a portion of the eligible cropland on his farm. Virtually all (98.8 percent) of the eligible acreage was enrolled in production flexibility contracts. The contract required that a participating producer comply with the existing conservation plan for the farm, including wetland provisions, and keep the land in agricultural uses.

The contract rules under the FAIR Act represented a movement toward a more market-based system in the sense that they provided farmers much *greater flexibility* in making planting decisions than under previous farm bills. The idling of land (crop base) required under the previous target-price system was eliminated, and there were no planting restrictions on noncontract acres so long as the producer followed the farm's conservation plan and did not violate wetland provisions. Moreover, on contract acres, participating farmers had the freedom to plant almost any crop, although there were limitations on growing fruits and vegetables. Producers participating in the FAIR program were not required to plant the crop for which the crop base was established and were allowed to plant all of their contract acreage plus additional acreage to any crop (except for fruits and vegetables) with no loss of payment. There were several exceptions to the prohibition on planting fruits and vegetables. First, dry peas, lentils, and mung beans could be planted on contract acreage without loss of payment. Second, any producer could double-crop fruits and vegetables without loss of payments in a region where there was a history of double-cropping fruits and vegetables with a contract commodity. Third, farms with a history of planting fruits and vegetables could plant fruits or vegetables on contract acres, but there was an acre-for-acre loss of payments.

Commodities defined as "contract commodities" under FAIR were those eligible for production flexibility, or contract, payments—wheat, corn, sorghum, barley, oats, rice, and upland cotton. The 1996 farm bill specified total contract payments for each year from 1996 to 2002 based on estimates of what deficiency payments would have been under the 1990 farm bill during that period. The bill also specified the allocation of the total annual payments among contract commodities.[13] The actual payment rate per unit (dollars per bushel or cents per pound) of a contract commodity in each year was based on the total contract payment to be allocated and the level of production that qualified for payments on contract acres. Thus, the more acres enrolled in a year, the smaller the payment rate per unit of product. The contract payment on an individual farm was the payment rate times the payment quantity of the commodity—the 1995 program yield for the farm times 85 percent of that farm's contract acreage. For example, consider a farmer with 100 contract acres of wheat and a program yield of 34 bushels per acre.[14] Production that qualified for contract payments, based on 85 percent of contract acres, was 2,890 (0.85·100·34) bushels of wheat. The average estimated payment rate for wheat during the seven-year period was $.61. In this case, the farmer received an average annual contract payment of $1,763 (= 2,890·$0.61).

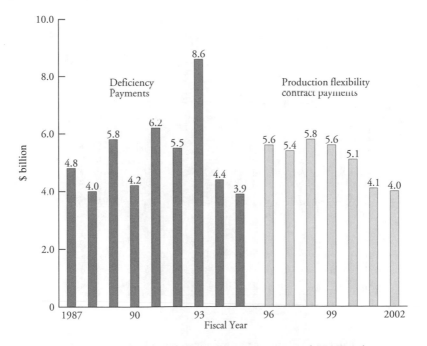

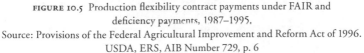

FIGURE 10.5 Production flexibility contract payments under FAIR and deficiency payments, 1987–1995.
Source: Provisions of the Federal Agricultural Improvement and Reform Act of 1996.
USDA, ERS, AIB Number 729, p. 6

A farmer's total contract payments would be the sum of such payments across contract commodities subject to a payment limitation of $40,000 per person, a $10,000 reduction from the previous $50,000 limit. The limit however, was porous—a farmer with a financial stake in three separate farms in some cases may have received up to $80,000 in contract payments per year under a "three-entity rule."

Although the contract payments were tied to the land with the base acreage, eligibility to receive payments under the 1996 farm bill hinged on who was bearing the risk of the farming operation. The owner operator who assumed the risk of producing a crop received the payment, but if the entire farm was cash leased, the owner was not entitled to any contract payments. If the farm was share leased, the contract payment was to be shared. This was an obvious area for conflict between producers and land owners because the bearing of risk was then a matter of degree, and a contract could be approved only if the producer and farm owner were able to agree on how the contract payments were to be shared.

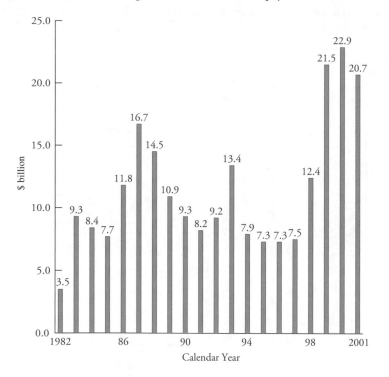

FIGURE 10.6 Direct government payments to agricultural producers and farm owners, U.S., 1982–2001.
Source: http://www.ers.usda.gov/data/farmincome/finfidmu.htm

Figure 10.5 shows the scheduled total payments made for contract commodities each year during the 1996–2002 period as specified in FAIR. The figure also contrasts the contract payments with annual deficiency payments made from 1987 to 1995. The scheduled contract payments declined between 1996 and 2002, reflecting the (stated) intent to phase out government support to agriculture upon the termination of the 1996 farm bill. In reality, total payments to farmers under the 1996 legislation—including contract payments and conservation, loan deficiency, and disaster aid—were dramatically higher than was specified in the FAIR Act, largely as a consequence of emergency-assistance legislation enacted in 1998, 1999, 2000, and 2001 (figure 10.6).

Loan Rates under the FAIR Act

Nonrecourse commodity loans, as previously discussed, permit farmers to receive a loan from the government at a designated rate per unit (the loan rate) by pledging and storing a quantity of a commodity as collateral. Under the FAIR Act, only producers who signed seven-year production flexibility contracts were eligible for price-support loans for wheat, feed grains, upland cotton, and rice. However, all production of these crops on a participating farm, regardless of the amount of contract acreage, was eligible for loans.

Loan rates for wheat and corn under the FAIR Act were based on 85 percent of the preceding five-year Olympic moving average (i.e., dropping the high- and low-price years) of farm prices. Loan rates for these commodities however, could be no higher than their 1995 levels—$2.58 for wheat and $1.89 for corn. Loan rates for grain sorghum, barley, and oats were to be set by the secretary of agriculture at levels considered "fair and equitable" relative to the feed value of corn. The loan period was not to exceed nine months for wheat and feed grains. Loan rates for rice were frozen at the 1995 level. The loan rate for upland cotton in any year was also based on 85 percent of the preceding five-year moving average of the spot-market price, excluding the highest- and the lowest-price years, but was not to be less than $0.50 per pound or more than $.5192 per pound. The loan period was limited to nine months for rice and ten months for cotton. The interest rate charged by the CCC was based on CCC's borrowing rate from the U.S. Treasury. The interest rate that the CCC charged to borrowers for 1995 and prior crop year loans was the rate the Treasury charged the CCC. For 1996 and subsequent crop year loans, the FAIR Act required the CCC to add one percentage point to its borrowing rate. In July 1997, for example, the CCC's borrowing rate was 5.75 percent for funds borrowed during July, so the July rate charged was 6.75 percent on funds advanced during July.[15]

The 1996 farm bill continued marketing loans and LDP provisions.

Marketing loan provisions allow repayment of nonrecourse loans at less than the loan rate, as previously explained. The secretary of agriculture was to make LDPs for the purpose of reducing administrative costs. Such payments are made to producers who agree not to obtain price-support loans, even though they are eligible. The LDP rate per unit is the announced loan rate less the CCC-determined repayment rate used in the marketing loan. The LDP made to a particular farmer is determined by multiplying the per unit payment rate times the amount of commodity eligible for loan. LDPs under the 1996 farm bill were available for all loan commodities (except extra-long staple cotton), including soybeans and oilseeds. LDPs became quite important under the 1996 farm bill during the "farm crises" of the late 1990s—totaling $1.8 billion in 1998, $5.9 billion in 1999, $6.4 billion in 2000, and $5.5 billion in 2001.[16] Annual marketing loan gains and LDPs were limited to $75,000 per farm but could be as much as $150,000 per person under the "three-entity rule" where the owner of a farm also had part interest in two other farms.

INCOME SUPPORT FOR OTHER COMMODITIES UNDER THE FAIR ACT

Soybeans and Other Oilseeds

Although there was no target price for soybeans prior to 1996, soybean price was supported through loans and purchases. The nonrecourse loan rate for soybeans, however, was often set below the market price. Producers of soybeans and other oilseeds did not have to sign seven-year production flexibility contracts to be eligible for nine-month loans under FAIR. Loan rates for these commodities were based on 85 percent of the previous five-year Olympic average of farm prices, but the soybean loan rate was to be no lower than $4.92 and no higher than $5.26 per bushel. Loan rates for other oilseeds could not be less than $0.087 or more than $0.093 per pound.

Sugar

Involvement by the U.S. government in sugar markets goes all the way back to 1789, when tariffs on imports were first imposed.[17] Such tariffs remained in effect for the most part until 1934. Although tariffs were initially used to raise revenues, the primary purpose of the tariffs changed in the late 1800s to providing protection for the domestic sugar industry.

The first federal sugar program was implemented in the Sugar Act of 1934 (also known as the Jones-Costigan Act), and, with the exception of a period in the 1970s, a sugar program has been in effect in the United States until the present time. The stated objectives of the program have been to retain sugarbeet and sugarcane production in the United States and to ensure adequate sugar supplies at reasonable prices for U.S. consumers. A primary policy tool in the sugar programs has been an import quota. Other policy tools used in the program at various times include price supports, processing taxes, acreage allotments, production quotas, and assessments on producers.

A reasonable characterization of the sugar program since 1934 is that policymakers attempted to set an import quota so that there would be no shortage or surplus at a particular support price. Figure 10.7 shows the impacts of the sugar program under this characterization. The U.S. sugar market is depicted as a small part of the world market so that the world price is not affected by policy changes in the United States.[18] With no sugar program, the price of sugar would be P_W, domestic production would be Q_0, domestic consumption would be Q_1, and imports would be $Q_1 - Q_0$.

Suppose now that a price support (in the form of a nonrecourse loan), P_S, is established.[19] If imports are not restricted in some manner, then domestic consumers will purchase only foreign sugar, and the government will have to purchase and store or dispose of all domestic production. Suppose policymakers restrict imports with an import quota equal to $Q_2 - Q_0$. Now the supply of sugar facing U.S. consumers is S_0ABS_1, the market-clearing price is P_S, domestic production is Q_3, domestic consumption is Q_4, and imports are $Q_4 - Q_3 = Q_2 - Q_0$. Domestic consumers are worse off because they pay a higher price than previously; domestic producers and processors are better off with the higher price; and (with the support price and import quota in figure 10.7) the program involves no Treasury costs. Those foreign producers who get the rights to import sugar may benefit from being able to sell at the higher price in the U.S. market.[20]

The sugar program has been successful in keeping the domestic price of sugar above the world price. From 1950 to 1974, in fact, the U.S. price was above the world price in all but one year. During this period, acreage restrictions were used to curtail the level of domestic production as U.S. producers made attempts to expand output. In 1974, world and U.S. sugar prices skyrocketed. Program opponents argued successfully that because prices were high enough that price supports were not necessary, there was no need to maintain the program. The sugar program was terminated.

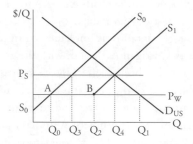

FIGURE 10.7 The economic effects of the U.S. sugar program.

By the end of the 1970s, however, prices had fallen considerably, and supporters of the sugar program lobbied for its reinstitution. The sugar program was formally reinstated in the Agricultural and Food Act of 1981 and has remained in effect since then. The central components of the program are the price supports and import quotas. Prices are supported through nonrecourse loans, and import quotas are divided on a country-by-country basis among (roughly) forty countries. The quotas, though quite valuable, are allocated among these countries free of charge.

The sugar program has encountered problems in recent years as a result of declining demand and increasing supply. The declining demand results from the development of sugar substitutes, primarily high-fructose corn sweeteners. The increase in supply has resulted from entry and expansion in production and acreage of both beets and cane sugar (there have been no acreage restrictions since prior to 1974). Under the Food Security Act of 1985, the sugar program was mandated to have no net costs to U.S. taxpayers. As can be seen from figure 10.7, either a decrease in demand or an increase in supply will create surpluses with accompanying Treasury costs. Such surpluses have been avoided in part by reducing import quotas; between 1977 and 1993, the level of sugar import quotas fell from 6.1 to 1.4 million tons. Political considerations—the import quotas are in essence a form of support to less-developed countries—limit policymakers' ability to reduce import quotas further. Responses to these problems under the 1990 farm bill included provisions for imposing marketing allotments on domestically produced sugar to limit production if "estimated sugar imports" were less than 1.25 million tons.[21] Also, marketing assessments of approximately 0.20 cents per pound on processors essentially reduced the level of the support price.

The 1996 farm bill left the structure of the sugar program largely intact. Sugar price was supported through nonrecourse loans so long as imports were greater than a trigger level (1.532 million short tons). Loan rates for sugarcane and sugar beets were frozen at their 1995 levels, 18 and 22.9 cents per pound, respectively. However, a penalty was imposed for using the nonrecourse loan forfeiture option—effectively reducing the level of price support for sugar by one cent per pound. The 1996 farm bill also eliminated the provisions for marketing allotments in the 1990 farm bill and the mandate in the 1985 farm bill that the sugar program operate at no cost to the federal government. It also raised marketing assessments on sugar processors. Sellers of domestic raw cane sugar and domestic refined beet sugar were required to pay assessments of approximately 0.25 cents per pound—25 percent higher than under previous legislation.[22] The sugar program ran into serious problems under the 1996 farm bill; with no restrictions on production, surpluses and Treasury costs increased to unsustainable levels.[23]

The 2002 farm bill reimposed the no-net-cost mandate on the sugar program. The bill also reauthorized the nonrecourse loan program for sugar at 18 cents per pound for cane sugar and 22.9 cents per pound for refined beet sugar. In addition, the new farm bill gave the secretary of agriculture authority to establish marketing allotments and to continue the PIK program.[24]

U.S. sugar markets are also affected by provisions of the Uruguay Round GATT agreement. The GATT required that the sugar import quota be converted to a tariff rate quota (TRQ)—the amount of sugar allowed to enter at a zero or very low tariff rate. The TRQ for U.S. sugar is 1.256 million short tons raw value of sugar per year. Imports greater than this face a prohibitively high tariff.[25] So long as U.S. imports are at least 1.532 million short tons, the price of U.S.-produced sugar continues to be supported, and the United States is in compliance with this trade agreement.

Although the Treasury costs of operating the sugar program are small, the sugar program is far from costless. The costs are borne largely by U.S. consumers.[26] The benefits of the sugar program are highly concentrated to the approximately ten thousand domestic producers of sugar and sugar substitutes. Domestic producers benefit by the difference between domestic price and world-market price. These benefits in the 1992–1994 fiscal years for each one-cent premium were estimated to average $39,000 per sugarcane farm and $5,600 per sugar beet farm.[27] Support for the sugar program is not limited to domestic sugar producers. The sugar program is highly beneficial to the corn-based sweetener industry, and the Washington lobbyists for corn refiners are highly effective advocates for sugar price supports. Archer Daniels Midland Corporation (ADM), for example, is a driving force behind the sugar lobby in the periodic congressional battles over sugar legislation.[28] Although ADM does not directly produce sugar, the sugar program has created a price umbrella under which ADM can profitably produce high-fructose corn syrup—a sugar substitute. As in the case of the tobacco and other farm programs, most of the benefits of the sugar program are transitional and tend to be capitalized into higher values of land and specialized production, harvesting, and processing facilities.[29]

Although benefits of the sugar program are highly concentrated to producers and processors of sugar and sugar substitutes, costs are highly dispersed among 290 million consumers. Because the average consumer uses only approximately one hundred pounds of sugar per year, it is easy to see why individual sugar producers are more concerned with maintaining the sugar program than individual sugar consumers are concerned with abolishing it. The sugar program increases retail sugar prices, but the cost to the individual consumer is quite small (probably less than $10 per consumer annually).

THE TOBACCO PROGRAM

Until enactment of the 2002 farm bill, both the peanut and the tobacco programs had marketing quotas. Tobacco had production controls from the 1930s until the program was eliminated in October 2004. The peanut program had similar controls until the late 1970s. From then until the 2002 farm bill, it had marketing quotas, but allowed more flexibility in production than under the tobacco program. In the 2002 farm bill, it was modified and now is essentially the same as other target-price programs.

Why has government policy been so important in tobacco production?[30] Although the harvested acreage of tobacco amounts to less than one-half of one percent of total U.S. cropland, tobacco has a high value per acre. The per acre gross revenue from tobacco, $3,000–4,000 per acre, is eight to ten times that from corn. Although tobacco is important regionally, two-thirds of all U.S. tobacco is produced in only two states—North Carolina and Kentucky.[31] Moreover, within the tobacco-production region, until recently, many farmers, non-farmers, and land owners who do not actually grow tobacco had an interest in tobacco production; that is, tobacco is grown in some twenty states on approximately 124,000 farms, but an additional 236,000 quota holders also had a financial stake in the tobacco price-support program.[32]

Historically, there have been at least three different dimensions to tobacco policy: (1) restrictions on smoking in public places, (2) efforts to reduce cigarette consumption generally, and (3) producer price supports. The first two dimensions have important implications for the future of the domestic tobacco industry, but we describe them only briefly here.

There are increasing and successful efforts to restrict smoking in public places, including work areas, airplanes, and restaurants. Most of the original impetus for this legislation was at the local or state level, but actions to ban or restrict smoking by the Federal Aviation Administration, the FDA, and other federal regulatory agencies have increased significantly since the 1980s.

A second theme of attempts to reduce consumption has a much longer history. Sumptuary taxes have been imposed on tobacco products since colonial times. Tobacco products are taxed at the local, state, and federal levels. If the demand for tobacco products is inelastic, a high tax rate may generate large revenues with relatively little effect on consumption of tobacco products. Revenues from taxes on tobacco products totalled approximately $20.6 billion in 2002—$7.7 billion by the federal government and $12.8 billion by state and local governments. Tobacco tax receipts amounted to more than twelve times the value of sales of tobacco at the farm level.[33]

Efforts to reduce consumption have intensified since 1964, when the U.S. surgeon general issued a report attacking smoking.[34] Radio and television cigarette advertising has been banned in the United States, and health warning labels are required on cigarette containers.[35] The future of the domestic tobacco industry is uncertain because of recent actions to restrict tobacco sales, including the 1996 FDA initiative to regulate the tobacco industry and the spate of recent law suits against cigarette manufacturers on the part of smokers suffering from lung cancer. Although per capita cigarette consumption in the United States and some other Western countries has been declining, cigarette sales continue to increase on a worldwide basis.[36]

A great deal of criticism was levelled at the federal government's role in administering the tobacco program. The tobacco program also faced increasing pressures both because of health problems associated with tobacco and because of the program's effect on tobacco exports. At the end of World War II, the U.S. share of flue-cured tobacco exports exceeded 60 percent. By 1995, that percentage was down to less than 15 percent.[37] The price-support program in the United States indirectly encouraged the production of tobacco in Canada, Brazil, India, and other countries that are major competitors of the United States in tobacco production.

Production Controls and Price Supports

Efforts in the United States to increase tobacco price by restricting production can be traced back to the 1600s. An effective producer cartel for tobacco was not achieved, however, until the AAA of 1933. Although the tobacco price-support program underwent various changes over time, until its elimination in 2004, it remained quite similar in many respects to the program of the 1930s.[38] In the beginning, the tobacco program had price supports with strict controls on land use. A national acreage allotment was determined and allocated among individual farmers. Prices were supported above the competitive level, and farmers were able to sell all the tobacco they produced on their allotted acreage. Farmers responded by increasing the per acre amounts of fertilizer, pesticides, and other inputs, and dramatic increases in yields resulted; the average yield for the years 1955–60, for example, was 60 percent higher than for the years 1940–45.[39] To maintain prices without costly buildups in government-held stocks of tobacco, acreage allotments had to be reduced again and again during this period. In 1965, in response to problems associated with high yields of low-quality tobacco varieties, the tobacco program was changed from an acreage allotment to a poundage marketing quota program. Under the poundage quota program, an individual tobacco grower could sell no more than his poundage quota at the support price. Sale of tobacco in excess of quota was taxed at prohibitive rates (roughly 75 percent of the support price).

The tobacco price-support level was originally based on parity. From the early 1960s until 1986, price-support levels were adjusted from year to year based on changes in the Prices Paid Index. The Tobacco Reform Act of 1986 gave the secretary of agriculture the authority to establish tobacco quotas and price supports using more market-oriented formulas.[40]

The loan and storage features of the tobacco program operated through grower-owned and operated cooperatives. For flue-cured tobacco, the Flue-Cured Tobacco Cooperative Stabilization Corporation ("Stabilization") assumed control of all tobacco that was placed under loan. At the time of the sales auction, Stabilization paid the farmer for tobacco going under loan with money borrowed from the CCC. Stabilization then stored the crop and arranged for sale to private buyers.

In response to widespread public criticism of government expenditures on the tobacco program, the "No Net Cost" Tobacco Act of 1982 established a producer-supported fund to repay the government for potential losses in operating the price-support program. (The government continued to bear the costs of administering the price-support program.) The fees assessed on growers were not large enough to cover operating losses, however, and the result was a federal bailout of the tobacco program in the Tobacco Reform Act of 1986. This act provided for the sale of large unsold stabilization inventories from previous crop years at greatly discounted prices, resulting in a loss to the CCC. This bailout amounted to a direct government subsidy to rescue the "no net cost" tobacco program.[41]

The 1986 legislation also reduced the average level of price supports by approximately 20 percent and established a formula for setting support prices based on a moving average of past market prices and the USDA index of prices paid by tobacco farmers.[42] Major domestic buyers were required to estimate purchases for the upcoming crop year in the spring. The secretary of agriculture then set the aggregate poundage quota based on these estimates and on export projections. Adjustments were made for inventory levels and other market conditions.[43]

The Determination of Quota Prices

As indicated earlier, to sell tobacco at the support price, a farmer was required to possess poundage quota. With this requirement, the demand for tobacco poundage quota could be derived from the demand for tobacco. Because the quota, or the right to produce and sell tobacco, did not enter the production process except as it constrained output, the demand for quota reflected the residual difference between the price of tobacco and the marginal costs of production (where such costs include all nonquota factors in the tobacco-production process). Figure 10.8 illustrates how market quota rental rates were determined if there were no restrictions on the leasing of tobacco quota.[44] Suppose the aggregate production quota were established by policymakers at Q_S^0 (panel a).[45] With this production quota, the annual market rental value of the quota was r_0 (panel a)—the difference between product price and nonquota production costs (as indicated by the tobacco supply curve). This quota rental value is also shown in the quota market (panel b). There, the demand for quota is derived as the vertical distance between the supply and the demand for tobacco (panel a), and the supply of quota is vertical at the level established by policymakers. Thus, the market-clearing rental rate for quota was determined by tobacco price, the nonquota costs of production, and the level of the production quota.

If the amount of quota was reduced—say, to Q_S^1—the market-clearing price of tobacco increased, the marginal cost of production decreased, and the rental rate for quota increased to r_1. Moreover, as the amount of quota (and the quantity of tobacco produced) was reduced and the rental price of quota rose, both the demand for and the returns to other specialized factors with upward-sloping supply curves (such as land) were reduced.

Tobacco policy required that tobacco be produced in the county to which the quota was assigned. From 1982 until the elimination of the program in 2004, owners of flue-cured tobacco quotas were allowed to sell these rights—but only within the same county.[46] Flue-cured quotas generally could not be rented out. Thus, production had to be on the same farm unit to which the quota was attached—owners had to produce their own quota, rent it in place, or sell the quota.[47]

These restrictions on the transfer of tobacco quota provide insights into why sale prices and rental rates for tobacco quota varied from county to county. County-level demand curves for tobacco quota could be derived using an approach similar to the approach used in figure 10.8. At the county level, how-ever, the demand for tobacco (shown in *panel a*) would be perfectly elastic (each county is a small part of the total market for tobacco). Thus, the demand for quota would be derived as the vertical distance between the fixed tobacco price and the marginal costs of production. Counties that produced tobacco at low cost had higher demands for quota. For any given amount of tobacco quota in a county, the lower the costs of production, the higher the demand for quota and the greater the observed rental rate (or sale price) of quota.

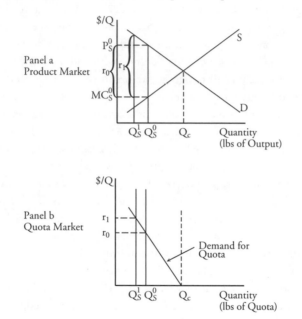

FIGURE 10.8 Rental price of tobacco quota is derived from the product market.

The market sale value of tobacco quota can be explained by capital asset-pricing theory. If the tobacco program were expected to last forever in its current state, the quota sale value would be determined by the capitalization formula

$$PV = \frac{r}{i},$$

where:

PV = Present value of a pound of quota
r = Current (and expected future) annual rental price per pound of tobacco quota
i = Discount rate

The capitalized value of quota varied considerably during the last thirty years of the program depending on price-support levels, no-net-cost assessment levels, and prospects for the future of the tobacco program. Average quota values, as high as $4.50 per pound in 1977, fell to below $1.50 per pound in 1985 as leaf surpluses accumulated, aggregate quota levels fell, and no-net-cost assessments increased.[48] The increased level of uncertainty regarding the future of the tobacco program was reflected in the capitalization formula as higher discount rates and reduced market prices for tobacco quota. In the 1990s, annual rental rates for flue-cured tobacco, mostly $.35 to $.45 per pound, ranged from $.25 to $.75 per pound (or even more widely) in North Carolina while the sale, or capital, values for flue-cured tobacco ranged from $2.00 to $3.00 per pound. Near the end of the program, the sale or capital value was as high as $6 per pound amid buyout speculation.[49]

Both rental and sales values varied from county to county, depending largely on differences in cost of production. For any given rental rate, the capital value varied with the discount rate and the expected life of the tobacco program—neither of which is observable. The riskier the investment, the larger the discount rate used by investors in valuing capital assets. A market value of quota that is three times the annual rental rate—for example, a rental rate of $.75 per pound and sale value of $2.25 per pound—is consistent with a discount rate of 12 percent and a four-year expected life of the tobacco program. It is, of course, also consistent with many other combinations of interest rates and planning horizons.

The tobacco program, which restricted overall output and the movement of quota between counties and states, led to higher costs of production because of two types of resource misallocation. There was too little production (the cartel problem), and restrictions on transfer of quota prevented production from moving from higher-cost to lower-cost production regions. Following many years of Congressional debate, legislation terminating the tobacco program was passed in October 2004.[50] The legislation (H.R. 4520) addressed corporate tax issues, and also funded a buyout in the amount of $10.1 billion to compensate tobacco growers and quota owners for costs they incur as a result of termination of the tobacco program. The buyout is to be funded by cigarette manufacturers and importers based on their share of the U.S. cigarette market but ultimately from smokers.[51] After the 2004 crop year, tobacco production and prices will be determined by market forces rather than by the federal tobacco program. Key provisions of the buyout call for quota owners to receive $7 for each pound of quota owned. Payments are to be made in equal annual installments (of $0.70 per pound) over a ten year period. Growers will receive up to $3 per pound of quota grown in 2002, 2003, and 2004, with payments again being made over a ten year period.[52] A quota owner/grower thus can receive (undiscounted) total payments of $10 for each pound of quota in his possession. This is considerably higher than the market sale value of quota in the 1990s (before expectations regarding the buyout started to influence quota prices) of $2–$3 per pound. As with most farm subsidy programs, most of the payments will go to a small percentage of the recipients. The top 1 percent of recipients will receive more than one-fourth of the payments, averaging about $600,000 over ten years. The bottom 80 percent, on the other hand, will each receive about $5,000 over ten years.[53] The buyout legislation also includes provisions to provide $500 million to assist in the disposition of tobacco stocks held by the grower associations and the Commodity Credit Corporation.

Transitional Gains Trap

The capitalization of increased product prices into prices of poundage quota and other specialized resources gave rise to what has been referred to as a *transitional gains trap*.[54] The producers who were assigned allotments when the tobacco program was initiated or who held allotments or poundage quota later when price-support levels increased (unexpectedly) received a windfall gain. Of course, as discussed in earlier chapters, political actions are often costly. Thus, costs of lobbying, campaign contributions, and so on offset to some extent the value of any windfalls received by owners of tobacco quota. The right to produce tobacco—through possession of tobacco acreage allotment in early versions of the program—immediately acquired a value when the program was instituted because production was legally restricted. The fact that the allotment acquired a value, however, also meant an increase in production costs. With the program in effect, the farmer who wished to produce tobacco had either to own tobacco allotment or to rent it from another owner. If allotment was rented, the rental payments represented an explicit cost. If a farmer produced tobacco using his own allotment, the rental income foregone represented an implicit cost. In either case, the rental payment was a relevant economic cost, and one effect of the tobacco program was to increase production costs significantly.

When increases in price supports led to increased prices of allotments, quotas, and other specialized resources used in producing tobacco, the individuals owning these resources received benefits at that time. Tobacco producers in later years, however, received little or no benefit because the higher product prices were largely offset by higher production costs. The conclusion is that the gain to producers from price supports is (at best) transitory or a once-and-for-all windfall.

Moreover, once a price-support program is begun, there is no way without a buyout to abolish the program and return to competitive markets without imposing windfall losses on all owners of quota and some owners of land, tobacco-production facilities, and other specialized resources—many of whom are not the ones who received the original windfall gain. (In the absence of a buyout, how would prices of farmland in different counties be affected if the tobacco program were terminated?)[55] This "transitional gains trap" problem— where the value of the right to produce is capitalized into the price of inelastically supplied inputs, thereby causing higher production costs—is inherent in price-support programs of all types.

THE PEANUT PROGRAM

Peanut production is in some respects quite similar to tobacco production. Both are high-value crops important on a regional basis, and the program provisions for both commodities were (until the 2002 farm bill, when the peanut program underwent substantial changes) binding on all producers if approved by at least two-thirds of the producers voting in the required referendum. The peanut program was begun in the 1930s, and peanut acreage allotments lasted until 1977. At that time, acreage allotments were replaced with poundage quotas.[56]

From 1977 until recently, the peanut program was a two-price plan, with a high price in the domestic market and a considerably lower price in the world market. Peanut growers were allocated poundage quotas based on the expected consumption of peanuts in the domestic edible market. The prices of peanuts produced for edible use in the domestic market—quota peanuts—were supported well above the competitive price level. Under the 1990 farm bill, the price support for quota peanuts was based on the previous year's loan rate adjusted upward (no more than 5 percent) each year for higher production costs. In response to concerns over Treasury costs (arising, at least in part, from increasing imports resulting from the NAFTA and the GATT), the 1996 farm bill revised the peanut program to make it a "no-net-cost" program, and the quota-support rate was reduced (from $678 per ton in 1995) and frozen at $610 per ton.[57] Further, the legislatively mandated minimum national poundage quota was eliminated.

Under the pre-2002 U.S. peanut program, quota holders and other producers were allowed to produce nonquota peanuts, or *additionals*, in unlimited amounts. Any additionals marketed directly for domestic edible use, however, were subject to a prohibitive penalty. Additionals could be sold without penalty either into the export market or into the crush market (where they are used for oil or meal) at market-clearing prices. Prior to the 1996 farm bill, peanut quotas (like tobacco quotas) could be sold or leased, but only within counties. The 1996 legislation permitted limited sale and lease of peanut quotas across county lines within a state.

Like the tobacco program, the pre-2002 peanut price-support program increased cost of production. The prohibition of quota movement across county or state lines prior to 1996 prevented the shifting of production to the most profitable production regions. Barriers to mobility in production can lead to substantial disparities in productivity between production regions. Indications that there may have been substantial losses from restricting the transfer of poundage quota include the observations that (prior to the 1996 farm bill, at least) (1) substantial amounts of production quota were not used in certain counties in Texas, and (2) lease rates in Texas were much lower than in most counties in Georgia, North Carolina, and Virginia. The increased, but still quite limited, mobility of peanut quota under the 1996 farm bill reduced but did not eliminate the resource misallocation inherent in the quota system.

Until fairly recently in the operation of the pre-2002 two-price plan, import restrictions virtually prohibited imports of edible peanuts.[58] Without such import restrictions, lower-priced imports would have been substituted for the higher-priced domestic quota peanuts, thereby undermining the program. Thus, the peanut program increased prices of edible peanuts to U.S. consumers, and the restrictions on sales into the domestic market resulted in a reallocation of peanuts out of the U.S. market. Estimates of the gains to producers (about $11,000 annually per peanut producer) and losses to consumers (less than $1.50 per consumer annually) from the pre-2002 peanut program indicate that this program represented another example of a program in which a relatively small homogeneous group (peanut producers) gained at the expense of a larger more diverse group (consumers) in political markets.

The short- and long-run effects of the pre-2002 peanut program on quota owners were similar to those of the tobacco program. The peanut program conferred once-and-for-all gains initially on producers who were granted peanut acreage allotments. However, the benefits of higher prices to current producers (mentioned in the preceding paragraph), whether they owned or rented quota, were largely offset by higher production costs. Thus, current producers actually benefited little from the peanut program, and domestic consumers paid higher prices for peanuts.

As a result of various problems faced by peanut growers (including the threat of high Treasury costs), the program was fundamentally altered in the 2002 farm bill. For a brief description of these changes, see the appendix on this bill. In a nutshell, the government paid quota owners for their poundage quota and converted the program to a target-price program with the same provisions as, for example, for wheat and corn.[59] Peanut growers and quota owners generally supported these program changes.

HONEY AND WOOL PROGRAMS—ELIMINATED AND REINSTATED

Two federal programs for individual commodities—for honey and for wool and mohair—were discontinued in the mid-1990s. Both of these programs were reinstated in the 2002 farm bill. Because it is unusual for such government programs to be eliminated (even temporarily), it is useful to recount the history of these two programs.

Honey

Honey was not included in the list of "basic commodities" covered under the initial AAA programs.[60] The honey program was instituted in 1950 as a result of events during and after World War II. During the war, honey was given the status of a "war essential" commodity because it was a substitute for sugar and because beeswax was used to waterproof bombs. The price of honey was high throughout the war, but dropped after the war. As prices dropped, beekeepers lobbied Congress for a price-support program. They claimed that many of them were being forced out of business and argued that beekeeping was essential for agriculture because of the pollination services provided by bees. Beekeepers argued, in essence, that pollination markets did not work well, and threatened that there would be large losses to agriculture if measures were not taken to keep them in business.

The basic structure of the honey program from 1950 to 1985 was a simple price-support program with nonrecourse loans. During most of this period, the program appears to have had little effect, with support prices set at levels less than the world price in virtually every year. The United States was a net exporter of honey in most years from 1952 through 1966. Since then, at least in part because of increased foreign production, the United States has been a net importer of honey. Throughout this period, the only subsidy associated with the honey program was the low interest rate on nonrecourse loans.[61]

From 1981 to 1985, in part as a result of increased support prices (that had nothing to do with any lobbying efforts by beekeepers), the support price for honey exceeded the world-market price. This change resulted in unacceptably high Treasury costs for the honey program. Why? The honey program did not include any provisions to restrict imports. Thus, domestic honey purchasers, when faced with the choice between U.S.-produced honey at the high support price and foreign honey at the lower world price, predominantly chose the foreign honey. The result was large increases in imports, CCC forfeitures, and Treasury costs. Imports increased from 77.3 million pounds in 1981 to 138.2 million pounds in 1985; CCC forfeitures jumped from 8.4 million pounds in 1981 to 106.4 million pounds in 1985; and Treasury costs skyrocketed from an average of $8.5 million in 1980–81 to an average of $86 million in 1984–86!

These costs were politically unacceptable, especially in light of the fact that in the mid-1980s there were only approximately two thousand commercial beekeepers. Steps were therefore taken to reduce Treasury costs related to honey in the 1985 farm bill. Support prices were reduced, and a buyback, or marketing loan, option was instituted. Under this option, a producer could enter a nonrecourse loan with the CCC and then buy the honey back at a government-determined repayment rate that was less than the loan rate (and often also less than the market price). In the 1990 farm bill, the program rules were modified so that producers did not have to put their honey under loan with the CCC to be able to receive the subsidy of the difference between the loan rate and the repayment rate. The buyback option greatly reduced producers' incentives to forfeit their honey to the CCC. Forfeitures fell from roughly 100 million pounds per year between 1983 and 1985 to approximately 3 million pounds for the period 1989–91.

In 1993, Congress reauthorized the honey program through 1998, but the 1994 and 1995 appropriations acts eliminated any government expenditures for honey for those fiscal years. The absence of any provisions for reviving the honey program in the 1996 farm bill (seemingly) drove the final stake into the heart of the program. Beekeepers, however, did not leave the political marketplace; rather, they tried a different tact. They filed claims with the International Trade Commission (ITC) and the International Trade Administration (ITA) claiming that Chinese honey was coming into the United States at too low of a price and requesting that a countervailing duty be imposed on Chinese honey imports. An agreement was reached between the United States and the People's Republic of China that called for limits on annual imports of Chinese honey and imposed a price support on Chinese imports. The impact of this action was to increase temporarily the price of (Chinese) imports, thereby reducing those imports, increasing domestic prices, and benefiting U.S. producers. Imports from Argentina, however, increased dramatically to more than offset reduced Chinese imports.

When the agreement with China expired in August 2000, new trade cases were brought almost immediately against both China and Argentina, alleging dumping (when a country sells a commodity below the "cost of production") by both countries and the provision of export subsidies by the government of Argentina. In December 2001, the Department of Commerce ruled in favor of levying import duties on both China and Argentina.

More direct subsidies to honey producers were granted in the form of marketing assistance loans and LDPs for the 2000 year honey crop. The nonrecourse loan rate was greater than market prices, and Treasury costs for 2000 crop year honey, associated with LDP and marketing loan payments, were approximately $22.7 and $6.3 million, respectively.[62] As a result of higher market prices, no loan program was enacted for 2001 crop year honey. Most recently, the resurrection of the honey program was completed with the inclusion in the 2002 farm bill of a nonrecourse loan rate of 60 cents per pound for honey, with provisions for marketing assistance loans and LDPs.

Thus, the honey program was sent to its grave in the 1990s by unacceptably high Treasury costs that resulted from policy changes (increased support prices) that did not result from beekeepers' lobbying efforts. During most of its existence, the program provided minimal benefits to beekeepers. During the mid-1980s, however, commercial beekeepers probably received annual benefits of approximately $10,000 each. The annual cost to the average consumer was probably only approximately 33 cents.

With the passage of the 2002 farm bill, the honey program has been revived. One explanation for this revival is that the political climate surrounding the 2002 farm bill was more generous than in the 1990s for reasons unrelated to honey price support. The fact that the wool and mohair program also was reinstated (see the next section) and that several other commodity groups were included in the farm bill for the first time supports this explanation.

A natural question to ask is whether the problems that led to the earlier elimination of the honey program are likely to recur. The 2002 honey program is a simple nonrecourse loan program similar to earlier versions. Moreover, although the loan rate of 60 cents per pound is less than the current market price for honey, it is likely that in the future the market price will fall below 60 cents, which will trigger subsidy payments. The fatal problem with the pre-1993 honey program was that when the market price fell below the loan rate, there were no restrictions on imports. What makes the 2002 program different is that the tariffs on imports levied by the Department of Commerce reduce the attractiveness of imports and likely will keep Treasury costs from ballooning.

Wool and Mohair

The United States is a relatively high-cost producer of wool, as evidenced by the fact that imports of wool are (and have been historically) substantial.[63] The first price supports for wool were authorized in 1938. The Agricultural Act of 1949 required that support prices be set to encourage annual domestic production of 360 million pounds of wool. Attaining this level of production was not a problem during World War II, but since then production has dropped well below that level. Average U.S. wool production (shorn) for the years 1995–97 was only approximately 58 million pounds.[64] The National Wool Act of 1954 established a system of direct "incentive payments" (similar in their impacts to deficiency payments made in target-price programs) to farmers. The level of these payments was based on the difference between the price support (computed by a complicated parity formula) and the market price. A farmer's incentive payments also varied with the quality of the wool she produced. These direct payments, which remained in effect for four decades, were terminated as of December 31, 1995.

The other primary policy tool used in the wool program was a tariff on imports. This tariff reduced the level of wool imports into the United States and raised revenues. These revenues were used to cover the costs of the direct payments to growers; in fact, a requirement of the wool program was that total direct payments to farmers could not exceed 70 percent of tariff revenues.

Some impacts of the wool program can be seen in figure 10.9, which shows the domestic demand and supply of wool and the world price. In the absence of the program, imports would be $Q_1 - Q_0$. With the direct incentive payments in place and a support level of P_T, domestic production is Q_2. With an import tariff of \$T per pound, the price at which domestic producers can sell their wool and the price paid by domestic consumers for either domestic or imported wool is $P_w + T$. Imports are now $Q_3 - Q_2$. Tariff revenues are the shaded *area b*, and total direct payments are the shaded *area a*. Under this program, domestic consumers pay more for wool (by \$T per pound), and domestic producers receive a higher price for their wool (P_T rather than P_w). From 1986 through 1993, the average direct payment rate was \$1.01 per pound, whereas the average market price was \$.85 per pound. Thus, the direct payments were a major portion of the revenues received by wool growers. The increase in price associated with these payments probably increased U.S. wool production by approximately 16 percent. Estimates are that wool producers gained approximately \$800 per producer from the direct payment portion of the program. In 1990, estimates indicate that although almost half of the direct payments to producers were for less than \$100, the (approximately) three hundred largest checks averaged \$98,000 and accounted for more than a quarter of the program's 1990 costs.[65]

The wool program was one of the programs targeted for elimination by the Clinton administration (1993–2000). Beginning in 1994, the direct payment portion of the program was phased out, and this price support for wool was terminated as of December 31, 1995. The import tariff portion of the program remained in effect, with recent tariffs set at approximately $.12 per pound (roughly 6 percent of the price of wool). Like government payments for honey, the direct payment portion of the wool program has been revived in recent years.[66] As a result of low market prices, Wool and Mohair Market Loss Assistance Programs were implemented that made producers eligible for payments of 20 cents per pound for wool shorn in 1999 and (up to) 40 cents per pound in 2000. Most recently, the 2002 farm bill includes provisions for marketing loans and LDPs for wool and mohair (see the appendix for actual loan rates).

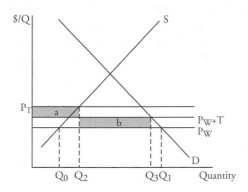

FIGURE 10.9 Impacts of the Price Support Program for wool.

As one might expect, the wool program has been largely a product of the lobbying efforts of the domestic wool industry.[67] A variety of reasons have been cited to justify the wool program, notably national security, but the rent-seeking theory of government action is the most persuasive.

Wool production declined markedly in the United States in spite of the government program to aid wool growers. When the program was terminated in 1995, domestic consumption of wool was less than half the level of the early 1960s, and domestic production was less than one-third of consumption.[68] It might be expected that the elimination of the direct payments portion of the wool program would not have a large impact on incomes in the U.S. sheep and lamb industry because their income is derived mainly from meat rather than from wool. Nonetheless, domestic production of shorn wool products in 1999 and 2000 was almost 30 percent less than in 1994 and 1995.

Mohair is the fleece from Angora goats. The United States is an important exporter of mohair, with approximately 90 percent of U.S. production being exported. The primary policy tool of the program is direct payments like those in the wool program. The program ran into serious problems beginning in the mid-1980s. Total price-support payments were $37 and $48 million in 1987 and 1988. In fact, direct payments in 1986–88 were more than half of all payments made under the program from 1962 to 1985. These payments continued to rise in the early 1990s and peaked at approximately $68 million in 1993. Approximately 80 percent of U.S. production of mohair comes from a few counties in Texas.

What can be said about the distribution of government payments among mohair producers? Approximately twelve thousand growers received government payments in 1986, with 13 percent receiving payments of $5,000 or more each. This group of growers (roughly sixteen hundred of them) received 86 percent of government mohair payments, with average payments of approximately $23,000 each.[69] As with wool, price supports for mohair were phased out during 1994 and 1995, terminated as of December 31, 1995, and then reinstated in the 2002 farm bill.

SUMMARY

Income support to farmers before the FAIR Act of 1996 was mainly through price-support programs. In the case of wheat, feed grain, cotton, and rice programs, participation was voluntary from the standpoint of the individual producer. Farmers were induced to participate by a compensatory payments program that assured the producer of a "target price." Participating producers received "deficiency payments" from the government when the market price fell below the target price. The cost of participation to an eligible producer was a mandatory reduction in the amount of land planted and the obligation to place such land in an approved conservation use. The impact of target-price programs on the overall output of these commodities depended on the extent of participation and the amount of diverted acreage required for participation. These target-price programs, which were based on artificially high output prices and voluntary diversion of productive land to less-productive uses, resulted in the misallocation of resources. These programs were both expensive to taxpayers and inconsistent with free trade.

The 1996 farm bill fundamentally changed the form of income support to producers of wheat, feed grains, cotton, and rice. Under the "freedom to farm" approach, as it is commonly referred to, farmers previously participating in any of these target-price programs were given the option of signing a seven-year contract with the USDA and receiving lump sum contract payments each year during the period 1996–2002. Under this program, farmers had much greater flexibility to make planting decisions than under previous programs because the lump sum contract payments made were independent of current production on the contract acreage. Farmers who elected to participate during a one-time sign-up period in 1996 were required to comply with existing conservation plans but were allowed to grow anything on contract acreage except fruits and vegetables. They could grow other crops, including other contract crops, graze or hay the land, or do nothing but control the weeds and continue to receive the payments. Virtually all eligible producers chose to sign up for the payments.

The 1996 FAIR Act established fixed dollar amounts for the aggregate lump sum payments for each crop for each year. The total (nominal) amount scheduled to be spent during the period 1996–2002 was only slightly less than the amount spent on price supports for these commodities during the seven-year period ending in 1995 ($35.6 billion versus $38.7 billion).[70] So although farmers were given increased freedom to make decisions about the production and marketing of wheat, feed grains, cotton, and rice, the farm bill as enacted in 1996 had little impact on the overall level of government spending on the farm sector. In reality, direct payments to farmers were dramatically increased in 1998, 1999, and 2000 through emergency-assistance legislation and through increases in marketing loan payments and LDPs. In 1999, for example, total direct payments to farmers were more than three times as large as in 1995. Moreover, whereas the lump sum contract payments were independent of current production, the marketing loan payments and LDPs (which came into effect when world-market prices fell) were dependent on current production. Consequently, it remains to be seen how much lasting impact the FAIR Act will have on the role of government in U.S. agriculture. Under the 2002 farm bill, target prices have been revived and a portion of government payments remains dependent on current production. Forecasted expenditures of roughly $18 billion annually do not suggest a reduced government role in agriculture in the near future.

Income-support programs continue under the 1996 and 2002 farm bill for oilseeds and sugar, but the sugar program is by far the most costly. Although the Treasury cost of the sugar program is typically small, import quotas are used to raise domestic sugar prices considerably above world-market levels. As is true for other commodity programs, a relatively small number of producers and processors in the sugar industry obtain considerable benefits from a large number of consumers—each of whom bears small costs.

Until its elimination in 2004, farmer participation in the government-sponsored and sanctioned tobacco program—a marketing cartel—was mandatory. The tobacco program was subject to the same criticism as other cartels. Moreover, it faced increasing pressures because of the greater awareness of the adverse health effects of tobacco use. Recent settlements of health-related law-suits imposed huge costs on the tobacco industry.[71] In November 1998, an his-toric agreement was reached between the tobacco industry and state attorneys general that requires manufacturers to reimburse states for the costs of treat-ing smoking-related illnesses. The twenty-five-year $206 billion settlement is the largest financial recovery in U.S. history. Four previously settled lawsuits in individual states commit the industry to an additional cost of $45 billion over twenty-five years. Higher cigarette prices (resulting from the settlement pay-ments) may cause consumption to decrease as much as 25 percent over the next ten years—with highly adverse implications for tobacco growers. Consequently, cigarette manufacturers established a $5.1 billion fund to aid tobacco farmers. Still, the huge financial settlements and the subsequent increases in cigarette prices and reductions in cigarette consumption meant added pressure on the tobacco price-support program—and on tobacco farmers. Flue-cured tobacco quotas in 2003 were approximately 46 percent lower than in 1997.

The elimination of the tobacco program abolished the value of tobacco marketing quotas. The effect will be a reduction in cost of production, with costs being reduced more in low-cost production areas where quota values were higher. There was a "transitional gains trap" in the case of the tobacco price-support program. Present producers did not benefit appreciably from such pro-grams because program benefits were capitalized into asset (including quota) prices, which resulted in higher production costs. Nonetheless, owners of quota and other specialized assets could have incurred substantial losses if the pro-gram had simply been terminated. Rather than simply eliminating the federal tobacco program, however, Congress enacted legislation that provided over $10 billion to compensate quota owners and tobacco growers for the elimination of the program.

Like the tobacco program, primary policy tools in the pre-2002 federal peanut program were marketing quotas and price supports. These supports, in combination with import restrictions, resulted in domestic prices (in the edible peanut market) that were substantially higher than world prices. The pre-2002 peanut program differed from the tobacco program insofar as peanut producers were allowed to grow and sell nonquota peanuts (known as *additionals*). These nonquota peanuts could be sold, however, only into the lower-price export or domestic crush markets. NAFTA and GATT created problems for the benefi-ciaries of the peanut program by relaxing restrictions on imports. These prob-lems were addressed in the 1996 farm bill by reducing both price supports and quota levels. In the 2002 farm bill, the peanut program was fundamentally altered and is now a target price–based program with the same provisions as wheat and corn.

Large farms receive larger gains from farm commodity programs because price supports, contract payments under the 1996 and 2002 farm bills, and other benefits usually increase with the amount of output. Indeed, income support goes primarily to farmers whose incomes are far above the median household income in the United States. Issues associated with this feature of government farm programs, the effect of increased asset prices on producers versus asset owners, and attempts by farmers to circumvent payment limitations are further explored in chapter 12.

In conclusion, U.S. agriculture remains encumbered with a multitude of rules and regulations under the 1996 and 2002 farm bills. To refer to the 1996 farm bill as "freedom to farm" legislation seems inappropriate for a program so complex that more than eighty pages in the *Federal Register* were taken to lay out the rules for making the newly instituted contract flexibility payments. Moreover, as described earlier, taxpayers remained heavily involved in newly instituted bankrolling of the production of farm commodities during the seven years of the FAIR Act. As one observer somewhat irreverently commented, to the extent that the "freedom to farm" label for the act is relevant, it really is freedom to farm at taxpayer expense! Taxpayer involvement under the 2002 farm bill is likely to continue at high levels.

The 1996 farm bill was supposed to set the framework for economic assistance to the farm sector for seven years—from 1996 through 2002. Perceived "farm crises" in 1998, 1999, and 2000, however, not only resulted in huge amounts of "emergency aid" (as previously described) but also evoked cries by some legislators to rewrite the 1996 farm bill—the presumed transition to a free-market agriculture—and to reinstitute production controls. One objective of the 2002 farm bill was to include provisions for sufficient levels of support to agriculture so that ad hoc emergency aid packages like those of the late 1990s would not be required. Thus, it seems highly likely that income transfer programs to the farm sector will continue to be a feature of U.S. agricultural policy for the foreseeable future. The exact nature and form of income support for producers of farm commodities under future farm policy, however, remain to be seen.

11

Cooperatives and Marketing Orders

Historically, there has been a widespread opinion that farmers suffer because of a lack of bargaining power. This attitude is related to the fact that the farmer's share of the consumer's dollar has decreased over time as processing and marketing services for food products have increased. Middlemen are often blamed for many of the farmer's woes. Farm income is thought to be lower because of the profits earned by middlemen as farm products move from the farm to the consumer. Thus, farmers and farm organizations have long sought ways to increase the share of the consumer's food dollar received by farmers. This chapter presents an analysis of cooperatives and marketing orders—marketing institutions designed to increase farmers' bargaining power and to reduce the role of middlemen in the marketing of farm products.

MARKETING AND SUPPLY COOPERATIVES

The underlying idea of a producer cooperative is that it provides a way for a voluntary association of individuals to avoid dealing with profit-seeking firms.[1] The basic objective of a co-op is to increase member profits by reducing or eliminating middleman margins. A group of farmers may band together to buy inputs or to market products. The farmers quite often have the goals of reducing the price they pay for inputs and of increasing the price they receive for their output by controlling supply. Agricultural co-ops are owned and controlled by member patrons and operated on a nonprofit basis. There are more than 47,000 rural and urban co-ops in the United States.[2] Most agricultural cooperatives either provide production inputs (*farm supply co-ops*) or market farm products (*marketing co-ops*). In 1984, there were 3,514 farm marketing co-ops and 2,136 farm supply co-ops in the United States.[3] By 2000, the number of marketing and farm supply co-ops had fallen to 1,672 and 1,277, respectively.[4] The co-op share of farm-level marketing activity increased from approximately 20 percent in 1952 to 30 percent in 1998.[5]

CAPPER-VOLSTEAD ACT

The co-op movement began in the early 1800s in the United States when dairy producers in Connecticut attempted to act together as a group in churning and marketing butter. The establishment of co-ops was an important activity of all the major farm organizations. However, the modern co-op movement received a major impetus with the passage of the Capper-Volstead Act in 1922. The act establishes conditions under which an organization might be defined as a co-op and attempts to increase farmers' bargaining power by protecting co-ops from the antitrust provisions of the earlier Sherman and Clayton Acts. Although "undue price enhancement" by co-ops is forbidden, enforcement is entrusted to the USDA rather than to the Department of Justice. In view of the subjective nature of the concept "undue price enhancement," it is not surprising that no secretary of agriculture since 1922 has found an instance in which a co-op was guilty of this practice. When prices are raised above free-market levels, it is a matter of opinion as to whether price has been "unduly" increased.

In the early 1980s, the Justice Department, the Federal Trade Commission, the General Accounting Office, and the Executive Office of the President expressed concern about the effects of co-op activities, but co-ops have retained their legal standing. Although the Capper-Volstead Act gives co-ops the right to form a common marketing agency, the extent to which co-ops can legally control their members' production is uncertain. It is clear that without the act many of the co-op marketing activities would be in violation of federal antitrust laws. Co-ops, for example, are allowed to engage in information-sharing activities that would almost certainly violate antitrust laws if done by a group of investor-owned firms. Cooperatives such as those involving marketing orders for milk, which significantly increase consumer prices, face constant scrutiny.

INCENTIVE PROBLEMS

Some economic analysts have argued that "most cooperatives are unable to compete with the large investor firms."[6] When a co-op attains any significant scale of operation, the absence or weakness of economic incentives is likely to create management problems. Although co-ops must have full-time employees and hired management, management functions in most co-ops are in the hands of people who are not residual claimants. The residual claimant of a proprietary firm is the owner. He or she reaps the profits or bears the losses of managerial decisions. In an investor-owned firm, there is a market for corporate stock. Consequently, equity prices in an investor-owned firm, unlike equity prices in a co-op, reflect the market's assessment of the firm's long-run prospects. There is also a market for corporate managers. Hence, market signals in investor-owned firms provide important information in monitoring management, despite the separation of ownership and control.

In a co-op, in contrast, management does not stand to gain or lose depending on the firm's success, at least to the same extent, as in a typical investor-owned firm. Thus, the co-op includes a separation of power and responsibility and the attendant incentive problems. Co-op managers' goals will vary, but it is predictable that when those who are not residual claimants make decisions, they are not likely to manage in a way that maximizes the present value of the co-op's stream of future residual returns.[7]

The residual claimants of a co-op's earnings are its members. When a new member purchases equity in a co-op, he or she does not acquire the right to sell the equity, unlike in the purchase of corporate stock, or the right to future residual co-op earnings beyond the period of co-op membership.[8] The rights to future residual earnings belong to future patrons. Upon admission to membership in a co-op, a new member-patron acquires the same rights to the organization's residual cash flows based on patronage (known as patronage refunds) as those held by existing members. Because co-op residual claimants can capture the benefits of investment decisions only over the time horizons of their expected membership, there is a general tendency to favor investment decisions with short payoff horizons.[9] Therefore, in view of the inherent incentive problems in the co-op form of business enterprise, the question arises: Why do co-ops survive?

TAX TREATMENT OF COOPERATIVES

A key to co-op survival appears to be the tax treatment afforded patronage refunds.[10] Patronage refunds are not counted as income to the co-op, but rather as personal income to the co-op members. Earnings retained in the business after they have been allocated to members' accounts are not taxable to the co-op, but are taxable to the members. In an investor-owned corporation, in contrast, dividend income is taxable both to the corporation at the corporate rate and to the individual shareholder when received. The result is a substantial tax break to the co-op as illustrated by the hypothetical example shown in table 11.1.

TABLE 11.1 Effect of Differences in Taxation of Corporations and Cooperatives.

	CORPORATION	CO-OP
Sales	$5,000,000	$5,000,000
Costs (operating and overhead)	4,500,000	4,500,000
Net Income	500,000	500,000
Dividends (patronage refunds)	200,000	200,000
Corporate taxes (34 percent)	170,000	0
Retained in business	130,000	300,000
Personal taxes (28 percent rate)	56,000	140,000
Owners' income after taxes	274,000	360,000
Owners' equity	3,000,000	3,000,000

In the example given in table 11.1, it is assumed that size of business, income, and operating costs are the same for the corporation and the co-op. It is also assumed that all of the co-op net income is distributed as patronage refunds or retained in the business and allocated to members' accounts. The corporation shareholders' income after taxes is $274,000, a rate of return of 9.1 percent of their equity. In contrast, the co-op shareholder's after-tax incomes is $360,000 and the after-tax rate of return for the co-op is 12.0 percent.

Sexton and Sexton contend that the preceding argument overlooks the fact that the cooperative-patron relationship is closely analogous to the stages of a vertically integrated business and that a vertically integrated corporation gets virtually the same tax break as a co-op.[11] In a vertically integrated poultry production, processing, and marketing corporation, for example, the earnings of the parts of the corporation pass to the parent company without being taxed. As shown by the table 11.1 example, however, it is the taxation of the parent company's earnings that appears to place the corporation-shareholder relationship at a disadvantage relative to the cooperative-patron relationship.

The example suggests why a great deal of effort is spent in maintaining the tax status of co-ops. Any co-op tax advantages, however, are offset to some extent by the inherent managerial incentive problems discussed earlier.

Depending on the severity of managerial problems, there might be a problem in financing co-op activities. Most equity capital in agricultural co-ops is raised, however, by retaining a share of net income in lieu of including it in member patronage refunds. Moreover, financing difficulties are offset by the federally chartered Bank for Co-Operatives, which the co-ops own and which provides a major share of co-ops' outstanding debt.[12]

Although co-ops generally raise questions of fairness in taxation, similar questions arise in the use of marketing co-ops to restrict competition and raise product price. Co-ops, however, generally do not have the power to restrict competition. Because there is free entry and expansion by competing sellers, co-op as well as nonco-op, agricultural marketing co-ops can do little to raise product price. Moreover, even if a marketing co-op were to include all sellers and attempt to restrict sales voluntarily, that would do little to raise product price because of the difficulties posed by free riders. That is, in the absence of legal sanctions, the free rider is likely to make cartelization ineffective.[13]

Some agricultural co-ops—notably marketing co-ops for dairy products, fruits, and vegetables—use government sanctions in the form of marketing orders to prevent entry by rival sellers. Marketing orders in these co-ops, as explained later, legally eliminate free riders who, if not prevented, would effectively undermine anticompetitive behavior.

MARKETING ORDERS

Marketing orders are government-enforced regulations that allow producers to work together, typically for the purpose of increasing prices. The enabling legislation for marketing orders was initiated under the federal Agricultural Marketing Agreement Act of 1937. Marketing orders were devised as a tool to achieve "orderly" marketing conditions and parity prices. Like other institutions and policies designed to support price, they were instituted at a time of strong sentiment to raise agricultural prices through restrictions on competition.

Marketing orders can be requested by producers and implemented after a hearing if two-thirds of the producers favor the proposed order (processors generally do not vote). The order defines the commodity and the market area to be regulated, and it typically empowers government-appointed panels of producers and middlemen to make industrywide marketing decisions about sales volume and standards.

There are both federal and state marketing orders. Although legislative provisions differ, order operation is basically the same for state and federal marketing orders. The discussion of this chapter focuses on federal orders. In federal orders, USDA employees assist producers of a specific commodity in developing the proposal for an order. If producers approve the order, the terms of the agreement are binding on all handlers. There is considerable variation in orders, but the basic principle is the same: market orders provide a means to enable producers to act together to limit competition.

MARKETING ORDERS AS A "SELF-HELP" PROGRAM

Marketing orders are often referred to as producer "self-help" programs. In reality, however, a marketing order, being a type of government-sanctioned and enforced producer cartel, is more aptly described as a "government help program." Government sanctions are used to negate the free-rider incentive that limits the effectiveness of voluntary cartels.

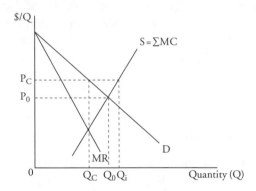

FIGURE 11.1 Voluntary cartels generally are ineffective because of free riders.

The free-rider incentive in voluntary cartels is shown in figure 11.1. Under competitive conditions, output Q_0 is produced and sold at the price P_0. If producers can agree to act together and restrict output to Q_C (where the marginal revenue to the producers as a group is equal to their marginal cost), short-run profits can be increased. However, such an agreement is usually unstable: just as all sellers together have a strong incentive to depart from the competitive solution, each seller separately has an equally strong incentive to depart from the cartel position. Each seller would maximize her income by producing a part of output Q_i rather than a part of the cartel output Q_C because P_C rather than MR would be the marginal revenue for each seller.[14] Because each seller has an incentive to cheat on a voluntary agreement to restrict competition in this way, the free-rider incentive is typically strong enough to maintain competition in the case of voluntary cartelization attempts. A federal marketing order is an institutional arrangement that allows producers to use the police power of government to enforce compliance with restrictions on competition.

Marketing orders exist for milk and for certain fruits, vegetables, and specialty crops. Federal marketing orders for fruits and vegetables contain quantity or quality controls, but price setting, in conjunction with a government-operated price-support program, is reserved for milk.

MILK MARKETING

Most production-control programs for agricultural commodities hinge on the fact that absent the production control, demand is inelastic so that revenues are increased by reducing output.[15] In some cases, where a product is used in two or more markets, sellers may be able to increase net returns by price discrimination even if total output is not restricted. Milk is the most important farm commodity in the United States in which a two-price program is used. Two government programs are involved in milk marketing: marketing orders and price supports.

Background of Milk Marketing Orders

In 1922, the Capper-Volstead Act effectively exempted dairy co-ops from antitrust actions, allowing producer organizations to restrict output and charge higher prices. During the early 1930s, many states passed laws regulating the pricing of milk. The marketing order system is the umbrella under which milk is marketed and sold throughout the United States today. The Agricultural Marketing Agreement Act of 1937 and its amendments still govern the federal marketing order for milk and other products.

Classified Pricing

Classified pricing is the system of pricing both fluid and "manufacturing" milk according to use. Under this system, different prices are charged depending on whether the milk is used for fluid consumption or for manufacturing. The classified pricing system for milk is incredibly complex. Although a number of federal and state marketing orders maintain and monitor classified pricing, the practice predates the Agricultural Marketing Agreement Act of 1937.

Grade A milk is milk that meets sanitation requirements for fluid milk. Approximately 95 percent of all milk produced in the United States is Grade A. The amount of Grade A milk produced greatly exceeds the demand for fluid milk at current supported prices. Consequently, much of this milk is sold for manufacturing uses, including cheese, ice cream, butter, and dry milk powder. Handlers pay different prices for Grade A milk based on the final use of the milk—that is, depending on whether the milk is used for fluid consumption or for manufacturing purposes.

Class I milk is for fluid consumption, and Class II is for manufacturing uses that have lower sanitation requirements. In some marketing orders, there is an additional classification, Class III, which is sold at a price below Class II but also is used for manufacturing purposes. Class II milk is used for fluid cream, ice cream, cottage cheese, yogurt, and other "soft" dairy products. Class III milk is used for "hard" products, including cheese, butter, and powdered milk. Grade B milk is milk that does not meet the sanitation requirements for Grade A milk. This milk can be used only for manufactured products. Thus, Grade B milk competes with Grade A milk in Class II and Class III uses.

Price Discrimination

Price discrimination provides one explanation for the existence of the classified pricing system of milk. Consider the situation depicted in figure 11.2. Suppose initially, a monopoly seller cannot (economically) distinguish between the two different types of buyers (buyers for fluid milk and buyers for milk to be used to manufacture other dairy products). He faces a single demand curve, D_{TOTAL}, sets marginal revenue (ΣMR) equal to marginal cost (MC), and charges a single price, P_0. Now, suppose the seller can economically distinguish the two types of buyers and prevent resale between them. If the demand for milk for fluid consumption is less elastic at the margin than the demand for milk for manufacturing uses, there is an opportunity to increase profits. The seller will attempt to allocate the product between uses in a way that will equate the marginal revenue in each market. Such an allocation will result in a higher price being charged in the less-elastic market (fluid milk). In figure 11.2, the prices charged are P_f in the fluid market and P_m in the manufactured market.

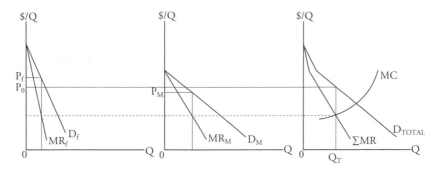

FIGURE 11.2 Price discrimination in selling milk.

Operation of the Federal Marketing Order

The marketing order is a legal instrument issued by the secretary of agriculture that regulates the terms under which processors within a specified area can purchase milk from dairy farmers. Approximately three-fourths of the Grade A milk marketed in the United States is delivered to manufacturing plants under federal orders.[16] Most of the remainder is marketed under state orders. Because the economic effects of state and federal orders are similar, the following discussion is devoted mainly to the operation of federal orders.

The Federal Milk Marketing Order system is used to set minimum prices of milk used for different purposes—fluid milk, cream, cheese, and so on, with the set prices varying from region to region in the United States. Under each marketing order, a market administrator uses formulas to sets the minimum prices that handlers in that marketing area must pay dairy farmers for different classes of milk. Class prices historically were based on the average price paid for manufacturing grade milk in Minnesota and Wisconsin updated by a product price formula.[17] The difference between the price of Class I milk and the prices of other milk classes varied from market to market.[18] A predetermined marketing order Class I price differential was added to the basic formula to determine the Class I price for each order. Milk processors in each order area then channelled as much milk into the high-price (fluid) market as could be sold at the set price. The rest of the milk was diverted to manufacturing uses. The price of manufacturing milk was and continues to be supported through a price-support system. The 1996 farm bill, as explained in a later section, eliminated the significance of Minnesota-Wisconsin prices in the classification scheme used in federal milk marketing orders, but did not fundamentally change the marketing system for milk.

Blend Price

All producers in a given market are paid the same average price for their output. This average price is referred to as the *blend price*. In a typical pooling arrangement, the marketing co-op pays each farmer the same per unit price for Grade A milk regardless of whether a particular farmer's milk is used for fluid consumption or for cheese and other manufactured products. The blend price received by producers is determined by the average ratio of Class I sales to all Grade A milk sold in the order area. That is, the blend price is a weighted average of the fluid and manufacturing prices, where the weights for the average are the proportions of Grade A milk going into Class I and Class II uses. For example, assume that half of the milk in an order area is sold for fluid use (Class I), and the rest is used for manufacturing purposes (Class II). If the price of Class I milk is $13 per hundredweight and the price of Class II milk is $11, *each* farmer selling milk in that market order area would receive a blend price of $12 per hundredweight for all milk sold, regardless of how much of any particular producer's milk was eventually sold as fluid milk. This system of marketwide pooling is used to keep producers from shifting among processors in an attempt to receive a higher blend price.

Operation of the Price-Support Program

In addition to marketing orders, price supports traditionally have played a key role in milk marketing. Since 1949, the federal government has supported the price of milk by setting a minimum support price to be paid to producers for manufacturing milk. The price of milk is supported through CCC purchases of butter, cheese, and nonfat dry milk from processing plants. Purchase prices for these products acquired by the CCC are set such that a weighted average of the product prices (based on the yield from 100 pounds of milk), less processing costs, will equal the manufacturing milk support price.[19] Products acquired by the CCC then are disposed of outside regular market channels and used in school lunch programs, military and veterans' hospital programs, and other government programs. Although the price of milk sold by processors as Class I (fluid) is not supported directly, the price-support program does indirectly support the price of Class I (fluid) milk by setting a floor under the market price of manufacturing milk products.[20]

Although the 1996 farm bill left the system of milk marketing orders in place, it did purport to make a significant change in the long-standing dairy price-support program. Under the FAIR Act, government purchases of butter, cheese, and dry milk to support the price of milk were to continue through

1999 at declining price-support levels. Milk price supports, which were scheduled to be eliminated on January 1, 2000, were later extended until May 31, 2002.[21]

State Orders

Approximately one-fourth of all milk produced in the United States is delivered to milk handlers under state marketing orders. California (which produces more milk than any other state) accounts for more than half of all milk produced under state marketing orders.[22] The economic effects of state orders are similar to those of federal orders, but the two types of orders operate a bit differently. Under state orders, there often is a type of quota system. A dairy farmer may be required to have a milk "base" (measured in pounds of milk per time period) to qualify to receive the higher Class I price for some of her milk. The value of milk base is determined competitively, and the base can be bought and sold. The base system does not restrict the amount of milk a farmer may sell, but rather determines how much of the milk sold is eligible to share in Class I receipts of the pool. Any milk a farmer produces in excess of her base is sold for the lower manufacturing price.

Effects of the Dairy Program

The dairy program has been widely criticized because it distorts the production and marketing of milk in a number of ways. First, it has caused an overproduction of milk; the extent of overproduction in any particular year depends on how much the price was held above the competitive level. Unless the support price is reduced, the surplus problem (reflected in stocks of manufactured dairy products) becomes greater over time because both demand and supply tend to become more elastic the longer the adjustment period. Figure 11.3 illustrates a situation in which a price support results in a surplus of S_0 in the short run. As time passes and demand and supply become more elastic, the surplus increases to S_1. Major expansions or contractions of the total milk supply are commonly viewed as long-term processes because the industry's physical plant capacity hinges on long-term investment decisions. Even in the short term, however, dairy farmers can alter supplies of milk, at least to some extent, by varying culling and feeding rates.[23]

Over the years, the government has tried various approaches, including paying farmers not to produce milk and purchasing dairy cows, in vain attempts to solve the overproduction problem created by high price supports. During the past decade, however, government stocks of surplus dairy products quite predictably have decreased dramatically in response to reduced price supports.

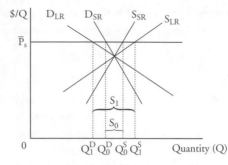

FIGURE 11.3 Demand and supply are affected by length of adjustment period.

Second, by increasing prices received by dairy producers above the competitive level, the program has imposed a substantial cost on consumers of milk as well as on taxpayers.[24] Economists Peter Helmberger and Yu-Hui Chen estimated that in 1990 the Federal Milk Marketing Order system led to 13 percent higher prices for fluid milk, with losses to consumers at just more than $1 billion per year.[25] Often overlooked is the fact that higher prices of fluid milk discourage consumption and contribute to an inadequate intake of calcium by American consumers.[26] A study reported in the *Journal of Consumer Affairs* found that elimination of the dairy price-support program would eliminate the calcium deficiency.[27]

Third, the price of fluid milk has been increased relative to prices of manufactured dairy products.[28] The proportion of Grade A milk not used for fluid consumption has increased over time and is now about two-thirds of Grade A production. Thus, more and more higher-value (Grade A) milk is being used for lower-value manufacturing uses. The increasing proportion of Grade A milk used for manufacturing purposes has come at the expense of Grade B production—now only approximately 3 percent of total U.S. milk output.[29] Thus, the dairy program has likely led to larger-size dairy farms, on average, because Grade A farms are larger than Grade B dairy farms.

Fourth, the dairy program creates a misallocation of resources, resulting in too many resources being used in milk production. Milk marketing orders, with their highly restrictive regulations on the marketing of fluid milk, have also increased the proportion of total milk produced in relatively high-cost areas at the expense of production in California, Minnesota, and Wisconsin, which appear to have a comparative advantage in milk production. Thus, the dairy program not only results in higher prices to consumers, but also allows higher-cost producers to continue in production.

Fifth, barriers to international trade have long been used to prevent lower-priced imports of butter, cheese, and other manufactured milk products from undercutting the U.S. dairy program. The implementation of recent international trade agreements will have significant implications for the U.S. dairy program.[30] The Uruguay Round GATT agreement, which was scheduled to be implemented over the 1995–2000 period, calls for U.S. dairy product import quotas to be reduced over time, and there is a clearly defined minimum-access requirement that allows more dairy products to enter the United States.[31] NAFTA, which became effective on January 1, 1994, also includes provisions for relaxing trade barriers between Canada, Mexico, and the United States. NAFTA is likely to benefit the U.S. dairy industry because Mexican demand for milk and dairy products will likely continue to outpace Mexico's domestic production.[32]

The result of lowering trade barriers on U.S. imports and exports of dairy products has become apparent. Since the implementation of GATT and NAFTA, imports of dried milk, cheese, and butter have increased when compared with imports from the period 1988–1993. At the same time, exports of cheese and ice cream also have increased.[33]

Persistence of the Dairy Program

In view of the distortions the dairy program creates in the production and marketing of milk, why does it persist? Political support for the program comes from dairy producers and other owners of specialized inputs benefiting from higher milk prices, suppliers of inputs to the dairy industry, and personnel who administer the programs. Moreover, there is a transitional gains trap, as in other farm programs that initially increase the profitability of production. The dairy program cannot be eliminated without imposing losses on owners of specialized inputs; losses would be heaviest for milk producers in high-cost production areas. A recent study estimated that annual rents resulting from the dairy program ranged from $1.59 billion to $2.29 billion per year. Dairy cows, as expected, were found to be a specialized factor, but land was not.[34]

In most milk marketing orders, there is no limit either on the volume of milk a farmer can market at the support price of milk for manufacturing or on the entry of new dairy farms. Thus, potential cartel profits tend to be transformed into increased prices (and costs) of specialized resources such as dairy cows, equipment, land, and the managerial skills required to produce milk as output expands or costs increase, or both, until firms are making normal profits. If the dairy program were terminated (unexpectedly), dairy farmers would suffer windfall losses regardless of when they went into the dairy business.

Classified pricing is often justified on the basis of the cost differential in producing Grades A and B milk. Without the price differentials under the dairy program, undoubtedly less Grade A milk would be produced. There is no persuasive evidence, however, that classified pricing is necessary to maintain adequate fluid milk production in the United States.

RECENT CHANGES IN THE DAIRY PROGRAM

Marketing Orders

As indicated by the preceding discussion, the federally administered and enforced dairy cartel has long been a highly regimented system of milk marketing in the United States.[35] The 1996 farm bill directed the secretary of agriculture to make changes to existing milk policies—including a consolidation of the number of milk marketing orders. Three years later, the secretary announced a number of superficial changes to the system that had been in place for the past sixty years, including the following:

1. reducing the number of federal milk marketing orders from thirty-one to eleven,
2. changing the price differentials for Class I milk,
3. creating a new Class IV, and
4. developing new methods for computing class prices.

As previously described, the price of Class III milk was historically based on prices that milk producers in the Minnesota-Wisconsin region received for Grade B milk. The price differentials for Classes I and II of milk in different regions of the country then were based on the Minnesota-Wisconsin manufacturing grade price for Class III milk.

The 1996 farm bill modified but did not fundamentally change the marketing order system used to set minimum prices paid to dairy farmers for Class I milk used for perishable fluid products. Moreover, the 2002 farm bill did not change the classification system. Class I was kept for fluid milk and Class II for soft dairy products, but the reformed Class III was restricted to cheese, and a new Class IV was created for butter and dry milk. The Class III and Class IV prices now are based on wholesale prices for butter, cheese, and dry milk instead of on Grade B prices. A price support keeps these prices from falling below $9.90 per hundredweight. Class II prices equal Class IV price plus $.70 per hundredweight. Class I price is the higher of the Class III or Class IV price plus a specific differential that varies by region and reflects, to some extent, differences in transportation costs.

The 2002 farm bill added a new layer of complexity to an already highly complex dairy program. It established a national dairy-market-loss payments program. Producers enter into contracts ending on September 30, 2005. Dairy farm operators receive a direct payment when the monthly Class I price in Boston is less than $16.94 per hundredweight. The payment is 45 percent of the difference between $16.94 per hundredweight and the Class I price in the Boston marketing order.[36]

In short, the market order reforms did not fundamentally reduce the market distortions inherent in the milk classification system of the federal order system. The 1996 farm bill left in place a highly constrained market process in the dairy industry wherein marketing order administrators rather than market conditions set different prices for Grade A milk, depending on whether milk is sold for fluid or manufacturing uses. The effect is to increase the price of milk used as Class I milk, thereby penalizing consumers of fluid milk.

Dairy Compacts

The 1996 farm bill allowed for the creation of the Northeast Dairy Compact in the six New England States in 1997. Such compacts establish a minimum price for Class I milk that is usually higher than the one in effect under Federal Milk Marketing Orders.[37] Although one effect of the Northeast Dairy Compact was to raise retail milk prices, it did little to keep small-scale dairy farmers in business.[38] Instead, it provided financial incentives for the remaining dairy farms to get bigger.

Congress considered expanding the Northeast Compact to nearby states and creating a Southern Dairy Compact. If dairy compacts were expanded and retail milk prices increased, the results would be predictable. There would be less consumption of fluid milk and increased production of lower-valued manufactured products, including cheese, butter, and dry milk—and quite likely a return to the era of CCC purchases of surplus stocks of dairy products. Dairy compacts, however, were not reauthorized in the 2002 farm bill.

In summary, the 1996 FAIR Act did nothing to change U.S. dairy policy fundamentally. First, the Federal Milk Marketing Order system remains in place. Second, the creation of the Northeast Dairy Compact created still another type of distortion in milk marketing.

The 2002 farm bill maintains a permanent price support of $9.90 per hundredweight for butter, cheddar cheese, and nonfat dry milk. Market loss payments are also established to replace ad hoc assistance payments made to producers in 1999, 2000, and 2001. This program provides direct payments to dairy producers if the monthly Class I price in Boston falls below a specified level. The Northeast Dairy Compact was not reauthorized, and no further changes were made to milk marketing orders in the 2002 farm bill.[39]

MARKETING ORDERS FOR FRUITS AND VEGETABLES

The number of federal marketing orders for fruits, vegetables, and specialty crops has ranged from around forty-five to fifty in recent years. These marketing orders typically affect the quality and quantity of product marketed.[40] Oranges and most other commodities marketed under marketing orders are subject to some form of quality control that reduces the amount available for sale. Such measures specify the minimum grades and sizes of products that may be marketed. Imports must also meet standards comparable to those specified in the marketing orders.

Approximately half of the federal marketing orders contain quantity control provisions that permit limitation of sales in the primary (fresh) market, with the remainder moved to a secondary (processed) market. Other provisions of marketing orders may specify varieties of products that may be planted, establish standard packs and containers, and fund research, development, advertising, and promotion. Although there is considerable variation across marketing orders for fruits and vegetables, the basic principle is the same: producers act together to limit competition. There are a number of state marketing orders, but the bulk of this activity is in California.

Total-Quantity Regulations

Total-quantity regulations are based on the idea that the elasticity of demand varies by use. *Market allocation* parallels federal milk orders except that quantity instead of price is set in the primary (fresh) market for a number of products, including walnuts, almonds, and raisins. A portion of the product is diverted from the less elastic market, and the handler pays members on the basis of the average price received in the entire order area. The product excluded may be destroyed, exported, or diverted to a more elastic secondary market.

In the case of *producer allotments*, marketing quotas or allotments are assigned to individual producers. Producer allotments have been used for cranberries, Far West spearmint oil, and Florida celery.[41] Each year a producer is permitted to sell an amount equal to a specified percentage of his base allotment. Another possibility is to *limit production*. For example, there was a "green drop" order provision for California cling peaches in which fruit was knocked from the trees while still small as a way of reducing production.

Rate-of-Flow Regulations

Rate-of-flow regulations are also based on the fact that demand is less elastic in the primary market. The amount of produce shipped to market in a given period may be limited in several ways. In *reserve pool* schemes, all producers are required to place a specified portion of their crop into storage, some or all of which may later be released for unrestricted sale or for sale in a secondary market. Reserve pools are authorized in orders for California walnuts, raisins, and prunes and for Far West spearmint oil.[42] *Shipping holidays*, a minor form of volume control that prohibits further commercial shipments, can be declared until a "temporary glut" disappears. Such holidays are typically limited to periods surrounding calendar holidays.[43]

In a *prorate* program, the total amount targeted for shipment to the primary market during a particular time period is specified and apportioned among shippers on a weekly basis. In this way, the flow per time period (e.g., week) is reduced, with all shippers covered by the order sharing in the reduction. These shipping restrictions are a close substitute for total quantity restrictions in the case of a perishable commodity. The fruit not marketed for fresh use is forced into processing uses or allowed to rot. No marketing orders have used prorates since three citrus orders were terminated in 1994.

A great deal of controversy surrounded the effects of the prorate provisions of the marketing order for California navel oranges. Marketing orders face the most public criticism when crops are deliberately destroyed. In 1981, a public outcry arose when photographs of oranges rotting in parking lots appeared in the press. In defense of government-enforced destruction of 40 percent of the California navel orange crop, a USDA official was quoted in the *New York Times* as saying, "Oranges are not an essential food. People don't need oranges. They can take vitamins."[44] The California navel orange marketing order was abolished in 1994.

Grade, Size, and Maturity Regulations

Provisions affecting quality are included in most marketing orders. These quality-control standards are enforced through mandatory federal inspection. When small-size produce is eliminated, the demand for the remaining portion of the crop is increased. Producer returns may or may not increase when there is a decrease in total quantity marketed, although producers would not support such marketing restrictions unless they expect to gain from them.

Consumers who prefer to buy lower grades and smaller sizes are affected most by eliminating the marketing of lower quality, small-size products. In some cases, grade and size restrictions measurably reduce imports, further restricting the choices of domestic consumers. Foreign shippers, who must meet the specifications of different orders for potatoes, tomatoes, oranges, and other products, view marketing orders as impediments to trade with the United States.

Advertising, Promotion, and Research

Advertising, promotion, and research provisions of marketing orders have become more important during the past decade. Producers or handlers may be assessed funds to support research, promotion, and advertising. These provisions of marketing orders differ from those previously discussed because they reduce income in the present period with the expectation of increasing it in the future. Advertising and promotion is undertaken on the assumption either that consumer information is incomplete or that consumer demand can be shifted through persuasion. It is difficult in practice to separate these two motives or to measure their individual impacts.

Advertising provisions of marketing orders are very similar to producer-funded advertising through "check-off" plans. A large number of state commissions are chartered to collect a levy from producers at the point of sale to the first handler. These levies are called check-off plans because the processor withholds or checks off a set amount per unit of product before paying the producer. Some of these plans have been defeated in the required referendum.

The object of producer-funded advertising is to increase the demand for the product. Such advertising is most likely to be effective when new information about the quality or the nature of a product is presented. Demand sometimes may also be increased without changing the nature of the product through an effective advertising program (e.g., "Pork, the other white meat").

FACTORS AFFECTING DEVELOPMENT AND LIFE OF MARKETING ORDERS

Agreement by producers is more likely to be reached if the benefits are evenly spread among a small number of producers in concentrated areas or under relatively homogeneous production conditions. If all producers have about the same costs, there likely will be less resistance than if there are some very low-cost producers. Producers in lower-cost regions or those with superior skills are more likely to oppose marketing orders. Thus, any increases in producer incomes from restrictions on competition come at the expense not just of consumers, but also of some producers who would prefer to operate without a marketing order. Because the proportion of the commodity that can be sold in the fresh market is fixed by fiat, the lower-cost producers are prevented from capturing a larger share of the market.

The potential to increase price by diverting some of the product is greater the lower the elasticity of demand. Furthermore, the expected life of a marketing order is likely to be longer if the elasticity of supply is low than it would be in a situation where the output response by producers to an increase in price is high. Thus, it is not surprising that most marketing orders cover products of considerable value concentrated among a small number of producers in a fairly small geographic area. California crops account for a high proportion of the active federal and state marketing orders.

EFFECTS OF MARKETING ORDERS

Consumers

Marketing orders increase the prices of fresh oranges and other products going to primary markets. Consumers are clearly adversely affected when marketing orders raise prices, in particular consumers who consumed the grades and quantities no longer offered for sale.

Handlers and Processors

Fresh produce handlers and processors have generally opposed the development and use of marketing orders for fairly obvious reasons. There is, for example, a loss of entrepreneurial freedom of action under rate-of-flow and other order provisions. There is also the possibility that the adoption of marketing orders makes the development of co-op-owned processing facilities more likely.

Producers

A successful price-discriminating marketing order cartel yields higher average producer prices.[45] The prospect of higher prices leads to increases in output by both existing and new producers because most marketing orders do not effectively limit entry.[46] Thus, production tends to increase so long as there are "pure profits"—that is, until cartel profits are dissipated.[47]

Overproduction is a predictable result of a cartel that does not limit entry while raising prices. In the case of the navel orange order, not only were oranges diverted to juice when consumers preferred fresh oranges, but resources were also diverted into growing oranges used for juice because doing so enabled a grower to share in the profits from fresh oranges.[48]

Orderly Marketing

The ostensible purpose of marketing orders is to establish "orderly" marketing conditions. Although this concept is not well defined, it presumably has to do with reducing marketing risks associated with price changes. Marketing orders, however, do not necessarily stabilize prices. It would be consistent with the stabilization objective to slow down the flow of crops to market in years of high production and then remove the restrictions in years of normal or low production. In fact, prorate and other market-allocation devices have been used in good and bad years alike.

Even if marketing orders reduce price variation, they will not necessarily reduce fluctuations in producer profits. If prices were constant in good years and bad, profits would plummet in bad years when producers had little to sell. Allowing prices to vary helps to stabilize profits by letting producers take advantage of higher prices in poor crop years.

It is sometimes argued that fruits and vegetables must be given special regulatory treatment because they are perishable. Perishable goods, however, often are subject to seasonal price fluctuations. Fresh asparagus, raspberries, hotel rooms, and oysters are highly seasonal commodities produced without marketing orders.[49] Trying to smooth out price fluctuations by setting a uniform price throughout the year deprives consumers of the benefits of the months of abundance without making the goods available during the months of scarcity.

Moreover, the orderly marketing argument implies that all agricultural products need regulation. Yet growers of many crops similar to those now under marketing orders operate without economic regulation. Oranges grown in Florida and Texas are under marketing orders, whereas those grown in California are not.

Finally, marketing boards have resisted innovations that would make the regulated commodities more storable. Until the lemon marketing order was terminated in 1994, the lemon committee blocked the introduction of shrink-wrap technology that would make lemons storable for six months or longer.[50] The USDA has blocked the reconstitution of milk from dry powder that would even out seasonal fluctuations in supply. Thus, the evidence suggests that the major purpose of marketing orders is to increase price and profits, not to stabilize them.

SUMMARY

Farmers and farm organizations have long sought ways to increase their "bargaining power." There is a widespread view that farmers would benefit from measures to decrease the role of the middleman in the marketing of farm products. Cooperatives and marketing orders are two institutional arrangements designed to increase farmers' bargaining power and to assume some of the middlemen roles.

Marketing and farm supply co-ops have increased in importance since the passage of the Capper-Volstead Act in 1922, although the number of co-ops has fallen in recent years. The potential for co-op activities is reduced by the inherent incentive problems. Management is not in the hands of residual claimants, and co-op members acquire rights to future co-op earnings only as long as they remain in the co-op. Because members can capture the benefits only over the time horizon of their expected membership, there is a bias toward investment decisions with short-run payoffs. A key to the success of co-ops appears to be the tax treatment of patronage refunds. Whereas dividend income in the case of investor-owned firms is taxable both to the corporation and when received by individual shareholders, patronage refunds of co-ops are not taxable to the co-op. The result is a substantial tax break to co-ops when compared with investor-owned firms.

Equity questions also arise in collective bargaining activities of co-ops involving marketing orders. A marketing order essentially is a government-sanctioned cartel that permits members of a producer group to act in concert to limit competition. Marketing orders operate under provisions of the Agricultural Marketing Agreement Act of 1937. Federal and state marketing orders are important in the production and marketing of milk, fruits, vegetables, and specialty crops. Marketing orders empower government-appointed panels of producers and middlemen to make industrywide marketing decisions about sales volume and standards. Oranges and most fruits and vegetables marketed under marketing orders are subject to some form of quality control. Approximately half of these orders also contain quantity-control provisions. Price setting under marketing orders occurs only for milk.

More than 95 percent of all milk produced in the United States is Grade A and qualifies for use as fluid milk. Under classified pricing for milk, a higher price is generated for Class I milk that is used for fluid consumption. Only about one-third of the Grade A milk is sold for fluid use. The remainder competes in the processing market with lower-cost Grade B milk, which has less-restrictive sanitation standards and cannot be used as fluid milk.

Marketing orders for all products are facing increasing criticism. There appears to be no more reason for the government to foster producer cartels of milk, fruits, and vegetables than of other products. Although marketing orders are often justified on the basis of "orderly marketing," the evidence suggests that the real purpose of marketing orders is to increase producer incomes. Marketing orders are of limited benefit to producers in the long run, however, because short-run cartel profits attract more producers to the industry. Consumers ultimately pay the price of these restrictions on competition through higher product prices. Further, the dairy program price-support activities have at times resulted in substantial taxpayer costs.

Marketing orders are not only inconsistent with the market process in the production and marketing of domestic products. Their implementation also requires restrictions on imports to prevent domestic consumers from substituting lower-priced imports for higher-priced domestic commodities. This is particularly important in the case of cheese, butter, and other dairy products, where U.S. prices historically have been significantly higher than the world price. Lower trade barriers achieved through GATT and other multilateral trade agreements inevitably can be expected to narrow the difference between U.S. and world prices of manufactured dairy products and to increase international trade.

12 | Effects of Agricultural Commodity Programs

Farm commodity prices for milk, cotton, sugar, wheat, feed grains, tobacco, and other products have been supported through a number of different programs since the 1930s. Supply controls have taken the form of acreage restrictions and allotments, land retirement, and marketing quotas. Prices have also been supported through direct purchases of products and through the use of nonrecourse loans, target prices, and trade restrictions. Various domestic and foreign food aid programs have also been used to increase the consumption of farm products and to bolster prices; these programs are described in chapters 13 and 14. In previous chapters, the major effects of various programs were described. This chapter summarizes the direct and indirect effects of the various commodity programs, shows why the benefits tend to be dissipated over time, and describes the major beneficiaries of these programs.

WHO ARE THE SHORT-RUN BENEFICIARIES?

Several different groups receive short-run benefits from farm price-support programs, but the amount of the benefit varies widely. Farmers may benefit as producers or as owners of land and other specialized resources. Those who develop, administer, and evaluate the programs may also benefit. In some cases, processors of farm products also benefit. For example, ADM, a large agribusiness firm, manufactures corn-based sweeteners and reaps huge benefits from the sugar program.[1] The peanut program, in contrast, raises costs to manufacturers of peanut candy.

Owners of Specialized Resources

Owners of land, allotments, and other specialized resources are the major gainers from farm programs that increase product prices. Of course, it is costly in terms of time and money to obtain and maintain farm programs, as emphasized in earlier chapters. As Gordon Tullock, a developer of the theory of rent seeking, suggests, however, it is likely that the gains from rent seeking "are immensely greater than the sum total of the lobbying expenses."[2]

Regardless of whether prices are supported above the competitive level by voluntary or mandatory supply controls, the benefits of price supports are largely capitalized into the values of land, production and marketing rights, and other specialized resources not reflected in farm income statistics. Thus, the gains go primarily to owners of specialized resources and not to farm operators as such. Moreover, when farm program benefits are capitalized into higher prices of land and other inputs, those who own more of the affected farm resources gain more.

Consider the example of land. The price of land is determined by the discounted stream of expected future returns. If there is an increase in product price so that the expected return to land increases, land prices will increase. In the mid-1990s, Tweeten found that expectations of continuing farm commodity programs had caused some $100 billion of such benefits to be capitalized into land prices—or up to 15 percent of total farmland value.[3] The increase in land price means that production costs increase.

The capitalization phenomenon is even more clear-cut in the case of programs involving acreage allotments or marketing quotas. In the tobacco price-support program, for example, the value of the marketing quota, which gave the producer the right to produce and sell tobacco, often exceeded $1,000 per acre per year. In such cases, the price-support program increased cost of production for the quota level of output by more than $1,000 per acre.

Although owners of land, allotments, and other specialized resources receive windfall gains when a price-support program is unexpectedly initiated (or when a price-support level is increased), any gains received by farmers are likely to be short-lived or transitional. That is, the first generation of resource owners receive most of the benefits. As benefits are capitalized into higher input prices, gains to later producers are largely negated by higher production costs (including higher land and allotment prices). Thus, price-support programs result in what has been called a "transitional gains trap." Once a price-support program is in operation, its elimination imposes losses on owners of specialized resources regardless of whether they benefited from the original windfall. In reality, at any given time, owners of specialized assets, including land and allotments, often are not the same people who received the windfalls when farm programs were initiated (or when benefit levels were increased).

Owners of specialized resources lose when the prices of the resource decrease, whatever the reason. For example, owners of land, capital facilities, and other farm assets in the United States incurred huge losses in real wealth when inflationary expectations and farm product prices decreased in the 1980s. Farm real estate prices plummeted more than one-third (in nominal terms) from 1982 to 1987. Further, inflation eroded almost 20 percent of the value of the dollar during this period.[4] When prices of farmland and other resources decrease, those who own more resources lose more wealth. Thus, it is not surprising that the large, highly leveraged commercial farmers were most affected by decreases in prices of farm assets in the 1980s.

Producers and Direct Payments

Producers who have more to sell stand to gain more from farm price supports. In contrast, small farmers are affected relatively little when product prices are increased because the benefits are tied to the volume of sales. For example, as discussed in chapter 6, farms with annual sales of less than $20,000 in 1998 constituted 64 percent of all U.S. farms and received payments averaging approximately $800 each—less than 10 percent of total direct government payments.[5] Further, the short-run benefits of price-support programs vary widely (even for farms of a given size), depending on crops grown.

Recent farm bills have included statutory limits on the amount of government payments received per person but legal loopholes limited their effectiveness. In the PIK program in 1983, for example, the PIK entitlements did not count toward the annual total payment ceiling of $50,000 per person. Similarly, the Milk Production Termination Program under the 1985 farm bill was also exempt from payment ceilings, and 112 dairy producers in California, Florida, Idaho, Texas, and Arizona received payments of more than $1 million each under the program.[6] Moreover, farmers often reorganized farming operations so that additional "persons" could receive payments.[7]

Payments of such magnitudes to farmers under target-price and other farm programs seemingly are inconsistent with the objective of supporting incomes of low-income producers.[8] Yet given that participating farmers typically had to reduce their output to receive the price-support payments, the establishment of a maximum payment level reduced participation rates of large producers, thereby limiting the effectiveness of efforts to increase product price through voluntary reductions in output. Because one-third of U.S. farms produce approximately 90 percent of total agricultural output, it is this output that determines the effectiveness of a supply-control program. The lower the maximum limitation was set, the less the incentive on the part of large farmers to participate in farm programs. A high-payment limitation had a regressive effect on incomes within the agricultural sector, but a low-payment limitation limited the effectiveness of programs in reducing output.

Price supports and supply controls were eliminated for most farm commodities under the 1996 farm bill, but a complicated set of rather porous payment limits continues. Under the 2002 farm bill, there is a $40,000 per "person" annual limit for direct payments.[9] In some cases, however, individual farmers can receive up to $80,000 per year on separate farming operations. Similarly, marketing loan gains and LDPs per "person" are limited to $75,000 per crop year, but in some cases individual farmers having separate farming operations can receive annual marketing loan gains or LDPs up to $150,000.[10] The total dollar limitation per person, including up to $130,000 in countercyclical payments, is $360,000 per year.

Mandatory supply-control programs are an alternative to voluntary price-support programs. Once the mandatory supply-control program is approved in the required producer referendum, the individual producer has no choice as to whether or not to participate. With mandatory supply controls, direct government outlays are likely to be much smaller than with voluntary supply-control programs because voluntary programs must use direct payments to induce farmers to participate. Mandatory supply-control programs, however, are necessarily protectionist and create pressure for import controls to prevent domestic consumers from purchasing lower-priced products from foreign producers. Tobacco was the only remaining example of a mandatory supply-control program in effect in the United States prior to its elimination in 2004.

Farmers as Producers versus Farmers as Asset Owners

The preceding discussion suggests that it is mainly farmers as resource owners rather than farmers as producers who are affected when prices of farm assets change. Thus, farmers as producers, as distinct from farmers as asset owners, gain little from farm programs. The benefits from price supports, subsidized inputs, tax preferences, and so on are largely offset by increased costs of specialized inputs. Thus, insofar as producers and asset owners are different entities, the distribution of gains between them depends on how quickly the expected benefits or costs of program changes are incorporated into asset values. The more quickly asset values rise when program benefits are increased, the more asset owners benefit from the gain. If the benefits from an unexpected program change are immediately incorporated into asset values, current producers (who do not own assets) will benefit only to the extent that they contracted to obtain land and other resources before the program change is made. In general, the adjustment in asset values hinges on expectations, and there is no reason to expect the speed of adjustment to be the same in all markets.

Competition ensures that resource costs will rise enough so that the expected rate of return in the production of farm products will be no higher than rates of return in other areas of productive activity, regardless of how much product prices increase. Consider what happens, for example, if price supports are increased for corn. The increased profitability of higher product prices is soon reflected in increased prices of specialized resources used in corn production. Only those renters who have rented land or purchased machinery and other resources before resource prices fully adjust to higher product prices will gain from increased product prices. The conclusion is that the benefits of higher product prices or lower input prices generally have little effect on farmers as producers except for these short-run transitional gains.

Labor versus Other Specialized Resources

Agricultural farm labor generally is not highly specialized. If farm labor were completely unspecialized so that the supply of labor were completely elastic, farm programs would provide no benefit to labor resources in agriculture. To the extent that farmers are owners of specialized farming skills, however, they benefit from programs designed to assist agriculture. Moreover, the effect of government farm programs on specialized labor is different in one respect from that on specialized land or capital resources. In the case of land, rights to produce, machinery, and other capital facilities, market price is determined by the properly discounted stream of expected future returns. However, the expected gains from government programs over time are incorporated into higher market prices of land or any other specialized resource only if property rights are well defined and the asset can be bought and sold. When the price of corn increases, for example, land prices increase to reflect the increased future returns to land only if there is a market in which land prices are determined by expected future supply and demand conditions. Benefits of increased future returns are capitalized or incorporated into current market prices of land and capital inputs when property rights are clearly defined and legally enforced. In the corn example, expected increases in corn prices in future years are likely to affect land prices immediately when the rights to land are privately owned and can be freely exchanged.

The situation is different in the case either of specialized labor or of an entrepreneur whose services can be hired for a period of time but cannot be bought and sold. Individual liberty dictates that each person has control over the disposition of his or her own time. An employer cannot legally negotiate a binding contract to obtain a worker's lifetime services, as can be done in the case of capital assets, including real estate, machinery, marketing quotas, and so on. When an asset cannot be owned and freely exchanged, its value is based on its expected contribution during the contracted time period. For example, an employer receives the benefits of a more productive laborer only during the time that he employs the laborer. Moreover, there is a well-functioning market for specialized labor skills in agriculture. An outstanding dairy herd manager, for example, might capture the returns to these skills either by tending her own dairy farm or by moving to other dairy employment opportunities. In this sense, the return to specialized skills is available to the individual who possesses those skills in the same way that returns are available to owners of allotments and other specialized resources.

How is specialized labor or management for the dairy farmer different from specialized land? When there is an increase in milk price, the increase in the price of land is based on the expected duration of the higher milk price. Thus, the gain to the farmer owning specialized land, as shown earlier, is transitional. The farmer's wealth increases as a result of an increase in land price, but after land prices adjust to higher milk prices, the dairy farmer, whether using or renting out the land, would expect to receive a normal rate of return on the investment in land.

Superior skill in milk production means that returns to labor or management or both are significantly lower if one is employed in nondairy production activities. The farmer who has superior labor or management skills in dairying receives a higher return when milk price is increased. He receives the increased return each year as long as the milk price remains higher. The increased milk price is not capitalized into higher market prices for labor or management in the same sense as in the case of real estate, allotments, machinery, and other capital inputs because property rights for labor are not transferable. Thus, the gain from an increase in product price in the case of labor is not transitory in the way that it is for private property that can be bought and sold.

Farm Operators and Farm Labor

Because increased returns are largely capitalized into higher costs, farm programs have little effect on the long-term profitability of agriculture. And, as suggested earlier, farm programs have little effect on the returns to farm labor because labor resources in general are not very specialized in agriculture (so that the supply of labor is quite elastic). When labor can flow readily between agriculture and the rest of the economy, the long-run return to labor and management in agriculture is determined mainly by opportunity cost—by the alternatives that farm laborers have for nonagricultural uses of their resources.[11]

Political Bureaucracy

Politicians and the political bureaucracy also benefit from price-support programs. Farm state legislators use farm programs to obtain and maintain political support. Farm programs are also important to the bureaucracies that administer and evaluate the effects of these programs. As shown in chapter 7, USDA employment in 1998 was more than four times larger than in 1929 even though the number of farms decreased dramatically during this period. Thus, a large group of people have a vested interest in maintaining and expanding the scope of farm programs.

INDIRECT EFFECTS OF PRICE-SUPPORT PROGRAMS

The direct effect of price-support programs is to increase producer prices of farm products. An important indirect effect previously discussed is the increase in production costs as the higher product prices are capitalized into input prices. A number of other indirect effects occur as well.

Effect on Market Process

Farm price-support programs delay economic adjustments. In the decentralized market, economic change and progress is characterized by business experimentation and a form of economic natural selection. Entrepreneurial decisions are guided by perceptions of profit opportunities, and where there are no price supports or other types of government subsidies, those enterprises that best anticipate market conditions are most likely to continue in business. In this way, market forces constantly tend to cause resources to be deployed from less-productive to more-productive firms.

Price supports of whatever kind hamper and stifle the entrepreneurial discovery process, thereby distorting the allocation of resources and the pattern of production. One can only surmise what the pattern of production for peanuts, tobacco, milk, or other price-supported products would be today if there were no restrictions on competition. It can be safely predicted, however, that compared with current production patterns, there would be shifts in production of milk, tobacco, peanuts, and other products both between regions and between farms. Price supports thus distort the pattern of resource use. The 1996 and 2002 farm bills significantly reduced distortions in the production of wheat, cotton, rice, and feed grains. Farmers no longer are paid to take productive land out of production as part of price-support programs. Choices regarding production decisions do, however, continue to be influenced to some extent by government policy through such programs as the Conservation Reserve Program (CRP) and through such policy tools as nonrecourse loans and concomitant marketing loans and LDPs.

Market prices provide correct signals to producers and consumers only when prices are free to change in response to changing economic conditions. Government price controls block the flow of information that prices communicate to consumers about product availability and to producers about consumers' choices. When the price of milk is raised above the market-clearing price, for example, producers are induced to produce "too much" and consumers to consume "too little." Recurring surpluses of butter, cheese, wheat, corn, tobacco, and other products are a direct result of government price-support programs. So long as prices are supported above the competitive level, surplus production will be a chronic feature of U.S. agricultural programs. Public dissatisfaction with farm programs increases during periods when support levels for milk and other products are set considerably above market-clearing levels so that huge government subsidies are required to operate the programs.

The higher prices resulting from price-support programs make it more difficult for consumers, especially those in lower-income groups, to buy food. Thus, price-support programs, ostensibly designed to increase incomes of low-income producers, not only make farm incomes less equal, but also worsen the income condition of low-income consumers.

Effect on Market Stability

Price supports and marketing orders are often justified as measures to "stabilize markets." As government policies are implemented through the political process, however, they often introduce artificial instability and uncertainty into agricultural markets. Incumbent administrations frequently manipulate short-run policies, hoping to affect upcoming elections. Prior to the 1976 election, for example, the Ford administration raised the loan rate on wheat and tripled the tariff on sugar.[12] President Carter increased dairy price supports significantly on the eve of the 1980 election.[13] Direct payments to dairy producers under the 1983 Dairy and Tobacco Adjustment Act also coincided with the 1984 presidential campaign, fortunately for the Reagan administration. More recently, the

1996 farm bill, enacted in the heat of a presidential and congressional campaign, provided contract payments to farmers guaranteeing little decrease in government support to farmers for seven years. And shortly before the election that year, President Clinton responded to Hurricane Fran by visiting North Carolina with a package of federal disaster relief.[14]

Every four years or so, Congress enacts a new farm bill. The periodic swings from relatively high to relatively low price supports tend to create instability in U.S. agriculture. The high price-support levels of the 1981 farm bill, along with the inflationary monetary and fiscal policies of the late 1970s, fostered unrealistic expectations by farmers about future farm product prices and set the stage for the financial chaos in agriculture in the 1980s. As emphasized previously, however, the primary effect of agricultural marketing orders and price-support programs in general is to increase farm incomes rather than to "stabilize markets."

Rent Seeking

Finally, price-support programs divert resources from the task of production of food and fiber to the scramble to obtain and maintain government transfers. The role of recent PAC contributions by dairy co-ops and supporters of the sugar program at the federal level, for example, is evidence of this rent-seeking phenomenon in which groups attempt to achieve income transfers through the use of government power.[15] Other commodity groups, farm organizations, and narrowly focused interests also frequently attempt to achieve income transfers through the use of government power.

SHORT-RUN VERSUS LONG-RUN EFFECTS

The short-run and long-run effects of price-support programs are likely to be quite different. In the short run, an effective price-support program provides windfall gains, primarily to owners of land and other specialized resources at the time the program is instituted. Competition causes prices of these inputs to increase until expected rates of return in agriculture are no higher than those in other sectors. As suggested earlier, resource prices tend to reflect opportunity costs, and the supply of farm labor is quite elastic. Consequently, farm labor incomes with or without price supports are determined largely by general economic conditions and nonfarm employment opportunities. Thus, price-support programs, aside from the windfalls received when the programs are initiated or benefit levels increased, have little effect on farm labor incomes.

Distortions in resource use are likely to increase with the passage of time when the pattern of production is frozen so that there is little opportunity to shift production to the lowest-cost production regions. The tobacco, peanut (until the 2002 farm bill), and dairy programs, for example, have prevented or impeded the production of tobacco, peanuts, and milk from shifting to the lowest-cost production regions within the United States.[16]

Effect on Exports

In the short run, when price-support programs increase domestic prices, there is an immediate adverse effect on exports. The longer the length of run, moreover, the greater this effect is likely to be. An increase in domestic price encourages production in competing countries. Flue-cured tobacco provides a good example of this phenomenon. The U.S. tobacco program, by essentially providing a price umbrella under which foreign producers are protected from U.S. competition, stimulated production in other countries. This has increased the competition faced by U.S. tobacco producers in both domestic and foreign markets. The U.S. share of total world flue-cured tobacco exports during the period from 1955 to 1959 was 60 percent. By 2000, as price was artificially increased through strict production and marketing controls, the U.S. share of flue-cured tobacco exports was reduced to less than 10 percent.

Substitution in Consumption and Production

Supply and demand become more elastic the longer the adjustment period. Given an increase in price in the United States, the longer is the adjustment period, the greater will be the response by producers of substitute products. Thus, the longer a price-support program remains in effect, the greater the pressures from competing products. The substitutes may come from producers of the same product in other countries or from producers of substitute products at home or abroad. Consider the cotton price-support program of the 1930s, which provided a stimulus for the development of substitutes. The U.S. cotton price-support program is responsible for at least some of the speed at which synthetic fibers were developed and adopted in the United States. At the same time, the higher cotton prices in the United States also encouraged cotton production in Egypt and other countries.

The cotton price-support program contributed to a dramatic reduction in the U.S. share of world cotton production. During the period 1928–30, before price supports were instituted, U.S. annual cotton production averaged 14 million bales per year, and all other countries' total production averaged 12 million bales. In 1995, after sixty years of price supports, U.S. cotton production had increased relatively little, to approximately 18 million bales, whereas foreign cotton production was more than five times larger at 65 million bales. The U.S. cotton program simultaneously throttled U.S. cotton production and encouraged production by foreign competitors by providing a price umbrella over the international market.[17]

The effect of a price increase on demand is also greater the longer the length of the adjustment period. The longer the length of run, the more likely consumers are to find and adopt substitutes for a given product. As the cotton price increased owing to the price-support program, it took time for synthetic fibers to be developed and for consumers to discover and adopt the substitutes.

Cotton's share of fiber consumption before price supports were instituted was approximately 85 percent. A half century later in the early 1980s the share had decreased to approximately 25 percent. Domestic use of cotton since then has increased significantly—reflecting, at least in part, a shift in consumer preferences back to natural fibers. Cotton accounted for 41 percent of U.S. total fiber consumption in 2001, up from 35 percent just a decade earlier.[18]

The milk price-support program increased the prices of butter, cream, and other dairy products and thus encouraged the development of substitutes for these dairy products. As the price of butter increased relative to the price of margarine over time, for example, per capita consumption of margarine increased at the expense of butter. There has also been a substitution of nondairy creamers for cream. The conclusion is that the initial benefits of price-support programs are eroded by competition over time. Moreover, the longer the adjustment period, the more likely it is that lower-priced substitutes will be developed and adopted by consumers.

RESTRICTIONS ON COMPETITION

Restrictions on competition are at the heart of price-support programs because all price-support programs are inconsistent with the competitive market process. All impose restrictions on mutually beneficial exchange. In the case of marketing orders and production quotas, for example, all producers are forced to abide by the conditions of the cartel-like organization once the restrictions on competition are instituted. Individual producers and consumers no longer have the right to engage in mutually beneficial exchange as in a free market.

If, as suggested earlier, there is no principled philosophic difference between individual economic freedoms and individual freedoms of other sorts, the notion of individual rights is relevant in assessing the effects of such restrictions on competition. Government policies that force prices above or below the competitive level increase the costs of information exchange between consumers and producers and thus involve a type of censorship. Indeed, it has been argued that price controls "violate the right of free expression just as if the government dictated the content of the daily newspaper."[19]

Price-support programs in agriculture invariably block the free flow of price information and restrict consumers' options to buy domestically produced or imported products at the lowest prices. In the case of the milk program, for example, where prices of dairy products are held above the world-market level, import restrictions must be imposed to prevent consumers from purchasing lower-priced imported products. Thus, consumers as taxpayers are hit twice by price-support programs: they must pay higher prices for the products, but must also pay higher taxes to finance the price-support programs.

SUMMARY

In recent years, the government has operated price-support programs for wheat, feed grains, cotton, peanuts, tobacco, rice, milk, soybeans, wool/mohair, and honey. The programs have differed in detail, are incredibly complex, and have changed frequently. The major beneficiaries of all types of price-support programs, however, are the owners of land, allotments, and other specialized resources when the programs are initiated or at the time when benefit levels are increased. Program benefits are capitalized into higher prices of farm land, allotments, and other specialized resources. Farmers who enter production after a price-support program is initiated (or price level increased) generally gain little because the increased costs of using specialized resources tend to offset any benefits from the increased product price. Thus, the effect of farm programs on nonlabor farm income is transitory. Although price supports increase labor returns to those with specialized skills in agriculture so long as the price supports persist, they do little to increase incomes for unspecialized labor, which includes many if not most farmworkers. The main determinant of returns to such labor is nonfarm employment opportunities and general economic conditions.

The government payments received from farm programs are positively related to farm size: farmers producing more output receive more benefits. Maximum payment limitations reduce large producers' advantage to some extent, but there are numerous loopholes in the limits on payments.

The direct effect of price-support programs is to increase prices of farm products for producers. Huge surpluses, fully predictable when prices are raised above the competitive market-clearing level, have been a continual feature of government price-support programs since the 1930s. One indirect effect of price-support programs is to delay economic adjustments within farms and between production regions. Another indirect effect is to increase the resources devoted by farm groups to political activity aimed at achieving income transfers at the expense of resources used in the production of goods and services.

In the operation of standard price-support programs, "benefits" to producers decrease the longer the length of run (see figure 11.3 in chapter 11). Over time, supply becomes more elastic as higher product prices encourage the development of substitute products. Demand for the product also becomes more elastic as consumers discover and adopt substitutes. The result is that the adverse effects on consumption become greater over time, thereby exacerbating the problem of surplus production.

All price-support programs are inconsistent with the competitive market process. Mandatory production-control programs prevent mutually beneficial exchange between domestic or foreign producers and domestic consumers. In addition, these programs typically hamper or prevent production adjustments within and between production regions. Price-support programs that tie producer participation to restrictions on land use also distort the allocation of resources, often causing large acreages of highly fertile land to be taken out of production. Moreover, price-support programs, as shown in chapter 14, are inconsistent with achieving a more open economy.

13

Subsidized Food Programs

Government-operated food assistance or domestic food programs are programs that provide food at no cost or below market prices to targeted groups of consumers. Although these programs originated in the 1930s, the scope of domestic food assistance programs has increased dramatically since 1970. Although the food stamp and school lunch programs are the best known, there are a number of other subsidized food programs. This chapter presents a brief history of these programs and describes their major features. It also discusses the inherent information and incentive problems that have plagued the implementation of these programs from the beginning.

BRIEF HISTORY

The original purpose of food stamp, school lunch, and other subsidized food programs was to facilitate the operation of price-support programs for farm products. The Federal Surplus Commodities Corporation (FSCC) of 1935, in cooperation with the AAA, purchased surplus agricultural commodities for direct distribution to the unemployed and their families. Surplus commodities have been used in various ways over the years, with the focus always being on finding politically acceptable means of disposing of surpluses acquired in conjunction with product price supports.

Legislation Providing for Commodity-Distribution Programs

The operation of the FSCC was facilitated by an amendment to the AAA of

1933 that long served as a cornerstone in funding food assistance programs: Section 32. This amendment and two other major pieces of legislation provide the basis for commodity-distribution programs today. Section 32 appropriates 30 percent of the import duties imposed on all commodities for use by the secretary of agriculture to encourage exports and the domestic consumption of "surplus" agricultural commodities. Under this program, meats, fruits, and vegetables have been purchased with Section 32 funds and donated to school lunch and breakfast programs. Dairy products, rice, peanuts, wheat, and other price-supported products have also been purchased and donated to schools and other nonprofit agencies under Section 416 of the 1949 Agricultural Act. Finally, Section 6 of the National School Lunch Act of 1946 provides additional authorization for the purchase of agricultural commodities to be donated to schools and service institutions.[1]

The government donates surplus commodities to a network of food banks and other programs. The importance of these government-donated commodities relative to cash subsidies has decreased over time in domestic food programs. Although there has been little increase in the dollar value of donated commodities, cash subsidies for food assistance have increased dramatically since the mid-1960s. The food stamp program is the largest of the cash subsidy programs. There is now an array of frequently overlapping federal food assistance programs, but the following discussion focuses mainly on the food stamp and school lunch programs.

FOOD STAMPS

The food stamp program of the 1930s grew out of dissatisfaction with earlier direct food-distribution programs, which reduced regular market food purchases and afforded no choice to recipients regarding the commodities received. In the initial food stamp program, low-income families were authorized to purchase orange-colored stamps equal to their average food expenditures. For each dollar of orange stamps purchased, households received 50 cents worth of blue stamps. The orange stamps could be used to purchase any type of food at regular prices, but the blue stamps could be used only for those foods declared in surplus by the secretary of agriculture. This food stamp program ended during World War II, but was resumed after the war. Permanent food stamp legislation was enacted in 1964.

The food stamp program is the major food assistance program in the United States, accounting for approximately two-thirds of all food assistance spending.

Outlays on the food stamp program continue to increase. Preliminary estimates for 2002 suggest that approximately 19 million people received food stamps at a cost of roughly $20.5 billion.[2] The total value of an individual's food stamp allotment is based on three factors: food costs, income, and family size. Before 1979, recipients were required to pay a portion of the value of food stamps. In 1979, the purchase requirement was eliminated, and food stamps now are provided free to qualified recipients.

The food stamp program modestly increases expenditures on food in the United States. The increased expenditure on food, however, is far less than federal outlays on the food stamp program. This is because food stamp recipients, at least to some extent, substitute food stamps for food purchases that they would otherwise make if they did not receive food stamps. Estimates of the extent to which food stamps increase food expenditures range from 20 cents to 45 cents for each dollar spent on food stamps, which suggests that food stamps increase total food expenditures less than 2 percent.[3]

SCHOOL LUNCH PROGRAM

The school lunch program was also begun in connection with surplus disposal activities of the FSCC in the 1930s. Food donations to schools dropped off during World War II, but a permanent program was established under the National School Lunch Act of 1946. Both the scope and cost of the school lunch and other nutrition programs for children have increased dramatically since that time. Annual federal expenditures on the National School Lunch Program were less than $100 million in 1947. By 2002, federal outlays for school lunch, school breakfast, and other child nutrition programs had increased to more than $10 billion.[4]

Under the National School Lunch Program, both a cash subsidy and a donated food subsidy are provided for *all* lunches. More than half of the students receive meals free or at greatly reduced prices. Indeed, of the estimated 28 million participants in 2002 , 13.6 million received free school lunches.[5]

In 2002, the per meal subsidy, including commodities, was estimated to be $.36 for "paid" school lunches, $2.46 for free lunches, and $2.05 for reduced-price lunches.[6] Such estimates are necessarily crude when commodities from CCC stocks are used because we do not know how much the products would be worth if placed on the market. We do know, however, that the opportunity cost of surplus commodities is likely to be considerably less than the government outlays incurred in obtaining them.

The operation of the National School Lunch Program poses a number of problems and issues. First, there are producer pressures to use the program as a means of surplus disposal and to increase the demand for particular farm products. In 1996, when milk and beef prices fell, for example, the USDA increased purchases for school lunch and other nutrition programs.[7] Use of the program for surplus disposal, however, influences what schools serve in their lunches. Moreover, surplus products such as cheese, butter, and honey are not likely to be the foods that schools would prefer to have.

Second, there are problems related to USDA dietary guidelines and minimum nutrient requirements for school lunches. These requirements, based on the government's recommended daily allowances of various nutrients, are controversial and politically sensitive. A Clinton administration (1993–2000) study found that school lunches exceeded the government's dietary guidelines for saturated fat by more than 50 percent and for sodium by nearly 100 percent; regulations were therefore changed so that school meals now must comply with the dietary guidelines.[8] For example, the USDA mandates more fruits and vegetables on school menus. Such efforts are controversial and politically sensitive because any increase in fruits and vegetables at the expense of beef and other meats is harmful to the meat industry, particularly to producers of red meat.

Third, the federal subsidy in school lunch programs is an important public-policy issue that has received little public attention. As indicated earlier, *all* school lunches are subsidized to some extent. The school lunch subsidy became a major issue in the early 1980s as the Reagan administration attempted to reduce costs. That attempt to reduce school lunch subsidies failed. However, the subsidizing of school lunches, particularly for children from upper- and middle-income families, remains an important public-policy issue. Why should the public at large, including low-income taxpayers, be taxed to provide school lunches at subsidized prices for those who can afford to pay?

OTHER FOOD ASSISTANCE PROGRAMS

The 1964 permanent food stamp legislation led to a tremendous expansion of subsidized food programs, not only in food stamp and school lunch programs, but also in food programs targeted toward nutrition for children and the elderly. Total food assistance increased from $1 billion in 1969 to approximately $39 billion in 2002.[9] According to the 1997 mission statement of the USDA's Food and Consumer Service, one out of six people in the United States receives domestic food assistance. However, no precise estimate of the number of people participating can be made, for two reasons: participation data are not collected for several of the programs, and the same person may receive assistance from several programs.[10]

Five food assistance programs were targeted toward children in 2002.[11] In addition to school breakfast and lunch programs, there is a summer food service for low-income children during school vacations, a special milk program for children where there are no federally supported meal programs, and a nutrition program for homeless children. A nutrition program for the elderly provides cash and commodities to states for meals for senior citizens. The food is served in senior citizen centers or delivered by Meals on Wheels.

The food program for the elderly has no income eligibility limits. Other programs are targeted to people in low-income areas, even though they have no income requirement. Moreover, as indicated earlier, upper-income children that participate in the school breakfast and lunch programs receive subsidized meals. The same is true for the Child and Adult Care Food Program. Providing food assistance to individuals in middle- and upper-income families, whatever the form, poses the same public-policy question raised earlier in connection with the operation of the National School Lunch Program.

FOOD STAMP REFORM

Reform of the food stamp program became a political issue during the Reagan administration of the early 1980s. Food stamp abuse has a long history. The USDA estimated that 25 percent of the $260 million in food stamp coupons distributed during the period from 1939 to 1943 were misused.[12] Although the extent of fraud and abuse has been reduced, misuse of food stamps continues to be a major problem. Indeed, the General Accounting Office found that overpayments of food stamp benefits totaled almost $2 billion in fiscal 1993.[13] Most of the problem was due to inaccurate information provided by food stamp recipients to those administering the program.

The USDA has now implemented "electronic benefit transfer" (EBT) to reduce fraud and abuse in the food stamp program. EBT allows a food stamp recipient to authorize the transfer of their government benefits from a federal account to a retailer to pay for products received. A plastic card is issued, and a personal identification number (PIN) is assigned to give access to the account. No money and no food coupons change hands when the consumer makes a purchase in this way.

The General Accounting Office found that EBT can potentially reduce misuse of food stamps—in particular counterfeiting and mail theft. It is doubtful, however, that EBT will have a large impact on fraud and abuse that occur when recipients apply for food stamp coupons and states make eligibility decisions.[14]

Indeed, there is an inherent bias toward overpayment in the food stamp program because of perverse incentives on the part of both recipients and those administering the program. People applying for food stamps have an incentive to understate their family income, a key factor in determining a family's food stamp allotment. More eligible recipients mean more political pressure to increase the agency's budget. And a larger budget, as explained in earlier chapters, is advantageous to those administering the program because it means more jobs and perks.

Cashing Out Food Stamps

Proposals have been made to "cash out" all programs of special assistance for a single cash payment.[15] Interest in cashing out food stamps ebbs and flows over time. What would be the effects if this were done? Cash is more fungible than food stamps and easier to transfer to other uses. Therefore, one might expect food spending to increase less in a cash assistance program. Indeed, the empirical evidence shows that the tendency is to spend only 5 to 15 cents of each additional dollar on food in a cash system—instead of the 20 to 45 cents of each dollar on food when people receive the food subsidy in the form of food stamps.[16] In short, a cash transfer system would decrease consumption of food when compared with direct food aid through food stamps.

What would be the effect on overall food expenditures of cashing out food stamps? As shown earlier, the increase in overall food expenditures from food stamps is small—less than 2 percent. Therefore, the increase in food expenditures with food stamps cashed out would be even less. Even though the negative effect of cashing out on total food consumption would be modest, it is not surprising that farmers are opposed to cashing out food stamps.

Cashing out conceivably may reduce budget costs if it were to reduce fraud and administrative costs. However, cashing out also might *increase* budget costs if it caused more people to elect to participate in the program. USDA figures show that as of 1998, only approximately 65 percent of eligible persons actually participated in the food stamp program.[17]

There has been a great deal of discussion about the relative merits of food stamps versus cash income transfers from a public-policy standpoint. It is sometimes argued that unrestricted income transfers are preferable to in-kind transfers, which in the case of food stamps are intended to encourage people to eat more food. The individual recipient, from his or her own standpoint, is necessarily at least as well off with cash as with an equivalent dollar value of food stamps because the range of choice is expanded with an unrestricted income transfer. That is, the consumer receiving cash can purchase, if he so desires, the same amount of food as with the food stamp, but the unrestricted increase in income also presents additional options to that individual. Thus, the argument goes, cashing out food stamps would be an improvement according to the Pareto criterion.

Other Policy Considerations

This analysis, although valid from the recipient's viewpoint, is flawed from a public-policy standpoint. Because taxpayers bear the cost of subsidized food programs, their wishes must be taken into account in determining the preferred type of assistance.[18] The taxpayer may not evaluate transfer programs in the same way that the applied welfare economist evaluates them. Taxpayers may prefer to provide food subsidies rather than income because they wish the low-income recipients to spend more income on food. Indeed, a great deal of the controversy about the food stamp program concerns the expenditures by food stamp recipients for nonfood items. Thus, if taxpayers' objective in food assistance programs is to have low-income people consume more food, it is likely that taxpayers will not evaluate the relative merits of food subsidies and unrestricted income transfers in the same way as welfare recipients.

Food assistance programs have been part of major farm legislation since the early 1970s, providing a reason for urban members of Congress to vote for farm commodity programs and for rural members of Congress to vote for welfare programs. If food stamps were cashed out, it would as a general income transfer program be administratively more appropriate in a federal department other than the USDA. The removal of food assistance programs from the USDA has farm policy implications because opponents of cashing out fear that it would weaken political support for these payments. Opponents of cashing out consider the restriction that food stamps must be spent on food to be the cornerstone of political support for the program.[19] The political support for food stamp programs has come from several sources, including food retailers, commodity groups, farm groups, and those more comfortable with providing food rather than cash support.[20] These groups also have opposed cashing out because, as shown earlier, it would reduce total food expenditures. Farm groups may have another reason to oppose cashing out of food stamps. Farm legislators have obtained support for traditional farm programs by trading votes with urban legislators interested in food and nutrition programs currently figured in the USDA budget. Without these programs, the USDA would be reduced to approximately one-third of its current size.[21]

NUTRITION AND HEALTH POLICIES

Nutrition information and education programs are nearly as old as the USDA. The center of responsibility for these programs is the Agricultural Extension Service. Prior to 1970, the main message of the nutrition programs was to eat a variety of food from the basic food groups. The programs posed no serious threat to anyone's economic interests because they were not intended to restrict food consumption.[22] The situation changed after the McGovern Senate Select Committee on Nutrition and Human Needs published a set of dietary goals in the mid-1970s. These goals were designed to restrict the intake of fat, processed sugars, cholesterol, and salt. Immediate adverse reaction to these goals came from affected livestock producers, dairy farmers, sugar producers, and other agribusiness interests. The reason is obvious. Widespread adoption of the dietary goals in the United States would have significantly decreased the demand for red meats, eggs, cheese, sugar, and fats and oils.[23] Criticism by farm groups, however, did not stop the momentum for change in nutrition policy.

Congress authorized the USDA to be the lead agency in nutrition policy in the 1977 farm bill. In 1980, the USDA and the Department of Health, Education, and Welfare (HEW—now the Department of Health and Human Services [HHS]) issued dietary guidelines related to the use of fats and cholesterol, starch and fiber, sugar, sodium, and alcohol.[24] The guidelines were not as specific as dietary goals. Nevertheless, farmers reacted negatively—both to the guidelines and to educational programs by extension nutrition specialists based on the guidelines.

During this period in the Carter administration (1977–80), there was a proposal to institute "nutrition planning." In this proposed approach, farm price-support programs would have been used to further nutrition goals. "Nutrition planning" was visualized as a clear-cut technical process. In this process, the first step would be to determine what people's nutritional needs are. After these data were obtained, the levels and types of production necessary to meet those needs would be determined. The final step in nutrition planning, as visualized by Secretary of Agriculture Bob Bergland, was to create a farm policy to meet the nutrition and trade needs.

Nutrition planning is subject to all of the problems inherent in central planning in general.[25] Consumers can meet their dietary requirements in many different ways, and their choices are influenced by tastes, preferences, and price as well as by nutritional data. So long as consumers are free to make consumption decisions and politicians respond to short-run political concerns, nutrition planning of the type visualized is likely to have little impact on domestic farm programs. No serious attempt was ever made to implement "nutrition planning" during the Carter administration. Moreover, it is not surprising that extension educational programs designed with the purpose of reducing the intake of sugar, milk, beef, and other farm products were challenged by farm groups, especially by cattle and dairy farmers.

In the 1980s, the dietary goals and guidelines became the basis for the food pyramid. The food pyramid presumably reflects a consensus of dietary authorities on the importance of different food groups in the diet.[26] Government development and dissemination of dietary goals and guidelines reflected in the food pyramid are consistent with the "market-failure" view of nutrition information. This view maintains both that consumers do not have the necessary information to make correct choices regarding their diets and that government is capable of making the appropriate information available. Although some changes in dietary patterns have occurred, the results fall far short of the recommended goals.[27]

Even if individual consumers wish to follow healthy dietary practices, they face formidable obstacles in obtaining the information necessary to do so. The costs of obtaining information on amounts of fat, cholesterol, sodium, fiber, and so on are likely to be prohibitively high to the individual. Moreover, the free-rider incentive can stymie action by a subset of consumers who are willing to pay for additional information. It is difficult and costly for food manufacturers to provide information to those consumers willing to pay without providing it also to those who have not paid. Therefore, it might be argued that government should force food manufacturers to provide nutrition information to all consumers. Indeed, legislation regarding nutrition labeling, implemented in 1994, requires food manufacturers to list nutritional data on the product label.[28]

The government-mandated information enables some consumers to make more informed dietary choices. However, it creates a new class of free riders; it enables those who use the required costly information to benefit at the expense of those who must pay for information they do not use. Therefore, the government action creates a new class of forced riders—those consumers paying higher prices for food who consider the benefit of the additional information to be less than the cost.[29]

Government control of nutritional information illustrates again the importance of "government failure." Government efforts to provide information about diet and disease lagged private manufacturers' actions by at least ten years.[30] Moreover, government actually banned food manufacturers from advertising food fat and cholesterol profiles in the 1960s. Although the ban was lifted in 1973, manufacturers were not allowed to explain the health reasons to be concerned with fat and cholesterol; diet and disease issues were supposedly too complex for advertisers to deal with. What is the policy implication of this example of government regulation of information about diet and disease? It is simply that information and incentive problems are just as formidable in government attempts to improve consumers' dietary knowledge as they are in other areas.

IMPLEMENTATION PROBLEMS

From the beginning, implementation problems have been formidable in food assistance programs. First, there is an incentive to overprovide subsidized food services for the same reasons described in the earlier discussion of the collective decision-making process (chapter 3). Hence, the growth of food assistance programs irrespective of increases in consumer incomes during the past generation is predictable from public-choice theory. Furthermore, efforts by members of Congress, the USDA, and other government departments to increase the number of food stamp recipients are consistent with the theory of bureaucracy.[31] Although early food assistance programs were motivated largely by surplus problems incurred through government price-support operations, the current programs have taken on a life of their own. The major constituency of food assistance programs is no longer commercial agriculture, but rather the groups advocating and benefiting generally from "poverty" programs. These groups include not only the recipients of food assistance, but also the government officials and employees who provide the funding and administration of the programs at local, state, and federal levels.

Incentive problems also arise in food assistance programs where recipients face means tests. If some specified level of income is required to be eligible for food stamps, school lunches, or other food assistance, a family slightly above that income level has an incentive to change its behavior in order to qualify. Consider the example of the person choosing whether to search for a better job. Food stamps generally are available to people even if they have quit their jobs. Thus, the availability of food stamps is likely to increase unemployment by reducing the cost of being unemployed.

In addition to incentive problems, there are also formidable information problems in monitoring the food stamp, school lunch, and any other food assistance programs where there is a means test. Not only is there an incentive to underreport income; there is also a severe information problem in discovering whether such underreporting has occurred. In the National School Lunch Program, for example, the determination of who is eligible for free or reduced-price school lunches is based on family income, as stated on the application form. The income levels necessary to qualify for free or reduced-price lunches are often publicized in local newspapers so parents will know whether or not their children qualify. The perceived cost of underreporting income is likely to be low because it would be quite difficult for the school system to verify the income reported on the application form. Thus, inherent incentive and information problems have plagued implementation of food assistance programs since the food stamp program was first begun.

AGRICULTURAL PRICE SUPPORTS AND FOOD ASSISTANCE

A fundamental inconsistency exists between government programs that raise product prices and food assistance programs. Government programs raise prices of milk, fresh fruit, sugar, peanuts, and other products at the same time low-income consumers are deemed to have too little money to afford an adequate amount of food. Domestic consumers are legally prevented from purchasing lower-priced dairy products, for example, by import restrictions that are typically necessary in price-support programs, which hold domestic prices above world prices. For example, in addition to administering the dairy program, which raises fluid milk prices, the USDA has prevented reconstituted milk from being sold for less than the price of whole fluid milk. In marketing orders for fruits, lower-income consumers are harmed most by quality-control provisions that restrict sales of lower grades and smaller sizes of commodities. It is ironic that billions of dollars are being spent on government programs to raise prices of milk and other commodities, while at the same time billions of dollars are also being spent on programs to lower the price of food to low-income consumers.

SUMMARY

Subsidized food-distribution programs were initiated during the 1930s to facilitate the operation of price-support programs. Food stamp, school lunch, and other subsidized food programs have increased dramatically since the late 1960s, when expenditures increased rapidly for welfare programs generally. Outlays for the food stamp and other USDA subsidized food programs are increased in the 2002 farm bill—and were estimated to be approximately $41 billion in 2003.[32]

Farmers initially provided the major support for food assistance programs because these programs provided a politically acceptable way to dispose of costly surpluses. The support for subsidized food programs is no longer restricted solely to beneficiaries of price-support programs. Indeed, the major support for food assistance programs now comes from urban interests and the "poverty lobby" rather than from commercial agriculture. In recent years, legislators from farm districts interested in maintaining farm price supports have formed alliances with legislators from urban districts who support food assistance programs.

Implementation problems have plagued subsidized food programs from the beginning of the food stamp program. Formidable information and incentive problems are inherent in food stamp, school lunch, and other programs that involve means tests. There is an information problem in determining whether an individual qualifies. There is also an economic incentive for individuals to adjust their behavior to qualify for food assistance programs. Thus, it is not surprising that chronic complaints are made about abuses in food assistance programs with income eligibility limits, especially food stamps.

Subsidized food programs pose the same problem as all other income-redistribution programs. There is no objective procedure for determining how large the expenditures on these programs *should* be. The growth of food assistance programs is consistent with the theory of public choice. The bureaucracy involved in administering the programs has an incentive to expand the scope of operations. Moreover, it is not difficult for an administrator—especially in the case of food aid to low-income people—to rationalize that what is in one's own interest is also in the public interest.

14 | International Trade and Trade Restrictions

For more than two decades after World War II, international trade of the United States was viewed primarily as a matter of rapidly expanding export markets and the acquisition of foreign assets by U.S. investors.[1] Over a relatively short time, the U.S. economy experienced a transition to a state of considerable international interdependence with respect to the provision of goods, services, and capital. In nominal terms, a sevenfold increase in international activity, including U.S. imports and exports and net capital transactions, occurred during the period from 1970 to 1985. The increase in international activity has been less dramatic since then, but has nevertheless risen more than two and one-half times.[2] Some of the reduction in the rate of increase is due to a reduction in the rate of inflation.

International trade is highly important to U.S. agriculture because exports represent approximately one-fourth of the total revenue from sales of U.S. farm products. Exports are particularly important for some U.S. farm commodities. For example, approximately 40–50 percent of the wheat, cotton, rice, and soybeans; 33 percent of the tobacco; and 25 percent of the corn produced in the United States typically are exported.[3]

Both exports and imports have increased over time. In 1969, the values of agricultural exports and imports totaled $5.7 billion and $4.9 billion, respectively. By 2002, the nominal value of imports had increased to $41.0 billion, and the value of exports had increased to $53.3 billion—a substantial real increase in both.[4] Agricultural exports reached all time highs in 1981 but decreased significantly during the mid-1980s. The decrease has been attributed to a host of factors—including global recession, Third World debt, a strong U.S. dollar, domestic farm programs, and rising farm productivity in other countries.[5]

By the mid-1990s, the export market for farm products recovered most of the ground lost at that time, but foreign sales weakened again in the late 1990s. Although much has been written about the adverse effect of the strong dollar on farm exports, Batten and Belongia found there to be only a weak link between exchange rates and exports. They determined the dominant factor to be real income in importing nations.[6]

From the mid-1970s until 1985, the value of agricultural imports was less than half the value of agricultural exports. In 1985, agricultural imports were approximately two-thirds as large as exports. Indeed, for several months in mid-1986, agricultural imports exceeded agricultural exports. Agricultural imports in the 1990s again were approximately two-thirds as large as exports, but that proportion decreased near the end of the decade. Economic turmoil in Japan and other Asian countries in the 1990s loomed large as an explanation for the weakened export market for farm products. An additional problem for exports of U.S. farm products also surfaced at that time: concern by consumer groups in Japan and western Europe about the safety in the production and use of biologically engineered crops, such as "Roundup Ready" soybeans.

There are two types of agricultural imports: (1) animal and vegetable products similar to those produced in the United States, and (2) products not produced here, such as coffee, bananas, and tea. Demand for the second group is less elastic because no close substitutes are domestically produced. Consequently, a given reduction in the supply of imports of coffee, bananas, or tea will have a greater effect on consumer prices than a comparable reduction in imports of animal and vegetable products.

Agricultural trade is a key factor in agricultural policy, and there appears to be a strong inverse relationship between the volume of exports of U.S. farm products and domestic price-support expenditures. Exports of agricultural products increased in value from $6.7 billion in 1970 to $21.6 billion in 1975.[7] During the same period, government expenditures on price-support programs decreased from $5.1 billion to $1.9 billion.[8] More recently, exports of agricultural products decreased from $40.5 billion in 1980 to $29 billion in 1985. As exports were declining, the cost of government price-support programs increased from $4 billion to $17 billion. Exports trended up sharply after 1985, totaling $54.7 billion in 1995. At the same time, income support to agriculture decreased from $17 billion to $7.3 billion. And in 1998, as U.S. farm exports decreased, largely because of reduced demand in Asia and strong competition from large supplies in Argentina and China, Congress enacted legislation providing a $6 billion emergency aid package. This package was followed by emergency aid of approximately $8.0 billion each year from 1999 to 2001 as farm exports remained below the 1998 level.[9] As the demand for exports of farm products decreases, political pressures intensify, and the cost of stabilizing domestic farm incomes increases. Thus, trade policy is highly important to U.S. agriculture. The multilateral trade agreements reached in the mid-1990s (discussed later) and the passage of the FAIR Act in 1996 increased the influence of comparative advantage on exports of U.S. farm products. Export subsidies, or expanded direct payments (including emergency aid) to farmers following the 1996 and 2002 farm bills, however, work against comparative advantage in the production and marketing of U.S. farm products.

The importance of international trade to U.S. agriculture was dramatically demonstrated during the Great Depression. The Smoot-Hawley Tariff Act of 1930 raised tariffs to the highest levels in the nation's history—52.8 percent on an ad valorem basis. Other countries followed suit, and protectionism was rampant. It was no coincidence that U.S. farm exports fell by two-thirds from 1929 to 1933. A dramatic increase in the value of agricultural exports occurred during the 1970s, from $6.7 billion in 1970 to $32 billion in 1979. However, it was not until the late 1970s that U.S. farm exports recovered the share of total farm marketings that they were sixty years earlier (approximately 25 percent).[10] Because U.S. agriculture is heavily dependent on exporting its products, U.S. farmers have a strong stake in maintaining an open economy. This chapter considers the theoretical case for international trade, discusses specific types of trade barriers for agricultural products and the effects of multilateral trade treaties, and stresses the fundamental contradiction between a policy of liberal international trade and protectionist domestic farm programs.[11]

COMPARATIVE ADVANTAGE

Comparative advantage provides a basis for trade between individuals in different countries (as well as between individuals in the same country). To pursue comparative advantage means to sacrifice that which is less valuable for the sake of acquiring something more valuable.[12] Comparative advantage is determined by opportunity cost. The opportunity cost to Farmer Jones of using an acre of land for corn production, for example, is the value of the land in the best alternative use. Corn land can also be used to produce soybeans. If U.S. farmers become more productive in growing soybeans, or if the price of soybeans increases, the opportunity cost of land used to produce corn increases. Thus, the more adept U.S. farmers become in producing soybeans (or any other product), the higher the cost of producing other products. No nation's producers can be most efficient or have a comparative advantage in the production of every good and service produced.

Consider the example in table 14.1, where two countries, the United States and Japan, are assumed to be able to produce two goods of equal quality. Which country has a comparative advantage in producing textiles? In answering this question, the focus should be on opportunity cost—the real cost of producing anything is the value of what is given up in order to produce it. What is the opportunity cost of one unit of textiles? Assuming that competition has resulted in price levels in both countries that reflect the opportunity costs of the two goods, the cost of one unit of textiles in the United States is two-thirds units of grain. That is, producing and selling a unit of textile means that two-thirds of a unit of grain is sacrificed. In Japan, however, the cost of a unit of textiles is only one-half units of grain. Therefore, Japan (in this example) has a comparative advantage in the production of textiles. This implies that the United States has a comparative advantage in the production of grain because it must sacrifice only one and one-half units of textiles in producing a unit of grain, whereas the Japanese must sacrifice two units. The conclusion is that the total output of goods produced will be greater through specialization and that each country can gain from trade by specializing in the production of goods in which it has a comparative advantage.

TABLE 14.1 Comparative Advantage.

	United States	Japan
	(Prices per unit of good)	
Grain	$30	¥9,000
Textiles	$20	¥4,500

If trade is freely permitted, goods will tend to flow across borders until the price in any given country differs from the price in other countries only by the amount of transportation costs. Consider the simplified two-country trading situation depicted in figure 14.1. In the absence of international trade, product price is considerably higher in the United Kingdom P_{UK}^0 than in the United States P_{US}^0. If trade is allowed, then the product will be exported from the United States. The quantity of exports supplied for any given price greater than the initial (no trade) price in the United States is simply the difference between the U.S. quantity supplied and the U.S. quantity demanded. Similarly, the product will be imported into the United Kingdom, and the quantity of U.S. exports demanded at any given price (below the initial no-trade price) is the difference between the U.K. quantity demanded and U.K. quantity supplied. The market-clearing price with trade is the price at which the quantity of exports supplied equals the quantity of exports demanded—P_W in figure 14.1.

At P_W, the quantity exported from the United States ($Q_2 - Q_1$) is equal to the imports by the United Kingdom ($Q_4 - Q_3$). This quantity is labeled Q_x^0 in the middle panel of figure 14.1. Trade causes the price to increase in the exporting country and to decrease in the importing country. The amount by which price changes in each country as a result of trade is determined by the elasticities of supply and demand. The more inelastic supply or demand is, ceteris paribus, the greater the change in price for a given amount of trade.

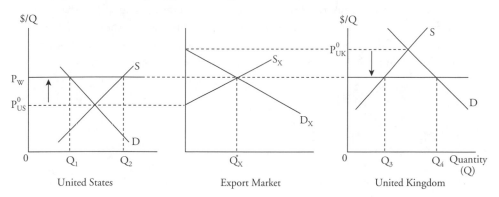

FIGURE 14.1 Effects of trade on exporting and importing countries.

International trade is beneficial to both the buyers and the sellers involved; otherwise, it would not occur. Moreover, restrictions on competition or barriers to trade inevitably are harmful to parties engaging in trade. It is not the case, however, that trade makes everyone better off. In the situation depicted in figure 14.1, for example, both U.S. consumers (who pay a higher price with trade) and U.K. producers (who receive a lower price with trade) are worse off. The fact that there are losers from trade explains the chronic efforts by producer groups in all countries to erect barriers to trade. Trade barriers, as shown in the next section, may take a number of different forms.

BARRIERS TO TRADE

Tariffs

Import barriers are the most common form of protectionism and tariffs are a common type of import barrier. Consider the effect of a tariff on a domestically produced and consumed good in an importing country (figure 14.2). At the world price, P_W, the amount imported is equal to $Q_D^0 - Q_S^0$ when there is free trade. If a per unit tariff of T is imposed, the price of imports increases to $P_W + T$, domestic consumption decreases and domestic production increases as the tariff provides a protective umbrella over domestic producers, at least in the short run. In the situation depicted, domestic production increases from Q_S^0 to Q_S^T and domestic consumption decreases from Q_D^0 to Q_D^T. The effect of the tariff on the quantity of imports is the sum of these two effects. Thus, after the tariff is imposed, the amount imported is $Q_D^T - Q_S^T$. This example shows why U.S. producers of dairy products, tobacco, steel, textile products, autos, and other products frequently lobby for tariffs and other restrictions on imports.

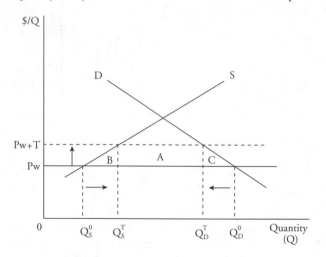

FIGURE 14.2 Effect of a tariff on U.S. imports.

The easier it is to make substitutions in consumption and production, the larger the effect of a tariff. If users of wheat can readily substitute other products when the price of wheat increases, an increase in the price of wheat will bring about a relatively large decrease in consumption. In general, the more elastic are demand and supply, the greater is the effect of a tariff on domestic production and consumption. This conclusion can be generalized even further. If a market is distorted through tariffs, taxes, price controls, and so on, the damage resulting from resource misallocation is less the more inelastic are demand and supply. That is, if something is done to misallocate resources, the effect will be less the more resistant the economy is to the movement of resources.

As direct effects of the tariff, domestic consumers pay higher prices, and domestic producers receive higher prices. Furthermore, the government collects tariff receipts equal to the quantity imported times the tariff—area A in figure 14.2. Indirect effects of the tariff include distortions in resource use. Producers are induced to increase output from Q_S^0 to Q_S^T with resources that (in the absence of the tariff) have higher value in other uses by the amount of area B in figure 14.2. Similarly, consumers reduce consumption from Q_D^0 to Q_D^T thereby foregoing consumption of units for which (again, in the absence of the tariff) marginal value exceeds opportunity cost by the amount of area C in figure 14.2.[13]

Nontariff Barriers

The most inflexible nontariff barrier is the *import quota*, which sets an absolute limit on the quantity of the product that may be imported. Import quotas typically are imposed at the urging of domestic producer groups. In the figure 14.2 example, a quota smaller than $Q_D^T - Q_S^T$ would increase the price in the importing country above the level $P_W + T$. Other import barriers include complex packing, content and labeling requirements, sanitary regulations, and foreign-exchange restrictions.[14]

"Voluntary" import controls represent another means of reducing imports. In this approach, used by the U.S. government in the 1980s, agreements are worked out with foreign governments to limit the number of automobiles, quantity of textile products, quantity of beef, and so on shipped to the United States. These restrictions on imports are "voluntary" in name only, however, because other countries are typically induced to restrict imports under the threat of quotas or other legislated import controls. The economic effects of such "voluntary" controls are similar to legislated restrictions. In each case, domestic producers receive short-run benefits at the expense of domestic consumers.

Import barriers are harmful to domestic consumers regardless of the means by which imports are restricted. What is sometimes overlooked, however, is that import controls also are harmful to domestic producers of other products. Import restrictions on Japanese autos, Hong Kong textiles, or German steel indirectly affect the exports of U.S. agricultural products. Import restrictions inevitably mean that these exports are reduced because the number of dollars available to foreign buyers to purchase U.S. soybeans, wheat, and other products hinges on the quantity of autos, televisions, steel, and other products imported by the United States.

Some people, in particular agricultural interests, view the United States as a free-trade island in a sea of protectionism. The actual situation is far different, however. U.S. agricultural trade, as shown later, has long been distorted by a host of import and export policies that give preferential treatment to domestic producers. Moreover, although considerably lower than in the European Union, the value of U.S. government transfers to agriculture from domestic consumers and taxpayers resulting from agricultural policies as recently as 2000 was much higher than in Australia and New Zealand.[15]

EXPORT SUBSIDIES AND RESTRICTIONS

The price-support and production-control programs instituted during the 1930s, in which domestic prices were held above world price levels, resulted in the chronic accumulation of surplus stocks. To reduce these stocks, there has been pressure over the years to subsidize exports. The effect of an export subsidy is shown in figure 14.3. In the absence of market intervention, the product price is P_W, and the quantity exported is $Q_S^0 - Q_D^0$. The implementation of an export subsidy gives domestic producers an artificial advantage in the export market. From the perspective of domestic producers, a subsidy of $\$S$ per unit of product exported essentially increases the demand for their product in the export market from P_W to $P_W + S$, where the amount of the per unit subsidy is paid by the domestic government. The increased price of exports causes an increase in the domestic amount produced. Domestic consumers face the higher price of $P_W + S$ because consumers must match the price that suppliers receive in the export market in order to purchase the product from domestic suppliers. Thus, domestic consumption falls, domestic production increases, and the level of exports increases to $Q_S^1 - Q_D^1$ (figure 14.3).[16]

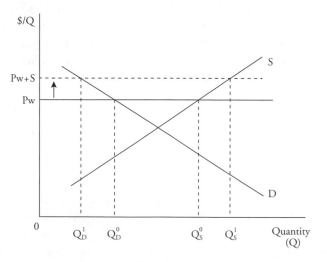

FIGURE 14.3 Effect of an export subsidy.

The seeds of export subsidies were sown in the 1920s in the proposed McNary-Haugen bills, which would have raised domestic prices by discriminating between domestic and foreign markets and by "dumping" exports. "Dumping" occurs when a country sells a commodity below the cost of production. There is a great deal of ambiguity in the concept of dumping. This ambiguity contributes to the huge disconnect in the United States between the rhetoric of antidumping supporters and the reality of antidumping practice. None of the calculation methods used by the U.S. Department of Commerce measure whether sales are truly below cost.[17] This should not be surprising because the subjective nature of opportunity cost poses the same problems in determining cost of production in this case as in the examples discussed in chapter 8.

Exports may also be restricted through the use of export taxes or quotas. The effect of an export tax, a fixed payment to government per unit of product exported, is to reduce the price received by exporters, effectively reducing the price received by domestic producers for goods entering the world market. The export tax causes domestic producers to produce less. It also causes domestic consumers to purchase more because the price they must pay to match the price domestic producers receive in the export market has fallen. An export quota places a specific limit on the quantity of a product that can be exported. An embargo makes it illegal to export any of the product. Export quotas are harmful to producers and are seldom used in the United States—perhaps because producers have a great deal of clout in the political arena. As we have seen, most government programs in agriculture benefit farmers—at least in the short run.

Section 32

Export subsidies began with an amendment to the 1933 AAA, Section 32, which authorized the use of 30 percent of import tariff revenues to subsidize agricultural exports and domestic consumption of "surplus" commodities.[18] Although Section 32 funds are no longer used to pay for export subsidies, they were generated by a continuing appropriation of 30 percent of the import duties collected on all commodities imported into the United States, both agricultural and nonagricultural. Subsidized shipments of exports remained small until federally financed shipments for famine relief rose sharply during and immediately after World War II. Section 32 funds could be used for purposes other than subsidizing agricultural exports. In fact, most of the Section 32 funds were spent on the purchase and domestic donation of agricultural commodities (mainly for the school lunch program), with export programs accounting for less than 10 percent of Section 32 expenditures between 1936 and 1976.[19]

Credit Programs Including Public Law 480

Public Law 480 (PL 480), which was a component of the Agricultural Trade Development and Assistance Act of 1954 (the 1954 farm bill), is commonly called the Food for Peace program. PL 480 was designed to reduce the CCC stocks acquired through price-support programs. Under Title I of this legislation, long-term sales to foreign buyers are made with repayment periods of up to forty years at low interest rates. Under Title II, food is donated to people in foreign countries in response to malnutrition, famine, and so on. The food is donated by the U.S. government and is distributed mainly through private voluntary organizations, cooperatives, and international organizations.

The PL 480 program has led export subsidies to become strongly embedded in U.S. farm policy. During the 1950s and 1960s, concessionary sales under government programs, including PL 480, often accounted for as much as one-third of export sales.[20] The gross taxpayer cost of financing such exports from 1955 to 1979 was approximately $40 billion.[21] PL 480 expenditures during the 1980s and 1990s, on average, typically have been somewhat less in real terms—running from $1 billion to $2 billion per year. In recent years, the United States has used targeted export subsidies as opposed to the general subsidies used in the 1950s and 1960s.[22]

PL 480 and other export subsidy programs historically have been strongly linked to low farm prices and the disposal of surplus farm products. Increases in foreign demand or decreases in domestic supply act to increase farm prices and to reduce surpluses under price supports. Thus, PL 480 sales and donations tend to decline when U.S. farm commodity prices increase.

Another program with substantial impacts on U.S. exports of farm products has been the Export Credit Guarantee Program. This legislation guarantees payment to U.S. lenders should a foreign buyer fail to repay any loan used to purchase U.S. agricultural commodities. From 1982 to 1986, the USDA provided approximately $22 billion in export credit guarantees.[23] This program increases exports to buyers where credit is necessary to make sales, but where financing may not be available without CCC guarantees that payments will be made. The USDA currently provides approximately $4 billion annually in export credit guarantees. Under the 1996 and 2002 farm bills, at least $1 billion of direct credit and credit guarantees must be targeted annually to "emerging markets" that are taking steps toward market-oriented economies.

Current laws require that certain proportions of U.S. exports be carried in U.S. flag ships when taxpayer money is used to fund the exports, as in PL 480 shipments. Shipment in U.S. flag ships may also be specified at other times, as in the Soviet grain agreement. Shipping in U.S. flag ships is generally more costly, which increases the cost of U.S. commodities to foreign buyers.

There has been a great deal of controversy about the impact in the recipient countries of PL 480 and other programs that encourage U.S. exports. The increase in supply available to recipient countries reduces prices received by local farmers, which leads to decreases in output and makes local farmers worse off. Thus, in the long run, U.S. export subsidies may reduce availability of domestically grown food in the recipient countries and aggravate rather than alleviate hunger problems.

Other Agricultural Export Subsidies

Another program that reduces export prices, the Export Enhancement Program (EEP), was initiated in 1985. Under the EEP, exporters are awarded bonus payments that enable them to be price competitive and thereby to make sales in targeted overseas markets where competitor countries are making subsidized sales.

An export-promotion program, the Market Access Program, formerly known as the Market Promotion Program, was authorized under the 1996 farm bill and has continued (and been expanded) under the 2002 bill. This program also subsidizes exports of U.S. commodities. Under the program, nonprofit trade organizations, state and regional trade groups, and private companies are reimbursed for expenses in carrying out approved promotional activities. Finally, the Dairy Export Incentive Program subsidizes exports of U.S. dairy products for purposes of "market development."[24]

In addition, in an effort to dispose of government stocks of farm products, the 1985 farm bill instituted marketing loans, which, like export subsidies, have the effect of increasing exports. Marketing loans permit prices of commodities placed under loan to fall below loan rates by enabling farmers to buy back their government-purchased crops at prices below those paid to them by the CCC. The 1996 and 2002 farm bills retained marketing loans for feed grains, wheat, rice, upland cotton, and oilseeds. LDPs, which are closely related to marketing loans (see chapter 10), averaged approximately $5.5 billion during the years 1999–2002.[25]

GATT, THE WORLD TRADE ORGANIZATION, AND AGRICULTURAL TRADE POLICY

The General Agreement on Tariffs and Trade (GATT) was a multilateral treaty among governments dating from 1947. The GATT's purpose was to liberalize and expand trade through negotiated reductions in trade barriers.[26] A number of GATT negotiating conferences or "rounds" were held, and several proved important to U.S. agriculture. The final round of GATT conferences was initiated in 1987 and was completed in 1994 with the signing of the Uruguay Round agreement.

The Uruguay Round created the World Trade Organization (WTO) among some 130 world governments to replace GATT as an institutional framework for overseeing trade negotiations to reduce trade barriers and adjudicate trade disputes.[27] Moreover, member countries agreed to resume negotiations in the agricultural reform process, beginning in 1999.

Until the Uruguay Round, agriculture had received special treatment under GATT trade rules through various loopholes, exceptions, and exemptions from most of the disciplines that applied to manufactured goods. As a result, GATT allowed countries to use export subsidies and various nontariff barriers that impeded agricultural trade. Under the Uruguay Round agreement, however, countries agreed to reduce protectionism by reducing import restrictions, domestic support of agricultural prices and farm income, and export subsidies. In addition, rules supposedly now prevent countries from using "arbitrary and unjustified" health and environmental regulations as disguised trade barriers.[28] The actions taken because of the Uruguay Round have likely had some effect on trade flows, although precise empirical measurement of these impacts is not possible. Americans are both better off materially because of the WTO and a bit freer from the power of government to decide what they produce and consume.[29] However, significant reductions in most agricultural tariffs, if they are ever made, remain for future rounds of WTO negotiations. A new series of WTO trade negotiations, the Doha Round, was initiated at Doha, Qatar, in September 2001.[30] Meetings followed in Cancun in 2003 and in Geneva in 2004. To date, no agreement has been reached and agricultural subsidies present one of the most contentious issues in the negotiations.[31]

REDUCTIONS IN AGRICULTURAL TRADE BARRIERS

The principal agreements achieved under the Uruguay Round include:[32]

- Reducing the value of export subsidies by 36 percent and the quantity of products subsidized by 21 percent.
- Reducing the level of domestic subsidies to agriculture by approximately 20 percent.

- Converting quotas to tariffs and tariff rate quotas and then phasing them out over a specified number of years.
- Providing minimum levels of market access for products previously barred from entering specific countries, such as rice into Japan, and then gradually increasing access levels.
- Establishing rules to make sanitary and phytosanitary regulations more science based.

Nontariff Trade Barriers

Without rigid import controls for price-supported products, consumers will substitute low-priced imports for high-priced domestically produced products. The GATT-WTO agreement banned all nontariff barriers, including import quotas and other quantitative import restrictions. The nontariff barriers were converted to ordinary tariffs, and all preexisting and new tariffs were subject to a schedule of reductions.[33] Members agreed to reduce all tariffs, including newly created tariffs, by an average of 36 percent by 2000—but no less than 15 percent for any tariff. To avoid any negative impact on trade, rules were established to maintain historical trade levels, and minimum import opportunities were provided where trade had been minimal.

The guidelines for tariff cuts provided for considerable flexibility that enables member countries to achieve the 36 percent *average* reduction with minimal cuts in tariffs on products more sensitive to competition.[34] Moreover, a country can minimize the effect of the tariff reduction by making large cuts in tariffs on commodities that do not compete with domestic products.

Moreover, imports can be restricted by means other than tariffs. The Agricultural Marketing Agreement Act, for example, provides that grade, size, quality, or maturity regulations established for fruits, vegetables, or nuts under a marketing order shall apply equally to imported products. This restriction on competition, necessary to the operation of marketing orders, is also an important impediment to trade that prevents consumers from purchasing lower-priced imports.

Technical Restrictions—Sanitary and Phytosanitary Measures

Some import restrictions affecting foreign producers may be similar to those imposed on domestic producers. For instance, it is U.S. policy that imported products must meet the same standards as U.S.-produced products for sanitary and phytosanitary measures to protect health or the environment or both from pests, diseases, and contaminants. The plants in which imported beef is slaughtered, for example, must meet the same standards as those for beef produced in the United States. Foreign plants are inspected periodically, and imported beef is checked for residues of banned chemicals or drugs when it enters the United States.

Sanitary and similar measures restrict imports and may be initiated and supported by producer groups for protectionist purposes. Consequently, whether sanitary and phytosanitary measures prove beneficial or harmful in promoting the public welfare hinges on the purpose and effects of the standards: Do the standards enable markets to work more effectively, or, alternatively, is the primary effect merely to restrict competition?

Sometimes it is not clear whether a health and safety regulation resulted from legitimate health concerns or was erected as a barrier to trade. Are current European and Japanese restrictions on imports and labeling of Roundup Ready soybeans and other genetically engineered commodities, for example, based on legitimate concerns, or are they designed to protect higher-cost European and Japanese producers? Under the Uruguay Round agreement, WTO settlement panels adjudicate such disputes to determine whether a particular country is in compliance when other countries challenge that country's sanitary and phytosanitary policies.[35]

DOMESTIC AGRICULTURAL POLICIES AND INTERNATIONAL TRADE

A fundamental inconsistency exists between domestic price supports and free trade.[36] The Uruguay Round recognized that domestic agricultural programs throughout the world were a major factor in the large-scale distortions in world agricultural markets. Before the Uruguay Round, an exemption from GATT provisions was in effect for agricultural products. The United States insisted on this exemption because of its own widespread use of price supports for dairy, sugar, peanuts, tobacco, and other products that held U.S. prices above world price levels.

Price supports hamper international trade in two ways. In the absence of production controls, price supports encourage production beyond levels that would otherwise occur, often resulting in import controls and a displacement of lower-cost imports. Price supports in the United States and in other countries also lead to surplus production and the use of export subsidies to make the higher-price commodities competitive on world markets.

Price supports, however, are not the only source of worldwide distortions in agricultural markets. Input subsidies, producer payments not accompanied by limitations on production (such as the lump sum payments under the 1996 farm bill), and export subsidies also work against production based on comparative advantage in agriculture.[37] Under the GATT-WTO agreement, countries were required to reduce total agricultural support by 20 percent during the period 1995–2000 (the specified base period is 1986–88).[38]

Under the GATT, governments are allowed to continue subsidizing their agricultural sectors and rural economies through a host of programs presumed to have relatively small effects on production and trade—such as domestic food aid, research, natural-disaster relief, crop insurance, environmental programs, and rural assistance.

Export Subsidies

The European Union employs most of the world's export subsides used to bridge the gap between high domestic prices and lower world-market prices.[39] As described earlier, however, the United States over the years has spent billions of dollars under PL 480 and subsidized credit programs that have effects similar to an export subsidy. Moreover, the United States has maintained a number of other export subsidy programs, such as the EEP and the Market Access Program, in the 1996 and 2002 farm bills. These export subsidy programs have helped to insulate U.S. producers from world-market prices.

Under the agreement reached in the Uruguay Round of tariff negotiations, the value of export subsidies by WTO members during the period from 1995 to 2000 is to be reduced by 36 percent, and the quantity of products subsidized by 21 percent (the base period is 1986–90).[40] Rather than reducing protectionist policies to comply with these provisions, however, some countries appear to be using various measures to circumvent the agreed upon reduction in export subsidies. The European Union, for example, "claims the right to export processed cheese that would otherwise exceed WTO commitment levels by applying export subsidies available for component ingredients—skim milk powder and butterfat—that are well below WTO commitment levels."[41] As indicated earlier, preliminary evidence suggests that the mechanism to adjudicate such disputes under the WTO is working reasonably well.

NORTH AMERICAN FREE TRADE AGREEMENT (NAFTA)

NAFTA is a regional trade agreement. The defining characteristic of the numerous regional trade agreements negotiated recently throughout the world is that they reduce trade barriers among member countries while each member country maintains its own domestic policies and trade policies toward nonmember nations. Under NAFTA, the United States, Canada, and Mexico agreed to lower or eliminate barriers to trade with other member countries over a fifteen-year period.⁴² This trade agreement was formed in 1989 between Canada and the United States and extended to Mexico in 1994.

There is no consensus on the overall effects of NAFTA and similar regional trade agreements. On one hand, NAFTA allows production to shift more among the member countries—the United States, Canada, and Mexico—and the principle of comparative advantage to operate more fully. On the other hand, by lowering barriers on internal trade between the members while retaining barriers to trade with nonmember nations, NAFTA (and other regional trade agreements) may reduce trade with nonmember producers and consumers in the rest of the world. A 1998 study of the effects of NAFTA and other regional trade agreements found that when fully implemented, NAFTA is expected to increase trade in agricultural products.⁴³

Of course, regardless of the ultimate effects of NAFTA, the United States (as well as other countries) stands to gain more from global free trade than from such regional trade agreements. Whether regional trade agreements throughout the world will increase or decrease global trade remains to be seen. Of course, NAFTA has proved controversial among some politicians and producer groups because it has adversely affected certain agricultural producers, other businesses, and employees—as generally happens when business conditions become more competitive, whether in domestic or international trade.

RECAP OF U.S. AGRICULTURAL AND TRADE POLICIES

The United States and other countries have used—and continue to use—trade policies and protectionist domestic agricultural programs to shield agriculture from international competition. Import controls, export subsidies, and other trade barriers in the United States have induced retaliation from other countries and have caused these other nations to be skeptical of the professed U.S. desire to achieve a more open economy. The unwillingness of the United States and other countries to subject their domestic farm programs to the discipline of unregulated international trade resulted in the GATT exemptions for agriculture. These exemptions for agriculture made it possible to hold domestic prices above world-market levels through price supports and other protectionist policies.

The Uruguay Round of trade negotiations resulted in a multilateral agreement to reduce protectionist agricultural policies by WTO member countries. Even under the WTO-scheduled reductions in trade barriers, however, farm products in the United States, the European Union, Canada, Japan, and other countries will remain sheltered from competition. In short, significant opportunity remains to reduce agricultural tariffs, export subsidies, and so on even further.

What are the policy implications for the United States? Agricultural resources would be used most productively and world GDP would be higher if all countries acted together in reducing trade barriers for farm products. There is a great deal of merit in the argument that the United States should reduce trade barriers further, regardless of whether other countries make similar reforms.[44]

U.S. trade policy is based on a faulty premise—that although current protectionist polices are good for the United States, we are willing to abandon our protectionist trade rules if other countries abandon theirs. Eliminating protectionist rules, however, is broadly beneficial to the United States, regardless of whether other nations reciprocate. There are, of course, political problems in doing so because lowering import restrictions is likely to reduce the incomes of U.S. producers of affected products. Moreover, free trade is not merely an economic concept; economic freedom is a human right. Individuals should be able to trade with whomever they wish—in other countries as well as in home markets—unless it poses a substantial threat to national security.[45]

Alternatively, as Nobel economist Milton Friedman suggests, the United States can assume a consistent and principled stance: "We could say to the rest of the world: We believe in freedom and intend to practice it. We cannot force you to be free. But we can offer full cooperation on equal terms to all. Our market is open to you without tariffs or other restrictions. Sell here what you can and wish to. Buy whatever you can and wish to. In that way, freedom and cooperation among individuals can be increased worldwide."[46]

International Trade and the Elasticity of Demand for Farm Products

The U.S. farm price-support programs were originally developed on the assumption that the domestic demands for the affected products were inelastic. World demand for U.S.-produced wheat, tobacco, and other products was thought to be more elastic than domestic demand because of the greater availability of substitutes. Demand for U.S. farm products has become more elastic (or less inelastic) during recent decades, however, as exports of farm products have increased. If the overall demand for a farm product were elastic at the farm level, a program to restrict output would reduce total receipts. Indeed, it may well be that for most of the U.S. commodities exported today, a price support would lead to a reduction rather than an increase in total income to agriculture.[47] Of course, a decrease in total receipts does not necessarily imply a reduction in profit because it costs less to produce less.

U.S. farmers reacted strongly to the export boom of the mid-1970s for farm products. More land was brought back into production, more machinery and equipment were purchased, and prices of farmland were bid up to unprecedented levels. When a global recession occurred in 1981, however, many recent entrants into agriculture and farmers who had expanded rapidly in highly leveraged operations during the 1970s suffered cash-flow problems. The increased role of exports, as suggested earlier, has made demand for farm commodities more elastic and most likely has increased the instability of markets for U.S. agricultural products. International trade creates a host of additional risks that influence foreign demand, including uncertainty of trade policies and changing exchange rates.

SUMMARY

Comparative advantage provides a basis for trade between countries. Trade, despite its generally beneficial nature, does not benefit everyone. Thus, we observe groups attempting to limit trade through tariffs, quotas, and other measures. Exports of farm products were drastically reduced by the protectionist legislation of the 1930s, and it was only in the late 1970s that farm exports recovered the share of farm marketings that prevailed fifty years earlier, approximately 25 percent. After increasing rapidly throughout the 1970s and peaking in 1981, agricultural exports decreased throughout the early 1980s. Exports increased substantially in the late 1980s and mid-1990s, recovering most of the recently lost ground. Foreign sales weakened again in the late 1990s and persisted through 2001 as economic turmoil increased, most notably in Russia and Asia.

As the proportion of farm products exported has increased over time, the demand for many farm products has become more elastic. Thus, with the increased importance of trade, protectionist farm programs may have become counterproductive to farmers, even in the short run. This may help to explain the change in U.S. farm policy away from domestic price supports to lump sum payments to farmers during the last two decades of the twentieth century.

Price-support programs create surpluses, which result in pressures to subsidize exports of farm products. During the past thirty years, concessionary sales under PL 480 and other government programs often accounted for a substantial proportion of export sales. Subsidized exports decreased in importance following the export boom for farm products in the early 1970s, but protectionist pressures led to new export subsidy programs for agricultural products in the 1985 farm bill. The 1990 and 1996 farm bills retained, in some form, most of the export subsidies enacted in earlier legislation.

In expanding opportunities for exports of farm products, the U.S. government must reduce (not increase) trade restrictions and work to reduce trade barriers in other countries. Foreign buyers must have dollars to purchase U.S. farm products. Consequently, "voluntary" import restrictions and other trade barriers for autos, steel, and so on are likely to prove especially damaging to the agricultural sector. It is inconsistent to attempt simultaneously to reduce imports and to increase exports.

Domestic agricultural programs are inconsistent with free trade. The U.S. price-support programs instituted during the 1930s spawned a host of protectionist import restrictions and export subsidies for farm products. These measures evoked or strengthened protectionism by agricultural interests in other countries. The harmful effects of protectionist policies prevent farmers, other workers, and consumers throughout the world from reaping the benefits that occur when individuals are permitted to engage in those activities in which they are most productive.

In reducing protectionism and expanding trade in agricultural products, the U.S. government has worked with other countries mainly through GATT (now the WTO) to reduce trade barriers in agriculture. The agreement reached in the Uruguay Round of GATT tariff negotiations and the development of NAFTA represent some progress in the multilateral approach to reducing agricultural protectionism. The alternative is for the United States to act unilaterally to reduce protectionist policies further, regardless of what other countries do. Politicians generally act to dismantle obstacles to free trade, however, only if consumer interests are sufficiently strong to offset lobbying efforts by domestic producer interests, but some countries have acted alone in adopting free trade policies. New Zealand, Singapore, and Hong Kong are conspicuous unilateral free traders and have done exceptionally well financially.

15

Crop Insurance, Market Stabilization, and Risk Management

Farming is a risky business because of weather, insects, disease, price variability, and so on. Public policies to stabilize markets and to reduce risk in agriculture have been rationalized on the grounds that these forces of nature, being difficult or impossible to control, warrant a sharing of risk by the public at large. The rationale favoring government intervention to stabilize agricultural markets and to reduce risk appears to be quite strong, at least when actual markets are compared with "perfectly competitive" markets. It is important, however, to compare agricultural markets with a realistic alternative—with government stabilization programs as they actually operate under real-world conditions. It is also important to compare the current agricultural sector including stabilization policies with the same sector excluding such policies, rather than to compare the current sector including stabilization policies with the agricultural world that existed prior to the advent of the New Deal farm programs.

This chapter demonstrates that the case in favor of relying on government programs to stabilize markets and to reduce risk is far weaker than is often assumed. It describes the results of an analysis of crop insurance throughout the world. It then briefly discusses the major federally subsidized crop insurance programs in the United States over the past half century and analyzes their effects. The results in the United States are shown to be similar to experiences with crop insurance throughout the world; in virtually all instances, a substantial proportion of the costs of government-provided insurance are borne by taxpayers. The chapter places emphasis on the problems inherent in government programs designed to stabilize markets or to reduce risk. In addition to "moral hazard" and "adverse selection"—which are important problems for both private and government insurance government crop insurance and other programs to reduce risk are also plagued by government-failure problems.

CROP INSURANCE: AN EXPENSIVE DISAPPOINTMENT

Crop Insurance Worldwide

Experience in both highly developed and less-developed countries demonstrates that crop insurance programs have many problems.[1] Crop insurance—like all insurance programs—is plagued with *moral-hazard* and *adverse-selection* problems. A moral-hazard problem exists when individuals are encouraged to take more risks by engaging in high-risk activities because they do not bear the full consequences of their actions. That is, insured individuals may deliberately (and illegally) suffer a loss or merely reduce precautionary actions to collect insurance benefits. For example, farmers faced with low prices may collect insurance benefits by setting fire to a field or by neglecting to protect the crop from pests. Moreover, moral-hazard problems in the administration of a government-subsidized crop insurance program are likely to be more severe than similar problems in private-sector insurance. Decision makers in a government-subsidized program are likely to take fewer precautions and use less care in establishing rates, monitoring compliance, and assessing losses because there is no residual claimant as there is in the private sector.

The adverse-selection problem is particularly acute in insurance markets. An adverse-selection problem arises when individuals know more about their own risk characteristics than do insurance companies and use that information to decide whether to insure. For example, a person having bad teeth is more likely to take out dental insurance if insurance premiums are not higher for people with bad teeth. The same goes for crop insurance. Adverse selection arguably is the most significant problem affecting the actuarial soundness of the crop insurance program.[2] Operating costs for a government crop insurance program may also be high because the program's payroll is bloated by political patronage. Such patronage may result in individuals being more likely (than in privately operated insurance companies) to be selected for leadership and other positions because of political considerations and other factors not related to job requirements.

Indemnity claims in most crop insurance programs are high in relation to premium income, especially when there is not much diversification by the insurance providers across types of crops or production regions.[3] Farming tends to be risky relative to many other businesses, so losses are higher. Moreover, a small program covering a small number of crops in a few areas is particularly vulnerable if disaster strikes. As a result of these problems, premiums have to be relatively high and a sufficient number of farmers must be willing to sign up in order for a crop insurance program to be self-financing. Even though the government subsidizes most crop insurance programs, many farmers have chosen not to participate when given the chance. A recent study of crop insurance in a number of different countries throughout the world concludes that "...with few exceptions, farmers in both developed and developing countries have been unwilling to pay the full cost of all-risk crop insurance."[4] Let us now consider the experience of crop insurance in the United States.

Federal Crop Insurance Corporation

The U.S. government became involved in crop insurance after several private-sector attempts to provide multiple-peril crop insurance failed.[5] A political decision was made in the New Deal era to provide subsidized crop insurance. The first national program began in 1938. The objective of the Federal Crop Insurance Corporation (FCIC, renamed the Risk Management Agency in the 1996 farm bill), a wholly owned government corporation, was to improve the economic stability of agriculture. Millions of farmers had been adversely affected by the droughts of the 1930s, and the purpose of the program was to insure against such catastrophes. The FCIC insured selected crops against major causes of crop losses, including weather, insects, and plant diseases. The FCIC in the beginning was authorized to set premiums at rates sufficient to cover crop losses but was not required to cover administrative expenses.[6] Thus, the government has subsidized federal crop insurance from its inception. Low participation and program losses—despite good weather—caused Congress to cancel the program in 1943.[7] It was revived the following year and operated from 1944 to 1979.

Crop insurance was initially limited to wheat and cotton, but coverage was broadened over time. Up through the 1970s, however, coverage continued to be available only on a limited number of crops and in only about half of the counties in the United States. Prior to 1980, FCIC contracts covered less than 5 percent of the total value of crops grown in the United States, and farmer participation averaged only 10–20 percent.[8] Thus, crop insurance had little effect on farm production.

Federal Crop Insurance Acts of 1980 and 1994

The 1980 Federal Crop Insurance Act (FCIA) provided "all-risk" crop insurance and supposedly replaced the old federal crop insurance program and disaster payments programs (see the next section). It was "an attempt to make crop insurance the federal government's means of dealing with natural disasters at the farm level."[9] The program was administered by the secretary of agriculture through the FCIC. The mandate of this agency is to supervise and administer crop insurance and other risk-management programs.[10]

All-risk or *multiple-peril* crop insurance now covers losses from drought, hail, insects, and disease for most crops in all regions of the United States. The USDA expanded the availability of crop insurance from thirty to sixty-seven crops between 1980 and 1998 and from approximately one-half of the nation's counties to virtually all areas of the country.[11] An initial goal of the 1980 act was to increase farmer participation to 50 percent of the eligible acres, but program participation fell considerably short of that goal.[12] The provision of disaster assistance—whether legislated normally or as emergency legislation—has a strong influence on producers' incentives to participate in federal crop insurance programs (discussed later).

The crop insurance program was revamped in 1994 and then was further modified by the 1996 farm bill, when it was also renamed. The program was not altered significantly by the 2002 farm bill. The program provides "catastrophic" coverage for a nominal processing fee for each crop insured.[13] This coverage guarantees 50 percent of the individual farmer's average yield and 55 percent of the expected market price. Farmers can also purchase additional coverage up to 75 percent of average yield and 100 percent of a government-determined expected price. The premiums are subsidized and vary from crop to crop and from county to county.

The crop insurance program historically has operated at a loss, with farmer payments generally covering approximately 75 percent of total cost (including administrative costs) prior to 1980.[14] From 1981 through 1996, traditional all-risk crop insurance paid an average of $1.26 in claims per $1 of premium.[15] After 1980, a 30 percent subsidy was built into the rate-setting procedures—the political price paid for ending the Disaster Payments Program (see the next section).[16] Moreover, premiums in any year may be decreased by decreases in farm product prices and political considerations. Insurance premiums in the 1999 crop year, for example, were reduced up to 30 percent under "emergency legislation" enacted in 1998. Loss ratios (the ratio of outlays to funds collected) vary widely from year to year depending on climatic and weather events. If premium subsidies are included as part of indemnity payments, producers received approximately $2.00 in indemnities for every dollar they paid in premiums during the period 1985–93.[17] The 1996 farm bill also mandated a number of pilot insurance programs—including federally subsidized crop revenue insurance plans (for crop years 1997–2000). Some farmers have been using crop insurance in combination with forward contracting or hedging in the futures market. The new insurance plans allow farmers to buy a single policy that insures against both production and price risks. In revenue insurance plans, as in multiple-peril crop insurance, the USDA subsidizes the premiums that farmers pay, pays private insurance companies to sell the insurance and process claims, and pays a large part of any company losses incurred if claims exceed premiums.[18] The coverage of this pilot program was increased in 2001 and 2002 and is to be continued under the 2002 farm bill until at least 2004.[19]

The FSA is not presently involved in the administration of crop insurance, and the 1996 farm bill restricted sales of "catastrophic" policies by local FSA offices to those areas that had an insufficient number of private insurers to provide "adequate service to producers."[20] Virtually all crop insurance is currently delivered and serviced solely by private companies.

Disaster Payments

The federal government has made "disaster payments" over the years under both formal and informal arrangements.[21] A formal Disaster Payments Program operated during the 1973–81 period, authorizing payments to producers of feed grains, wheat, cotton, and rice who lost their crops or were prevented from planting. The basic objective of the program was to cover the producers' out-of-pocket costs. It amounted to free insurance for these farmers at a Treasury cost that averaged approximately half a billion dollars a year.

The "prevented plantings" provide a striking example of the moral-hazard problem. When farmers received compensation for losses from the inability to plant crops because of drought or flood, their behavior was affected by the existence of the program. Disaster payments generally were made when yields fell below two-thirds the normal level. Disaster payments made it less rewarding for farmers to avoid risks of crop failure, which made it more likely that loss would be incurred. Hence, in one sense it was a disaster subsidy program.

Payments were concentrated in high-risk arid areas of states where land was the most fragile, especially subject to erosion by wind and water, and where production was least efficient, including New Mexico, Texas, Oklahoma, North Dakota, and South Dakota. Thus, the program discouraged soil conservation by subsidizing crop production on marginal lands in the Southwest and the Western Great Plains. When the formal Disaster Payments Program was terminated following the passage of the all-risk insurance program of 1980, federal crop insurance was provided on fragile lands where FCIC insurance previously had not been available.

Following the provision of all-risk crop insurance and the termination of the formal Disaster Payments Program, payments continued to be made on an ad hoc periodic basis for natural disasters, including droughts (1988) and floods (1993). Regardless of their justifications, disaster payments undermine formal crop insurance programs—whether public or private. Recognizing the problem, in 1994 Congress made the provision of disaster payments to farmers more difficult by stipulating that such payments would have to come from budgeted amounts for other farm subsidy programs.

However, Congress, responding to political pressure, reinstated disaster payment after the floods of 1996–97 in the West and Upper Midwest. The incentive for farmers to participate in the federal crop insurance program was further undermined by the $6 billion "emergency package of farm aid" enacted by Congress in 1998. Half of the 1998 package went to farmers receiving Freedom to Farm transition payments *regardless of yields or market price received*![22] And "emergency" farm legislation in 1999 provided $8.7 billion. Of this, more than $5 billion in Market Loss Assistance payments matched amounts that farmers received in production flexibility payments under the 1996 farm bill. Similar legislation was enacted in 2000 and 2001, with Market Loss Assistance payments in 2000 equal to those under the 1999 legislation and payments in 2001 approximately 15 percent less than in 1999. In reality, politics often overrides common sense in crop insurance—as in many other areas. In short, disaster payments both discourage farmers from taking out crop insurance and encourage them to spend more time in rent-seeking activity at the expense of time engaged in production and exchange of farm commodities.

Emergency Loans

In addition to crop insurance, the FSA provides emergency loans to farmers in areas experiencing damage from physical events such as tornadoes, floods, hurricanes, or other natural disasters. Eligibility hinges on the designation of the county as a disaster area by the president, secretary of agriculture, or FSA administrator. Such designations are affected both by the extent of crop loss and by political factors (e.g., an upcoming election). Emergency loans are made at a fixed interest rate well below the market rate.[23] A producer receiving an emergency loan must be an established farmer who suffered a qualifying physical loss or a production loss of at least 30 percent in any essential farm or ranch enterprise. Farmers receiving emergency loans must have demonstrated the ability needed to succeed in farming and be unable to receive credit from commercial sources.

Economic Implications

Insurance involving the substitution of a small known cost for the possibility of a large loss is a key means of coping with risk in many areas of life. Some agricultural risks, such as losses due to hail, are better suited for an actuarially sound insurance program than are others. Hail losses are not affected by management decisions and occur frequently enough to induce farmers to purchase hail insurance. In contrast, the large variability in annual losses combined with incentive problems in years with marginal moisture levels makes the provision of drought insurance by private companies more difficult.[24]

Gardner and Cramer estimate that it would take a large subsidy—probably more than 50 percent of premiums charged—to get a majority of U.S. farmers enrolled in crop insurance.[25] A lack of participation in insurance at levels high enough to cover costs is sometimes taken as evidence of market failure and, consequently, as a justification for subsidized crop insurance. This conclusion follows if one measures real-world markets against the norm of perfect competition where all risks would be fully insured. In the real world, however, where risk reduction is achievable only at a cost, it is economic to shift risk only when the expected gains exceed the expected costs. Thus, the absence of insurance in a given area of economic activity does not imply market failure. It may merely be evidence of an unwillingness to participate in an insurance program when premium levels are set high enough to cover the full cost of providing the insurance.[26] There is no known way to determine whether crop insurance is economic in the absence of a market test.

It is commonly held that former private crop insurance programs were unsuccessful because the insurance firms were unable to cope either with moral-hazard problems or with geographically widespread disasters. Thus, it is argued, the current federal crop insurance program is justified. As suggested earlier, however, it is not economic to insure against all risks. If farmers are willing to pay enough for insurance, private firms will provide it. However, if the government provides crop insurance (for whatever reason), there is no economic justification for farmers' paying less than the actuarial value. Under current conditions, the subsidized crop insurance program is an effective barrier to the provision of crop insurance by private firms. Moreover, the subsidized crop insurance program appears to be better explained by political than by economic factors, and, as described later, other private-sector innovation in risk management is now quite often discouraged by such subsidies.

MARKET STABILIZATION AND RISK MANAGEMENT

The public interest is often given as the justification for crop insurance and other programs to decrease risk or to stabilize farm prices and income. That is, it may be argued that crop insurance and price supports are not merely transfers to farmers, but rather programs that benefit the public at large. It is important, however, to judge the effects of programs on the basis of outcomes rather than stated objectives.

If government is to stabilize individual commodity markets, the planners must overcome the same kinds of problems faced in attempting to stabilize the entire economy. The stabilization idea is based, at least to some extent, on the "genie" concept of government, which assumes that government wants to, knows how to, and is able to coordinate economic activity. In reality, information and incentive problems are always present in the collective-choice process. Stabilization policies, whether of individual markets or of the entire economy, are not administered by impartial and omniscient experts, but through a political process in which decision makers act in light of their own interests and incentives.[27]

How Government Policies Increase Market Instability

Consider some of the ways in which government actions destabilize the agricultural sector. First, inflationary monetary and fiscal policies have had a destabilizing effect on U.S. agriculture. Monetary disturbances affect relative prices, in particular interest rates, a key factor in investment decisions. High interest rates are especially problematic in agriculture, which is characterized by a high ratio of capital investment per unit of labor. Many farm bankruptcies in the early 1980s involved highly leveraged operations that had borrowed money at the historically high interest rates of the late 1970s. Anticipated inflation is the product of government's monetary and fiscal policies and is the primary cause of high interest rates. Thus, the government's inflationary monetary and fiscal policies of the late 1970s created major problems in the farm sector.

Second, government actions are often ineffective or counterproductive in market stabilization. During the Carter administration (1977–80), for example, CCC storage was supplemented by the FOR program, ostensibly to stabilize the market. The FOR, as explained in chapter 9, was a complex system of incentives and subsidies to encourage farmers to store grain when prices were low and to encourage them to release it when prices were high. Subsequent study of the price patterns of that time, compared to the pre-FOR period, however, "showed no significant improvement in stability" because of the program.[28]

Similarly, the Dairy and Tobacco Adjustment Act of 1983 paid dairy farmers to reduce milk production in an attempt to alleviate the dairy surplus problem. This program ignored the fact that the surplus of dairy products is caused by high price supports dictated by political rather than economic considerations. Many other examples in the operation of farm programs show where short-run political considerations have dominated stabilization concerns (see chapter 5). There is also a great deal of uncertainty about future benefit levels of federal farm programs. High price supports that are later lowered in response to pressures to decrease government expenditures may foster unrealistic expectations by farm investors. Indeed, USDA economist John Lee, before passage of the 1996 farm bill, concluded that the single greatest source of uncertainty for many farmers (and for other agribusiness firms) is not weather or international markets, but federal farm programs.[29] Moreover, following passage of the 1996 farm bill, there was considerable uncertainty as to the direction of farm policy upon its expiration in 2002. Although current farm programs appear relatively secure under the 2002 farm bill, the structure and level of payments after it expires are highly uncertain.

Third, government-subsidized and government-sponsored credit programs create an incentive to expand the size of farm operations through borrowing. (Government credit programs in agriculture are described in chapter 16.) Moreover, when the cost of capital is decreased, farmers are induced to substitute capital for labor. "Too much" credit is more likely to be extended when credit is subsidized and when lenders do not bear the full consequences of their actions. Easy government credit was probably an important factor contributing to the increase in farm bankruptcies in the early and mid-1980s.[30] Moreover, as shown in the analysis of government credit programs in agriculture in chapter 16, huge amounts of farm loan losses persisted through the 1990s.

Fourth, agriculture is heavily dependent on international trade and consequently is greatly affected by government policies that disrupt trade. The suspension of grain sales to Russia by President Carter in 1980, for example, increased uncertainty in domestic grain markets. Moreover, it is not only the measures directly affecting agricultural exports that are important. Import restrictions on autos, steel, textiles, and other products, as described in chapter 14, are especially damaging to U.S. agriculture.

Because much of the instability in U.S. commodity markets during the 1970s, 1980s, and 1990s can be traced to government policies, it is apparent that government can make an important contribution to the stability of agricultural markets. That contribution, however, does not hinge on the provision of price supports, subsidized crop insurance, and other government programs designed explicitly for agriculture. As suggested earlier, farm programs may increase rather than decrease instability because they introduce artificial instability into agricultural markets. Instead, government can make its greatest contribution to the stability of U.S. agriculture by reducing trade restrictions and, perhaps most important, by adopting noninflationary monetary and fiscal policies. That is, government policies should not introduce artificial instability into agricultural markets. Consequently, when the inherent information and incentive problems are taken into account, government might make its greatest contribution to agricultural stability by attempting to do *less*.[31] That is, if government policies are destabilizing, a reduction in the scope of government programs may well increase market stability.

Ways to Reduce Risk and Stabilize Income

Recent advances in agricultural technology are likely to change significantly the traditional methods of coping with risk in agricultural production.[32] Genetic engineering is being used by vertically integrated agricultural chemical and seed companies throughout the world to produce differentiated and value-enhanced farm products to meet consumer demand for food products with unique characteristics—lower fat, increased protein, and so on. Globalization, the gradual worldwide reduction in trade barriers (see chapter 14), coupled with genetic developments by multinational corporations, means that U.S. farmers increasingly must compete with producers in other countries. Moreover, the ongoing change toward more integration in the food production process at the farm level (discussed later in this chapter) is creating new alternatives for farmers in coping with risk.[33]

Methods of economic coordination and shifting of risk are changing rapidly in U.S. agriculture. Vertical integration (through both contracting practices and ownership integration) provides one mechanism for farmers to decrease risk and has long been dominant in poultry production. Production contracts in broiler production and in other agricultural production contracts shift price and production risk from farmers to contractors. The result is that farmers accept lower returns in exchange for letting large contracting companies bear more risk.[34] Knoeber and Thurman, for example, found that broiler contracts, when contrasted with independent growers, shifted almost all risk (97 percent) from growers to integrators.[35] Vertical integration is increasing rapidly in hog production. With recent advances in biotechnology, such integration is increasingly likely to become common in the production and marketing of soybeans, corn, wheat, and other commodities. Vertical integration facilitates coordination between suppliers of inputs, producers of raw commodities, and food manufacturers in developing consumer products with selected product characteristics (low fat, high protein, etc.). Farm output coordinated by vertical integration increased from one-third in 1970 to 40 percent in 1994.[36]

How can agricultural policy promote the development of methods of economic coordination and other institutional changes that affect market participants' ability to shift risk? Most important, perhaps, government can create a climate in which it facilitates rather than impedes the development of alternative methods of economic coordination and institutions that affect farmers' ability to cope with weather, market, and political risks. The current government-subsidized crop insurance program, as suggested earlier, is an effective barrier to the privatization of crop insurance and exacerbates moral-hazard and adverse-selection problems. Therefore, *an important first step in the development and adoption of institutions to reduce risk is to phase out subsidized crop insurance.* This conclusion is bolstered by a recent comprehensive analysis of crop insurance and disaster-relief programs that finds that the programs are rooted in political expediency and rent seeking instead of in "market failure."[37]

Futures Markets

Risk-management policy can also be improved by encouraging private-sector alternatives to government programs. Producers will insure against risk so long as the expected benefits exceed the expected costs of obtaining the insurance coverage. The futures market is an effective way of generating and transmitting information about expectations of future market conditions. It also provides an important means of shifting risk in the production of crop and livestock products in those markets for which futures markets exist.

Futures contracts are agreements to deliver (or to accept), at some specified future date, amounts of a commodity at a price determined now.[38] Farmers might use futures markets, for example, to hedge against decreases in product price. A corn farmer might sell a futures contract at planting time, then buy back the futures contract at harvest. If corn prices go down, the farmer would receive less money than anticipated when selling his corn crop but would be compensated for the reduction in spot price when buying back at a lower price the futures contract that was sold at planting.

Trading in futures for agricultural products is now limited by the fact that for many commodities, available contracts extend only about a year into the future. There have been proposals to extend trading in selected futures contracts two or three years into the future to enable the private sector to take a longer view.[39] It is suggested that in such an approach, a government agency might buy and sell futures contracts to keep prices close to market-clearing levels based on expected supply and demand conditions.[40] There would presumably be no government stockpile of commodities because the program would operate through the purchase and sale of futures contracts. This type of program, according to its proponents, would provide buyers and sellers with a mechanism "to put current supply and demand conditions into perspective with expectations about the future" so that producers and processors would be able to eliminate price risks up to three years in advance.[41]

This mechanism would theoretically provide a relatively stable environment in which producers and processors of farm products can hedge production and storage decisions over a much longer period than currently is possible. Unfortunately, however, this approach involves a government trading agency and thus is also rooted in the "genie" concept of government. Any program of this type faces information and incentive problems similar to those endemic to all other actions by public agencies. The fundamental problem is that the political process has a short-run orientation. It is unrealistic to expect government officials to ignore political considerations in making decisions affecting storage. Consequently, problems are likely to arise when a government agency trades in futures markets. These problems are similar to those that arise when the government attempts to stabilize markets directly through storage operations. Even if government officials have the necessary information and know what "should be done," their actions are likely to be dominated by short-run political considerations. In view of the inherent incentive and information problems associated with government intervention in commodity markets, it may well be that government can make the greatest contribution in the case of futures markets simply by providing a stable legal framework for private traders. There is, after all, nothing to prevent longer-term futures contracts from developing with no government assistance should traders demonstrate a desire for such contracts.

In any comparison of government and private-sector stabilization programs, the basic question is whether government is better able than the private sector to develop, coordinate, and implement production, marketing, and storage decisions. There are good reasons to expect that risk-taking entrepreneurs, who are placing their own money on the line, will on average make better decisions than will politicians and other individuals in public agencies who do not fully bear the consequences of their decisions.

During the 1960s and early 1970s, for example, the government held large stocks acquired in price-support programs. The CCC was committed to sell commodities from storage whenever the market price rose above the loan rate by 15 percent or more. Thus, neither U.S. nor foreign grain users had any incentive to store grain because they assumed that supplies could always be obtained at the release price from government stocks.[42] During 1972 and 1973, however, the CCC sold off its long-held inventories when prices first began to rise during the grain sales to Russia. Then, when there was a corn crop shortfall in 1974, U.S. consumers were left vulnerable to large price increases.[43] Because neither the politicians who formulate policy nor CCC personnel who administer it are residual claimants, it is predictable that management of government-owned stocks would be more short-run oriented than decisions by managers of privately owned stocks.

Option Markets

Option markets are another private-sector device providing a potentially attractive substitute for current government programs in insuring against risk in agricultural markets. Agricultural options are contracts that give farmers the right but not the obligation to buy or sell a futures contract at a predetermined "strike price" over a stipulated time interval.[44] For example, at planting time a corn farmer might purchase a put option giving the grower the right to sell a corn futures contract at harvest at a specified strike price. If the market price of corn at harvest time exceeds the strike price, on the one hand, the option would not be exercised, and the farmer would receive the benefits from the higher market price. If corn price at harvest falls to a level below the option strike price, on the other hand, the farmer can either exercise the option or offset the original option purchase with a sale. The gains from these transactions offset (at least partially) the losses from the fall in the market prices of corn.[45] The purchaser of a put option, which entitles the purchaser to sell a commodity at a specified price, is thus insured against a decrease in price. The put option, like the conventional futures market hedge, provides security against price decreases. Unlike the conventional hedge, however, the put option allows a farmer to reap the benefit of an increase in price. Of course, this method of reducing risk involves a cost. The farmer incurs the initial cost of the option (the premium), regardless of whether the option is exercised.

There were no markets for put options in agricultural products from the New Deal era until 1984. The absence of option markets in agriculture was not a result of market failure, however, but rather resulted from a congressional ban on agricultural commodity options in 1936 following allegations of market manipulation. The 1982 Futures Trading Act lifted the 1936 ban and authorized a three-year pilot program; actual trading of agricultural commodity options began in late 1984.[46] Agricultural futures options markets now exist for a number of farm commodities, including corn, soybeans, wheat, and cotton.

Options markets would have advantages over current farm programs.[47] First, the trading of options facilitates rather than hinders the operation of markets in at least two ways. Options markets provide information to producers and consumers based on the underlying supply and demand conditions and provide another market mechanism for the farmer to reduce price risk. Second, unlike traditional price-support programs that are financed by taxpayers, farmers pay for price protection in options markets. Moreover, the farmer may choose the level of price protection desired. Of course, the cost is higher the more protection obtained.

There are also some drawbacks to the use of options markets.[48] From the farmer's standpoint, price protection through options markets is costly—when compared with conventional price-support programs financed by taxpayers. In addition, as in the case of futures markets, option markets may not offer price protection for sufficiently long periods of time. Agricultural options contracts currently extend for only approximately six months. As with futures markets, however, there are no restrictions on the use of longer-term contracts if the demand and supply from traders develops.

Agricultural options are traded for only a few commodities and are unlikely ever to be traded for some farm products where the demand would be too small to create a market. In spite of such practical difficulties, options markets for agricultural products are one way to stabilize markets for farm products without cost to taxpayers. Taxpayer-financed farm programs, however, significantly reduce the demand for futures and option-market contracts.[49]

SUMMARY

Farmers face a multitude of risks from weather, disease, pests, and changing market conditions. Countries around the world have instituted multiple-risk crop insurance programs to deal with these problems. The record shows that most crop insurance programs have not been successful because they are plagued by moral-hazard and adverse-selection problems, high administrative costs, and high indemnity claims in relation to premiums. Premiums on an actuarially sound basis may have to be quite high (and farmers must be willing to pay the premiums) to make crop insurance programs self-financing.

Individuals do not find it in their interest to insure against all risks. If a particular type of insurance is worth less to consumers than the cost of providing it, the insurance will not be provided. The fact that the private market does not supply such products, however, does not imply "market failure." Self-financing crop insurance, where farmers are willing to pay enough to operate an actuarially sound crop insurance program, may be one such product.[50]

A host of government programs, including product price supports and crop insurance, have been instituted to reduce risk and to stabilize agricultural markets in the United States since the 1930s. Federally subsidized crop insurance was available on a limited basis until 1980. Between 1980 and 1998, the USDA expanded the availability of crop insurance from approximately one-half of the nation's counties to virtually all areas of the United States.[51]

In the real world, where risk reduction is achievable only at a cost, it is economic to shift risk only when the gains exceed the costs. The optimal amount of insurance can be determined only through a market test. The current heavily subsidized all-risk crop insurance program is an effective barrier to the provision of crop insurance by private firms. Moreover, incentives for actuarial soundness are likely to be much greater when crop insurance is provided privately.[52] Crop insurance premiums have historically been rooted in political expediency, exacerbating moral-hazard and adverse-selection problems endemic in all insurance.

There is a strong a priori case for decentralized competitive markets as the most effective means of coping with changing economic conditions.[53] The outcomes of government attempts to stabilize the overall level of economic activity in the United States during the past twenty years suggest that government policies (as they are implemented through the political process) often introduce artificial instability into markets, including agricultural markets. This experience provides an important lesson for agriculture: government may well make its greatest contribution to economic stability by attempting to do less. Noninflationary monetary and fiscal policies and a more open economy are likely to be more beneficial to agriculture in the long run than are stabilization policies designed specifically for agriculture.

Government can also encourage the development of institutions and mechanisms that help farmers deal with risk. As suggested earlier, the current government-subsidized crop insurance program is an effective barrier to the privatization of crop insurance. And, more generally, government can facilitate rather than impede the development of alternative methods of economic coordination and institutions that affect farmers' ability to cope with weather, market, and political risks. The long-term government ban on agricultural commodity options is a case in point. More positively, by working to reduce trade restrictions on farm commodities and consumer products throughout the world, especially the fruits of genetic engineering, the U.S. government can facilitate the adoption of contractual arrangements in agriculture that enable farmers to reduce risk.

16

Subsidized Credit in U.S. Agriculture

Farm spokespersons have long held that the credit needs for agriculture are not adequately met by conventional financial institutions.[1] Today the commonly cited rationale for public intervention in credit markets includes credit gaps in the form of market failure and credit rationing as well as social objectives and priorities affecting the allocation of resources and the distribution of income.[2] In this view, private lending procedures, sources of funds, and loan terms are not well suited to the "needs" of agriculture. Government began to make direct loans to farmers and ranchers to meet short-term credit "requirements" in the 1920s. During the 1930s, the establishment of the Farm Credit System (FCS) was completed, and the FmHA, the Rural Electrification Administration (REA), and the CCC were created. All of these agencies continue their operations at present, although, as described later, the names and scope of authority of some of the agencies have changed over time.

There are a number of different types of government lending programs, and it is difficult to get a complete picture of federally assisted borrowing. The USDA lending agencies in agriculture make direct loans and, in some cases, guarantee private loans. In addition to direct loans and loan guarantees, federally assisted borrowing is offered in agriculture through the FCS, a government-sponsored enterprise. In this case and in others described later, the outlays reported in the official federal budget do not accurately portray the full extent of federal credit activity in agriculture. Some of these problems are discussed in this chapter following a description of the major government credit agencies and programs in U.S. agriculture.

Federal support has affected a substantial share of the agricultural credit market for several generations. The role of subsidized credit in the agricultural finance market, however, has changed significantly since the mid-1980s. The share of agricultural debt held by private lenders has gone up, whereas the federally supported share of agricultural credit (USDA's FSA and the FCS) has gone down (table 16.1). The focus of this chapter is on the rationale behind and the economic effects of federally subsidized credit.

TABLE 16.1 Distribution of Total Farm Business Debt by Type of Lender, 1985 and 2000.

	Debt Owed by Type of Lender	
Lender	1985	2000
	Percentage distribution of total debt	
FCS	31.6	26.4
Commercial Banks	25.0	41.6
FSA	13.8	4.1
Life Insurance Companies	6.3	6.4
Individuals*	23.2	21.5
Total	100.0	100.0

*Includes land for contract, merchants, and dealers' credit, and so on; CCC storage and drying facilities loans; and Farmer Mac loans.
Source: USDA, Economic Research Service, *Agricultural Income and Finance: Situation and Outlook Report*, AIS-77 (Washington, D.C: U.S. Government Printing Office, September 2001), table 10, p. 27.

THE FARM CREDIT SYSTEM

The roots of federal government intervention into agricultural credit policies predate the New Deal era, reaching back to the Federal Farm Loan Act in 1916.[3] This act set up the first unit of what was later designated the FCS to make long-term loans on farm real estate. Later units were added to make operating loans and to finance marketing cooperatives. The FCS has undergone continual changes in authority and structure over time.

Types of FCS Loans

Long-term FCS loans are made to farmers and ranchers, corporations producing farm products, farm-related businesses, and rural homeowners. The loans can be used to acquire land, equipment, and livestock or to refinance existing debt. The largest holders of farm real estate debt are the FCS and commercial banks. As of 2000, each of these lenders held slightly less than one-third of total farm real estate debt (table 16.2).

TABLE 16.2 Distribution of Farm Business Debt, by Lender, 2000.

Lender	Type of debt		
	Real Estate	Non-Real Estate	Total
	Percentage of total		
Commercial banks	17.3	24.3	41.6
FCS	17.3	9.1	26.4
FSA	1.9	2.1	4.0
Life Insurance Companies	6.4	–	6.4
Individuals and Others	10.2	11.4	21.6
CCC	0.0	–	0*
Total	53.1	46.9	100.0

*Excludes CCC Crop loans, which were estimated at $5 billion at the end of 2001.
Source: USDA, Economic Research Service, *Agricultural Income and Finance: Situation and Outlook Report*, AIS-77 (Washington, D.C.: U.S. Government Printing Office, September 2001), table 10, p. 27, and USDA, Economic Research Service, *Agricultural Income and Finance: Annual Lender Issue*, AIS-78 (Washington, D.C.: U.S. Government Printing Office, February 2002), p. 7.

Short- and intermediate-term FCS loans can be used for a wide range of activities in farming and farm-related businesses, including the production of farm products, the production and harvest of aquatic products, and the purchase or repair of rural homes. The FCS share of non–real estate farm debt in 2000 was approximately 20 percent—less than half the amount held by commercial banks, the largest holder of non–real estate debt (table 16.2).

The FCS also makes short-term and long-term loans directly to cooperatives of farmers and commercial fishers. Long-term loans are made for constructing or remodeling facilities or for purchasing land, buildings, or equipment.

The FCS—a "Government-Sponsored Enterprise"

Federal farm credit in the form of federal land banks initiated the concept of the "government-sponsored enterprise" (GSE).[4] A GSE is privately owned and operated and is limited to a specified economic sector.[5] The FCS, which began as a government-sponsored effort to provide a cooperative system through which farmers could provide their own credit, is considered self-supporting within the rules under which it operates. The FCS, as a GSE, can obtain its funds at only slightly above U.S. Treasury rates on comparable issues of federal debt because of the GSE's perceived relationship with the federal government—making the FCS a formidable competitor for commercial banks and other private lenders. There is an implicit guarantee that the federal government stands behind FCS loans. Consequently, there is also an implicit subsidy by the federal government to FCS borrowers.

The implicit subsidy to users of FCS-provided credit (relative to credit from commercial banks) is affected by the fact that government sponsorship of the FCS provides a number of direct tax benefits. Although the FCS operates under a different and complicated preferential tax structure, most of the advantage in taxation relative to that of commercial banks reflects the FCS's cooperative status. As a result, the effective federal tax rate on earnings of commercial banks is more than twice that of the FCS.[6] A further advantage is that interest income derived from FCS securities is exempt from state and local income taxes. Perhaps the most important subsidy, however, is the implicit government guarantee that FCS loans will be repaid. The net result is that interest rates on long-term agricultural real estate loans from the FCS were approximately one and one-half percentage points lower than commercial bank rates in 2001.[7]

FCS Independence

The FCS became wholly user owned when the last government loan was repaid in 1968. The events of the mid-1980s, however, indicated that the FCS still remained dependent on government support. The FCS lost some $2.7 billion in 1985 through mortgage and loan defaults. Several of the FCS banks had become insolvent, and Congress responded with a federal bailout, rescuing the financially troubled system. The bailout legislation provided a multi-billion-dollar package of federal assistance and mandated a substantial restructuring and reorganization of the FCS. Despite these measures, the FCS has to date not regained the one-third share of the nation's farm debt that it held before the bailout in the mid-1980s. In 2000, it held slightly more than one-fourth of the nation's farm business debt (table 16.1).

The FCS's credit policies are supervised, administered, and coordinated by the Farm Credit Administration (FCA), an agency of the executive branch of the U.S. government. The FCA was an arm of the USDA from 1939 to 1953 but is now a separate agency. The FCS obtains funds through the sale of securities to investors on the national money market.

The USDA

The USDA has a number of government credit programs—both for agriculture and for other purposes in rural areas. The FSA is the direct lending arm in agriculture. In addition, the USDA engages in a range of credit activities in housing, utility services, and business assistance programs for business and industry in rural areas (described later).

The FSA and the FmHA

The USDA has a long history in extending operating and ownership loans to farmers. USDA farm credit programs were administered by the FmHA for almost fifty years.[8] The agency was created in 1946, but its roots go back to the New Deal era of the 1930s, when the USDA made loans to assist poor or tenant farmers in purchasing farms. There was a presumption that owners were better stewards of land and that widespread land ownership would improve rural incomes and wealth.[9]

The FmHA was created to implement all direct lending, loan insurance, and grant programs for low-income farmers. It was designed to be a "lender of last resort," extending credit to farmers who were "unable to acquire commercial credit at reasonable rates and terms."[10]

The agency's role has been broadened a number of times since 1946, enlarging and extending its credit programs to farm and nonfarm housing and a variety of rural development programs. The greatest increase in coverage, however, occurred in 1972, when loans for community facilities, including fire departments, hospitals, and recreational facilities were greatly expanded. The FmHA was abolished in 1994, and its farm credit programs were transferred to the newly created FSA.[11]

The FSA—a Lender of Last Resort

A long-time goal of agricultural policymakers has been to increase farm incomes through farm credit markets. Of particular interest have been farmers not considered creditworthy by commercial banks.[12] Indeed, in its early lending activities, the USDA was viewed as a social welfare agency as much as a credit agency because its lending activities placed a high priority on keeping struggling farmers on their farms. The FSA continues to function as a "lender of last resort" for farm ownership and operating loans where borrowers must refinance through conventional lenders when "sufficiently qualified." So-called limited-resource loans are made for the same purposes as farm ownership and operating loans, but to owners and tenants who "need" a lower interest rate to have a "reasonable chance" of success. Finally, "emergency loans" are also available to help farmers recover from low production and other physical losses inflicted by natural disasters. For a farm to qualify for an emergency loan, the county in which it is located must be designated a disaster area.

Interest rates on FSA limited-resource loans are significantly lower than commercial bank rates. Rates for FSA agricultural real estate loans in 2001, for example, were more than one-half point lower than for FCS loans and more than two points lower than rates on farm real estate loans obtained from commercial banks.[13] The interest rate on FSA limited-resource loans was fixed at 5 percent—providing a 3–4 percentage point subsidy to FSA borrowers when compared with rates paid by borrowers from commercial banks.[14]

The FSA held 4.1 percent of total U.S. farm business debt in 2000—which was (roughly) evenly divided between real estate and non–real estate debt (table 16.2). This share of total farm business debt was less than one-third that of the 1980s (table 16.1).

The FSA faces the dilemma of avoiding troubled loans while providing credit to high-risk farmers who are not deemed creditworthy by private lending agencies. Thus, it should not be surprising that loan delinquencies and defaults are common on FSA loans. The problem becomes especially acute during times of severe economic stress in agriculture, such as in the mid-1980s, when more than half of the borrowers were either technically insolvent or had extreme financial problems.[15] The proportion of delinquencies on FSA loans was substantially less in the late 1990s. The percentage of delinquent loans (loans at least thirty days past due) was approximately 19 percent in mid-2001.[16] In stark contrast, only 1.0 and 1.5 percent of outstanding farm loan volume was delinquent at the FCS and commercial banks, respectively.[17]

Rural Development

The Rural Housing Service administers the rural housing programs—direct loans, loan guarantees, and rental assistance payments for low-income families who reside in "rural areas"—which includes cities with populations up to 50,000! The Rural Business-Cooperative Service administers the business assistance programs—primarily loan guarantees for business and industry in rural areas. Thus, the original FmHA credit programs in agriculture have been expanded to encompass borrowers far removed from the farm sector. There is an implicit subsidy on loans for rural development. Interest rates are below the market rate (being adjusted depending on the income level of the county) because Rural Development office loans are guaranteed, eliminating risk to lenders.

The Rural Utilities Service administers loan and loan guarantees for electricity—formerly handled by the REA—and for water and sewer activities, handled by the FmHA before 1994. The Rural Utilities Service, too, has gone far beyond the REA's original mission to provide electricity and telephone service to rural areas. It has expanded its utility programs to include subsidized lending to electric cooperatives serving high-income urban and suburban areas throughout the United States. In short, the rural-development credit programs appear to be consistent with the theory of bureaucracy discussed in earlier chapters. A government program, once started, tends to expand its jurisdiction, regardless of changes in economic conditions affecting the rationale for the initial program.

The CCC

The CCC historically was an important source of agricultural credit. Farmers would pledge a quantity of a commodity as collateral and thereby obtain a nonrecourse loan from the CCC. The demand for CCC loans varies from year to year depending on the difference between the loan rates of various programs and commodity market prices. CCC loan debt outstanding has been much less during the late 1990s than it was during the mid-1980s. For example, CCC loan debt was $16.9 billion in 1985, but only approximately $5 billion at the end of 2001.[18]

Credit obtained through CCC loans represents a double break for borrowers. First, the amount of money a farmer can obtain as a nonrecourse loan on a given amount of collateral in the form of wheat, corn, or other commodity often exceeds the amount that she can obtain from private lending sources. Second, the interest rate charged on loans is lower than the commercial rate whether or not the borrower elects to repay the nonrecourse loan. However, the 1996 farm bill reduced the amount of the direct interest subsidy on CCC loans. The interest rate now is 1 percent over the rate that the CCC is charged to borrow from the U.S. Treasury. The rate charged previously was equal to the rate that the U.S. Treasury charged the CCC.

The borrower can either repay a CCC nonrecourse loan with interest during a specified period and regain control of the commodity or forfeit the commodity to the CCC in full satisfaction of the loan—including the accumulated interest. Thus, there is an interest subsidy to the farmer borrower, whether or not the loan is repaid. Moreover, large farmers get more benefits from CCC loans (and other subsidized credit programs) because benefits tend to vary directly with volume of production.

Under the 1996 farm bill, so-called recourse loan programs were to be instituted for dairy products (following the scheduled elimination of price supports in 1999), and, under some circumstances, loans for sugar might have become recourse loans. Under recourse loans, borrowers *must* repay loans with interest within a specified period. Recourse loans were never actually implemented for either dairy (price supports were not eliminated) or sugar (import levels were sufficiently high), and recourse loans are not used in the 2002 farm bill.

Government-Assisted versus Private Credit in U.S. Agriculture

The objective of federal credit programs is quite different from that of profit-seeking private credit institutions. The purpose of federal credit programs is to offer terms and conditions to selected borrowers that are more favorable than those otherwise available from private lenders. When compared with fully private loans, government-assisted credit may include lower interest rates or loan guarantees, less-stringent credit risk thresholds in making credit available, and more generous repayment schedules.[19] Moreover, as is also the case with other government activities, a federal credit program has no standard measure of performance, such as profit, in assessing success. A large increase in federal outlays on agricultural credit programs during the farm financial stress of the 1980s is not surprising.

Problems arise, however, when a lending agency deals with only one sector of the economy, whether the agency is public or private. In recent years, many private commercial banks in farm areas have also been in trouble. A problem is likely to arise when a bank at a given location is not able to diversify its risk outside of its geographic area and outside of agriculture. This inability to diversify risks is an inherent problem in federal agricultural credit institutions. It is also a problem with commercial banks located in predominantly agricultural areas, such as the Corn Belt, that retain a large share of agricultural loans in their loan portfolio. For example, farm loans in so-called farm banks—in which agricultural loans constitute at least 25 percent of their loan portfolios—averaged 36 percent of total loans at all farm banks in 1997 and reached almost 49 percent for farm banks with less than $25 million in assets.[20]

The potential significance of portfolio diversification is illustrated by the situation in California, where statewide branch banking has long been allowed. Agricultural lenders there fared much better than agricultural banks in other areas during the 1980s because large banks, which accounted for most of the lending in agriculture, held less than 5 percent of their portfolios in agricultural production loans.[21] The conclusion is that nationwide banks are able to diversify their risks much more effectively than banks restricted to a given geographical area. A bank that makes loans in several regions does not have its fate tied to the economy of one region. Moreover, with interstate banking, a bank in a farming region will not have all its loans dependent on the state of the farm economy.[22] Thus, restrictions on interstate banking played an important role in the farm credit woes of the 1980s.

More recently, large agricultural banks generally diversify their risks more effectively. In mid-2001, for agricultural banks with less than $25 million in total assets, agricultural loans constituted almost half the banks' loan portfolios.[23] For banks with more than $500 million in total assets, agricultural loans constituted only approximately 22 percent of bank loans.[24]

Outlays versus Opportunity Cost of Credit Programs

The federal budget is based on expected outlays and receipts for various government programs. Government outlays for agricultural credit activities, however, understate the opportunity cost of these activities for a number of reasons. First, outlays for direct and guaranteed loan programs are either excluded or presented in net terms after repayments and sales of assets are considered. Government loan guarantees are excluded because a guaranteed loan commitment by itself does not affect budget outlays because it is only a contingent liability. By assuming this liability, however, the government induces lenders to invest in loans and thereby redirects capital as effectively as through direct loans.[25] Second, outlays in the federal budget do not reflect the implicit subsidies received by borrowers through interest rates that are lower than those charged by private lenders. In short, the opportunity cost of farm loans and loan guarantees is much higher than the nominal budget outlay for these activities.

The USDA Office of Budget and Program Analysis estimates "program levels" of credit and other agricultural activities.[26] The program level of any activity is an estimate of the total financial economic cost of the activity. The estimated outlay for FSA farm loan and grant programs in year 2003, for example, is $244 million, but the estimated "program level" is $4.0 billion.[27] The full economic cost of a subsidized loan program is much higher than the outlays from the federal Treasury because of interest subsidies and the estimated value of contingent liabilities on guaranteed loans.[28] Thus, the budget outlay greatly understates the actual economic costs of these programs.

EFFECTS OF EASY-CREDIT POLICIES IN U.S. AGRICULTURE

Subsidized credit is in effect an income-redistribution program. Consequently, as emphasized in chapter 6, economic theory cannot be used to justify subsidized credit programs, which benefit some farmers at the expense of other farmers and of taxpayers generally. Economic theory is useful, however, in analyzing the information and incentive problems inherent in publicly funded credit programs. Easy-credit policies in agriculture also lead to a number of indirect and unintended effects.

Information Problems

What is the "optimal" amount of credit in agriculture? Unlike with private banks, there is no standard measure of performance to assess the success of federal credit programs. In the absence of a market test, there is no reliable procedure to determine how federally provided credit should be allocated, either within agriculture or between agriculture and other sectors of the economy. The lack of a measurement tool makes it impossible to determine how effectively credit is being used in federally assisted agricultural credit programs.

A number of arguments have been used to justify easy credit in agriculture—arguments that fall under the broad justifications of reducing "market imperfections" and enhancing "equity." As shown throughout this book, however, programs that are instituted—ostensibly at least—to increase equity almost always inherently create economic distortions, reduce economic output, and have other unintended consequences. This thesis is supported by a recent analysis of arguments made in defense of easy credit in agriculture, wherein the authors concluded that it is increasingly difficult to make a case for subsidizing credit.[29] Although the authors of this analysis acknowledge that it is the case that credit markets in agriculture are not perfectly competitive, they stress that government programs suffer from their own set of imperfections so that "society must choose between imperfect market outcomes and imperfect government remedies."[30]

Incentive Problems

Incentive problems arise in subsidized credit programs as they do in all other situations where resources are allocated through the collective-choice process. In the case of the FSA's so-called limited-resource loans, for example, credit is to be extended when farmers "need a lower interest rate to have a reasonable chance of success."[31] There is however, no defensible criterion by which USDA officials can determine which farmers "need" a lower interest rate.

There is also a moral-hazard problem in all cases where the USDA acts as a "lender of last resort." If subsidized credit is available for farmers who cannot obtain credit elsewhere, the farmer has an incentive to demonstrate that credit cannot be obtained from commercial sources. Similarly, holders of FSA farm ownership loans are legally supposed to refinance when sufficiently qualified to obtain credit from conventional sources. Clearly, however, FSA borrowers have an incentive, regardless of their economic condition, to demonstrate that they are not sufficiently qualified for such commercial credit.

Politicians are likely to be motivated by political considerations in making decisions about subsidized credit programs. During the late 1970s and early 1980s, there was a shift in policy toward "easier credit" for farmers in financial difficulty. In response to the American Agriculture Movement's lobbying efforts, for example, the Emergency Agriculture Act of 1978 supplemented the long-standing USDA emergency loan programs with a new $6 billion program of "economic emergency" loans. These loans were made to farmers already in financial trouble who could not obtain credit from commercial sources.[32] Such loans simply postponed the failure of some farms until the next round of depressed farm product prices in 1981–82. Credit programs of this type substitute lending officials' politically influenced judgment for market profit-and-loss signals.

The 1984 USDA debt deferral and adjustment program is another example where political considerations appear to have influenced a farm credit program. The program, initiated in the heat of the 1984 presidential election campaign, allowed the USDA to grant its farmer borrowers deferrals on the repayment of up to 25 percent of the borrower's indebtedness. It also permitted the agency to guarantee 90 percent of a problem farm loan held by other lenders provided that the lender reduced by specified amounts the principal amount of the debt or the interest rate charged on the indebtedness.

Any change in USDA lending rules, especially rules related to foreclosure, is politically sensitive. Secretary of Agriculture Bergland imposed a moratorium on farm foreclosures during much of the Carter presidency in the late 1970s. Secretary John Block of the Reagan administration lifted the moratorium after the 1980 election, but reimposed it again in 1982 in response to political pressure. Without a clearly defined and firmly enforced foreclosure policy, government lending agencies are likely to get dragged into more and more hopeless economic ventures. This problem is inherent in lending activities when judgment based on political pressure is substituted for the discipline of the marketplace. When credit is available only from those who hope to profit from lending, there is much less likelihood of overexpansion of landholding or capital facilities.

The problem inherent in government lending policies in agriculture is a chronic one that is magnified during periods of economic downturn in agriculture. When such economic conditions occur, it is fully predictable that the delinquency problem will be much more acute for FSA borrowers than for other users of farm credit.

Indirect Effects (Resource Allocation)

Subsidized credit programs enable participating farmers to obtain additional credit at interest rates lower than can be obtained from commercial banks for loans of comparable risk. The effect of a subsidized credit program in agriculture that competes with private lenders, such as the FCS, is shown in figure 16.1. In the absence of subsidized credit, the market-clearing amount of credit is Q_0 at interest rate r_0. Under a subsidized credit program and increase in the supply of credit in agriculture, the interest rate decreases to r_1, and the amount of farm credit increases to Q_1. The short-run effects of credit subsidies on interest rates paid by farmers obtaining the loans are obvious—the indirect effects, however, are not so obvious. First, subsidized credit affects which producers remain in production. If credit is subsidized, some less-productive producers are kept in production beyond the level dictated by market forces. The increased output also results in lower product prices. Thus, farmers not receiving subsidized credit are harmed because their product prices are reduced. The result is that those less-productive farmers who receive subsidized loans benefit at the expense of more-productive farmers, thereby reducing overall productivity.[33]

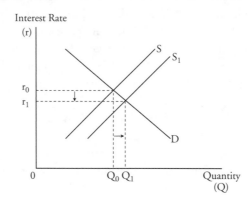

FIGURE 16.1 The direct effect on recipients of subsidized credit in U.S. agriculture.

Second, subsidized credit policies tend to boost asset values and may benefit owners of capital assets more than they benefit the recipients of the subsidized credit.[34] Land values increase because subsidized interest rates increase the prices that prospective land buyers are willing and able to pay. These benefits come at the expense of taxpayers, borrowers, and competitors.[35] Further, it is likely that easy credit has led to the substitution of machinery and other capital inputs for labor in agriculture, resulting in more highly mechanized farms. Moreover, federal credit policies may contribute to the consolidation of farming assets in another way. The FCS focuses its lending activities on larger commercial farm operations.[36] In view of widespread public concerns about farm size and capital requirements in commercial agriculture, it is ironic that government-operated and government-sanctioned credit programs have contributed to the trends toward larger and more highly mechanized farms.

SUMMARY

The FCS, FSA, CCC, and Rural Utilities Service are the major credit agencies for U.S. agriculture that are operated or supervised by the federal government. The FCS provides credit for farmers, ranchers, and agricultural cooperatives. Although privately owned, it is a GSE that enjoys special legal advantages that enable it to borrow at rates only slightly higher than those paid by the U.S. Treasury. Moreover, the federal government implicitly backs FCS loans as evidenced by the $4 billion in bailout assistance provided to assist the financially troubled FCS in the mid-1980s.

The FSA and the CCC are the primary federal agencies providing explicit credit subsidies through direct loans to agricultural borrowers. The FSA is in transition from direct lender to guarantor of loans. For example, guaranteed loans constituted approximately 33 percent of FSA loan obligations in the mid-1980s. By 2001, however, the share was approximately 71 percent.[37] Loan guarantees, however, are no less important than direct loans in redirecting lending activity. Moreover, it is difficult to measure the extent of federal credit programs in agriculture. Outlays in the official budget greatly understate the magnitude of federally assisted borrowing because guaranteed and direct loan programs are presented in net terms.

The alleged "need" for subsidized credit to farmers is based on the argument that private lenders will not supply credit on terms and in amounts required by farmers. The fact that a farmer cannot profitably obtain credit from a private lender does not imply, however, that subsidized credit is warranted. It is likely that the would-be borrower does not meet private-sector standards and is denied credit because the loan is viewed as potentially unprofitable.[38]

The immediate effects of subsidizing credit is to reduce interest rates and to increase the amount of credit used in agriculture. The reduction in interest rates has contributed to increased production and to the trends toward larger and more highly mechanized farms. Subsidized credit is harmful to nonusers of subsidized credit in agriculture because it increases output and decreases product prices.

Finally, subsidized credit poses the same problems posed by all other government intervention affecting market prices. The market process allocates capital on the basis of its expected productivity and profits. In federal credit programs, in contrast, there is no standard measure of performance. In the absence of a profit benchmark, there is no objective procedure to determine how much credit *should be used* in agriculture. Incentive as well as information problems arise when credit decisions are made through the collective-choice process. Where the FSA operates as a lender of last resort, for example, moral-hazard problems arise because borrowers have an incentive to demonstrate that they "lack other sources of credit." Political decision makers have an incentive to respond. In contrast, when credit is made available on the basis of profit and loss expectations by private lending agencies, farmers are less likely to overexpand land and capital facilities.

Government regulations that adversely affect the ability of agricultural credit institutions to diversify portfolios are also harmful. Problems arise when lending institutions deal with only one sector of the economy, whether the credit agencies are public or private. Government restrictions on nationwide banking reduce diversification in bank loan portfolios, thereby increasing risk and the likelihood of bank failure. Financial markets, however, are changing rapidly as a result of advances in technology and deregulation. Many restrictions that once contributed to credit-market inefficiencies, such as geographical limitations on bank activities and limitations on permissible activities of commercial banks, have been or are being liberalized.[39] In view of these changes, the persuasiveness of commonly cited reasons for federal intervention in agricultural credit markets has greatly diminished so that today "it is increasingly difficult to make a case for subsidizing credit to agriculture."[40]

17

Conservation and "Protection" of Natural Resources

The conservation movement in the United States was formally initiated in 1908 when President Theodore Roosevelt called together a conference of state governors. The conventional wisdom at that time was that natural resources were being used too rapidly and that political controls should be instituted to conserve resources for future generations. The conservation movement led to large quantities of forest, mineral, park, and other lands being kept under public ownership. It also led to the creation of several new government agencies including the Forest Service, the Grazing Service, and the Fish and Wildlife Service.

The conservation movement probably had its greatest impacts on agriculture through programs and policies that affected soil conservation practices. Soil conservation efforts received a major impetus with the creation of the Soil Conservation Service (SCS) in 1935 in the New Deal era. The SCS was augmented in 1937 by a system of conservation districts that now governs the soil and water conservation policies in most counties of the United States through locally elected boards. A new USDA agency, the Natural Resources Conservation Service (NRCS), was created in 1994 by merging the SCS and the conservation cost-sharing programs of the Agricultural Stabilization and Conservation Service.[1] The NRCS provides assistance to landowners and farm operators in developing and carrying out soil conservation plans and projects. Conservation provisions of the 1996 and 2002 farm bills are described in a later section.

This chapter analyzes the meaning of the concept "conservation" and explains why private ownership promotes wiser stewardship of natural resources. It discusses the rationale for government soil- and land-conservation programs along with the problems inherent in achieving optimal levels of resource use through the collective-choice process. The economic problems involved in the conservation and efficient use of water resources, although not discussed in this chapter, are similar to those for land resources.[2] The "free-market environmentalism" approach to natural-resource problems that is used in this chapter involves a blend of the economics of property rights, public choice, and entrepreneurship.[3]

WHAT IS CONSERVATION?

Conservation is frequently taken to mean "not consuming." During the decade of the 1970s, for example, *energy conservation*, as the term was used, typically referred to measures to reduce energy consumption. Conservation, in the sense of not consuming today so that resources are preserved for future generations, provides no guidance, however, to the proper rate of resource use over time. The relevant conservation problem for petroleum, timber, copper, soil, or any other resource concerns the optimal *rate of use*.

Conservation involves capital investment, and the conservation problem is one of choosing among alternative patterns of resource use over time.[4] Sound conservation practices can be determined only by comparing properly discounted costs and benefits that hinge on future conditions that are uncertain or unknown at the time the decision is made. Setting the most profitable rate of resource use is an entrepreneurial decision and is necessarily based on a subjective assessment of the uncertain future conditions. Whether it is economic to "conserve energy" by insulating the walls of a house, for example, depends on heating costs over time and insulation costs—both of which are uncertain. Let us turn now to the relationship between the institutional arrangement and resource conservation.

CONSERVATION AND THE MARKET

There are two methods of organizing the use of natural resources: the market and central direction. The history of past "resource crises" contains an important lesson in analyzing today's resource problems. To understand this lesson, consider the importance of private property as a social institution.

Common Property versus Private Property

The nature of ownership is no less important for natural resources than for other assets. More than two thousand years ago, Aristotle aptly described the problem associated with the use of "common property resources": "What is common to many is taken least care of, for all men have greater regard for what is their own than for what they possess in common with others."[5] Private ownership, in sharp contrast to ownership in common, encourages resource owners to conserve for the future because current market values of transferable private property reflect expected future income.

So long as property is transferable, a current resource owner will have a strong incentive to take the preferences of future generations into account even though she does not expect to reap the future harvest personally: "Suppose a 60 year-old tree farmer is contemplating whether or not to plant Douglas fir trees which will not reach optimal cutting size for another 50 years. When ownership is transferable, the market value of the farmer's land will increase in anticipation of the future harvest as the trees grow and the expected day of harvest moves closer. Thus, the farmer will be able to capture his contribution at any time, even though the actual harvest may not take place until well after his death."[6] The conclusion is that the private-property system is highly important in motivating current resource owners to take the interests of future generations into account.

The Market and Resource Crises

The price system is a way of rationing scarce resources both at a given point in time and over time. It is in the owner's interest to use a resource in a way that will maximize wealth or the present value of the resource, whether the resource is petroleum, timber, or land. A key argument proposed by many conservationists is that market price signals typically cause natural resources to be used too rapidly. However, forecasts of "doom and gloom" have existed for as long as civilization has existed. Yet these forecasts have been wrong, and there is no persuasive evidence that current resource problems are different from those of the past.[7] Indeed, history provides a great deal of hope that market forces have the power to eliminate resource crises today as in the past.

Historically perceived economic crises relating to the use of whale oil, minerals, petroleum, timber, and other resources were solved by freely functioning markets with individuals acting in their own self-interest. The lesson from the past is that if the operation of market forces is not suspended by government edict, crises will be short-lived as people react to higher prices both by substitution in consumption and by the implementation of technological changes. In a market economy, approaching resource scarcities trigger price increases that provide the motivation for actions that mitigate the effect of these scarcities.[8] The actions may involve increased exploration, recycling, or development of substitutes.

Throughout history, people have assumed a fixed amount of particular natural resources such as whale oil, petroleum, and coal to predict doom. In a fundamental sense, however, natural resources are not fixed in amount but are functions of capital accumulation, science, and technology. The available quantity or supply of petroleum, for example, hinges on price. As price increases, it becomes profitable to dig deeper wells, to make petroleum and petroleum substitutes from coal or grain, and so on.[9]

It is often argued that mineral resources have been extracted too rapidly and that conservation programs should be legally mandated. A study analyzing prices of fourteen depletable natural resources—aluminum, bauxite, coal, copper, crude petroleum, gold, iron ore, lead, lime, magnesium, nickel, silver, tin, and zinc—from 1900 through 1975 contradicts this argument, however.[10] In looking at price changes over time, the study found that mandated conservation programs would not have paid off. For none of the fourteen depletable resources analyzed would conservation from 1900 through 1975 have been a superior economic alternative to selling the resource in 1900 and investing the proceeds at the AAA corporate bond rate.[11] During the period analyzed, enforced long-term conservation of mineral resources would thus have been bad public policy both for the people forgoing consumption at the time and also for later generations that obtained the use of the resources.

Has the situation changed during the past quarter century? Are we now in a new era of resource scarcity? More recent evidence suggests that raw material scarcity problems have not worsened. Of thirteen major metals, the only one that rose in price relative to wages during the twentieth century was platinum.[12] The prices of most of the rest fell an average of fivefold after 1900.[13] Thus, the trend in mineral prices continues to tell a tale of *decreasing* scarcity of mineral resources.[14]

From 1980 to 1990, Julian Simon and Paul Ehrlich conducted an interesting market experiment about the scarcity of mineral resources. In 1980, Simon (economist) bet Ehrlich (prominent environmentalist) $10,000 that natural resources would become cheaper rather than more expensive. Ehrlich selected five metals—copper, chrome, nickel, tin, and tungsten—and a ten-year time period. At settling time in 1990, the sum of the prices (and the price of each metal) had fallen.[15] Simon's confidence was rooted in the fact that the costs of raw materials have fallen sharply over the period of recorded history. These results do not suggest that conservation, properly defined, is unwise, but that market prices are likely to take into account expectations about future economic conditions more accurately than can be done through central direction.

What are the implications of these results for agriculture? Rapid increases in knowledge and technology have permitted farmland and other resources in agriculture to be used much more productively.[16] A greater improvement in the world's availability of food occurred during the last half of the twentieth century than had occurred in all previous history.[17] Moreover, world-market prices for wheat, corn, and rice (adjusted for inflation) at the end of the period were the lowest of the twentieth century.[18]

Although there is concern in the United States that too much farmland has been lost to urban uses, here, too, market prices take into account expectations about current and future economic conditions more accurately than can be done through central direction.[19] The inherent problem of attempting to allocate resources in the production of food and other commodities without decentralized market prices was demonstrated in the former Soviet Union and other communist countries (see chapter 1). In short, market signals are no less important in determining the most productive pattern in the use of land and other resources in agriculture than in conservation of raw materials generally.

Time Preference

It is sometimes suggested that a high rate-of-time preference (RTP) is likely to cause resource owners to use resources too quickly.[20] *Time preference* refers to the value placed on consumption in the near future relative to the more distant future. If a decision maker's RTP is high, the individual is willing to forgo a relatively large amount of future income in order to obtain income in the present time period. Thus, the higher the RTP, the less likely is an individual to save, and if an individual's RTP increases, that person will save less and consume more in the present time period.

It is often assumed that the conservation of soil and other depletable resources is socially beneficial even though judged uneconomic by the resource owner. That is, the resource owner might exploit the resource in the sense of disinvesting even in cases where the cost of conservation is less than the value of resources saved. As an example, assume that the value of a forest is increasing at 15 percent per year and that the market interest rate is 10 percent. In this case, it appears desirable to let the trees grow because the return from an additional year's growth is more than the opportunity cost of capital. Would the tree owner with a high RTP cut the trees in order to obtain income now? Not necessarily. The owner might either borrow, using the timber as collateral, or sell the timber at the discounted value of its expected future yield and let the new owner harvest the trees at the "proper time." Thus, under competitive conditions, a high RTP by a resource owner need not imply uneconomic exploitation or disinvestment.

Where the landowner is not able to borrow money (or sell the forest land) on the basis of the timber's future value, the problem is not the landowner's high RTP, but rather a difference in expectations concerning the present value of the timber stand. In the real world, where future prices are always uncertain, there is no reason to expect people to have similar expectations about timber prices or other production risks. Moreover, transaction costs may also make a loan unprofitable.[21] In selling timber land, for example, transactions costs might include such factors as time and expense of locating and paying someone to estimate timber values, haggling over price, hiring legal counsel, potentially filing a lawsuit if the timber buyer fails to perform, and so on.

SOIL EROSION

Although the preceding discussion suggests that freely functioning markets with people acting in their own self-interest will conserve resources and eliminate resource "crises," public concern about soil erosion increased during the late 1970s and early 1980s. The concern was about whether farming practices were exhausting soil resources, making future food supplies uncertain. The concern about the effects of soil erosion may have abated somewhat during the past two decades. Nonetheless, a host of new soil conservation programs was instituted in the 1980s, and conservation provisions were further expanded in the 1996 and 2002 farm bills. Moreover, as shown later, an alarmist attitude exists among some conservationists (exemplified by the American Farmland Trust) about the adequacy of future food supplies.[22] Is the soil conservation problem unique in the sense that the market does not work to husband soil resources properly? Consider the evidence.

A Growing Problem?

There was little reliable information about the extent and severity of the soil erosion problem in the United States until 1977, when the SCS completed a national resource inventory of soil and water conservation problems (the first such inventory since 1938).[23] Three inventories of soil erosion in the United States have been taken since the 1977 inventory—most recently in 1997.[24]

These surveys show that although high rates of soil erosion continue to be a problem on some cropland, soil erosion does not pose an immediate threat to the nation's ability to produce food and fiber.[25] As one might expect, most erosion occurs on cropland. Erosion problems tend to be more severe on cropland because tilling exposes more of the soil to rainfall, thereby increasing the amount of water-borne soil runoff. Indeed, more than half of all erosion on U.S. cropland is concentrated on "highly erodible land"—which constitutes only approximately one-fourth of total cropland.[26]

Nobel laureate T. W. Schultz, after analyzing available soil erosion survey results, concluded that soil resources in the United States have improved over time.[27] When compared with soil resources of the 1930s, crop yields have increased, and row-crop acreage has decreased. Acreages of corn and cotton have declined and are now produced on soils not as prone to erosion.[28] Schultz determined that the severity of the soil erosion problem has been greatly exaggerated. A comparison of recent inventories of soil erosion with that of the 1930s survey shows that cropland erosion has, indeed, substantially declined over the past fifty years.[29]

It is important to realize that not all soil erosion *can* be stopped.[30] Even if there were no agriculture, there would still be erosion. Moreover, the fact that soil is a renewable resource adds an additional complication in determining the optimal level of soil erosion. As shown later, it is difficult, because of information and incentive problems, to determine when there is a soil erosion problem that warrants government action.

Possible Reasons for the Problem

It is often assumed that there is a general soil erosion problem and that it can be attributed to three factors. First, farmers allegedly lack knowledge concerning the effects of soil erosion. In this view, present rates of erosion will force up future production costs to unacceptably high levels. Second, it is held that farmers renting land overexploit soil resources. As more and more land is rented, it is argued, those who lease land pay less attention to conservation practices. Third, it is contended that runoff creates externality problems associated with land use.

What is the evidence on these points? First, the success of U.S. agriculture over time is evidence that farmers are knowledgeable and competent entrepreneurs.[31] The increasing productivity of cropland per acre in the United States suggests that farmers do not lose their entrepreneurial ability when making investment decisions about soil resources. Moreover, an American Agricultural Economics Association task force, after reviewing the evidence in the mid-1980s, was not convinced that present rates of erosion would force up future production costs of farm products.[32] This conclusion is strengthened by inventories of soil erosion in the 1990s showing that erosion per acre of U.S. cropland had decreased one-fourth since the task force report.[33] Soil is only one ingredient in production, and some loss of soil productivity can be compensated for by increases in nonsoil inputs. The costs of nonsoil inputs relative to the potential costs of yield loss and erosion-control measures are the key variables in determining the "optimal" level of soil conservation.

Second, even in the case of land rented out, landowners have a large stake in maintaining soil resources because the rented value of their farmland for agricultural uses is determined by its productivity. Moreover, long-term renters, even if acting in terms of narrowly defined self-interest, have an economic incentive to maintain the productivity of the soil on rented land. Thus, there appears to be little evidence supporting the first two of the proposed reasons for the alleged misuse of soil resources.

Government efforts to reduce soil erosion have been justified mainly on the basis of the third factor, *externalities*. A spillover or externality problem arises when property rights are not clearly defined and effectively enforced. In the case of soil erosion, the argument is made that farmers do not use sufficient conservation practices. In the situation depicted in figure 17.1, for example, farmers on the basis of private costs and benefits would purchase the quantity Q_1 of terracing and other conservation practices. If there are benefits of these practices to society over and above those to the individual farmer, as indicated by VMP_{social}, the farmer would invest too little in conservation practices. In this case, the socially optimal level of conservation practices is Q_2 instead of Q_1. Thus, the argument goes, conservation practices should be subsidized to reduce the cost, thereby inducing the decision maker to invest in the "optimum" level of conservation expenditures. In figure 17.1, the appropriate subsidy (S) reduces marginal cost by an amount sufficient to increase conservation practices to Q_2.

There undoubtedly are spillover effects associated with soil erosion. Soil carried as suspended sediment may harm fish and other aquatic life and reduce the aesthetic value of water for recreational uses. Suspended sediment also decreases the value of water for residential and industrial uses.[34] Gully erosion on land owned by farmer Jones that spills over and damages farmer Smith's land is another common type of externality in agriculture.

A spillover occurs, as in water erosion, when an action (or lack of action) by one person infringes on the property rights of another. Offsite damage occurs also by dust from wind erosion—mainly in the drier western areas of the United States. In the Southern Plains, Mountain States, and Northern Plains, offsite damages from wind erosion can exceed those from water erosion.[35] Dust damages machinery, increases maintenance costs, and can adversely affect health.[36]

The presence of a spillover effect, however, does not imply that there is a spillover problem that warrants action through the collective-choice process.

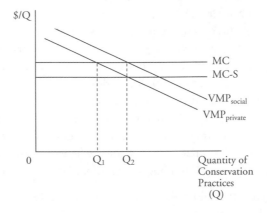

FIGURE 17.1 The externality rationale for subsidized conservation practices.

In the traditional approach to soil erosion (and other externalities), the presence of a spillover effect is considered to be evidence of a spillover problem that requires government intervention. That is, a difference between private and social cost is simply postulated. In the determination of whether government intervention is warranted, however, soil conservation under market arrangements must be compared with government solutions because soil conservation agencies actually operate under real-world conditions.[37] When an attempt is made to determine and mandate an optimal level of soil conservation, a problem similar to that in any other government program arises. As the discussion in the next section demonstrates, transaction costs associated with "market failure" in land markets do not disappear when government addresses those externalities.[38]

Implementation Problems in Soil Conservation Programs

A national soil conservation program is likely to be a model of inefficiency.[39] Soil erosion that is economically important occurs on particular farms in specific locations, and a small percentage of the total amount of land in crops, pasture, range, and forests is affected.[40] Yet the NRCS provides funds and services to *all* parts of U.S. agriculture. Why does the NRCS spend funds in counties with few (if any) erosion problems? The answer is that these decisions are basically dictated by political rather than by economic considerations. Members of Congress have an incentive to provide jobs and federal spending in their own legislative districts, regardless of whether such expenditures are economic. John

B. Crowell Jr., assistant secretary of agriculture, presented evidence on this point in a letter to the editor of the *Wall Street Journal*:

> Congress appropriates almost $1 billion a year for conservation activi-
> ties. . . . In the past these funds have not sufficiently reached the areas
> with the most serious erosion. . . . In 1983 the Administration initiated a
> five-year program to target an increased share of total conservation and
> financial assistance . . . to areas most needing erosion control. Despite the
> fact that targeting clearly was controlling erosion . . . on more acres with
> the same Federal dollars, Congress this year ordered that from 1985 on,
> no increase in targeting . . . should be attempted. . . . Congress felt heat .
> . . from constituents in non-targeted areas who were fearful that "their"
> traditional conservation funding was in jeopardy.[41]

The 1985 farm bill established the Conservation Reserve Program (CRP), which retired land from production for an extended period of time. The CRP, unlike the earlier Soil Bank program, targeted highly erodible lands and stipulated that farmers of highly erodible lands or wetlands who did not implement approved conservation plans would lose eligibility for USDA program benefits (see the next section).

The CRP might appear to be an exception to the preceding discussion that government conservation decisions frequently are heavily influenced by political considerations—rather than by dispassionate government analysis dedicated to promoting the public weal. Agricultural policy analyst, Luther Tweeten, however, contends that the CRP is not cost effective in protecting the environment. Many acres enrolled in the CRP have no environmental hazards, and much of the land, classified by the USDA as "highly erodible," can be farmed with modern conservation tillage and other conservation practices without harm to the environment.[42]

The key public-policy issue in soil conservation, even in areas where erosion appears to be a serious problem, is not how many tons of soil are lost annually. The basic issue concerns the relative merits of market versus nonmarket approaches in protecting soil quality. The political or nonmarket "failure" resulting from information and incentive problems is no less important in government programs to reduce soil erosion than in other decisions made through the collective-choice process.

The information problems that arise in attempts to mandate optimal soil conservation practices are formidable. Because conservation is an investment, it can be judged by criteria similar to those used in judging other investments. Profitable soil management and conservation practices, however, can be determined only by comparing the discounted expected costs and benefits. Because the costs and benefits occur over time, there is a great deal of uncertainty about their magnitudes, and there is no reason to expect the evaluation of a particular conservation measure by an outside observer to correspond to that of the landowner. Thus, attempts to determine and mandate optimal levels of soil conservation face the same problems as other attempts to second-guess real-world decision makers.[43]

Conservation programs often have been inconsistent with other government programs. Price-support programs and subsidized crop insurance give farmers an incentive to cultivate fragile lands. Farmers have been paid to create new cropland from forests and swamps, while other farm programs simultaneously paid farmers to idle already productive cropland.[44] The use of agricultural lime, which increases output and places downward pressure on product prices that are already considered too low, has been subsidized for conservation reasons. The conclusion we draw is that formidable nonmarket or "government-failure" problems must be taken into account in any objective analysis of the relative merits of market versus government approaches to soil conservation.

Current Conservation Policies

The SCS, as previously indicated, was the major conservation agency in the USDA from 1935, when it was created, until it was renamed the NRCS in 1994. As such, it provided assistance to landowners and operators for soil conservation plans and projects. The range of agency activities and environmental-control programs related to soil and water conservation programs was greatly expanded by the 1985 farm bill. The 1996 and 2002 farm bills expanded even further the range of USDA soil and water conservation and environmental programs, with an increased focus on wildlife habitat.[45] A substantial increase was made in funding for conservation programs under the 2002 farm bill.[46]

A primary purpose of the NRCS is to assist land users, communities, units of state and local government, and other federal agencies in planning and implementing conservation. The stated goal is to "reduce erosion, improve soil and water quality, improve and conserve wetlands, enhance fish and wildlife habitat, improve air quality, improve pasture and range condition, reduce upstream flooding, and improve woodlands."[47]

So-called swampbuster, sodbuster, and conservation-compliance provisions affect farm program benefits for farmers who drain wetlands or cultivate highly erodible land. The conservation-compliance requirement means that a farmer in violation of conservation policies loses farm program benefits—including contract payments, crop insurance payments, CCC storage loans, and FSA loans for all crops during the year of violation.

No attempt is made here to describe all of the existing USDA conservation programs. The USDA administered seventeen incentive-based conservation programs prior to the 1996 farm bill. Several new conservation programs were created by this bill.[48] The 2002 farm bill added even more programs and generally maintained or increased the level of funding for existing programs.[49] A variety of cost-sharing conservation programs are designed to assist crop and livestock producers with environmental and conservation improvements on the farm. More of the conservation is now targeted toward environmental concerns associated with livestock production.[50]

Despite the large number of conservation programs, more money each year is spent on the CRP—approximately $1.9 billion in 2003—than is spent on all other USDA conservation programs combined.[51] The CRP, initiated in the 1980s, is a voluntary program that provides producers cost-sharing plus annual rental payments for a ten- to fifteen-year period "to remove highly erodible cropland and other environmentally sensitive land from production."[52] The 2002 farm bill expands the amount of land that may be enrolled in the CRP, from the previous limit of 36.4 million acres to 39.2 million acres.[53]

The CRP and other conservation programs are no panacea in achieving the most appropriate conservation and environmental policies related to the production of crop and livestock products. Implementation problems, similar to those affecting other government programs, also limit the effectiveness of federal agricultural conservation policies.

PROTECTION OF AGRICULTURAL LAND

During the late 1970s, the USDA and other agricultural agencies throughout the United States became concerned about the loss of "prime agricultural land." In support of this concern, the USDA published a study contending that agricultural land markets were not working properly and that the conversion of cropland to nonfarm uses posed a major threat to future agricultural production in the United States.[54] Twenty years later there remains concern about the effects of converting agricultural land to nonagricultural uses—including "urban sprawl."[55] Two reasons are commonly cited for protecting agricultural land beyond the level dictated by market forces. First, it is alleged that agricultural land must be protected to ensure future production of sufficient food and fiber.[56] There appears, however, to be little or no basis for this argument. Indeed, there is a great deal of evidence that land markets are unique in their ability to allocate land among agriculture, housing, business, recreation, and other competing uses. Luttrell, for example, shows that the amount of cropland in the United States has varied over time according to the relative demands for farm products.[57]

Second, the theory of externalities is another possible justification for preserving agricultural land. It has been contended that agricultural land should be protected to provide "visual amenities," to ensure more "orderly" development, and to provide local economic benefits that derive from a viable agricultural industry. In essence, this argument suggests that a landowner who converts his land from agricultural to other uses does not bear the full costs of his actions. Most economists, however, place little weight on these factors. It seems just as likely that measures to restrict arbitrarily the conversion of agricultural land to other uses will hold land in lower-valued uses and impede "orderly" economic progress. Moreover, the disamenities associated with livestock production, pesticide use, and so on may more than offset any visual amenities associated with agricultural production.

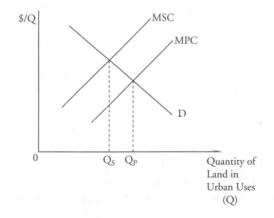

FIGURE 17.2 The externality argument for protecting agricultural land.

The theoretical case for restricting the conversion of agricultural land to urban uses is depicted in figure 17.2. If the cost and benefits of land for urban uses were as depicted, too much land would be converted from agricultural to urban uses (Q_p rather than Q_S). The fact that the marginal social cost (MSC) is higher than the marginal private cost (MPC) suggests that there are externalities; that is, certain costs of using agricultural land for nonfarm uses are not included in costs paid by developers. The difference between marginal private costs and marginal social costs in this example, however, is merely asserted. Even if such a difference exists, it has not been demonstrated that a nonmarket method of land allocation is preferable to the market process. Government efforts to allocate land are imperfect, and if the pattern of land use cannot be improved by government measures to protect agricultural land, there is no basis for implementing such measures. Despite the lack of empirical or theoretical justification for public policies to reduce the conversion of agricultural land, several different policies have been widely adopted to "protect" agricultural land.

State and local governments throughout the United States have been "protecting" farmland for more than forty years. All states now provide property tax relief for owners of agricultural land and "right-to-farm legislation" for farmers as protection from nuisance lawsuits. Many states have instituted a wide range of additional programs that are intended to "prevent conversion of farmland and improve the economic viability of farms."[58] Several of the most widely used techniques to protect farmland are discussed in the next several sections.

Property Tax Relief

Every state now reduces property taxes for farmland, and differential assessment is the most widely used type of property tax relief. Differential assessment permits qualifying agricultural and forestry lands to be assessed for property tax purposes on the basis of present-use value rather than market value. This approach is effective in giving a tax break to farmers, but it is subject to criticism both in terms of effectiveness and efficiency of land use.

Despite the dubious benefits of differential assessment from the standpoint of the public at large, enabling legislation in the various states often was instituted at the behest of the USDA and land grant colleges and universities. Indeed, the research supporting differential-assessment policies for agricultural land—important in getting the legislation enacted in the various states—was carried out by the Cooperative Extension Service and experiment station network.[59]

Right-to-Farm Legislation

Responding to farm versus nonfarm conflicts over noises, odors, and dusts associated with farming, all states also have enacted nuisance suit legislation. In general, this "right-to-farm" legislation provides that an agricultural operation will not become a nuisance because of changed economic conditions if the farm has been in operation for a specified period of time and is properly managed. Disputes between farmers and nonfarm interests have become frequent in recent years—particularly in areas with large hog and livestock operations. Right-to-farm legislation, however, provides no protection to farmers where water pollution occurs as a result of farming activities, and whether such laws can provide protection to farmers from other types of spillover effects is in doubt.[60] The Iowa Supreme Court, for example, ruled that Iowa's right-to-farm law violated the Fifth Amendment to the U.S. Constitution.

Agricultural Districts

The creation of agricultural districts is another widely used method to maintain land in agriculture. In such districts, incentives are used to encourage farmers to maintain land use in agricultural production. The range of incentives used, which varies from state to state, includes tax relief, limits on the use of eminent domain, limits on annexation, and limits on the enactment of local government ordinances that adversely affect agriculture.

Purchase of Development Rights

Still another approach used to protect agricultural land is to permit farmers to retain title to land while public agencies and private organizations purchase the rights to develop land for nonfarm purposes.[61] Farmers are offered compensation for giving up the right to develop their land. After selling their development rights, farmers would be able to continue farming the land, but would not be able to convert it to nonagricultural uses.

Evaluation

Property tax relief, right-to-farm protection from nuisance lawsuits, agricultural districts, purchase of development rights, and other legislative approaches have had little effect in restricting the conversion of land to nonagricultural uses. The potential economic gain to the landowner from converting land to nonagricultural uses in rapidly urbanizing areas is likely to swamp any tax and other economic incentives to keep land in agriculture. The purchase of development rights is a potentially effective way to keep land in agriculture, but, if widely used, it involves a high cost to taxpayers. The effectiveness of right-to-farm legislation against nuisance lawsuits is unclear because its legal status is still unsettled. As suggested in the next section, however, government measures designed to control land use, even if effective in doing so, may impede rather than promote the most productive pattern of land use.

THE MARKET VERSUS CENTRAL DIRECTION IN LAND-USE DECISIONS

Most of the research concerned with preserving agricultural land has focused on the relative effectiveness of different programs, whether the goal is to decrease erosion or to maintain land in agriculture. The problem in determining the "optimal" amount of land in agriculture (or the "optimal" amount of soil erosion) has largely been ignored, as has the more fundamental question of whether land-use controls to protect and conserve agricultural land are beneficial.

Information Problems

The basic problem in the allocation of land among competing uses is how to employ the knowledge of all affected members of society to secure the most economic use of land resources. The market process is unique in its ability to allocate land to different uses, taking into account the multitude of factors affecting demand and supply. Market prices coordinate and transmit widely dispersed information more effectively than is possible through any other known method. The information that influences choices by buyers and sellers of land is decentralized and cannot be objectively determined, except as revealed by the actions of market participants.[62] Thus, there is inevitably a loss of valuable information when land-market price signals are overridden by administrative land-use controls.

The importance of price signals in coordinating and transmitting information has been largely ignored in the land-use planning literature. In proposals to institute "comprehensive" land-use planning, for example, land classification is often suggested as a means of land allocation. A proposed land policy program for North Carolina recommended that all land in the state be classified on a county-by-county basis into one of five different classes: developed, transition, community, rural, and conservation.[63] Preservation of "prime" agricultural land is often a major focus of efforts to plan land use through central direction. Although prime agricultural land may currently be highly productive in agriculture, it is often even more valuable in other uses. The land-classification approach fails to take into account that, aside from the land market, there is no objective procedure to weigh the merits of competing uses of land—of determining which parcels of land should be in agriculture and which should be in other uses both now and in the future.

Incentive Problems

Although political land-use planning is presumably based on widespread citizen participation, any land-use plan must be carried out by government officials. Decisions are reached through a political process that is short-run oriented and dominated by special-interest groups concerned with only a narrow set of issues. Thus, low-income and other groups that participate least effectively in the political process are likely to be most disadvantaged by political land-use controls.[64]

There is also a problem in obtaining an objective evaluation of the relative advantages of the alternative measures available for affecting land use. Any such evaluation is costly and in most cases will be financed by the government. Moreover, the type of evaluation system used is likely to affect the findings. Consider, for example, an analysis of the cost-effectiveness of government conservation programs in agriculture. If the personnel doing the evaluation are employees of the USDA land grant university system, they are likely to have a vested interest in maintaining government support for the programs being evaluated. Consequently, they are unlikely to conclude that there is a reduced need for public expenditures on conservation measures in agriculture.

SUMMARY

Conservation is a capital-investment problem, and sound conservation practices can be determined only by comparing costs and benefits over time. Economic crises of the past relating to whale oil, petroleum, timber, and other products were solved through freely functioning markets with people acting in their own self-interest. Approaching resource scarcities trigger price increases, which motivate actions by consumers and producers that mitigate the effects of these scarcities. The conclusion is that resource scarcities are likely to be handled best in decentralized markets, where decision makers have the most information and where economic actors bear the consequences of their own decisions.

In recent years, there has been a great deal of discussion about two land policy issues. First, it is said that there is a serious and worsening problem of soil erosion. Increasing productivity of cropland over time suggests, however, that the problem of soil erosion has been exaggerated. Indeed, evidence indicates that the soil erosion of cropland has declined and that the quality of soil resources in the United States has improved over time. Second, it is argued that too much land is being converted from agriculture to urban uses. On this issue, none of the commonly cited reasons to "protect" agricultural land will withstand careful scrutiny. Thus, an assessment of the available evidence suggests that neither of these allegations is correct. Despite the evidence that the soil erosion problem has not worsened, new soil conservation programs were instituted in the mid-1980s, and conservation provisions were expanded even further in the 1996 and 2002 farm bills.

The problem of spillover effects related to soil erosion occurs when downwind or downstream deposition of soil particles has negative impacts. If such spillover occurs and contracting costs are too high for upwind and downwind parties to contract over erosion's harmful effects, a prima facie case can be made for government action.[65] The case for government measures to reduce soil erosion and to protect agricultural land rests on two basic assumptions. First, it assumes that spillover or externality problems are important in a significant number of land-use decisions. Second, it assumes that the problem of "political failure" in political land-use controls to correct for spillover problems will be less than the "market-failure" problems that the political controls are designed to correct. When transaction and information costs are taken into account, however, little if any basis exists for thinking that a greater government role in protecting land and soil resources is warranted. There simply is no persuasive evidence that land conservation problems are unique in economic analysis, suggesting that freely functioning land markets will eliminate inappropriate loss of farmland, excess soil erosion, and other "crises" affecting agricultural land, just as the market has eliminated resource crises in the past.

18

Agricultural Research and Extension Activities

Agricultural research today often evokes mixed emotions. On the one hand, publicly and privately funded agricultural research has both reduced the price and greatly expanded the range and scope of fresh, frozen, and processed food products available to the American consumer. Everyone benefits from this increase in choice of food products throughout the year. During the past twenty years, however, increasing concerns have been voiced about the effects of agricultural research and the application of new technology on agricultural labor, family farms, health, and the environment. Despite the dissatisfaction with some aspects of agricultural research, many people continue to view publicly funded research and extension activities in U.S. agriculture as a model to be followed in other sectors of the U.S. economy and in other countries throughout the world.[1]

The view that the level of public investment in agricultural research and educational activities in the United States is too low is well established in the agricultural economics literature. This conclusion is based on cost-benefit studies suggesting that the return to past investments has been quite high. In addition to discussing limitations in the evidence supporting this underinvestment hypothesis, this chapter investigates a number of other issues and questions. It addresses the following questions specifically: When did the federal and state research activities in U.S. agriculture begin? Who are the beneficiaries of new technology? What is the rationale for publicly funded research and extension activities? Is the theory of bureaucracy applicable in agricultural research and educational programs? If so, what are the implications of public-choice theory in publicly funded agricultural research and extension activities?

THE BEGINNING

The publicly financed research and educational activities in agriculture were begun more than 140 years ago. A few states instituted agricultural experiment stations in the early nineteenth century, but it was in 1862 that the USDA was created as an information agency for farmers.[2] Also in 1862, Congress passed the Morrill Act to encourage the establishment of an agricultural and mechanical college in each state. The Morrill Act provided for a grant of thirty thousand acres of land to each state for each representative and senator in Congress. The proceeds from sale of the land were to be used for the endowment and support of at least one land-grant college in each state. Although the development of these institutions would probably have occurred even if there had been no Morrill Act, the rate of development quite likely would have been slower.[3]

A second step in the creation of the nationwide system of agricultural education and research agencies was the Hatch Act passed by Congress in 1887. This act initiated the system of state agricultural experiment stations associated with the land-grant colleges and universities. The Smith-Lever Act of 1914 offered aid to the states in developing a nationwide system of publicly supported agricultural extension activities to disseminate the research results from the experiment stations to farmers and their families. Finally, the Smith-Hughes Act of 1917 provided federal support for the teaching of vocational agriculture in high schools.

CHANGE IN SCOPE OF USDA ACTIVITIES OVER TIME

From 1862 to 1932, the USDA was mainly a scientific and statistical agency. Agricultural research was conducted on crops, soils, and animals with the primary objective of discovering cost-reducing methods of producing and marketing farm products. The extension and educational activities were designed to disseminate the latest research findings from the experiment stations to farmers. From the beginning, publicly funded agricultural research received support from three types of political supporters: "public-interest" advocates who wished to improve agriculture through science, agricultural scientists, and farmers.[4] The first two groups were instrumental in founding the agricultural research institutions described previously.

The nature of USDA activities changed dramatically during the New Deal era. During that era, a host of action programs (discussed in earlier chapters) were initiated, including programs involving product price supports, soil conservation, rural electrification, subsidized credit, crop insurance, food assistance to low-income families, and so on. Although spending on food assistance programs has increased relative to outlays on other USDA programs (including agricultural research and education) since the 1980s (see chapters 13 and 20), publicly funded research and extension programs (with an annual outlay of approximately $2 billion) continue to play an important role in U.S. agriculture.

WHO ARE THE BENEFICIARIES?

The primary focus of agricultural research and extension activities continues to be the enhancement of agricultural productivity. Farmers in the U.S. Midwest, for example, planted the world's first hybrid wheat in 1984, with yields 25–30 percent higher than yields of varieties previously available.[5] The effect of a technological innovation of this type is to increase supply, resulting in an increase in output and a decrease in price (figure 18.1). Consumers, benefiting from lower food and fiber prices, are the main beneficiaries of improvements in agricultural technology. The magnitude of the effect of new technology on product prices hinges on consumers and producers' responsiveness to price changes.

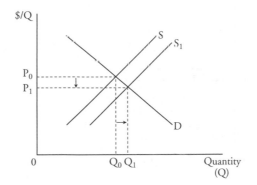

FIGURE 18.1 The effects of technological advances in U.S. agriculture.

The effect of a technological innovation is not the same for all producers. Producers who adopt a cost-reducing innovation first—the innovators—stand to gain the most (at least in the short run). For the innovators, costs are lower and output higher (figure 18.2), but as long as the number of innovators is small, neither total output nor price is appreciably affected. Thus, innovators' profits are increased by the amount of the shaded area in figure 18.2.

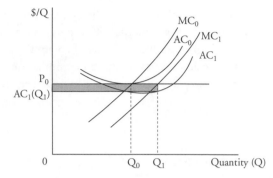

FIGURE 18.2 Technology reduces cost and increases profits to innovators (before product price decreases).

The situation is quite different, however, after a technological innovation is widely adopted and the product price decreases because of the increase in supply (figure 18.1). Competitive forces lead producers to increase output enough so that the expected rate of return is no higher than it was before the cost-reducing innovation. The individual producer following these adjustments faces lower costs, but she also receives lower product prices (figure 18.3).

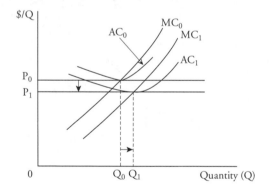

FIGURE 18.3 Effect of technology on producer after innovation is widely adopted.

The price decrease following the widespread adoption of new technology tends to eliminate the cost advantage of the new technology to the innovating firms. The producer who does not adopt the new technology faces the same cost but lower product price and is worse off because of the new technology. Some technology is appropriate only for large-scale producers. Thus, an advancement in technology affects individual producers differently, depending on time of adoption, nature of the innovation, and so on.

There is an inconsistency between research to increase agricultural productivity and USDA-administered supply-control programs. On the one hand, the USDA funds research to develop new technology and to increase output of crops and livestock through varietal and breeding programs, development of better cultural and husbandry practices, and so on. On the other hand, huge government expenditures have been incurred for more than six decades to maintain or increase the price of various farm products—often through acreage allotments and land set-aside programs. In the case of programs based on acreage allotments or marketing quotas, the greater the improvement in technology, the more acreage or output must be reduced to achieve a given level of prices.

RATIONALE FOR PUBLIC FUNDING OF RESEARCH AND EDUCATION

The public and private sectors invest approximately $7 billion annually in agricultural research in agricultural chemicals, food products, plant breeding, farm machinery, and animal health.[6] Private-sector research in agriculture, which doubled in real terms from 1975 to 1995, now exceeds and is increasing more rapidly than government-funded research.[7] Moreover, it is likely that this shift of research in agriculture from land-grant colleges to the private sector will continue.[8]

Scientific advances in genetic engineering and other types of biotechnology as well as increases in "intellectual property" protection for biological inventions are closely linked to vertical integration, and these developments have been important in driving the growth of privately funded research.[9] Moreover, as genetic engineering and vertical integration increase in agriculture, more and more agricultural research is likely to reflect production requirements of integrators, such as commodities with unique traits, instead of information useful to independent producers. It is notable that as total funding of private research increased almost fivefold between 1966 and 1995, the share devoted to plant breeding and agricultural chemicals doubled.[10]

In addition to agricultural research, private companies provide farm planning, crop consultants, price information, and other extension-type services to U.S. farmers. In view of the large amount of research and educational services provided by private firms, what possible justifications can there be for public funding of research and educational activities in U.S. agriculture?

Public Goods

Public funding of research and education in U.S. agriculture is usually justified on the basis that these goods and services are "public goods."[11] It may be recalled from chapter 3 that public goods have two distinguishing characteristics: nonrivalness and nonexcludability. First, the fact that Farmer Jones makes use of a new cultural practice—no till, for example—does not prevent Farmer Smith from also doing so. In contrast, a *private* good such as fertilizer that is used by Farmer Jones cannot also be used by Farmer Smith. Much of the information arising from agricultural research is largely consistent with the nonrivalness aspect of a public good. In general, the use of information by one person does not preclude other people from using the same information.

Second, if the firm providing a good or service cannot exclude nonpayers, market provision is not likely to be feasible. The extent to which exclusion is feasible depends to some extent on whether it is basic science, applied science, or the development of technology and its extension to information users. Basic research is often published in scientific journals accessible to everyone. In this and other cases where much of the gain from research is captured by other firms and consumers rather than by the innovating firm, private-sector research may not induce enough research investment.[12]

This justification is thus for public investment in "social overhead capital" in agriculture, where investment benefits accrue to a wide variety of individuals who do not themselves incur the cost of making the investment. But such a justification can be used as an argument for government intervention in a virtually unlimited range of activities. Raising children to be honest, for example, is an investment made by parents, but "credit card companies, self service stores, and the Internal Revenue Service are among the beneficiaries."[13] Yet most people would not conclude that the separation of costs and benefits necessarily implies a role for government in this case. In assessment of the appropriate role of the public sector in subsidizing new knowledge, it is useful to take a comparative-institutions approach. In this and other situations where there may be a divergence between those who bear the costs and those who reap the benefits, the outcome of the market allocation of resources to these activities must be compared not with unattainable ideals, but with the results when resources are allocated through actual governmental processes.

Furthermore, the public-goods rationale is less and less valid as one moves from basic science to the development and extension of new technology. Developers of new technology in agriculture can often appropriate the returns from goods and services through patents, copyrights, and fees. A new plant variety or a new machine can be patented. Printed information can be copyrighted.

Admission fees can be charged for information provided through lectures, demonstrations, and so on. The conclusion is that much agricultural research and education does not meet the nonexcludability condition of the public-goods model. That is, it is often possible to exclude nonusers by charging for the types of goods and services commonly provided by agricultural research and extension specialists. Moreover, even in the case of research that meets the public-goods criterion, the potential gains from public-sector investment must be weighed against distortions of resource usage through the political process (discussed in the next section). Thus, public-goods theory alone is not sufficient to justify governmental financing of research and education in agriculture.

In a recent analysis, Alston and Pardey suggest a number of other "market-failure" reasons for the apparent underinvestment in agricultural research.[14] Research typically is long term, large scale, and risky, and firms developing new technology may not be able to appropriate the benefits fully. Moreover, research involves externalities in those instances where research benefits (or costs) accrue to people other than those who use the results.

Spillovers and Research Funding

The fact that new technology developed by researchers in one state often has beneficial spillover effects in other states is also cited as a justification for public funding of research. A new variety of corn developed by the North Carolina Agricultural Research Service, for example, may be useful to farmers in nearby states. Thus, it is sometimes contended that when research is funded at the state level, research expenditures are too low because of this beneficial spillover effect. The argument is that because the beneficial spillover effects are not properly taken into account at the state level, the level of investment in state-funded research is "too low," and this is taken as a justification for increased decision making or funding of agricultural research at the federal level.[15]

However, the conclusion that spillover effects of this kind warrant a shift of research funding from the state to the federal level does not necessarily follow. First, as suggested earlier, the benefits of new machinery, new varieties, and so on developed at the state level can often be appropriated through patents and copyrights.[16] Second, the argument that federal funding is warranted where there are beneficial spillovers also ignores the fact that centralization of decision making at the federal level *creates* inefficiencies and spillovers as a result of nonmarket failure.

In reality, agricultural research appropriations at the federal level appear to be influenced more by political considerations than by public-goods or externality theory. For example, legislators often are motivated largely by the pork barrel—the desire to place buildings, jobs, and research missions within their own states. Thus, 44 percent of all research construction authorized between 1958 and 1977 occurred in the home states of the twelve sitting members of the Senate Appropriations Subcommittee on Agriculture.[17] Hadwiger graphically describes Senate pork-barreling: "Senate pork-barreling has been a mixed blessing for agricultural research. The pork-barrel impulse has been useful in gaining support for new activities. . . . But the demand for state laboratories has obliged the federal Agricultural Research Service to operate a 'traveling circus' opening new locations in current Senate constituencies, while closing some in states whose senators are no longer members of the subcommittee."[18]

Thus, the existence of spillovers associated with state funding of research does not imply that publicly funded research in agriculture should be further centralized at the federal level. Indeed, significant bureaucratic inefficiencies are inherent in the current system of funding agricultural research.

Complementarity of Research and Higher Education

The current institutional structure integrates the state experiment stations (and often extension services) with publicly financed colleges of agriculture. This structure—with the state-owned land-grant colleges having close ties to the USDA—was initially justified on the grounds of the "complementarities" associated with the productive interaction between research, teaching, and extension in the agricultural sciences in land-grant colleges and universities. Although this rationale is still widely cited, "the precise nature and magnitude of these complementary effects remains largely speculative."[19]

Moreover, any benefits deriving from complementarity must be weighed against the problems associated with the current structure of government-supported agricultural research and higher education. In a comprehensive analysis of the current system, Alston and Pardey conclude that it is questionable whether the current number and structure of land-grant colleges can be justified on the basis of economic efficiency.[20] They suggest that it might be more economical to consolidate some college programs and research programs across states.

A relatively minor change in the current institutional arrangement of agricultural education and research of the type Alston and Pardey propose, however, does not exhaust the possibilities for reform. For example, Edwin Mills suggests that substantial benefits from privatization of state-owned and operated educational institutions would be generated by greater competition and removal of distortions, such as excessive enrollments, induced by underpricing higher education.[21] The implications of privatization of the land-grant system would be profound for agricultural research as well as for agricultural education.

How important are the information and incentive problems of the political process in analyzing the funding of agricultural research and educational activities? The next section explores other problems with rate-of-return estimates on publicly funded research in agriculture and further demonstrates why it is difficult or impossible to get a definitive answer to the question of the "optimal" system for funding agricultural research and educational activities.

THE THEORY OF BUREAUCRACY AND AGRICULTURAL RESEARCH

The theory of bureaucracy suggests that there is a tendency for services provided through the public sector to be oversupplied. The head of a USDA research bureau or of a state agricultural experiment station is faced with incentive and information problems similar to the problems faced by other decision makers in the collective-choice process. The agricultural bureaucrat cannot acquire the information on individual preferences and production opportunities that is required to determine the overall level or the pattern of research expenditure that would be in the public interest.[22] Thus, because of limits on information, even the most selfless research or extension decision maker must choose some feasible, lower-level goal such as budget maximization. Incentive problems also occur because of the separation of power and responsibility (see chapter 4). In the collective-choice process that determines publicly funded research and extension activities, budgets tend to be treated as common-pool resources that no one owns. Thus, there are strong a priori reasons to expect that public financing will lead to an oversupply of research and extension services in agriculture, just as in other areas.

Vernon Ruttan once argued that agricultural research is not consistent with this component (oversupply) of the theory of bureaucratic productivity.[23] He cited a number of studies finding that the rate of return of publicly funded agricultural research typically falls in the 30–60 percent range. On the basis of these results, Ruttan concluded that there was underinvestment rather than overinvestment and that government should increase spending on agricultural research until the rates of return are driven down to comparable rates elsewhere in the economy—"to below 20 percent."[24]

In a recent exhaustive summary of 289 studies of returns to agricultural research and extension since 1958, including 164 studies during the 1990–98 period, Alston and colleagues also found returns to agricultural research to be very high. With implausible extreme values being ignored, the annual rates of return estimated in the studies reviewed varied widely at any point in time, but showed no tendency to decline over time and averaged 65 percent overall.[25] In a related study, Alston and Pardey analyzed the effects of U.S. agricultural research-and-development policy and agreed with Ruttan that even with existing government involvement, too little is being done.[26]

A recent USDA study also reexamines the role of the public sector in agricultural research.[27] This analysis of empirical studies found the estimated annual social rate of return to agricultural research between 1915 and 1985 was approximately 60 percent. After adjusting for a number of possible errors that biased the estimates upward, the authors conclude: "the rate of return was likely to be about 35 percent."[28] The adjusted relatively high rate of return is taken to mean that "further allocation of funds to agricultural research would be generally beneficial to the U.S. economy, even if it meant reducing other investments."[29]

There are a number of reasons, however, to be skeptical both of claims that rates of return on public funding of agricultural research are extraordinarily high and that increased government intervention is warranted.[30] First, as suggested earlier, the developer of agricultural research can appropriate a large part of the returns from new technology through patents, copyrights, and other means. If agricultural research is largely a private good, one would expect entry of new firms producing these services until expected rates of return are similar to returns from other investments of similar risk. Consequently, in the absence of significant barriers to entry, estimates of abnormally high returns to publicly funded research and extension activities must be viewed as suspect.

Recent increases in the amount of privately funded agricultural research—most notably in biotechnology—are consistent with the thesis that there are no significant barriers to the entry and expansion of firms engaged in this activity. The fact that it has taken so long for significant increases in privately funded agricultural research (relative to the amount of government-funded research) to occur is also consistent with the thesis that the potential rents are not as large as suggested by published rate-of-return estimates of publicly funded research and extension activities.

Second, rates of return on public-sector research are commonly overstated because the full social cost of using government revenues for research are not incorporated into the calculations.[31] It has been common practice in the evaluation of agricultural policy in the past to assume that the opportunity cost of a dollar of government spending is one dollar. In fact, the opportunity cost of a dollar spent by a government agency is likely to be much higher than one dollar, in large part because of the costs of tax collection and misallocation of resources inherent in taxation and government spending.[32]

Consider, for example, the administration and compliance costs of the

Internal Revenue Service. These costs, although generally ignored by economists studying the distortionary effects of public funds, are quite substantial.[33] The direct costs of funding the IRS and other agencies to administer the tax system are obvious. Business firms and households, however, also incur huge compliance costs in the form of time and money spent in keeping records, hiring tax accountants and lawyers, learning about the tax code, preparing forms, responding to audits, and so on—all of it amounting to more than 5 billion hours annually. When the opportunity cost of time was taken into account, Payne estimated compliance costs to be 24 percent of tax revenues collected.[34]

In addition, disincentive effects and market distortions are associated with taxation—sometimes described as a "deadweight loss" or "excess burden." In figure 18.4, the introduction of a tax of $T per unit reduces output from Q_0 to Q_1 and results in an "excess burden" represented by the shaded triangle. With the tax, the units from Q_0 to Q_1 are not produced even though their marginal value exceeds their marginal cost. A number of studies have estimated the deadweight losses of taxes, but the estimates vary widely.[35] Alston and Pardey, in evaluating the importance of these costs in government-funded agricultural research, concluded that the appropriate value is between $1.07 and $1.25 per dollar of taxes collected.[36] The resource-misallocation costs of public expenditure were estimated by the President's Council of Economic Advisers to range between 20 and 50 cents per additional dollar collected.[37] Payne, after considering the compliance, disincentive, and other costs associated with taxation, estimates that the opportunity cost is $1.65 for each dollar collected.[38]

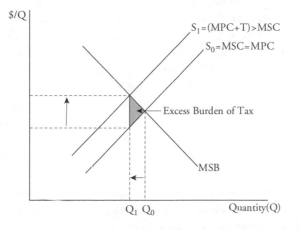

FIGURE 18.4 Taxes and efficiency—the excess burden of a tax on output.
Source: Hyman, *Public Finance: A Contemporary Application of Theory to Policy*, pp. 60–63

Thus, estimates of rates of return for agricultural research generally do not fully account for the opportunity cost of expenditures by government. This shortcoming casts doubt on the validity of the high estimated rates of return and suggests that rate-of-return estimates for publicly funded research are likely to have a strong upward bias. Consider, for example, a government investment of $1million that yields benefits measured to be equal to $1.75 million. If, on the one hand, the opportunity cost of the government investment is assumed to be $1 million, then this investment appears to yield a return of 75 percent. If, on the other hand, after the incentive, administrative, and collection costs are taken into account, the opportunity cost is assumed to be $1.65 million, then the rate of return on the investment is only 6.1 percent.

A third reason why rates of return on publicly funded research in agriculture appear higher than they really are is that state and federal research agencies, unlike private firms, pay no taxes.[39] Therefore, even if returns for public and private investment in agricultural research were the same, rates of return in the private sector (after accounting for taxes) would appear to be lower than estimated rates of return on publicly funded research. A study investigating the magnitude of this effect on one thousand private firms demonstrates that adjusting the rates of return of investments by private firms for taxes raised the average rate of return from 10.8 percent to 20 percent.[40] Thus, meaningful comparisons of estimated rates of return on government-funded and privately funded research must take into account the taxes paid on funds invested by private firms.

Fourth, there is the problem of specifying the appropriate costs and benefits to be used in rate-of-return studies. All rate-of-return studies are based on *ex post* data. Current investment decisions, however, are based on *ex ante* data, and a high *ex post* return does not imply a high *ex ante* return. Thus, the fact that the rate of return is high on the development of a new tobacco harvester, for example, does not necessarily imply that the rate of return on future research in tobacco mechanization will be high. Underinvestment in a choice context implies that the *ex ante* internal rate of return is high relative to the opportunity cost of capital. Of course, a high *ex ante* return in a world of uncertainty does not imply a high *ex post* return. Moreover, the economic analyst has no way to measure the *ex ante* costs and returns that influence collective-choice decisions. Once taxes are collected, what is the cost of the government's spending, say, an additional billion dollars on agricultural research? It is the *opportunity cost* of these funds in their best alternative use, whether that use is for prisons, roads, defense, welfare, private goods, or lower taxes.

Although the market rate of interest in many cases provides a good indication of the opportunity cost of capital, its usefulness in investment decisions is limited when the alternatives being considered include nonmarket activities.

Consider the problems of determining the opportunity cost of spending an additional $1 billion on agricultural research if, say, national defense is the sacrificed alternative. The expected benefits from additional defense expenditures are highly subjective, and there is no reason to expect different observers to make the same assessment of these benefits. A similar problem arises in evaluating the benefits of expenditures for prisons, income transfers, and so on, where such benefits are often not reflected in market prices. Yet it cannot be said that there is underinvestment in publicly funded agricultural research unless the rate of return is higher than it would be on these spending alternatives. Moreover, an increase in publicly funded research tends to displace private research. Kealey suggests that the amount spent on research might be just as great if there were no government subsidized research.[41]

Undesirable spillovers associated with changes in agricultural technology present still another problem in specifying the costs and benefits of agricultural research. New agricultural technology has had enormous consequences, "most of them unintended."[42] The potential problems in the use of chemical pesticides were dramatized by Rachel Carson's *Silent Spring* in 1962.[43] Carson imagined a farm on which human and nonhuman life had been blighted by deadly chemicals, resulting in a "silent springtime." The influence of environmental groups on pesticide decisions in commercial agriculture has increased dramatically since that time. It was not until 1977, however, that the USDA announced a goal of reducing reliance on chemicals by increasing research on strategies that use a combination of biological, chemical, and other controls.[44] The uncertainties, lack of information, and lack of consensus about the risks associated with pesticide use pose formidable problems to the economic analyst in estimating rates of return to agricultural research for improved pest control.

Uncertainty regarding the results of uses of biotechnology in agriculture also complicates rate-of-return estimates for agricultural research. Biotechnology is the application of living organisms to improve economically important processes. Frost-inhibiting bacteria, soil-dwelling microbes with insecticidal properties, growth hormones, and plant and animal vaccines using live, biologically novel organisms are examples of the application of recombinant DNA techniques in the development of products for agriculture. Proposals for the release of genetically engineered microbes, plants, and animals for widespread use raise questions about the potential effects on human health and the environment because the dimension of the risk is unknown.[45]

Genetic modification of grains and other farm commodities can enhance input or performance traits, including herbicide tolerance, increased protein or reduced fat, and drought tolerance. There is, however, widespread concern— particularly in western Europe—about the effects of genetically engineered products on human health. More than half of the consumers in Germany, Austria, Portugal, and Sweden, for example, consider genetic engineering to pose a serious food risk.[46] The production of farm commodities is driven by consumer demand. Hence, current European (and Japanese) restrictions on imports of genetically modified farm commodities and food products have the potential to decrease significantly the demand for U.S. farm products, at least in the short-run, thereby reducing the expected rate of return on investments in biotechnology in agriculture.

Agricultural research, including genetic engineering, also is likely to affect the structure of U.S. agriculture. Critics of research conducted by the USDA land-grant system have argued for a long time that this research focuses on problems of large agribusiness firms and that government agricultural and education agencies have abandoned their function of serving family farmers.[47] Recent breakthroughs in genetic engineering and the associated increased vertical integration in the production and marketing complex for farm commodities are likely to intensify these arguments.

Large agribusiness firms—including Monsanto, DuPont, and Dow—are the primary patent holders in genetic engineering. These firms are rapidly consolidating with traditional agricultural seed and processing firms with the goal of reaping the benefits accruing to developers of new technology. How quickly will the rapidly developing biotechnology be adopted? What will be the effect of these structural changes on the "family farm?" How will the changes affect the demand for farm products? It is impossible to identify, let alone measure, all of the indirect spillover effects associated with labor-saving technology, genetically engineered pesticides and seeds, and other fruits of agricultural research.[48] Yet these effects are relevant in any realistic measurement of the costs and benefits associated with government expenditures on agricultural research.

In view of the problems in isolating and measuring the costs and benefits associated with publicly financed investments in agricultural research, "policymakers must estimate the prudent level of investment without exact quantitative evidence of rates of return," weighing the costs of diverting resources from other productive uses.[49] Moreover, there may be little or no relationship between the objectively defined costs and benefits that any particular economic analyst projects and the evaluations that public officials (or the public at large) place on various alternatives. Collective-choice decisions inevitably are based on subjective considerations by members of the legislative process. Consequently, the problem of identifying inefficiency on the part of decision makers in the collective-choice process appears to be quite similar to the problem of identifying inefficiency on the part of private entrepreneurs (recall the discussion in chapter 2 that concluded that efforts along these lines are futile). In view of these considerations, there are ample reasons for skepticism about both the high rate-of-return estimates and the conclusion that there is underinvestment in publicly funded agricultural research.[50]

SUMMARY

There is a long history of publicly funded research and extension activities in U.S. agriculture. The goal of these activities is to improve technology, which increases supply and places downward pressure on prices of farm products. Improvements in technology, however, do not have the same effect on all farmers. Successful innovators gain from improvements in technology because their costs are reduced before the innovation has a significant effect on product price. After a technological innovation is widely adopted and the product price decreases, consumers receive most of the benefits of new technology. Expenditures that improve technology are inconsistent with farm price supports because increases in product supply make it more costly to support prices at any given price level.

More than half of the expenditure on agricultural research is privately funded. Publicly funded research is often justified on the basis of public goods and externality theory. However, most agricultural research and extension activities involving new varieties, new machinery, books, demonstrations, and fees do not conform to the public goods model because developers of these types of new technology can generally appropriate the returns through patents, copyrights, and user fees.

Despite the fact that agricultural research and educational activities appear to be mainly private goods rather than public goods, it is widely held that there is underinvestment of publicly funded research activities in U.S. agriculture. This proposition is based on empirical estimates of rates of return that are quite high. The high estimated rates of return from publicly funded research and educational activities in agriculture do not necessarily imply underfunding, however.

There are a number of reasons to be skeptical of the apparently high rates of return. First, the rates of return are not comparable with rates of return in the private sector because of tax considerations. Second, the estimates fail to consider costs associated with the misallocation of resources resulting from taxation. Third, there is a problem of specifying the appropriate costs and returns when there is no market measure of opportunity cost, as in the case of national defense, prisons, and so on. Fourth, the cost of undesirable spillovers associated with new technology are not taken into account. Finally, returns from publicly financed agricultural research are unlikely to be much higher than returns from privately financed agricultural research, as the rate-of-return estimates suggest, because returns from most agricultural research and education activities can be appropriated by the private developer through fees, patents, copyrights, and so on. In a competitive system, private investment will increase as long as returns to agricultural research are appreciably higher than from other investments of comparable risk.

In any analysis of the merits of public versus private funding of agricultural research, it is important to consider how each system operates under real-world conditions, taking into account information and incentive problems. Private firms have incentives to invest the amount that yields the greatest net return, but governments do not face comparable incentives or constraints.[51] In comparisons of public and private investment, it is just as important to consider pork-barreling and other non-market-failure problems associated with publicly funded research as it is to consider the market-failure problems associated with privately funded agricultural research and educational activities. Given these government-failure problems, it can be argued that governments may best encourage efficient levels of research investment by defining and enforcing property rights so that privately funded research can be profitably undertaken.[52]

The analysis in this chapter demonstrates that even in basic agricultural research, where much of the gain is captured by other firms and consumers rather than by the innovating firm, it is important to take into account problems inherent in collective decision making. When this is done, there is no persuasive evidence that an increase in government spending on agricultural research is warranted.[53]

19

Taxation in Agriculture

Federal tax laws historically have extended special treatment to individuals engaged in agricultural production. Prior to the Tax Reform Act of 1986, the tax benefits available to farm operators were also available to nonfarm investors who qualified as farmers for income tax purposes. Consequently, nonfarmers often used farming as a tax shelter because of the incentive to invest in farming by people in higher marginal tax brackets. As a result, aggregate farm "losses" for tax purposes exceeded farm "profits" reported on tax returns for several years prior to the Tax Reform Act of 1986. The 1986 tax legislation curtailed tax shelters and significantly reduced the attractiveness of investments in agriculture to nonfarm investors. The Taxpayer Relief Act of 1997 brought about the most significant tax reforms since 1986 by providing targeted tax relief to many groups, including farmers. The Economic and Tax Reconciliation Act of 2001 phases in a series of tax reductions over ten years. However, this act also greatly increases the uncertainty of tax law because it includes a provision that repeals all of the 2001 tax law changes at the end of 2010!

Farmers are subject to a variety of taxes at all levels of government. This chapter focuses on tax laws that extend special treatment to farmers—mainly in federal income and estate taxes. A number of legislative changes have been made in federal tax legislation since 1986, but the effects of taxation remain an important issue both for farmers and public policy.

The special tax treatment of farmers raises a number of questions. What are the major tax advantages in agriculture? How are tax advantages related to the system of progressive tax rates? What are the implications of tax preferences for agriculture? These questions are addressed following a discussion of "progressive" income taxes and the importance of marginal tax rates in decisions made by taxpayers.

MARGINAL TAX RATES AND THE PROGRESSIVE INCOME TAX

Taxation affects personal decisions related to work that generates taxable income, and hence it also affects individual productivity. Moreover, the marginal tax rate is important in individual decisions affecting resource use. It can be expressed as follows.

$$\text{Marginal Tax Rate} = \frac{\text{Change in tax liability}}{\text{Change in taxable income}}$$

For an increase in income, the marginal tax rate reveals how much of the additional income must be paid in taxes by the wage earner. For example, if an individual's marginal tax bracket is 28 percent and the worker earns $100 of additional taxable income, $28 of this income must be paid in taxes.

Much of the attractiveness of U.S. agriculture as a tax shelter over the years has been due to the fact that the structure of federal income tax rates in the United States is *progressive*. That is, as income increases, the marginal tax rate increases, and the tax takes a larger percentage of taxable income. The maximum marginal federal income tax rate in the United States in 2002 was 38.6.[1]

The importance of economic incentives on individual behavior has sometimes been heavily discounted, even by economists. The income-expenditure or Keynesian approach to the overall performance of the economy, for example, stresses the importance of maintaining a high level of aggregate demand. In the Keynesian approach, increased government spending will lead to economic growth, regardless of tax rates. In this view, taxes are merely a transfer, and tax rates can be varied with little impact on production.

The more recent supply-side school of thought, in contrast, stresses the disincentive effects of taxes. This emphasis on the importance of economic incentives and disincentives is not new. In fact, it is rooted in the ideas of Adam Smith and other classical economists. Taxes affect incentives in a number of different ways. First, as the marginal tax rate increases, the opportunity cost of leisure decreases. Consider a North Carolina worker in, say, the 31 percent federal income tax bracket, who is also subject to the North Carolina state income tax at the 7 percent rate. For taxpayers who itemize deductions, state income taxes are deductible from federal taxable income. If this worker earns an additional $100, he will pay $7 more in state taxes, and his federal tax payment will increase by $28.83 = (100−7)·0.31. Thus, his effective marginal tax rate is 35.83 percent. In contrast, the worker in the 15 percent federal tax bracket must pay $20.95 for federal and state income taxes if she itemizes deductions and earns $100 additional income. Thus, as tax rates increase, people can be expected to substitute leisure for work by taking longer vacations, doing less overtime work, taking earlier retirement, and so on.

Second, high marginal tax rates not only discourage work, but also cause people to work on jobs where they are less productive. An individual in the 36 percent tax bracket, for example, must earn $1,000 additional income to have $640 after taxes. Thus, a lawyer or teacher may be induced to paint her own house, repair the automobile, or perform other tasks where she is less productive. In this way, progressive income taxes can result in a pattern of labor use that is not consistent with the law of comparative advantage.

Third, high rates increase individuals' incentive to engage in illegal activities and to evade taxes on legal economic transactions. Economists refer to these unreported and consequently difficult to measure activities as the underground economy.[2] Unreported illegal transactions include drug trafficking, smuggling, prostitution, and so on. However, a large proportion of the underground economy involves legal goods and services that go unreported to avoid taxes. The legal but unreported transactions include such things as tips received by waiters and other service employees, and unreported cash sales or income by small businesses, plumbers, and other craftsmen working "off the books."

There is no way to determine the precise magnitude of the underground economy because the transactions are not reported. Estimates of these unreported economic transactions in the United States, however, range from 10 to 15 percent of total output (as measured by nominal GDP).[3] This suggests that unreported transactions in the United States totaled $1 to $1.5 trillion in 2001. The size of the underground economy quite likely is even larger in western Europe, where tax rates are higher, and in South America, where government regulations often make it more difficult and costly to operate a legal business.[4]

Finally, high marginal tax rates mean that many valuable resources are devoted to the tax shelter industry. Thousands of tax lawyers, accountants, and financial planners in the United States are employed in assisting physicians, lawyers, teachers, and other taxpayers in finding ways to reduce their taxes.

The 1986 Tax Reform Act significantly reduced the progressivity of the federal income tax. The marginal tax rate structure was simplified from fourteen brackets—ranging from 11 percent to 50 percent—eventually to only three brackets in 1991—ranging from 15 percent to 31 percent.[5] Two higher brackets were added in 1993, raising the maximum marginal rate from 31 to 39.6 percent. The 2001 tax legislation further modified tax brackets and reduced taxes, phasing in reductions over a six-year period. As of 2002, there were six income tax brackets, ranging from 10 to 38.6 percent. Although simplification of the tax system was supposedly a primary goal, the complexity of the federal income tax system has increased considerably since 1986 (recent significant changes were enacted in 1993, 1997, and 2001). Lawmakers, in seeking to be reelected, discovered that they could give targeted benefits, such as family benefits, with one hand while taking it away with the other hand by imposing ceilings, floors, phase-ins, and phase-outs. Many middle-income families are not eligible for the college tuition tax credit enacted in 1997, for example, because their incomes exceed the threshold to qualify for the credit.[6] Targeted benefits and other special provisions greatly complicate the tax code—and the difficulty of completing one's income tax return!

Let us now consider specific tax-based investment incentives in U.S. agriculture (table 19.1). We first consider major provisions of the federal income tax code that provide preferential tax treatment for farmers.

TABLE 19.1 Tax-Induced Investment Incentives in U.S. Agriculture.

Type of Incentive by Type of Tax	Advantage to Farmers
A. Federal Income Tax	
Cash accounting	1. Simplicity of record keeping 2. Reduces input costs (and increases post-tax income)
Favorable depreciation rules	Reduces taxable income
Estimated taxes	Not required to pay
B. Federal Estate Tax	
Use of agricultural use values in valuing farm estates	Reduces value of estate taxed
Extended time to pay estate tax	Installment payment plan—fourteen years rather than nine months
C. Local Property Taxes	
Special-use valuation (farm value rather than fair market value)	Reduces assessed value and federal estate taxes on qualifying farm real estate

THE FEDERAL INCOME TAX AND AGRICULTURE

The individual income tax, as suggested earlier, is designed to impose a progressive tax on an individual's net income each year. In order to tax net income, there must be rules for determining both gross income and offsets against gross income.[7] Although cash receipts from the sale of farm products are easy to measure, making offsets to obtain net or taxable income becomes complicated, especially where production involves more than one time period, as is often the case in agriculture. The most important tax advantages for agriculture are cash accounting and favorable depreciation rules, including the deductibility of certain capital expenditures.

Accrual versus Cash Accounting

The use of accrual accounting is generally required in calculating net income in the ordinary course of business. Under accrual accounting, income from the sale of, for example, an agriculture-specific commodity is matched with the expenses of producing the commodity. This matching of income and expenses requires that records be kept on expenses, production, inventories, and sales for each year. Under this system of record keeping, all sales in a given year are treated as income regardless of whether payment is actually received during that year. Expenses related to goods sold, whether paid or not, are taken as offsets against income in the year of sale. Under accrual accounting, unsold goods and purchased inputs are inventoried and included with income from sales of products in determining profits for tax purposes. That is, inventories of unsold goods are counted as revenues even though they have not been sold.

Under cash accounting, income from the sale of a commodity is taxed in the year payment is received. Moreover, with the exception of livestock purchased for resale (the cost of feeder cattle purchased one year and sold the following year, for example, cannot be deducted until the year of sale), expenses generally can be deducted from taxable income in the year the expenses are paid rather than in the year in which the goods are sold. The deductibility of prepaid expenses of most variable inputs, such as feed, seed, and fertilizer, is limited to half of other deductible farm expenses in the year of payment. Inventories of unsold goods are ignored under cash accounting, but the costs related to these goods are deducted when the costs are paid.

How does the cash method of accounting differ from the accrual method? In the accrual method, there is an attempt to match expenses with income from sales in the year that the sales occur. With this method, outlays on fertilizer and other inputs bought in the fall for use in the following spring, for example, are effectively matched against income from sales of the crop on which the inputs are used. Under the accrual method, farm business expenses are deductible in the tax year in which the farmer becomes liable for them. Thus, the fertilizer or other input would be deductible when purchased but must be inventoried so that its cost, in effect, is matched against income from sale of products that the fertilizer or other input is used to produce. In cash accounting, in contrast, the fertilizer or other input expense is deducted in the year bought, regardless of when it is used. As a result, expenses of production are matched with income from sales of those products under cash accounting only in cases where expenses are paid and payment is received for the resulting products during the same year. For example, expenses are matched with income if all costs of producing corn are paid and the entire crop is sold within a tax period. In farming, however, the payment received in one year often results from production in an earlier year (e.g., stored corn may be sold), and the expenses paid in one year frequently relate to production in a future year. When compared with producers operating under the accrual system, this mismatching of income and expenses in different tax years reduces farmers' tax liabilities because it is always beneficial to receive a benefit sooner rather than later. Stated differently, cash accounting causes taxable income to be lower in present value than the economic income accrued.[8]

Farmers and other small business firms are permitted to use cash accounting rather than accrual accounting presumably because of the complex record-keeping requirements required in accrual accounting. The ability to use cash rather than accrual methods is justified on the grounds that the more complicated accrual bookkeeping methods would impose a substantial burden on small firms. Farmers tend to benefit more from the use of cash accounting than nonfarm firms eligible to use it because of the relatively longer time lag in production between the purchase of inputs and the sale of products—particularly in the production of annual crops.

The use of cash accounting by corporations engaged in farming is allowed only for those with gross receipts of $1 million or less per year (or for those corporations organized as S corporations).[9] However, corporations engaged in certain types of farming activities are exempt from this restriction on cash accounting. Thus, nurseries (including sod farms) and agricultural firms involved in the growing or harvesting of trees (except fruit and nut trees) may elect to use cash accounting.

Prior to tax legislation enacted in 1987, corporations that met the qualifications to be defined as a "family farm" or a "closely held corporation" were permitted to use cash accounting no matter how large their gross receipts were in any year.[10] Consequently, it is not only farmers with simple bookkeeping systems who have benefited from the use of cash accounting. Tyson Foods, a corporate "family farm" poultry producer with sales of $1.1 billion in 1985, was permitted to use cash accounting prior to the 1987 Revenue Act. Hudson Foods Inc. and Perdue Farms Inc. were also considered family farms for tax purposes and received huge tax benefits from cash accounting.[11] "Family farming corporations" now must use the accrual method if their annual gross receipts exceed $25 million. A corporation (other than an S corporation) that is also engaged in a nonfarming business activity cannot use the cash method for the nonfarming activity if annual gross receipts (farm plus nonfarm) are more than $1 million.[12]

Expensing versus Depreciation

Operating expenses incurred by farmers and other businesses are generally deductible as an offset to earned income. Capital expenses as offsets to income, however, generally are treated differently from operating expenses; they are not deductible, but must be depreciated. A capital expense is a payment or debt incurred for the acquisition of an asset having a useful life of more than one year. Beginning in the tax year 2003, however, farmers and other businesses have been able to expense (deduct) up to $25,000 of newly acquired depreciable tangible personal property, such as machinery and equipment.[13]

Depreciation periods generally are short relative to the expected life for most types of farm property. For example, farm machinery and equipment items have a seven-year recovery period; single-purpose agricultural buildings (hog houses, milking parlors, and greenhouses) have a ten-year recovery period. That is, these assets can be fully depreciated over seven- or ten-year periods. When contrasted with a system in which tax write-offs correspond exactly to the life of the asset, there are tax benefits if costs of depreciable assets are written off before the property stops contributing to income. Moreover, recovery periods of depreciable assets generally are less than the expected life for nonfarm and farm investments. Thus, the special tax treatment in the depreciation rules for capital (as opposed to land and labor) leads to use of too much capital in agriculture, relative to labor and land.

As suggested earlier, expenditures incurred in the production of some farm products can be expensed, or fully deducted, in the year of purchase. Examples include: (1) costs of lime, fertilizer, and other materials that enrich the land for more than one year; and (2) soil and water conservation expenditures on USDA-approved conservation projects. Costs of growing plants that take two years or longer to reach the productive stage must currently be capitalized and either depreciated or subtracted from the sale price to determine the taxable gain when the property reaches the productive stage.[14] Farmers eligible to use cash accounting can still deduct preproduction expenses for these enterprises if they use the straight-line depreciation method on all farm assets put into use in the year the deduction is taken. However, most farmers find it advantageous to use the declining balance depreciation method and consequently must capitalize the preproduction costs of these productive enterprises.

There is a tax benefit from being able to deduct the entire amount of a capital expenditure in the year of purchase rather than merely deducting the amount of depreciation because the benefit from a cost deducted now is greater than if deducted later. Consider, for example, a farmer purchasing and applying lime that costs $10,000 and is expected to last for ten years. The entire amount can be deducted in the year of purchase. In contrast, if the farmer were required to depreciate the cost over a recovery period of ten years, only $1,000 could be deducted in the year of purchase (under straight-line depreciation). In this case, the cost of the lime for tax purposes is spread over ten years rather than being recovered in the year of purchase. Moreover, the reduction in taxes because of expensing for a given amount of capital expenditure will be greater the higher the marginal tax rate.

Gains on the Sale of Capital Assets

A change in value of a capital asset is not treated as income for tax purposes until the asset is sold. That is, only when a capital asset is sold is its increase (or decrease) in value recognized for income tax purposes. Capital gains tax rates were reduced by the Taxpayer Relief Act of 1997 for taxpayers in lower and higher tax brackets. Capital gains tax rates, as of 2002, ranged from 8 percent to 28 percent.[15] The capital gains provision of the tax law is especially important to farmers because they are three times more likely to report capital gains than are nonfarmers.[16]

Estimated Taxes

Taxpayers generally are required either to have federal income taxes withheld on income received during the year or to make quarterly estimated tax payments (on April 15, June 15, September 15, and January 15) and to file Form 1040 by April 15 of the following year. If more than two-thirds of income is from farming, however, quarterly estimated tax payments are not required. Qualified farmers, however, must file their tax returns and pay all taxes by March 1 of the following year. There is, of course, an economic advantage to delaying the date on which taxes must be paid because of the time value of money.

THE ESTATE TAX

The federal estate tax is a progressive tax on wealth transferred because of death.[17] The tax is computed on the value of the property owned by the deceased, and the tax is generally due nine months after death. There are exceptions to both of these rules in agriculture. First, the federal estate tax may be calculated on the basis of "agricultural use value" rather than on the basis of market value (table 19.1). In addition, qualifying farms and other small businesses are given an extended time to pay the tax, during which time interest on estate taxes due accrues at a rate well below market rates.

CORPORATE FARMING

Federal law generally does not place direct restrictions on the corporate form of ownership in farming. Nine states, however, currently restrict the ownership of farmland or operation of farm businesses by corporations except for family corporations or corporations with few shareholders and limited nonfarm income— Kansas, North Dakota, Oklahoma, Minnesota, South Dakota, Missouri, Iowa, Nebraska, and Wisconsin. Other states—Texas, West Virginia, and South Carolina—also impose "minor restrictions of various types."[18] Moreover, farm corporations are not eligible to borrow from the FmHA, and income earned by corporations and distributed to shareholders is taxed twice. Corporate income is taxed at the corporation income tax rate (maximum 39 percent), and income distributed to shareholders is also taxable.

There are two methods of taxing the income of farm corporations. The standard method, alluded to earlier, taxes income to the corporation. An alternate method permits shareholders to choose to have corporate income taxed to them individually (Subchapter S). Several potential benefits cause some farmers to incorporate.[19]

First, the total tax cost on corporate income will sometimes be lower than would be the case if the income were earned by an individual. Corporation profits not paid out as dividends may be accumulated at lower tax cost than if the profits had been earned by individuals because corporate tax rates are lower than individual rates at lower income levels. Second, with the incorporation and then transfer of shares of stock each year, farm transfers can be made more easily without physically dividing a farm. Third, the cost of fringe benefits such as meals, health insurance, and group life insurance can be deducted by the corporation, but their value need not be included in the gross income of shareholders (or other employees).[20] In addition, corporate ownership has the advantages of limited liability, and it provides a means of pooling capital. Aside from tax considerations, the disadvantages of incorporation are the initial cost and the time and expense of maintaining records.

There are two types of farm corporations—family-held corporations and those with nonfamily stockholders. Of these two types, family-held corporations are far more common, and most have no more than ten stockholders.[21] Although family-held corporations constitute only 4 percent of all farms, these farms accounted for approximately 23 percent of all farm product sales in 1997—up approximately 8 percent from two decades earlier.[22]

Similarly, neither the importance of nonfamily corporate farms nor the share of farm products produced on these farms has changed much in the past twenty years.[23] Nonfamily corporate farms constituted less than one-half of one percent of all farms in 1997, but accounted for approximately 6 percent of total farm product sales.[24] Most nonfamily corporate farms have fewer than ten stockholders.[25]

FARMING AS A TAX SHELTER

A tax shelter is an investment that allows taxpayers to reduce or eliminate tax liabilities on income by using preferential provisions of income tax laws. Tax liabilities are lowered to the extent that deductions are claimed against income earned from other sources while income from the tax shelter is delayed or reported in a way that subjects it to a relatively low tax rate.

Prior to the Tax Reform Act of 1986, U.S. tax laws favored agricultural investments in four ways. Investors in agriculture were provided (1) the option of using cash rather than accrual accounting, (2) the opportunity to expense certain capital investments, (3) a lower tax rate on capital gains than on ordinary income, and (4) investment tax credits. All of these provisions have been significantly affected by the 1986 and subsequent legislation.

An investor now cannot use a loss from a "passive activity" to shelter "active income" from other sources (including salary and portfolio income). For example, tax losses from farming cannot be written off against income from other sources received by nonfarm investors. The limitation on passive losses is intended to preserve tax advantages for bona fide farmers. Farmers who qualify as "material participants" in production are not affected by the passive-loss rules.

IMPLICATIONS FOR AGRICULTURE

Tax laws have a significant impact on agriculture for at least three reasons.[26] First, tax preferences are more valuable the higher the marginal tax rate. Thus, investments in agriculture are more likely to find their way into the hands of higher-bracket taxpayers because of various tax preferences. Consequently, tax laws have tended to concentrate farmland ownership in the hands of higher-income farmers. Moreover, tax preferences, to the extent that they increase demand for farmland, exert upward pressure on prices of farm real estate.

Second, and perhaps more important, the federal tax system affects the resource mix within agriculture. Tax policies tend to encourage the use of capital and to discourage the use of labor. The cost of investments in capital facilities is reduced through expensing and accelerated depreciation of depreciable property. Some capital inputs are depreciated much more quickly than other capital inputs relative to their expected economic lives. For example, farm buildings are depreciated over twenty years, whereas "single-purpose" agricultural structures are depreciated over ten years. Thus, tax policies both encourage the use of capital relative to labor and alter the capital mix in farming.

Third, preferential tax policies tend to attract additional resources into agriculture, bringing about an increase in farm output. The Tax Reform Act of 1986, however, reduced the attractiveness of agriculture as a tax shelter and the incentive to invest in agriculture. To the extent that current tax policies continue to attract more resources into agriculture relative to a tax-neutral policy, of course, the result is lower prices for farm products.

SUMMARY

Federal tax laws historically have extended favorable treatment to individuals engaged in agricultural operations. In the case of income taxes, farmers are permitted to use the cash rather than accrual method of accounting. Accelerated depreciation rules effectively reduce the cost of investment in capital assets. The depreciation schedule for a capital asset also is frequently shorter than the economic life of the asset. In addition, some capital expenditures—such as outlays for fertilizer, lime, and USDA-approved soil and water conservation practices—can be expensed (deducted). Further, farmers are not required to make estimated tax payments. In the case of estate taxes, it is often possible to have farmland valued on the basis of its "agricultural use value" instead of its market value, and farmers are allowed a longer time to pay the tax.

The federal income tax is progressive, taxing higher incomes at higher rates. Consequently, the tax preferences in agriculture are more valuable to the individual taxpayer the higher the marginal tax rate. The favorable treatment of agriculture in federal tax laws—when compared to a situation without tax preferences—is to increase costs that are deductible and consequently to decrease near-term taxable income. For example, assume that tax preferences decrease taxable income by $10,000 each for Mr. Smith and Mr. Jones—with Smith in the 15 percent bracket and Jones in the 36 percent bracket. The benefit of the tax preference is $1,500 to Smith and $3,600 to Jones. That is, a similar reduction in taxable income yields a much larger benefit to the farmer in the higher tax bracket.

Moreover, marginal tax rates have been increased since being reduced in 1986, and capital gains in agriculture (relative to ordinary income) again receive preferential taxation. Tax shelters are now curtailed so that only those involved in farming on a regular, continuous, and substantial basis can use farm losses to offset wage and salary income. The long-run tendency of the progressive tax system and the various tax preferences in agriculture—to the extent that they have persisted, however—is to increase investment and output in agriculture and to decrease prices for farm products.

Taxation in agriculture is an important public-policy issue. Moreover, taxation is but another example of the phenomenon described throughout the preceding chapters: unintended and indirect effects of government policies that benefit particular groups are quite often antithetical to other goals of government policies. For example, accelerated depreciation rules affecting the amount of federal income taxes farmers must pay increase short-run profits. Competition, however, causes prices of agricultural land and other specialized agricultural resources to increase as long as expected returns in agriculture are higher than those of alternative investments. Moreover, capital tends to flow between or within sectors of the economy until expected rates of return, net of taxes, are equal at the margin. Thus, as in the case of any other farm program, any tax break in agriculture has only a transitory effect on net farm income.

20

The Effects of Government Farm Programs

The economic evaluation of U.S. farm programs is not a simple task. The impacts of different programs are often offsetting. In this chapter, farm programs and the related expenditures are classified into several broad categories, and the major winners and losers from these programs are identified. Most of the effects of specific programs described in this chapter have already been discussed in earlier chapters in connection with the analysis of particular programs. The objective of this chapter is to describe the major effects of government programs in agriculture as a whole.

PROGRAMS THAT INCREASE PRODUCT PRICES TO FARMERS

The data in table 20.1 represent an attempt to separate budget outlays for various programs on the basis of their impact on commodity supply and demand.[1] Product prices may be increased by decreasing supply or by increasing demand. Expenditures on stabilization programs (the second column in table 20.1) historically included outlays that tended to increase producer prices of U.S. farm products through reductions in supply. Since enactment of the 1996 farm bill, or the FAIR Act, however, most of the effect of column 2 has been in the form of direct income transfers rather than programs that increase prices of farm products.

Programs may reduce supply in a number of ways, depending on the specific nature of the particular program. Production controls reduce the supply of farm

TABLE 20.1 U.S. Department of Agriculture Expenditures (Millions of Dollars).

DATE	(1) TOTAL[a]	(2) STABILIZATION OF FARM PRICES AND INCOME[b]	(3) FOOD AND NUTRITION PROGRAMS	(4) FINANCING FARMERS AND RURAL DEVELOPMENT	(5) FINANCING RURAL ELECTRIFICATION AND TELEPHONES[c]	(6) CONSERVATION OF LAND AND WATER RESOURCES	(7) RESEARCH EXTENSION, AND OTHER SERVICES[d]
1929	172	–	–	6	–	–	166
1935	1,218	749	–	81	10	–	378
1940	1,416	1,013	–	241	38	29	95
1945	2,265	1,470	–	340	16	325	114
1950	2,956	1,844	–	146	293	337	336
1955	4,636	3,506	84	180	204	286	376
1960	5,419	3,693	234	292	330	368	302
1965	7,298	5,084	300	285	392	425	812
1970	8,307	5,090	960	142	338	459	1,318
1975	14,977	1,855	6,174	3,252	274	652	2,770
1980	34,823	4,022	13,555	9,918	3,413	915	3,000
1985	55,530	19,488	17,994	11,093	1,555	984	4,456
1990	46,012	8,774	24,043	6,713	278	2,464	3,739
1995	56,667	7,293	37,492	2,052	120	2,876	6,834
2000	75,728	35,481	32,477	946	-1,855	976	7,704
2002	68,978	19,748	37,815	2,150	-1,766	1,280	9,751

Source: Data from 1929 to 1980 were taken from Clifton B. Luttrell, *Down on the Farm with Uncle Sam* (Los Angeles: International Institute for Economic Research, 1983), p. 17. Data from later periods are from Department of the Treasury, *Final Monthly Treasury Statement* (Washington, D.C.: U.S. Government Printing Office, various years).

[a] Includes off-budget outlays of $5 billion for FmHA and $255 million for electrification and telephones in 1975; and $6.881 billion and $3.387 billion for these purposes, respectively, in 1980. Rural Utilities Service loan programs through the Federal Financing Bank and FSA farm ownership loan programs are no longer off-budget and are included in spending totals for 1985, 1990, 1995, and 1999.

[b] Includes outlays for the FSA and Risk Management Agency.

[c] Net expenditures may be negative (or receipts exceed outlays) because of payments of principal and interest on outstanding loans.

[d] Includes outlays for Forest Service, plant and animal inspection, and administrative expenses.

products, thereby increasing prices to farmers. The impact of a generic supply-shifting program is depicted in figure 20.1. The 1996 farm bill eliminated production controls for wheat, rice, cotton, feed grains, and sugar, the 2002 farm bill dismantled the system of peanut marketing quotas, and in October 2004 the tobacco program was eliminated.

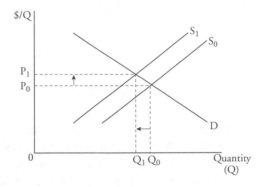

FIGURE 20.1 Production controls reduce supply and increase product prices.

The supply of farm products is also reduced by restrictions on imports of price-supported products, which were imposed to prevent consumers from consuming lower-priced imported products. Regardless of how production is reduced, however, the result is to reduce supply and to increase product prices to farmers.[2]

Various domestic and foreign food assistance and nutrition programs (table 20.1, column 3) increase the demand for farm products through government purchases, food subsidies, and export subsidies, thereby increasing product prices. The impacts of a generic demand-shifting program are displayed in figure 20.2. Price supports for milk are implemented through government purchases of manufactured milk products. Food stamp, school lunch, and other assistance programs increase the demand for farm products by subsidizing food purchases. Indeed, in the original New Deal food stamp and school lunch programs, the emphasis was much more on the disposal of surpluses than on adequate and suitable diets for the undernourished.[3] Similarly, much of the political support for PL 480 ("Food for Peace") as a program of foreign food aid over the years has arisen from its role in increasing the demand for farm products.[4] A wide range of domestic and foreign food aid programs continue to be important in maintaining the demand for U.S. agricultural products.

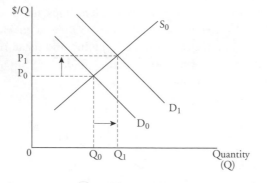

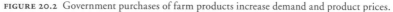

FIGURE 20.2 Government purchases of farm products increase demand and product prices.

International grain agreements (with Russia in 1975 and China in 1980 for five- and four-year periods, respectively) were designed to stabilize prices and to increase overall demand for U.S. grain. The agreements specified a range of grain exports to these nations each year at market prices. However, such agreements have relatively little impact on world demand and prices because any increase in U.S. exports is likely to be largely offset by reductions in trade with other nations. But the agreements may, at least to some extent, increase the demand for U.S. farm products. In general, government programs that increase demand have the effect of increasing prices of farm products and food prices to those who are not the direct beneficiaries of the programs.

PROGRAMS THAT REDUCE PRICES

USDA Programs

Columns 4 through 7 in table 20.1 include expenditures for programs that increase the supply of farm products and reduce farm product prices.[5] Government subsidies for agricultural credit and electric power, conservation of land and water resources (including flood control, irrigation, and land reclamation), and research and extension services reduce farm production costs, increase output, and decrease product prices (figure 20.3). Subsidized credit by the FSA, for example, adds to total resources in agriculture by providing more credit than would be available at competitive market rates and terms. Farmers are able to acquire equipment, livestock, fertilizer, seed, and other farm inputs at reduced costs and to improve the productivity of land through subsidized drainage, irrigation, flood control, and rural electric power. Research and extension activities reduce per unit costs and increase total farm output. The NRCS provides cost sharing to farmers to carry out conservation and environmental practices and is also involved in the development of soil and water conservation programs. Subsidized soil conservation and research activities tend to increase production in the long run, whereas irrigation and floodwater control provide immediate increases in output. Other government programs affecting agriculture—such as export controls on farm products, embargoes, tax preferences, and domestic wage and price controls—may have sizable impacts on farm product prices, but probably have relatively little effect on direct budget outlays.

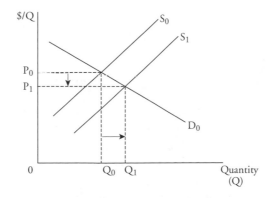

FIGURE 20.3 Subsidized credit, conservation practices, and research and extension services increase supply and decrease product prices.

Department of Interior Water and Power Subsidies in the West

Irrigation is highly important to agricultural production in the West, and water is frequently priced to farmers below its value in nonagricultural uses.[6] Substantial subsidies for surface water to agriculture in the West have been provided through water projects of the Bureau of Reclamation.[7] Irrigation districts also use artificially low-priced electricity produced by federally funded dams to pump groundwater for irrigation.[8] Although only approximately 150,000 farms benefit from federal water projects, the per farm stakes may be quite large. The capitalized value of the irrigation subsidies for a 160-acre California farm, for example, may be in excess of $100,000.[9] Although it is difficult or impossible to determine the magnitude of these water and power subsidies over time, "certainly it is in the billions [of dollars]."[10] These subsidies arise through programs of the Department of Interior rather than the USDA and are not included in the government outlays shown in table 20.1.

Agricultural production in the West has been significantly increased through Department of Interior water and power subsidies. There is a basic inconsistency, however, between such subsidies that increase agricultural output and USDA programs designed to decrease farm output. Without subsidized irrigation water, California would be relatively unimportant in agricultural production.[11] With subsidized irrigation water, California is the leading agricultural state in the United States. The water and power subsidies in the West not only distort the geographical pattern of agricultural production within the United States, but also increase the scarcity of water for recreation and urban uses in the West.

NET EFFECTS: WHO WINS? WHO LOSES?

Because some programs increase product prices received by farmers at the same time that other programs decrease prices, some of the expenditures are offsetting. USDA expenditures that increase demand and prices received by farmers totaled approximately $37.8 billion in 2002 (column 3, table 20.1). At the same time, expenditures that increase supply and decrease farm product prices— including outlays on credit, irrigation, research and extension subsidies—totaled approximately $11.4 billion (columns 4 through 7, table 20.1). Thus, although $38 billion was spent on farm programs to *increase* farm product prices received by farmers, almost one-third as much was spent on programs that *decreased* farm product prices. If the dollars spent on programs were equally efficient in achieving their conflicting objectives, expenditures that decrease product prices would offset an equal amount of expenditures that increase product prices. This suggests that $22 billion in 2002 may have been spent on activities having little (or no) net impact on food costs, farm prices, or total farm incomes. It does not suggest, however, that the programs were neutral in impact. There are important gainers and losers from farm programs, even if the expenditures, on average, are self-defeating. The identification of winners and losers is important in understanding the political support for farm programs.

Consumers and Taxpayers

The Treasury outlays on government programs that increase supply and place downward pressure on product prices are quite large, as shown in the previous section. The potential beneficial effects of reduced prices to consumers, however, are often negated by other programs that raise domestic product prices above world-market levels. Because of the network of farm programs, most of which are quite similar to their New Deal predecessors, prices of sugar, milk, fresh oranges, and a number of other products are higher than they would otherwise be. In the absence of domestic price-support programs and the accompanying import restrictions, U.S. consumers would be able to purchase many food products at prices lower, in some cases much lower, than those now paid. Consumers also pay for farm programs through higher taxes that are required for the operation and administration of these programs.

USDA budget outlays were approximately $69.0 billion in 2002 (table 20.1). This figure includes only federal outlays. "Outlays" are cash disbursements from the Treasury. These outlays, however, do not accurately reflect the total magnitude of federal activities in U.S. agriculture because interest subsidies and costs of guaranteed and direct loan programs in general are either excluded or presented in net terms after repayments and sales of assets are considered. The USDA also develops a "program-level" budget that purports to represent the actual economic cost of all financial assistance provided to the public. This calculation includes direct or guaranteed loans (including interest subsidies) and in-kind benefits, such as commodities distributed, for example, through the National School Lunch Program. The program-level budget for 1999 totaled $92 billion—almost $30 billion higher than the official "budget outlay." Even this figure does not represent the full impact of government influence because it does not include, for example, the value of subsidized interest on loans made by the FCS, which is a government-sponsored enterprise.

Owners of Specialized Resources

Within the agricultural sector, owners of land, allotments, and other specialized resources are the biggest gainers from farm programs. Owners of specialized resources receive windfall gains when price-support programs are initiated.[12] In the case of the tobacco price-support program, for example, the market value of the right to produce often exceeds $1,000 per acre per year. In addition, some farmers have received major gains in the form of subsidized credit and conservation subsidies. Gains achieved through the political process, however, require costly lobbying efforts. Thus, some of any benefit derived through the political process is dissipated through the lobbying and political contributions required to initiate (and maintain) the program.

Although owners of land and other specialized factors receive windfall gains either when a price-support program is initiated or when a price-support level is increased, the gains to later entrants into production are largely negated by higher production costs as expected benefits are capitalized into higher prices of land, allotments, and other specialized factors. Moreover, once a price-support program is in operation, its elimination imposes windfall losses on owners of affected specialized resources, regardless of whether they benefited from the original windfall. In reality, owners of land and production rights at any given time quite often are not the same people who received the windfalls when the programs were initiated (or when benefit levels increased).

Farmers as Producers versus Farmers as Asset Owners

The distribution of gains between producers and asset owners depends on how quickly the expected benefits or costs of program changes are incorporated into asset values. The preceding discussion suggests, however, that it is resource owners rather than farmers as producers who are the major gainers when prices of farm assets increase. And many owners of land and other farm assets are not farmers.

Labor versus Other Specialized Resources

Farmers as owners of specialized skills benefit from programs to assist agriculture. However, the effect of government programs on specialized labor is different in one respect from that of programs affecting specialized land or capital resources. The gains from government programs that reduce input prices or increase product prices are incorporated into higher market prices of land and other assets if property rights are well defined and assets can be bought and sold. In such cases, the farmer's wealth increases as a result of the increases in asset values. Following this increase, however, the asset owner can then expect to receive a normal rate of return.

The situation is different in the case of specialized labor or entrepreneurship, where the service provided is hired for a period of time but cannot be bought or sold (see chapter 12). In this case, asset value is based on the expected contribution during the contracted time period. Moreover, the asset owner receives an increased return each year as long as product price remains higher. Thus, the gain from an increase in product price in the case of specialized labor is not transitory in the way that it is for the owner of private property that can be bought and sold.

Farm Operators and Farm Labor

Price supports and subsidized inputs provide incentives for increased agricultural production, but competition for labor and entrepreneurial skills in other sectors tends to equate returns throughout the labor market. D. Gale Johnson concludes, on the basis of a number of empirical studies, that the supply of labor in agriculture is highly responsive to changes in wage rates.[13] If this conclusion is correct, it indicates that specialization of labor is not very important in analyzing the effects of farm programs. It also suggests that changes in product prices and the demand for labor result mainly in changes in farm employment rather than in changes in returns to farm labor (figure 20.4). Thus, whether the demand for labor increases (as depicted from D to D_1 in figure 20.4) or decreases (as from D to D_2) has little effect on wage rates. Johnson concludes that the return to labor in the rest of the economy is the main determinant of incomes to farm labor.[14] Any tendency for agricultural wages to increase when farm output increases as a result of farm programs provides an incentive for workers to move into the agricultural sector. The highly elastic supply of labor implies that nonfarm labor readily moves into (out of) agriculture if farm wage rates increase (decrease).

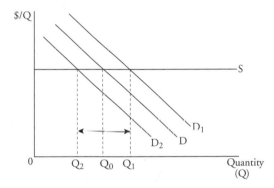

FIGURE 20.4 The effects of price support programs on the market for farm labor.

Some farm programs increase the demand for labor, whereas others decrease the demand for labor. On the one hand, an increase in product price, other things being constant, will increase the quantity of output supplied, which will (typically) increase the demand for labor. On the other hand, subsidized credit and tax preferences in agriculture reduce the cost of capital relative to labor and increase the rate of substitution of capital for labor, thereby reducing the demand for farm labor. Because the supply of labor is quite elastic, however, the effect of agriculture programs on farm wage rates is likely to be relatively small. Consequently, whether farm product prices are high or low has little effect on the return to farm labor.[15]

The effects of subsidized credit, conservation, research, and education programs that reduce cost and increase supply vary widely between farm operators. In the case of programs that increase technology, innovators gain in the short run, whereas those who adopt the technology later benefit little because of the increases in output and reductions in product prices. Although some farm operators gain from subsidized credit and conservation programs that reduce their costs of production, programs that increase output and decrease product prices have a harmful effect on those producers who do not receive the subsidies.

Government Employees

Government employees also gain from farm programs. The number of USDA employees increased more than fourfold from 1929 to 1999 even as the number of farms and farmers decreased at a dramatic rate. As the number of commercial farms and farmers has decreased, USDA activities have expanded into rural development, rural recreation, nutrition, and other areas, as predicted by the theory of public choice. Consequently, various USDA agencies now have a huge number of employees who have a vested interest in maintaining and expanding the scope of agricultural programs.

Resource Allocation

In a market system, resources are allocated to various uses on the basis of market prices. When resources are allocated on the basis of political priorities, the pattern of resource use will change. Consider the example of agricultural credit. In the market, lenders lend money at different rates to various borrowers depending on the perceived credit risk. Competition equalizes the rates charged in agriculture with those in other sectors for loans of similar risk. Subsidizing agricultural credit may lead to increased credit in agriculture and less credit extended to other sectors. Producers will use credit (and other inputs) as long as the expected value of the marginal product exceeds the interest rate. If the use of credit in agriculture is subsidized, producers will use more credit, and at the margin the rate of return on investment will be lower in agriculture than in other sectors.

It is important to recognize that a program that subsidizes credit is similar to other programs that arbitrarily change market prices. When the market price of credit is subsidized to a particular group, there is no objective procedure for determining how large the subsidy should be and no objective basis for allocating credit between agriculture and other sectors. For example , there is no standard measure of performance, such as profit, for assessing the success of federal loans or loan guarantees.

Similarly, land use, when allocated by market forces, is based on the expected return. Thus, land having the highest expected use in agriculture is used for agricultural production, land having the highest use for housing is used for housing, and so on. Prior to the 1996 farm bill, production-control programs in agriculture diverted some of the world's most productive farmland into nonproductive uses through various land set-aside programs. More generally, there has been a movement by proponents of "managed growth" or "smart growth" in recent years to ignore market price signals for land and to determine the pattern of land use through the political process. In the absence of market prices, however, there is no realistic way to determine which land to use for agriculture, for recreation, for housing, or for other purposes. That is, there is no known way by which public planners can obtain the necessary information on consumer preferences, resource supplies, and production opportunities to determine the pattern of land use that will best accommodate the competing demands for land. Indeed, there is a strong a priori case for decentralized competitive markets as the most effective means of coping with changing economic conditions in land use and other areas.

POLICY IMPLICATIONS

We pointed out earlier that there are two explanations for farm programs—income redistribution and the public interest. In the latter view, it is held that programs designed to increase and stabilize farm income benefit the public at large. Regardless of the rationale for the initiation of the programs, the continued existence of most farm programs such as price supports and credit subsidies appears to be better explained by income redistribution. These programs benefit mainly large farmers whose incomes, on average, already exceed incomes of the nonfarm population. The largest 8 percent of farms (in terms of gross value produced) received 47 percent of payments to farmers in government farm programs.[16]

At least on the surface, the inherent uncertainties associated with agriculture suggest that the argument that farm programs are necessary to stabilize agricultural markets appears to be stronger than the justification based on income redistribution. The stabilization rationale for farm programs also is weak, however. Indeed, much of the instability in U.S. agriculture since World War II has been caused or exacerbated by government policies, including inflationary monetary and fiscal policies, subsidized credit, and trade restrictions. Government attempts to stabilize agricultural markets are limited by the same incentive and information problems that thwart government attempts to stabilize the overall level of economic activity. Moreover, as the dependence of U.S. agriculture on international trade increases, domestic policies that reduce the competitiveness of U.S. farm products are increasingly counterproductive. The important lesson for U.S. agriculture is that government might make its greatest contribution to economic stability by attempting to do less.[17] Specifically, noninflationary monetary and fiscal policies and a more open economy are likely to be more beneficial to agriculture in the long run than government action programs designed specifically for the farm sector.

Protectionism and the Deregulation of U.S. Agriculture

In the late 1980s and early 1990s, there was increased recognition of the fundamental inconsistency between government farm programs and free international trade. Huge outlays on farm programs and domestic budget pressures, especially in the United States and the European Community, also were important in developing the climate necessary for a consensus to reduce protectionist farm policies—both domestically and in the global agricultural trading system. The result was the GATT Uruguay Round trade agreement in 1994, which created the WTO. Under the WTO, more than one hundred world governments agreed to reduce agricultural protectionism by reducing import restrictions, domestic support of agricultural prices, and farm income and export subsidies.

NAFTA was a less-comprehensive agreement to lower or eliminate regional barriers to trade over a fifteen-year period. It was formed between the United States and Canada in 1989 and extended to Mexico in 1994. Although more trade is beneficial, there is, of course, more to be gained from global free trade than from such regional trade agreements.

Despite the success of recent trade agreements in moving toward freer trade in agricultural products, much scope remains to reduce or eliminate protectionist agricultural policies throughout the world, including the United States. Most agricultural tariffs, for example, were not significantly reduced under the GATT. Furthermore, a host of other agricultural subsidies of various kinds continue to distort the pattern of agricultural production throughout the world. Another controversy and potentially highly significant barrier to trade in farm commodities cropped up in the late 1990s—mainly in western Europe and Japan—over the safety of genetically engineered farm products. In short, despite the reductions in trade barriers under NAFTA and the GATT, protectionist policies continue to shackle international trade of agricultural products in countries throughout the world.

The FAIR Act of 1996 followed in the wake of the GATT and NAFTA trade pacts. For a period after its passage, the FAIR Act appeared to represent a major change in the nature and direction of U.S. commodity programs. Target-price programs were eliminated, and farmers received "decoupled" lump sum contract (or transition) payments. The magnitude of the decoupled payments was not dependent on a farmer's current level of production of any particular commodity. This feature of the FAIR Act provided farmers greater flexibility in making planting decisions than under previous farm bills. Moreover, a widely held notion was that government payments would be eliminated or, at a minimum, be substantially reduced when the FAIR Act legislation expired.

Then, in the late 1990s, commodity prices fell dramatically. Loan rates, which were set at levels that seemed extremely low in 1996, became effective at the low market prices of the late 1990s. The government payments associated with the loan rates (primarily marketing loans and LDPs) were not decoupled. That is, these payments *were* dependent on the current quantity of a commodity that a farmer produced. In addition, for each of the years 1998–2001, Congress responded to low market prices by supplementing the lump sum contract payments with huge amounts of "temporary" disaster relief for U.S. farmers.

The Farm Security and Rural Investment Act of 2002 in some ways represents a return to pre-1996 policies. In particular, target-price programs have been reinstituted, albeit in a somewhat different form than the programs that were eliminated in 1996. The 2002 bill provides farmers with a three-piece safety net designed (in part) to maintain farm incomes without requiring Congress to enact annual ad hoc disaster-relief legislation. In other ways, the 2002 farm bill represents a continuation of FAIR Act provisions. A large proportion of the payments to farmers continues to be decoupled from current production under the 2002 bill, implying that the increased flexibility in making planting decisions is maintained.

Government spending on the agricultural sector was not reduced under the 1996 farm bill. Nor does it appear that expenditures will decline significantly under the 2002 bill. Thus, the income-transfer programs to the farm sector seem likely to continue as a feature of U.S. agricultural policy for the foreseeable future.

As indicated earlier, the rules for receiving lump sum payments under the 1996 and 2002 farm bills provide farmers much greater flexibility in making planting decisions than was the case under previous farm bills. However, the system of lump sum payments continues to increase the cost of producing farm commodities because payments to farmers are tied to the land under contract, thereby maintaining farmland values above their competitive levels. Despite the fact that the 1996 and 2002 farm bills continue to hold cost of production of farm products above competitive levels, "transition payments" unrelated to current production are more compatible with the spirit of WTO rules than are payments made under previous farm bills. That is, current U.S. farm program payments distort domestic consumers and producers' choices and international trade less than did the previous system of price supports and other foreign and domestic impediments to exchange. Activity in production and international trade of U.S. farm products is nevertheless significantly distorted when compared with a decentralized competitive norm.

Finally, the 1996 and 2002 farm bills continue the long-standing practice of transferring income from the nonfarm sector to the farm sector of the U.S. economy. Income redistribution, however, is determined by political considerations rather than by economics. No system of transferring income from taxpayers to farmers can be justified with claims that it increases social utility when any single interest group is benefited at the expense of the taxpaying public. Thus, the desirability of welfare payments to farmers is a separate issue from other types of government regulation of agriculture. Elimination of price supports and other impediments to trade is beneficial, regardless of whether income transfers continue to be made to farmers.

SUMMARY

U.S. agricultural policies have distorted markets for milk, sugar, tobacco, peanuts, cotton, wheat, and other products since the New Deal era. Persistent agricultural surpluses during most of that period can be attributed directly to price-support programs. Attempts to solve these problems through government payments, land retirement, and other means brought about a misallocation of resources and required that restrictions be imposed on imports to prevent consumers from purchasing less-expensive imported products. A fundamental inconsistency existed between these programs and the WTO goal of eliminating international barriers to trade in farm products. This inconsistency has, to some extent, been addressed in the 1996 and 2002 farm bills. These bills support farmers mainly through direct payments instead of with price supports for farm products, which often require trade barriers to function. Both bills, however, indicate a continued willingness to transfer substantial amounts of income to the agricultural sector.

Most of the benefits of farm programs—both in the past and under the 1996 and 2002 farm bills—are received by large farmers whose incomes already exceed, on average, incomes in the nonfarm sector. Price supports, for example, provide short-run gains mainly to owners of land, allotments, and other specialized resources because the higher product prices received by farmers are quickly offset by higher production costs. Price supports, lump sum transition payments, and subsidies for credit and other inputs also encourage farmers to over-invest in land and capital facilities. Finally, marketing orders, import controls, export subsidies, and other restrictions on competition distort the allocation of resources and restrict individuals' freedom to engage in mutually beneficial exchange. These domestic policies also are inconsistent with the WTO and NAFTA objective of achieving a more open economy.

The WTO objective of liberalizing trade is no less appropriate in agriculture than in other sectors. There is no persuasive evidence that the competitive market process is incapable of coordinating economic activity in agriculture. Indeed, with more than one-third of U.S. wheat, soybeans, rice, tobacco, and cotton being exported, the paradox of free trade and protectionist domestic farm programs was reflected in passage of the 1996 U.S. farm bill, which substituted direct payments to farmers for high price supports for products. However, the inconsistency between protectionism in agriculture and free trade was heightened with passage of the 2002 farm bill. Thus, there is a great deal of evidence that farm programs are better explained by income redistribution than by the public interest.

Finally, the notion of individual rights, including the right to make voluntary economic transactions, is central to questions concerning the appropriate role of government in agriculture and in other sectors. We feel that a convincing argument can be made that an appropriate public-policy objective with regard to agriculture is the development of an institutional framework that provides the maximum scope for individual choice. Only in this way can the nation's agricultural resources be used most effectively and the interests of farmers, consumers, and taxpayers best be served.

Appendix

The Farm Security and Rural Investment Act of 2002: How It Updated Existing Law

TITLE I: COMMODITIES

An important commodity program–related change made in the 2002 farm bill is the implementation of a system referred to as a three-piece safety net.[1] The components of this safety net are:

Marketing Loan Provisions. The new farm bill will continue the current marketing loan program at increased loan rates for all crops except soybeans. All production is eligible for the marketing loan.

- The $5.26 per bushel soybean loan rate was deliberately high in the 1996 farm bill to compensate for the fact that soybean growers did not receive AMTA payments. The new farm bill brings soybeans into the three-piece program with other commodities and lowers the loan rate to $5.00 per bushel, a level that is considered to be equitable to the loan rates for other commodities.
- Sorghum is a feed grain that trades on the same market as corn, but has a lower loan rate that has resulted in decreased plantings of this crop. The new bill raises the sorghum loan rate to a level equivalent to corn.

Direct Decoupled Payments. The amount of the direct, decoupled payment is equal to the product of the payment rate, the payment acres, and the payment yield. A producer can elect to receive up to 50 percent of the direct payment beginning December 1 of the year prior to the year the crop is harvested and the balance of the direct payment in October of the year the crop is harvested.

TABLE A.I Loan Rates, Direct Payment Rates, and Target Prices.

Crop	$/Unit	Loan Rates			Direct Rates		Target Prices		
		Current	2002 Farm Bill (2002-2003)	2002 Farm Bill (2004-2007)	AMTA	2002 Farm Bill	1995	2002 Farm Bill (2002-2003)	2002 Farm Bill (2004-2007)
Wheat	Bu.	2.58	2.80	2.75	0.46	0.52	4.00	3.86	3.92
Corn	Bu.	1.89	1.98	1.95	0.26	0.28	2.75	2.60	2.63
Sorghum	Bu.	1.71	1.98	1.95	0.31	0.35	2.61	2.54	2.57
Barley	Bu.	1.65	1.88	1.85	0.19	.024	2.36	2.21	2.24
Oats	Bu.	1.21	1.35	1.33	0.02	0.024	1.45	1.40	1.44
Up. Corn	Lb.	0.5192	0.5200	0.5200	0.0554	0.0667	0.7290	0.7240	.07240
Rice	Cwt.	6.50	6.50	6.50	2.05	2.35	10.71	10.50	10.50
Soybeans	Bu.	5.26	5.00	5.00	NONE	0.44	NONE	0.0980	0.1010
Minor Oilseeds	Lb.	0.093	0.096	0.093	NONE	0.0080	NONE	0.0980	0.1010

Countercyclical Payments. Countercyclical payments will be made whenever the effective price for a covered commodity is less than the target price. The effective price is equal to the sum of (1) the *higher* of the national average market price during the twelve-month marketing year for the commodity or the national average loan rate, *and* (2) the payment rate for direct decoupled payments for the commodity. The payment rate for countercyclical payments is equal to the difference between the target price and the effective price for the commodity. The payment amount for countercyclical payments is the product of the payment rate, the payment acres, and the payment yield. If, for example, market prices are above target prices (as they would have been in 1996), the producer would not receive a payment, and there would be no government expenditures.[2]

Table A.1 shows the loan rates specified in the 2002 farm bill for various commodities and how those rates compare to the loan rates in effect prior to passage of the bill.

Additional details regarding commodity-related provisions of the 2002 farm bill include:

· Base Acres. Producers are allowed to retain their current AMTA base acres and add oilseed acres or to update base acres to all covered commodities using 1998–2001 acres planted and prevented planted.

· Payment Yields. Producers who choose to update base acreage to the average of 1998–2001 plantings are also allowed to update yields for countercyclical payments. The update is the higher of 70 percent of the difference between current AMTA yields and a full yield update based on 1998–2001 yields on planted acreage *or* 93.5 percent of 1998–2001 yields on planted acreage. Provides a "plug" of 75 percent of the county average yield for years in which the actual farm yield is less than the county average yield.

· Timing of Payments. A producer can elect to receive up to 50 percent of the *direct payment* beginning December 1 of the year prior to the year the crop is harvested and the balance of the direct payment in October of the year the crop is harvested. For *countercyclical payments*, a producer can receive up to 35 percent of the projected payment in October of the year the crop is harvested; an additional 35 percent beginning in February of the following year; and the balance after the end of the twelve-month marketing year for the specific crop.

· LDPs. Includes authority for LDPs on grazed wheat, oats, barley, and triticale. Provides for LDPs for the 2001 crop on non-AMTA farms and waives beneficial interest requirements for the 2001 crop. Also implements a program of incentive payments to develop marketing opportunities for Hard White Wheat.

· Corrects USDA error to provide certain producers payments that were undelivered for crop years 1998, 1999, 2000, and 2001.

Dairy. Maintains a permanent $9.90 (per hundredweight) Milk Price Support Program and establishes a three-and-one-half year National Dairy Program to provide assistance to all U.S. producers. The program will provide a federal payment each month equal to 45 percent of the difference between $16.94 and the Boston Class I price. Payments are made on up to 2.4 million pounds of production for a producer annually.

Peanuts. Provides a quota buyout of 11 cents per pound annually for 5 years (55 cents total); provides a target price of $495 per ton; and allows for the payment of storage costs for peanuts under loan. Provides $355 per ton loan rate and $36 per ton fixed payment rate.

Sugar. Eliminates the one-cent per pound loan-forfeiture penalty and gives authority to the secretary of agriculture to establish quota allotments.

Wool and Mohair. Provides marketing loans or LDPs based on a loan rate of $1.00 per pound for graded wool, $.40 per pound for nongraded wool, $4.20 per pound for mohair, and $.40 per pound for unshorn pelts.

Honey. Provides marketing loans or LDPs based on a loan rate of $.60 per pound.

Apples. Provides assistance for apple producers who have suffered low market prices.

Pulse Crops. Establishes marketing loans and LDPs for small chickpeas, lentils and dry peas at the loan rates shown in table A.2.

Specialty Crop Purchases. Increases carryover-spending authority for Section 32 commodity purchases. Directs additional commodity purchases by requiring not less than $200 million of Section 32 funds per year to be used to purchase fruits and vegetables and other specialty food crops. At least $50 million of that amount is to be used for fresh fruits and vegetables for schools through the Department of Defense Fresh Program.

TABLE A.2 Loan Rates for Chickpeas, Lentils, and Dry Peas.

Small Chickpeas		Lentils		Dry Peas	
2002–2003 $/cwt	2004–2007 $/cwt	2002–2003 $/cwt	2004–2007 $/cwt	2002–2003 $/cwt	2004–2007 $/cwt
$7.56	$7.43	$11.94	$11.72	$6.33	$6.22

Step 2 Adjustment. Suspends the 1.25 cent price differential threshold for Step 2 marketing payments through July 31, 2006.

Payment Limitations. Relative to the House-passed bill, the framework reduces the limit on direct payments from $50,000 to $40,000; reduces the limit on countercyclical payments from $75,000 to $65,000; reduces limit on LDPs and market loan gains from $150,000 to $75,000; contains a separate payment limitation for the peanut program; retains current rules on spouses, three-entities, and actively engaged requirement; adopts a $2.5 million adjusted gross income cap on eligibility for participation in farm programs; retains the use of generic certificates in the loan program. Total dollar limitation is reduced from $550,0000 in the House bill to $360,000 in the conference framework.

· Creates a new commission to study and make recommendations regarding farm program payment limitations and the impact of payment limit policy changes on farm income, land values, and agribusiness infrastructure.

TITLE II: CONSERVATION

The 2002 farm bill greatly expands soil and water conservation programs. Federal expenditures on these programs increase by more than 80 percent above pre-2002 program levels. Specific programs are listed in table A.3, along with the costs of each program.[3]

TABLE A.3 Soil and Water Conservation Programs and Costs.

Program	Notes	Cost
Conservation Reserve Program (CRP)	Increases acreage cap from 36.4 million to 39.2 million acres. Retains priority areas. Expands wetlands pilot to 1 million acres with all states eligible.	$1.517 billion
Wetlands Reserve Program (WRP)	Increases acreage cap to 2.275 million acres.	$1.5 billion
Grasslands Reserve Program	A new program to enroll up to 2 million acres of virgin and improved pastureland. Program would be divided 40/60 between agreements of ten, fifteen, or twenty years, and agreements and easements for thirty years and permanent easements.	$254 million
Farmland Protection Program (FPP)	Since 1996, the program has provided $53.4 million to protect 108,000 acres. Funding increased nearly twenty-fold over amount committed to this program since the previous farm bill.	$985 million

TITLE III: TRADE

Roughly 40 percent of U.S. commodities are exported. Title III of the 2002 farm bill substantially increases funding for programs designed to maintain and expand foreign markets for U.S. agricultural products. These programs and their associated costs are listed in table A.4.

TABLE A.4 Foreign-Market Programs and Costs.

Program	Notes	Cost
Market Access Program (MAP)	Increases program spending to $200 million annually by 2006.	$650 million
Technical Assistance for Specialty Crops (TASC)	Provides exporter assistance to address barriers that restrict U.S. specialty crop exports.	$19 million
Foreign Market Development Cooperator Program (FMD)	Increases program spending from $27.5 to $34.5 million per year, with a continued significant emphasis on the importance of the export of value-added agricultural commodities into emerging markets.	$67 million
Food for Progress	Increases funding caps for transportation and administrative costs and sets a minimum level of commodities to be purchased for use in this food aid program.	$308 million
Global Food for Education Initiative	Continues pilot program for fiscal year 2003.	$100 million
Total		$1.144 billion

TITLE IV: NUTRITION

The 2002 farm bill maintains the linkage between agriculture and nutrition programs by allocating $6.4 billion to nutrition programs. It makes several changes to the food stamp program and other nutritional programs. Among other things, it

- Reinstates benefits for legal immigrants who have lived in the United States for at least five years. Also restores benefits for legal immigrant children and disabled individuals without minimum residency requirements.
- Provides five months of transitional benefits for households leaving Temporary Assistance to Needy Families (TANF).
- Includes provisions to simplify and streamline the food stamp program so that it better aligns with other public assistance programs and helps both recipients and state administrators.
- Reforms and streamlines the food stamp program quality-control system.
- Increases funding for the Emergency Food Assistance Program to $140 million per year. Provides commodities to food banks and soup kitchens and expands other commodity-distribution programs.
- Provides an increase in funding for both the Senior and WIC Farmers' Market Nutrition Programs.
- Provides additional commodities for the National School Lunch Program and includes a pilot program through which fresh fruits and vegetables will be provided free in schools.

TITLE V: CREDIT

The 2002 farm bill generally reauthorizes USDA lending programs and provides greater access to USDA farm credit programs for beginning farmers and ranchers. The bill also increases the percentage that USDA may lend for down payment loans, extends the duration of the loans, and establishes a pilot program to encourage beginning farmers to be able to purchase farms on a land contract basis.

TITLE VI: RURAL DEVELOPMENT

The Farm Security and Rural Investment Act of 2002 expands funding for rural development programs. These programs are designed to aid development of rural infrastructure and create jobs in rural areas. Specific programs are listed in table A.5.

· Community Water Assistance Grant Program. Sets aside appropriated funds for communities facing emergency drinking water shortages.

TABLE A.5 Rural Development Programs and Costs.

Program	Notes	Cost
Rural Local Television Broadcast Signal Loan Guarantees	Provides funds to allow rural residents in unserved or underserved areas to access their local television stations.	$80 million
Broadband Service in Rural Areas	Provides funds that allow rural consumers to receive high-speed, high-quality broadband service.	$100 million
Value-Added Agricultural Market Development Grants	Provides $40 million a year for grants to assist producer-owned value-added businesses.	$240 million
Rural Strategic Investment Program	Creates regional investment boards that may receive up to $3 million for economic development.	$100 million
Rural Business Investment Program	Provides $280 million in guarantees for rural business investment companies to provide equity investment for businesses.	$100 million
Funding for Rural Development Backlogs Program	Funds backlogged applications for water and wastewater programs.	$360 million
Rural Firefighters and Emergency Personnel Grant Program	Provides funding to train rural firefighters and emergency personnel.	$50 million
Total		$1.03 billion

TITLE VII: RESEARCH

The 2002 farm bill reauthorizes and establishes new agricultural research and extension programs. Funding for the Initiative for Future Agriculture and Food Systems is increased incrementally from $120 million a year to $200 million annually in fiscal year 2006.

· Cost: $1.3 billion.

TITLE VIII: FORESTRY

The 2002 farm bill commits funding for a new cost-share program to assist private nonindustrial forest landowners in adopting sustainable forest-management practices.

TITLE IX: ENERGY

The Farm Security and Rural Investment Act of 2002 is the first farm bill to contain a separate title devoted to energy programs. Programs funded under this title and their costs are listed in table A.6.

TITLE X: MISCELLANEOUS

Among the many other programs and policies covered in the 2002 farm bill, which has a length of six years, are the following.

Country of Origin Labeling. For meat, fruits and vegetables, fish, and peanuts. Required the secretary to provide guidelines for voluntary labeling by September 30, 2002.[4] For a commodity to be labeled a U.S. product, it must be born, raised, and processed in the United States. Commodities that are ingredients in processed products would not fall under the labeling requirement.

Family Farmer Bankruptcy Protection. Extends Chapter 12 Bankruptcy provisions to December 31, 2002.

Swine Production Contracts. Provides growers who have swine production contracts the same statutory protections as those provided to livestock sellers and poultry growers.

Disclosure. Clarifies that livestock and poultry producers can discuss contacts with state and federal agencies and other individuals having a fiduciary or familial relationship.

TABLE A.6 Energy Programs and Costs.

Program	Notes	Cost
CCC Bio-energy Program	Provides mandatory funding for the CCC Bio-energy Program, which will enable the secretary of agriculture to continue making payments to bioenergy producers who purchase agricultural commodities for the purpose of expanding production of biodiesel and fuel-grade ethanol.	$204 million
Biobased Product Purchasing Preference	Establishes a new program for the purchase of biobased products by federal agencies. Funding will be used to test biobased products.	$6 million
Bio-diesel Fuel Education	Creates a grant program to educate government and private fuel consumers about the benefits of biodiesel fuel use.	$5 million
Renewable Energy System & Energy Efficiency Improvements	Establishes a loan, loan guarantee, and grant program to assist farmers in purchasing renewable energy systems and making energy efficiency improvements.	$115 million
Bio-mass Research and Development Act of 2000	Reauthorizes and funds the Bio-mass Research and Development Act through fiscal year 2007.	$75 million
Total		**$405 million**

Notes

FOREWORD

1 C. Lowell Harriss, "Free Market Allocation of Land Resources," in A. M. Woodruff, ed., *The Farm and the City* (Englewood Cliffs, N.J.: Prentice-Hall, 1980), p. 144.

CHAPTER I

1 Frank H. Knight, *The Economic Organization* (Chicago: University of Chicago Press, 1933).
2 Don Lavoie, *National Economic Planning: What Is Left?* (Cambridge, United Kingdom: Ballinger, 1985).
3 Ibid.
4 Milton Friedman and Rose Friedman, *Free to Choose* (New York: Avon, 1980), p. 2.
5 Sven Rydenfelt, *A Pattern for Failure* (New York: Harcourt Brace Jovanovich, 1984).
6 Knight, *The Economic Organization*, p. 31.
7 F. A. Hayek, *Studies in Philosophy, Politics, and Economics* (New York: Simon and Schuster, 1967), pp. 96–105.
8 For a vivid illustration of how voluntary exchange enables thousands of widely dispersed people to cooperate with each other, see Leonard E. Read, "I, Pencil," *The Freeman*, December 1958, pp. 1–5.
9 Hayek, *Studies in Philosophy, Politics, and Economics*, pp. 91–92.
10 The discussion at this point is adapted from E. C. Pasour Jr., "The Institutional Framework and Agricultural Development: Implications of the Economic Calculation Debate," *European Review of Agricultural Economics* 19 (1992): 365–75.
11 Oscar Lange and F. M. Taylor, *On the Economic Theory of Socialism*, edited by Benjamin E. Lippincott (Minneapolis: University of Minnesota Press, 1938).
12 See selections by Mises and Hayek in F. A. Hayek, ed., *Collectivist Economic Planning* (London: Routledge, 1935; reprint, London: Augustus M. Kelley, 1975).
13 In the 1989 edition of their textbook *Economics*, Nobel laureate Paul Samuelson and W. D. Nordhaus assert that "the Soviet economy is proof that, contrary to what many skeptics had

earlier believed, a socialist command economy can function and even thrive." P. A. Samuelson and W. D. Nordhaus, *Economics*, 13th ed. (New York: McGraw-Hill, 1989), p. 837. Similarly, Soviet Nobel laureate Leonid V. Kantorovich ignored the importance of information problems in touting the use of mathematical approaches to economic planning, even as the death knell sounded for Soviet collectivism: "I am looking optimistically on the prospects of widespread mathematical models . . . in economic science and in all-level economic control. It can give us a significant improvement of planning activity, better use of resources, increment of national income and living standards." L. V. Kantorovich, "Mathematics in Economics: Achievements, Difficulties, Perspectives," *American Economic Review* 79 (December 1989), 22. On a more positive note, the 2001 Nobel Prize in Economics was awarded to George Akerlof, Michael Spence, and Joseph Stiglitz for their work on the economics of information. For a commentary on the shortcomings in these economists' treatment of issues related to the distinction between decentralized private information and centralized government information, see David R. Henderson, "What the Nobel Economists Missed," *Wall Street Journal*, October 12, 2001, p. A14.

14 M. Rothschild, *Bionomics: The Inevitability of Capitalism* (New York: Henry Holt, 1990), p. 334.

15 Robert Heilbroner, "Reflections: After Communism," *The New Yorker* (September 10, 1990): 91–99.

16 Terminology is attributed to Nobel laureate James Buchanan by Charles K. Rowley, "The Limits of Democracy," in *Property Rights and the Limits of Democracy*, edited by C. K. Rowley (Brookfield, Vt.: Edward Elgar, 1993), p. 20.

17 Jack Hirshleifer and David Hirshleifer, *Price Theory and Applications*, 6th ed. (Englewood Cliffs, N.J.: Prentice-Hall, 1998), p. 410.

18 A brief summary of the efficiency conditions associated with perfect competition is presented in the next paragraph. For a more detailed description and explanation of these conditions, see Hirshleifer and Hirshleifer, *Price Theory and Applications*, pp. 481–83, or other intermediate economics price theory texts.

19 F. A. Hayek, *Individualism and Economic Order* (Chicago: University of Chicago Press, 1948), chap. 4.

20 See F. A. Hayek, "Competition as a Discovery Process," in *New Studies in Philosophy, Politics, Economics, and the History of Ideas* (Chicago: University of Chicago Press, 1978), pp. 179–90; and Don Lavoie, *Rivalry and Central Planning* (New York: Cambridge University Press, 1985).

21 Israel M. Kirzner, "On the Method of Austrian Economics," in *The Foundations of Modern Austrian Economics*, edited by Edwin G. Dolan, 40–51 (Kansas City: Sheed and Ward, 1976).

22 Ibid.

23 Israel M. Kirzner, *Competition and Entrepreneurship* (Chicago: University of Chicago Press, 1973).

24 Ibid., p. 40.

25 Israel M. Kirzner, *The Perils of Regulation: A Market Process Approach* (Coral Gables, Fl.: Law and Economics Center, University of Miami School of Law, 1978).

26 James M. Buchanan, *What Should Economists Do?* (Indianapolis: Liberty Press, 1979), pp. 62–63.

CHAPTER 2

1 Paul Heyne, *The Economic Way of Thinking*, 9th ed. (Upper Saddle River, N.J.: Prentice Hall, 2000), p. 131.

2 Thomas Sowell, *Knowledge and Decisions* (New York: Basic, 1980), p. 52.

3 E. C. Pasour Jr., "Economic Efficiency: Touchstone or Mirage?" *Intercollegiate Review* 17 (1981): 33–46.

4 Harold Demsetz, "Information and Efficiency: Another Viewpoint," *Journal of Law and Economics* 12 (April 1969): 1–22.

5 James M. Buchanan, "Positive Economics, Welfare Economics, and Political Economy," *Journal of Law and Economics* 2 (October 1959): 125–38.

6 William J. Baumol, *Economic Theory and Operations Analysis*, 4th ed. (Englewood Cliffs, N.J.: Prentice-Hall, 1977), p. 530.

7 Ibid.

8 Jack Hirshleifer and David Hirshleifer, *Price Theory and Applications*, 6th ed. (Englewood Cliffs, N.J.: Prentice-Hall, 1998), pp. 207–22.

9 Lionel Robbins, "Economics and Political Economy" *American Economic Review* 71 (1981), p. 8.

10 "Any attempt to construct a rigorous and universally applicable criterion for distinguishing what policy change is an economic improvement must founder on the problem of interpersonal comparisons. Where a policy change affects some persons favorably and others adversely, as is usually the case, there is no a priori way of weighing the net results." Baumol, *Economic Theory*, p. 526.

11 Robbins, "Economics and Political Economy," and Robert H. Bork, "A Lawyer's View of Constitutional Economics," in *Constitutional Economics: Containing the Economic Power of Government*, edited by R. B. McKenzie (Lexington, Mass.: D. C. Heath, 1984), p. 228.

12 Milton Friedman and Rose Friedman, *Free to Choose* (New York: Harcourt Brace Jovanovich, 1980), p. 287.

13 William Breit, "Constitutionalizing the Regulatory Process: Comment," in *Constitutional Economics*, edited by Richard B. McKenzie (Lexington, Mass.: D. C. Heath, 1984), p. 210.

14 Ronald Coase, "The Market for Goods and the Market for Ideas," *American Economic Review* 64 (May 1974): 384–91.

15 Milton Friedman, *Capitalism and Freedom* (Chicago: University of Chicago Press, 1962).

16 B. Delworth Gardner, *Plowing Ground in Washington: The Political Economy of U.S. Agriculture* (San Francisco: Pacific Research Institute for Public Policy, 1995), chap. 6. See also Bruce Gardner, *Agriculture's Revealing—and Painful—Lesson for Industrial Policy*, Backgrounder no. 320 (Washington, D.C.: Heritage Foundation, 1984).

17 U.S. General Accounting Office, *Sugar Program: Changing Domestic and International Conditions Require Program Changes*, GAO/RCED-93-84 (Washington, D.C.: U.S. Government Printing Office, April 1993).

18 Ibid.

CHAPTER 3

1 Paul Heyne, *The Economic Way of Thinking*, 9th ed. (Upper Saddle River, N.J.: Prentice Hall, 2000), p. 159.

2 For a more complete discussion of the undesirable consequences of private choice, see Peter H. Aranson, *American Government: Strategy and Choice* (Cambridge, Mass.: Winthrop, 1981), pp. 79–98, and W. C. Mitchell and R. T. Simmons, *Beyond Politics: Markets, Welfare, and the*

Failure of Bureaucracy (Boulder, Colo.: Westview Press for The Independent Institute, 1994), chap. 1.

3 Heyne, *The Economic Way of Thinking*, p. 321.

4 David N. Hyman, *Public Finance: A Contemporary Application of Theory to Policy*, 6th ed. (New York: Dryden Press, 1999), chap. 4.

5 Ibid., p. 157.

6 For a discussion of the Edgeworth box analysis of the exchange process, see Jack Hirshleifer and David Hirshleifer, *Price Theory and Applications*, 6th ed. (Englewood Cliffs, N.J.: Prentice Hall, 1998), pp. 388–93.

7 F. A. Hayek, *The Mirage of Social Justice*, vol. 2 of *Law, Legislation, and Liberty* (Chicago: University of Chicago Press, 1976), p. 9.

8 E. C. Pasour Jr., "Pareto Optimality as a Guide to Income Redistribution," *Public Choice* 36 (1981): 75–87.

9 Ibid.

10 Heyne, *The Economic Way of Thinking*, p. 184.

11 Dominick T. Armentano, *Antitrust and Monopoly: Anatomy of a Policy Failure* (New York: Wiley, 1982), p. 42.

12 George Stigler, "Imperfections in the Capital Market," *Journal of Political Economy* 75 (1967), p. 291.

13 Heyne, *The Economic Way of Thinking*, p. 518.

14 Ibid., chap. 19.

15 Joseph N. Boyce, "Landlords Turn to 'Commando' Patrols," *Wall Street Journal*, September 23, 1996, p. B1.

16 Heyne, *The Economic Way of Thinking*, chap. 14.

17 For a more complete discussion of the undesirable consequences of collective choice see Aranson, *American Government*, pp. 98–113, and Mitchell and Simmons, *Beyond Politics*, chap. 4.

18 Paul Johnson, "Movement in the Market: Mobility and Economics in the Free Society," in *On Freedom*, edited by John A. Howard, 39–58 (Greenwich, Conn.: Devin-Adair, 1984).

19 An economic shortage occurs when quantity demanded is greater than the quantity supplied at the prevailing money price. We spot a shortage in real life whenever we find that the non-money cost of acquisition, such as waiting in line, rises to ration scarce goods. See Heyne, *The Economic Way of Thinking*, p. 83.

20 For a more detailed discussion of cartels and the incentive for individual members to "chisel," see Hirshleifer and Hirshleifer, *Price Theory and Applications*, pp. 249–52.

21 James M. Buchanan, R. D. Tollison, and G. Tullock, eds., *Toward a Theory of the Rent-Seeking Society* (College Station: Texas A&M University Press, 1980).

22 "Regardless of the particular justification for agricultural policies, however, they are currently supported principally by what economists call rent-seeking behavior." Thomas Gale Moore, "Farm Policy: Justifications, Failures, and the Need for Reform," *Federal Reserve Bank of St. Louis Review* 69, no. 8 (October 1987), p. 7. See also Mitchell and Simmons, *Beyond Politics*, chap. 6.

23 The discussion here draws heavily on E. C. Pasour Jr., "Rent Seeking: Some Conceptual Problems and Implications," *Review of Austrian Economics* 1 (1987): 123–43.

24 D. H. Song and M. C. Hallberg, "Measuring Producers' Advantage from Classified Pricing of Milk," *American Journal of Agricultural Economics* 64 (February 1982), p. 7.

25 Aranson, *American Government*, p. 107.

26 Kenneth J. Arrow, *Social Choice and Individual Values*, 2d ed. (New York: Wiley, 1963).

27 James M. Buchanan and Gordon Tullock, *The Calculus of Consent: Logical Foundations of Constitutional Democracy* (Ann Arbor: University of Michigan Press, 1967), p. 334.

28 Peter J. Boettke, "Hayek's Serfdom Revisited: Government Failure in the Argument Against Socialism," *Eastern Economic Journal* 21 (Winter 1995), pp. 19–20.

29 Harold Demsetz, "Information and Efficiency: Another Viewpoint," *Journal of Law and Economics* 12 (April 1969): 1–22.

30 Ibid.

CHAPTER 4

1 For a good introduction to public-choice theory, see James Gwartney and Richard E. Wagner, "The Public Choice Revolution," *Intercollegiate Review* 23 (Spring 1988): 17–26.

2 Peter H. Aranson, *American Government: Strategy and Choice* (Cambridge, Mass.: Winthrop, 1981), p. 18.

3 See Ronald D. Knutson, J. B. Penn, and B. L. Flinchbaugh, *Agricultural and Food Policy*, 4th ed. (Englewood Cliffs, N.J.: Prentice-Hall, 1998), chap. 3, for a more detailed description of government institutions.

4 See Richard Posner, *Analysis of Law*, 5th ed. (New York: Aspen Law and Business, 1998), on the judicial decision-making process.

5 Bernard Grofman, "Models of Voter Turnout: A Brief Idiosyncratic Review," *Public Choice* 41 (1983), p. 57.

6 Aranson, *American Government*, p. 243.

7 Ibid., p. 250.

8 Ibid., pp. 250–54.

9 Ibid., p. 252.

10 William S. Maddox and Stuart A. Lilie, *Beyond Liberal and Conservative: Reassessing the Political Spectrum* (Washington, D.C.: Cato Institute, 1984).

11 Aranson, *American Government*, p. 356.

12 The discussion here draws heavily on Knutson, Penn, and Flinchbaugh, *Agricultural and Food Policy*, chap. 3.

13 Barry R. Weingast, "The Congressional-Bureaucratic System: A Principal Agent Perspective (with Applications to the SEC)," *Public Choice* 44 (1984): 147–91.

14 Ibid., p. 155.

15 Aranson, *American Government*, p. 446.

16 William A. Niskanen Jr., *Bureaucracy and Representative Government* (Chicago: Aldine-Atherton, 1971), p. 39.

17 For a critical discussion of related issues, see Ronald N. Johnson and Gary D. Libecap, *The Federal Civil Service System and the Problem of Bureaucracy* (Chicago: Chicago University Press, 1994). Johnson and Libecap argue, for example, that careful analysis of available data indicates no significant relationship between agency growth and salary. They attribute this finding to the elaborate set of rules governing salary structures in the federal civil service system.

18 James T. Bennett and T. J. DiLorenzo, *Underground Government: The Off-Budget Public Sector* (Washington, D.C.: Cato Institute, 1983), p. 5.

19 Weingast, "The Congressional-Bureaucratic System," pp. 149–50.

20 William C. Mitchell, "Fiscal Behavior of the Modern Democratic State: Public Choice Perspectives and Contributions," in *Political Economy*, edited by Larry C. Wade (Boston: Kluwer-Nijhoff, 1983), p. 89.

21 William C. Mitchell, "Efficiency, Responsibility, and Democratic Politics," in *Liberal Democracy*, edited by J. R. Pennock and J. W. Chapman (New York: New York University Press, 1983), p. 346.

22 Herman E. Talmadge, "Political Realities Affecting Agricultural Legislation," in *Farm and*

Food Policy: Critical Issues for Southern Agriculture, edited by M. D. Hammig and H. M. Harris Jr. (Clemson, S.C.: Clemson University, June 1983), p. 85.

23 The reason a federal government budget surplus finally emerged in 1998 after continuous budget deficits from 1967 is discussed in chapter 5.

24 Edward R. Tufte, *Political Control of the Economy* (Princeton, N.J.: Princeton University Press, 1978).

25 George S. Stigler, "The Theory of Economic Regulation," *Bell Journal of Economics and Management Science* 2 (Spring 1971): 3–21.

26 Richard Stroup and John Baden, "Property Rights and Natural Resource Management," *Literature of Liberty* 2 (September–December 1979), p. 12.

27 Bruce Benson and John Baden, "The Political Economy of Governmental Corruption: The Logic of Underground Government," *Journal of Legal Studies* 14 (June 1985): 391–410.

28 Such efforts, in fact, have a long history. See Johnson and Libecap, *The Federal Civil Service System*, for a historical account of the federal civil service system. See in particular chapter 1 for a description of efforts made over time to "reform" the system.

29 Both the concept and examples of privatization at local, state, and federal levels are discussed in Lawrence W. Reed, *Private Cures for Public Ills: The Promise of Privatization* (Irvington on-Hudson, N.Y.: Foundation for Economic Education, 1996).

30 See E. S. Savas, *Privatizing the Public Sector* (Chatham, N.J.: Chatham House, 1982), or, more recent, William C. Mitchell and Randy T. Simmons, *Beyond Politics: Markets, Welfare, and the Failure of Bureaucracy* (Boulder, Colo.: Westview Press, 1994), chapter 13.

31 E. C. Pasour Jr. and F. G. Scrimgeour, "New Zealand Economic Reforms: Implications for U.S. Farm Policy," *Choices* 10 (1995): 15–18.

CHAPTER 5

1 Robert Higgs, *Crisis and Leviathan: Critical Episodes in the Growth of American Government* (New York: Oxford University Press, 1987), p. 171.

2 Ronald D. Knutson, J. B. Penn, and B. L. Flinchbaugh, *Agricultural and Food Policy*, 4th ed. (Englewood Cliffs, N.J.: Prentice-Hall, 1998), p. 44.

3 See Don Paarlberg, "A New Agenda for Agriculture," chap. 12 in *The New Politics of Food*, edited by D. F. Hadwiger and W. P. Browne (Lexington, Mass.: D. C. Heath, 1978), and Knutson, Penn, and Flinchbaugh, *Agricultural and Food Policy*, chap. 4.

4 Knutson, Penn, and Flinchbaugh, *Agricultural and Food Policy*, chap. 4.

5 George P. Schultz, "Reflections on Political Economy," selection 32 in *The Economic Approach to Public Policy*, edited by R. C. Amacher, R. D. Tollison, and T. D. Willett (Ithaca, N.Y.: Cornell University Press, 1978).

6 B. Delworth Gardner, *Plowing Ground in Washington: The Political Economy of U.S. Agriculture* (San Francisco: Pacific Research Institute for Public Policy, 1995), p. 226.

7 Bruce Ingersoll, "Big Sugar Seeks Bailout, Gives Money to Help Get Way," *Wall Street Journal*, April 27, 2000 at: http://online.wsj.com/article/0,,SB956797227674205904,00.htm. Other commodity groups with contributions in excess of $1 million during this period included livestock ($5.7 million), dairy ($5.1 million), fruits and vegetables ($4.6 million), poultry and eggs ($2.9 million), rice and peanuts ($1.3 million), and cotton ($1.1 million).

8 Gardner, *Plowing Ground in Washington*, chap. 9.

9 See the appendix on the 2002 farm bill and the discussion of the 1996 farm bill in chapter 10 for more information on the specific provisions of these bills.

10 Bruce L. Gardner, "Causes of U.S. Farm Commodity Programs," *Journal of Political Economy*

95 (April 1987): 290–310.

11 Don F. Hadwiger, "Agricultural Policy," in *Encyclopedia of Policy Studies*, edited by Stuart S. Nagel (New York: Marcel Dekker, 1983), p. 513.

12 Paul Heyne, *The Economic Way of Thinking* (Upper Saddle River, N.J.: Prentice Hall, 2000), p. 520.

13 *Economic Report of the President* (Washington, D.C.: U.S. Government Printing Office, 1999), p. 420.

14 Ibid.

15 Edwin S. Mills, *The Burden of Government* (Stanford, Calif.: Hoover Institution Press, 1986).

16 Mancur Olson, *The Rise and Decline of Nations* (New Haven, Conn.: Yale University Press, 1982).

17 F. A. Hayek, *The Political Order of a Free People*, vol. 3 of *Law, Legislation, and Liberty* (Chicago: University of Chicago Press, 1979), p. 150.

18 This section draws heavily on F. G. Scrimgeour and E. C. Pasour Jr., "A Public Choice Perspective on Agricultural Policy Reform: The New Zealand Experience," *American Journal of Agricultural Economics* 78 (May 1996): 257–67.

19 For a discussion of the prisoners' dilemma and a lucid introduction to game theory, see Jack Hirshleifer and David Hirshleifer, *Price Theory and Applications*, 6th ed. (Upper Saddle River, N.J.: Prentice Hall, 1998), chap. 10.

20 R. E. Wagner, *Parchment, Guns, and Constitutional Order* (Brookfield, Vt.: Edward Elgar, 1993).

21 The dinner check analogy is borrowed from Richard H. Thaler, "Illusions and Mirages in Public Policy," *The Public Interest* (Fall 1983): 60–74.

22 Heyne, *The Economic Way of Thinking*, p. 519.

23 William C. Mitchell and Randy T. Simmons, *Beyond Politics: Markets, Welfare, and the Failure of Bureaucracy* (Boulder, Colo.: Westview Press, 1994), chap. 11.

24 James M. Buchanan, "Alternative Perspectives on Economics and Public Policy," *Cato Policy Report* 6 (January 1984): 1–5.

25 Norman J. Ornstein, "The Politics of the Deficit," chap. 11 in *Essays in Contemporary Economic Problems 1985: The Economy in Deficit* (Washington, D.C.: American Enterprise Institute, 1985).

26 T. L. Anderson and P. J. Hill, *The Birth of a Transfer Society* (Stanford, Calif.: Hoover Institution Press, 1980).

27 F. G. Scrimgeour and E. C. Pasour Jr., "The Public Choice Revolution and New Zealand Farm Policy," *Review of Marketing and Agricultural Economics* 62 (August 1994): 273–83.

28 J. D. Gwartney and R. E. Wagner, "The Public Choice Revolution," *Intercollegiate Review* 23 (spring 1988): 17–26.

29 James M. Buchanan is the individual most closely identified with this subfield of public-choice theory. See, for example, James M. Buchanan, "The Domain of Constitutional Political Economy," chap. 1 in *The Economics and the Ethics of Constitutional* (Ann Arbor: University of Michigan Press, 1991); James M. Buchanan, "Clarifying Confusion about the Balanced Budget Amendment," *National Tax Journal* 48 (1995): 347–55; James M. Buchanan, "The Balanced Budget Amendment: Clarifying the Arguments," *Public Choice* 90 (March 1997): 117–38. The academic journal *Constitutional Political Economy* was initiated in 1990 to focus on this subfield of public-choice theory involving the study of rules, how rules work, and how rules might be chosen.

30 Buchanan, "Alternative Perspectives," p. 5.

31 F. A. Hayek, *The Essence of Hayek*, edited by C. Nishiyama and K. Leube (Stanford, Calif.: Hoover University Press, 1984), p. 404.

32 Olson, *The Rise and Decline of Nations*, p. 109.

33 Ornstein, "The Politics of the Deficit," p. 333.

34 Terry L. Anderson and Peter J. Hill, *The Birth of a Transfer Society* (Stanford, Calif.: Hoover Institution Press, 1980), p. 93.

35 James M. Buchanan, *Freedom in Constitutional Contract: Perspectives of a Political Economist* (College Station: Texas A&M University Press, 1977).

36 Richard B. McKenzie, ed., *Constitutional Economics: Containing the Economic Powers of Government* (Lexington, Mass.: D. C. Heath, 1984). A line item veto bill of a sort was signed into law by President Clinton on April 9, 1996. It merely strengthened the president's existing power to propose to rescind items in bills already signed into law. Moreover, it was soon ruled unconstitutional by the U.S. Supreme Court. A true line item veto—one that would allow the president to strike individual lines of bills unless overridden by two-thirds of both houses—requires amending the Constitution.

37 Dennis S. Ippolito, *Congressional Spending* (Ithaca, N.Y.: Cornell University Press, 1981), p. 250.

38 Ornstein, "The Politics of the Deficit," p. 331.

39 Richard M. Weaver, *Ideas Have Consequences* (Chicago: University of Chicago Press, 1948).

40 Scrimgeour and Pasour, "A Public Choice Perspective on Agricultural Policy Reform."

41 E. C. Pasour Jr., "Economists and the Public Policy Process: What Can Economists Do?" *New Zealand Economic Papers* 27 (June 1993): 1–17.

42 *Economic Report of the President*, p. 420.

43 Hayek, *The Political Order of a Free People*, p. 134.

CHAPTER 6

1 E. C. Pasour Jr., "Economic Growth and Agriculture: An Evaluation of the Compensation Principle," *American Journal of Agricultural Economics* 55 (November 1973): 611–16.

2 For other perspectives on the farm problem, see Ronald D. Knutson, J. B. Penn, and Barry L. Flinchbaugh, *Agricultural and Food Policy*, 4th ed. (Upper Saddle River, N.J.: Prentice Hall, 1998), chap. 9, and Steven C. Blank, *The End of Agriculture in the American Portfolio* (Westport, Conn.: Quorum, 1998). Blank argues, in fact, that American agricultural production will end as a result of a natural process that makes producers better off.

3 U.S. Bureau of the Census, *Statistical Abstract of the United States: 1998* (Washington, D.C.: U.S. Government Printing Office, 1998), and USDA, Agricultural Statistics (Washington, D.C.: U.S. Government Printing Office, 1995–96).

4 E. C. Pasour Jr., "The Free Rider as a Basis for Government Intervention," *Journal of Libertarian Studies* 5 (Fall 1981): 453–63.

5 Mark Lilla, "Why the 'Income Distribution' Is so Misleading," *The Public Interest* 77 (Fall 1984): 62–76.

6 W. Michael Cox and Richard Alm, *By Our Own Bootstraps: Economic Opportunity and the Dynamics of Income Distribution*, Annual Report (Dallas: Federal Reserve Bank of Dallas, 1995), pp. 2–24.

7 Ibid., p. 8.

8 Mark Lilla, "Why the 'Income Distribution' Is so Misleading.".

9 During the 1960s, in contrast, farmers derived more than 40 percent of total household income from farm earnings.

10 See data on farm income in the USDA Web site at: http://www.ers.usda.gov/data/farmincome/finfidmu.ht.

11 David N. Hyman, *Public Finance: A Contemporary Application of Theory to Policy*, 6th ed. (Orlando, Fl.: Dryden Press, 1999), p. 431.

12 See the Environmental Working Group Farm Subsidy Database, 1996–2001, at http://www. ewg.org/farm/.

13 F. A. Hayek, *The Mirage of Social Justice*, vol. 2 of *Law, Legislation, and Liberty* (Chicago: University of Chicago Press, 1976).

14 Chiaki Nishiyama and K. R. Leube, *The Essence of Hayek* (Stanford, Calif.: Hoover Institution Press, 1984), pp. 77–78.

15 John Hospers, "Justice versus Social Justice," *The Freeman* 35 (January 1985), p. 24. Hospers defines a just wage as "the wage that one's services can command on a free market" (p. 19).

16 See Robert Nozick, *Anarchy, State, and Utopia* (New York: Basic, 1974); F. A. Hayek, *The Political Order of a Free People*, vol. 3 of *Law, Legislation, and Liberty* (Chicago: University of Chicago Press, 1979); James M. Buchanan, *The Economics and the Ethics of Constitutional Order* (Ann Arbor: University of Michigan Press, 1991).

CHAPTER 7

1 See B. Delworth Gardner, *Plowing Ground in Washington: The Political Economy of U.S. Agriculture* (San Francisco: Pacific Research Institute for Public Policy, 1995), chap. 1. Some economic analysts consider the 1996 farm bill to represent a "watershed change" in farm policy. See Ronald D. Knutson, J. B. Penn, and Barry L. Flinchbaugh, *Agricultural and Food Policy*, 4th ed. (Upper Saddle River, N.J.: Prentice Hall, 1998), p. 276.

2 Bruce L. Gardner, *The Governing of Agriculture* (Lawrence: Regents Press of Kansas, 1981), p. 48.

3 An important source for the material in this section is James D. Gwartney and Richard L. Stroup, *Economics: Private and Public Choice*, 9th ed. (Fort Worth, Tex.: Dryden Press, Harcourt Brace College, 2000), pp. 383–84.

4 Christian Saint-Etienne, *The Great Depression, 1929–1938* (Stanford, Calif.: Hoover Institution Press, 1984).

5 Ibid., p. 38.

6 Benjamin M. Anderson, *Economics and the Public Welfare* (Indianapolis: Liberty Press, 1979), p. 229.

7 Daniel J. B. Mitchell, "Wage Flexibility in the United States: Lessons from the Past," *American Economic Review* 75 (May 1985): 36–40.

8 Robert Higgs, *Crisis and Leviathan: Critical Episodes in the Growth of American Government* (New York: Oxford University Press, 1987), p. 178.

9 Anderson, *Economics and the Public Welfare*.

10 Gwartney and Stroup, *Economics*, p. 383.

11 Saint-Etienne, *The Great Depression*, p. 41.

12 Robert Higgs, "The Sources of Big Government," *Intercollegiate Review* 20 (1984): 23–33.

13 Quoted in Alan Nevins, *Grover Cleveland: A Study in Courage* (New York: Dodd, Mead, 1933), p. 332.

14 Higgs, *Crisis and Leviathan*, p. 30.

15 Ibid., p. 171.

16 William A. Niskanen, "The Growth of Government," *Cato Policy Report* 7 (July–August 1985): 8–10.

CHAPTER 8

1 Harold G. Halcrow, *Food Policy for America* (New York: McGraw-Hill, 1977), p. 11.
2 USDA, National Agricultural Statistical Service, *Agricultural Statistics: 2002* (Washington, D.C.: U.S. Government Printing Office, 2002), available at: http://www.usda.gov/nass/pubs/agr02/acro02.htm. The index used in this calculation is the index of prices paid by farmers for commodities, interest, taxes, and wage rates.
3 Ibid.
4 Lloyd D. Teigen, *Agricultural Parity: Historical Review and Alternative Calculations*, USDA, Economic Research Service, no. 571 (Washington, D.C.: U.S. Government Printing Office, 1987), p. 7.
5 Ibid.
6 USDA, National Agricultural Statistical Service, *Agricultural Statistics: 2002.*
7 Ronald D. Knutson, J. B. Penn, and B. L. Flinchbaugh, *Agricultural and Food Policy*, 4th ed. (Englewood Cliffs, N.J.: Prentice-Hall, 1998), p. 260.
8 Teigen, *Agricultural Parity*, p. 11.
9 James M. Buchanan, *Cost and Choice* (Chicago: Markham, 1969).
10 Based on unpublished summary of farm records from the Farm Business Management System, Department of Agricultural and Resource Economics, North Carolina State University, Raleigh.
11 Clifton B. Luttrell, "Farm Price Supports at Cost of Production," *Federal Reserve Bank of St. Louis Review* 59 (December 1977): 2–7.
12 Milton Friedman, *Price Theory* (Chicago: Aldine, 1976), p. 146.
13 E. C. Pasour Jr., "Cost of Production: A Defensible Basis for Agricultural Price Supports?" *American Journal of Agricultural Economics* 62 (May 1980): 244–48.
14 The authorization for the board was extended under the 1985 and 1990 farm bills but finally expired in 1995.
15 Lionel Robbins, "Economics and Political Economy," *American Economic Review* 71 (1981), 9.

CHAPTER 9

1 The dairy price-support program under the 1996 farm bill was slated to end after 1999. Supporters of the program were able to delay the end, however, and milk price supports were continued in the 2002 farm bill.
2 Numerous studies of the various economic impacts of federal and state dairy programs have been published. See, for example, R. A. Ippolito and R. Masson, "The Social Cost of Government Regulation of Milk," *Journal of Law and Economics* 21 (1978): 33–65; R. N. Johnson, "Retail Price Controls in the Dairy Industry: A Political Coalition Argument," *Journal of Law and Economics* 28 (1985): 55–75; and Daniel A. Sumner and Christopher A. Wolf, "Quotas Without Supply Control: Effects of Dairy Quota Policy in California," *American Journal of Agricultural Economics* 78 (1996): 354–66.
3 USDA, National Agricultural Statistical Service, *Agricultural Statistics 1999*, available at: http://www.usda.gov/nass/pubs/agstats.htm, p. XI-2.
4 For a detailed discussion of these events, see Randal R. Rucker, "Endogenous Policy Dynamics, the Visibility of Rents, and Changes in the Transferability of Production Right: The Case of Flue-Cured Tobacco," unpublished manuscript, Department of Agricultural Economics and Economics, Montana State University, Bozeman, June 1995.
5 Although acreage allotments were maintained, the poundage quota was typically the binding

constraint on producers from 1965 until the tobacco program was eliminated in October 2004.

6 Marketing quotas also are used to restrict agricultural output in other countries. Examples of such programs in recent years include marketing quota for dairy, eggs, and poultry in Canada; dairy production quota in the European Union; and (recently eliminated) quotas for tobacco, eggs, and milk in Australia.

7 Jack Hirshleifer and David Hirshleifer, *Price Theory and Applications*, 6th ed. (Upper Saddle River, N.J.: Prentice Hall, 1998), chap. 11.

8 This section draws heavily on Clifton B. Luttrell, *The High Cost of Farm Welfare* (Washington, D.C.: Cato Institute, 1989).

9 Ibid., p. 31.

10 The origin and operation of the CCC is explained later in this chapter.

11 The Supreme Court declared unconstitutional the processing taxes levied on cotton for the purpose of financing the 1933 act. The 1936 act (see text) retained most features of the original act but dropped the processing tax. Luttrell, *The High Cost of Farm Welfare*, p. 15.

12 Ibid., p. 32.

13 This problem is explored further in chapter 12.

14 Ronald D. Knutson, J. B. Penn, and B. L. Flinchbaugh, *Agricultural and Food Policy*, 4th ed. (Englewood Cliffs, N. J.: Prentice Hall, 1998), p. 261.

15 Public Law 480 has continued until the present. See chapter 14 for further discussion of the nature and effects of this program.

16 Target prices, as indicated in an earlier section in this chapter, are an example of "compensatory payments" proposed by Secretary of Agriculture Charles Brannan in the Truman administration in the late 1940s.

17 The target-price method of price supports is further explained in chapter 10.

18 This paragraph draws heavily from B. Delworth Gardner, *Plowing Ground in Washington: The Political Economy of U.S. Agriculture* (San Francisco: Pacific Research Institute for Public Policy, 1995), chap. 1.

19 Farmers have received generic certificates in lieu of cash under many other farm programs, including paid land diversion, marketing loans, disaster payments, and emergency feed programs. Grain merchants also have been issued generic export subsidy certificates. Knutson, Penn, and Flinchbaugh, *Agricultural and Food Policy*, pp. 271–72.

20 Ibid., p. 277, and Fred H. Sanderson, "A Retrospective on PIK," *Food Policy* 8 (May 1984): 103–10.

21 Sanderson, "A Retrospective on PIK," p. 103.

22 Knutson, Penn, and Flinchbaugh, *Agricultural and Food Policy*, p. 269.

23 Lewrene K. Glaser, *Provisions of the Food Security Act of 1985*, USDA Agriculture Information Bulletin no. 498 (Washington, D.C.: U.S. Government Printing Office, 1986), p. 36.

24 Ibid., p. 37.

25 Luther Tweeten, *Foundations of Farm Policy*, 2d ed. (Lincoln: University of Nebraska Press, 1979), p. 469.

CHAPTER IO

1 As shown later in this chapter, the scheduled annual government payments to farmers were not appreciably decreased under the seven-year life of the 1996 farm bill. Moreover, huge amounts of "emergency assistance" were provided to farmers in response to the farm crises of 1998, 1999, and 2000.

2 Following the 2002 farm bill, producer participation in the peanut program is optional.

3 The crop acreage bases continue to be used in making contract payments to each participating farm under the 1996 and 2002 farm bills (as described later).

4 Bruce L. Gardner, *The Governing of Agriculture* (Lawrence: Regents Press of Kansas, 1981), p. 24.

5 Steven R. Guebert, *Changing Role of CCC Loans*, Agricultural Situation Report (McLean, Va.: Farm Credit Administration, 1987).

6 The CCC determined value is computed for each county and changes daily.

7 Despite the fact that receipts obtained when redeeming a loan and selling the commodity may be the same as the amount of the loan ($2 in the previous example), a farmer may find it profitable to participate in the marketing loan program. By immediately selling a commodity under loan, the farmer may avoid incurring additional storage and delivery costs of the commodity to a government-owned facility if the producer eventually defaults on the loan. Moreover, if the producer expects the market price to rise, he may repay the loan at the CCC repayment rate in anticipation of future gains.

8 Marketing loans are equivalent to an export subsidy in the following sense. The CCC nonrecourse loan program tends to support a U.S. price higher than the world price so that U.S. products are not competitive in world markets. The marketing loan program makes it profitable for producers to redeem loans (when the loan rate is higher than the world price or CCC determined rate for repayment) and then sell the product at the world price, thereby enabling U.S. products to be more competitive in international markets.

9 A useful way of thinking about the effects of target-price programs is that prior to production, the demand facing producers becomes perfectly elastic at the target price, P_T, and the level of production, Q_T, is determined by the supply curve. When the level of production is determined, the available supply is vertical at Q_T, and the market price is determined by the intersection of this supply with the market demand curve. If the loan rate, P_L, exceeds the market price (as in figure 10.3), then the relevant postproduction demand curve becomes perfectly elastic at P_L.

10 The CCC paid a portion of the cost of planting the cover crops under a complicated cost-sharing arrangement.

11 The 1985 farm bill, by legislating target prices to 1990, may have reduced uncertainty about farm product prices. If uncertainty is reduced, risk-averse farmers will produce more at a given price than without the price guarantees. Any resulting increase in supply would offset some of the decrease in supply associated with the acreage-set-aside features of the target-price system. Geoff Edwards, "U.S. Farm Policy: An Australian Perspective," *Federal Reserve Bank of St. Louis Review* 69, no. 8 (October 1987): 20–31.

12 Note that in the absence of export subsidies, the loan rate relative to world market prices is the key factor influencing the competitiveness of U.S. exports of farm products in international trade. Prior to the 1985 farm bill, high loan rates for U.S. commodities in effect provided an umbrella for farmers in other countries, enabling these producers to undersell U.S. farmers. Marketing loans, initiated in the 1985 farm bill, amounted to an indirect export subsidy and made U.S. farm products more competitive in world markets (see chapter 14).

13 For example, the bill specified that for fiscal year 1999, the total amount available for contract payments for all contract commodities was $5,603,000,000, and that 46.22 percent of that total was to be allocated to contract payments for corn.

14 Data for this example are from a USDA briefing booklet dated April 1996.

15 Information provided by David Nichols, assistant treasurer, CCC, July 23, 1997.

16 See USDA, Economic Research Service, "U.S. and State Farm Income Data," at: http://www.ers.usda.gov/data/farmincome/finfidmu.htm.

17 The discussion in this section relies heavily on Frederick J. Nelson and Lyle P. Schertz, eds., *Provisions of the Federal Agriculture Improvement and Reform Act of 1996*, USDA, Economic Research Service, Agriculture Information Bulletin no. 729 (Washington, D.C.: U.S.

Government Printing Office, September 1996), pp. 20–21; Ron Lord, *Sugar: Background for 1995 Farm Legislation*, AER no. 711 (Washington, D.C.: USDA, Economic Research Service, 1995); and Anne Krueger, "The Political Economy of Controls: American Sugar," in *Public Policy and Economic Development: Essays in Honour of Ian Little*, edited by Maurice Scott and Deepak Lal, pp. 170 - 216 (Oxford:, Clairdon Press, 1990).

18 This assumption seems appropriate in light of the observation that for the years 1995–97 U.S. sugar imports were less than 10 percent of total world imports (USDA, National Agricultural Statistical Service, *Agricultural Statistics*, 1999 [Washington, D.C.: U.S. Government Printing Office, 2001), available at: www.usda.gov/nass/pubs/agstats.htm). Moreover, this assumption simplifies the analysis compared to assuming that the foreign supply of sugar is upward sloping, but it does not qualitatively alter the substance of the analysis.

19 Price-support payments for sugar are made to processors, who (to qualify for loans) must agree to pay producers at least minimum amounts established by the USDA. See Nelson and Schertz, *Provisions of the Federal Agricultural Improvement and Reform Act of 1996*, pp. 21–22. Most commodity support payments are made directly to producers. Sugar support payments are made to processors because sugarcane and sugar beets are bulky and highly perishable and must be processed before they can be stored or traded. See the information provided in USDA, Economic Research Service, "Features—Farm Bill 2002: Analysis of Selected Provisions: Sugar," at http://www.ers.usda.gov/Features/FarmBill/Analysis/sugar2002act.htm.

20 How these benefits are distributed among foreign producers, importers, and foreign government agents is an issue on which little or no information seems to be available.

21 Lord, *Sugar*, p. 27.

22 For the 2000 crop, the USDA implemented a PIK program for sugar to reduce the domestic supply of sugar and hold down treasury costs. The essence of this program (which is continued in the 2002 farm bill) is that producers are allowed to offer bids that represent the dollar value of the payment they will accept not to harvest beets in their fields. The USDA has established maximum per acre bids, and processors have demanded a share (roughly one-third) of the PIK payments, ostensibly to offset costs associated with the reduced quantity of beets going through their plants. The resulting payments to growers appear to be low enough that many eligible producers have chosen not to participate in the program.

23 For contemporary discussions of these problems and issues, see Bruce Ingersoll, "Big Sugar Seeks Bailout, Gives Money to Help Get Way," *Wall Street Journal*, April 27, 2000, p. A-28, and "Sugar Producers Get $1.6 Billion of Federal Help," *Wall Street Journal*, May 15, 2000, p. B-4.

24 See the information provided in USDA, Economic Research Service, "2002 Farm Bill, ERS Analysis: Selected Provisions, Title I: Commodity Programs, Sugar," at http://www.ers.usda.gov/Features/FarmBill/Analysis/sugar2002act.htm.

25 Under GATT, the U.S. duty on overquota sugar was set initially at 17.62 cents per pound beginning January 1, 1995, and was lowered 0.46 cents per year until it reached 15.36 cents per pound in the year 2000. The impacts of this two-part tariff on U.S. sugar prices, surpluses, and import levels are qualitatively similar to the impacts of the import quota shown in figure 10.5.

26 Insofar as the foreign supply of sugar shown as P_W in figure 10.5 is really upward sloping, foreign producers who are not allowed to import sugar into the United States also will be adversely affected. The limits on imports into the United States will cause sugar to be redirected into foreign markets, thereby driving down the price in non-U.S. markets.

27 Lord, *Sugar*, p. 28.

28 James Bovard, *Archer Daniels Midland: A Case Study in Corporate Welfare*, Policy Analysis no. 241 (Washington, D.C.: Cato Institute, 1995), p. 21.

29 Recent estimates indicate that the price of irrigated farmland used to produce sugar in Montana would fall by 19 to 35 percent in the absence of sugar beet production. See Mykel R. Taylor and Gary W. Brester, "The Effects of Sugarbeet Production on Montana Land Prices,"

unpublished manuscript, Department of Agricultural Economics and Economics, Montana State University, Bozeman, December 2002.

30 Although several other kinds of tobacco are grown, flue-cured and air-cured (mainly burley) tobaccos account for more than 95 percent of total production. Verner N. Grise, *Tobacco: Background for 1995 Farm Legislation*, Agricultural Economics Report no. 709 (Washington, D.C.: USDA, Commercial Agriculture Division, 1995), p. 4.

31 In North Carolina, the tobacco industry is estimated to contribute some $200 billion annually to the North Carolina economy (approximately 6 percent of gross state product). However, only approximately 1 percent of this contribution is at the farm level. Estimate by Michael Walden, Department of Agricultural and Resource Economics, North Carolina State University.

32 Grise, *Tobacco*, pp. 2 and 11.

33 Tom Capehart, "The Changing Tobacco User's Dollar," Electronic Outlook Report from the Economic Research Service (Washington, D.C., USDA, Economic Research Service, October 2004) p. 5, (available at: http://www.ers.usda.gov/publications/tbs/OCT04/tbs25701/tbs25701.pdf) and USDA, National Agricultural Statistical Service, *Agricultural Statistics*, 2004, p. II-27.

34 Paul R. Johnson, *The Economics of the Tobacco Industry* (New York: Praeger, 1984).

35 The effectiveness of these actions in reducing smoking is problematic. One study found that restrictions on advertising have tended to undermine improvements in cigarettes while doing nothing to reduce smoking. John E. Calfee, "The Ghost of Cigarette Advertising Past," *Regulation* 10 (November–December 1986): 235–45.

36 Unpublished data provided by Pete Burr, Foreign Agricultural Service, USDA, August 1997.

37 Ibid.

38 Blake Brown, "U.S. Flue-Cured Production: Four Decades of Change," *The North Carolina State Economist*, Department of Agricultural and Resource Economics, Raleigh, N. C., (July 1995), p.1.

39 Randal R. Rucker, "Endogenous Policy Dynamics, the Visibility of Rents, and Changes in the Transferability of Production Rights: The Case of Flue-Cured Tobacco," unpublished manuscript, Department of Agricultural Economics and Economics, Montana State University, Bozeman, June 1995.

40 Grise, *Tobacco*.

41 Ibid.

42 Daniel A. Sumner, "A Study of the Recent History and a Projection of Budget Costs of the 'New' Tobacco Program," paper presented at the annual meeting of the American Agricultural Economic Association, Reno, Nevada, July 27–30, 1986.

43 Ibid.

44 See Randal R. Rucker, Walter N. Thurman, and Daniel A. Sumner, "Restricting the Market for Quota: An Analysis of Tobacco Production Rights with Corroboration from Congressional Testimony," *Journal of Political Economy* 103 (February 1995): 142–75, and Rucker, "Endogenous Policy Dynamics," for discussions of issues related to the restrictions on the transfer of quota in the tobacco program.

45 The tobacco program also includes a price support. The discussion hereafter implicitly assumes that policymakers simultaneously set the support price and the production quota so that, for any given price support, the quantity of tobacco demanded is equal to the production quota. We believe this process to be a reasonable characterization of current tobacco policy because it avoids costly surpluses and excess Treasury costs—a mandate of the tobacco program since 1982.

46 Grise, *Tobacco*, p. 3. See also Rucker, "Endogenous Policy Dynamics," for a discussion of the history of the rules for transferring acreage allotment and poundage quota.

47 The restrictions on quota renting were circumvented in part through the formation of "farm combinations" arranged through local USDA offices (Rucker, "Endogenous Policy

Dynamics"). Because these arrangements were fairly common, industry observers and partici- pants knew (at least approximately) the level of lease rates from year to year.

48 Grise, *Tobacco*, p. 11.

49 E. C. Pasour, Jr., "The Tobacco-Quota Buyout: More Legal Plunder," *The Freeman: Ideas on Liberty* 55 (January–February, 2005): 38–41.

50 The primary source for information regarding this legislation is "A Summary of the Tobacco Buyout," by A. Blake Brown, Department of Agricultural and Resource Economics, North Carolina State University, Nov. 12, 2004 at http://www.ces.ncsu.edu/depts/agecon/tobacco_ econ/Buyout_Summary_nov04.pdf.

51 The actual additional cost burden of the buyout to cigarette manufacturers is less than $10.1 billion because about $2 billion of scheduled Phase II payments (from the Master Settlement Agreement in the litigation between manufacturers and the state attorneys general) to tobacco producers and quota owners ceased with enactment of the buyout.

52 A grower's total quota payment will be based on his 2002 effective marketing quota, with the producer of a quota receiving the full $3 per pound if he produced the quota in all three years from 2002–2004. If the quota was only produced in one year, a producer receives $1 per pound. Similarly if quota is produced in two years during the 2002–2004 period, the producer receives $2 per pound. See Brown, "A Summary of the Tobacco Buyout" for additional details.

53 John Corsiglia and Liz Moore, "EWG Analysis of House Tobacco Buyout Bill," Environmental Working Group's Farm Subsidy Database, News Release, June 22, 2004 at: http://www.ewg. org/farm/tobaccobuyout.php.

54 Gordon Tullock, "The Transitional Gains Trap," *Bell Journal of Economics* 6 (Autumn 1975): 671–78.

55 In answering this question, there are two issues to consider. First, what is the impact of a quota program (with no restrictions on transfer of production rights) on land values? Second, if there are restrictions on the transfer of production rights that are binding (in the sense that if they were removed, there would be movement in production), how would land prices be affected by the removal of such restrictions? The answer to the latter question depends on whether the land is in counties with high or low costs of production.

56 See Randal R. Rucker and Walter N. Thurman, "The Economic Effects of Supply Controls: The Simple Analytics of the U.S. Peanut Program," *Journal of Law and Economics*, 33 (October 1990): 483–515, for an analysis of the causes and consequences of the peanut program.

57 *Special Supplement: Provisions of the 1996 Farm Bill, Agricultural Outlook* (April 1996), p. 11.

58 The Uruguay Round GATT and the NAFTA agreements require increases in peanut imports. See Randal R. Rucker, Walter N. Thurman, and Robert B. Borges, "GATT and the U.S. Peanut Market," in *Regulations and Protectionism under GATT and NAFTA: Case Studies in North American Agriculture*, edited by Andrew Schmitz, 160–179, (Boulder, Colo.: Westview Press, 1996), for analysis of the effects of these agreements on U.S. peanut markets.

59 As indicated in the appendix, quota owners are to be paid 11 cents per year for five years for each pound of quota they owned. This price appears to exceed substantially the market price of poundage quota. For analysis of the effects of these program changes, see Jan Chvosta, Walter N. Thurman, A. Blake Brown, and Randal R. Rucker, "The End of Supply Controls: The Economic Effects of Recent Change in Federal Peanut Policy," unpublished manuscript, Department of Resource and Agricultural Economics, North Carolina State University, Raleigh, October 2002.

60 The primary source for the historical and institutional details in the discussion here is Mary K. Muth, Randal R. Rucker, Walter N. Thurman, and Ching-Ta Chuang, "The Fable of the Bees Revisited: Causes and Consequences of the U.S. Honey Program," *Journal of Law and Economics*, 46 (October 2003): 479–516, and sources cited therein.

61 Taxpayers, of course, also bore the costs of administering the program.

62 See Farm Service Agency, Online Price Support Division Reports, National LDP Summary for Honey, available at: http://www.fsa.usda.gov/dafp/psd/reports.htm.

63 The primary source for the historical and institutional details in the discussion here is John V. Lawler and Robert A. Skinner, *Wool and Mohair: Background for the 1990 Farm Legislation* (Washington, D.C.: USDA, Economic Research Service, November 1989).

64 USDA, National Agricultural Statistical Service, *Agricultural Statistics, 1999*, p. VII-38.

65 See Lawler and Skinner, *Wool and Mohair*, p. 26, and Richard Stroup, "Political Behavior," in *The Fortune Encyclopedia of Economics*, edited by David R. Henderson (New York: Warner Books, 1993), p. 47.

66 In addition, duties on lamb meat imported into the United States were significantly increased following the termination of the wool program.

67 Harold G. Halcrow, *Agricultural Policy Analysis* (New York: McGraw-Hill, 1984), p. 149.

68 USDA, *Agricultural Statistics 1995–96* (Washington, D.C.: U.S. Government Printing Office, 1996), p. VII-40. Market prices for wool have fallen dramatically since 1995, and domestic production of shorn wool products in 1999 and 2000 was almost 30 percent less than in 1994 and 1995 (USDA, National Agricultural Statistical Service, *Agricultural Statistics 2002*, available at: http://www.usda.gov/nass/pubs/agstats.htm), p. VII-35.

69 Lawler and Skinner, *Wool and Mohair*, pp. 28–29.

70 Nelson and Schertz, *Provisions of the Federal Agriculture Improvement and Reform Act of 1996*, p. 6, and USDA briefing booklet dated April 1996, p. 12.

71 Thomas C. Capehart, Jr., "Trends in the Cigarette Industry After the Master Settlement Agreement," Electronic Outlook Report from the Economic Research Service, TBS-250-01, October 2001, available at: http://www.ers.usda.gov/publications/tbs/oct01/tbs250-01/tbs250-01.pdf.

CHAPTER II

1 Bruce L. Gardner, *The Governing of Agriculture* (Lawrence: Regents Press of Kansas, 1981), p. 46.

2 National Cooperative Business Association Web site, available at: http://www.ncba.org/primer.cfm.

3 USDA, *Agricultural Statistics 1986* (Washington, D.C.: U.S. Government Printing Office, 1987), p. 438.

4 Figures on co-op numbers are from Farmer Cooperative Statistics, 2000, and are available at: http://www.rurdev.usda.gov/rbs/pub/sr60.pdf.

5 Walter J. Armbruster, Dennis R. Henderson, and Ronald D. Knutson, *Federal Marketing Programs in Agriculture* (Danville, Ill.: Interstate, 1983), p. 206; co-op share of U.S. farm marketing activity in 1998 is from *Rural Cooperatives* (January–February 1998), available at: http://www.rurdev.usda.gov/rbs/pub/jan00/contents.

6 Leon Garoyan, "Developments in the Theory of Farmer Cooperatives: Discussion," *American Journal of Agricultural Economics* 65 (December 1983), p. 1098.

7 Peter Vitaliano, "Cooperative Enterprise: An Alternative Conceptual Basis for Analyzing a Complex Institution," *American Journal of Agricultural Economics* 65 (December 1983): 1078–83.

8 Charles R. Knoeber and David L. Baumer, "Understanding Retained Patronage Refunds in Agricultural Cooperatives," *American Journal of Agricultural Economics* 65 (February 1983): 30–37.

9 Vitaliona, "Cooperative Enterprise," p. 1082.

10 Gardner, *The Governing of Agriculture*, p. 47.

11 Richard J. Sexton and Terri Erickson Sexton, "Taxing Co-ops: Current Treatment Is Fair, but Not for Reason Given by Co-op Leaders," *Choices* 1 (1986): 21–25.

12 Knoeber and Baumer, "Understanding Retained Patronage Refunds," p. 30.

13 E. C. Pasour Jr., "The Free Rider as a Basis for Government Intervention," *Journal of Libertarian Studies* 5 (Fall 1981): 453–64.

14 Gary S. Becker, *Economic Theory* (New York: Alfred A. Knopf, 1971), p. 99.

15 For discussions and economic analyses of various aspects of milk-marketing programs, see, for example, Reuben E. Kessel, "Economic Effects of Federal Regulation of Milk Markets," *Journal of Law and Economics* 10 (1967): 51–78; Richard A. Ippolito and Robert T. Masson, "The Social Cost of Government Regulation of Milk," *Journal of Law and Economics* 21 (1978): 33–65; and Ronald N. Johnson, "Retail Price Controls in the Dairy Industry: A Political Coalition Argument," *Journal of Law and Economics* 28 (1985): 55–75.

16 Only Grade A milk is regulated under federal orders. USDA, Economic Research Service, *Dairy: Background for 1995 Farm Legislation*, AER no. 705 (Washington, D.C.: U.S. Government Printing Office, 1995), p. 15.

17 Class prices historically were based on the Minnesota-Wisconsin price because this was considered to be the low-cost production area.

18 Frederick J. Nelson and Lyle P. Schertz, eds., *Provisions of the Federal Agriculture Improvement and Reform Act of 1996*, USDA, Economic Research Service, Agriculture Information Bulletin no. 729 (Washington, D.C.: U.S. Government Printing Office, September 1996), p. 14.

19 Ibid., p. 13.

20 The price-support program, which is closely linked to the marketing order program, enables the market order officials in each order to set a minimum price for Class I milk.

21 Larry Salathe and James Langley, *Federal Agriculture Improvement and Reform Act of 1996: A Description of U.S. Farm Commodity Programs under the 1996 Farm Bill*, Briefing Booklet (Washington, D.C.: USDA, Office of the Chief Economist and Farm Service Agency, April 1996), p. 24. The 2002 farm bill fixed the minimum support price for milk at $9.90 per hundredweight.

22 For an economic analysis of the California dairy program, see Daniel A. Sumner and Christopher Wolf, "Quotas Without Supply Control: Effects of Dairy Quota Policy in California," *American Journal of Agricultural Economics* 78, no. 2 (May 1996): 354–66.

23 USDA, Economic Research Service, *Dairy: Background for 1995 Farm Legislation*, p. 5.

24 If price supports are phased out, taxpayer costs of the program will be reduced mainly to administrative costs of operating the federal system of milk-marketing orders.

25 Peter Helmberger and Yu-Hui Chen, "Economic Effects of U.S. Dairy Programs," *Journal of Agricultural and Resource Economics* 19 (December 1994): 225–38.

26 Kevin McNew, "Milking the Sacred Cow: A Case for Eliminating the Federal Dairy Program," *Policy Analysis* 362 (December 1, 1999), p. 8.

27 Dale Heien and Cathy R. Wessells, "The Nutritional Impact of the Dairy Price Support Program," *Journal of Consumer Affairs* 22 (Winter 1988): 201–19.

28 McNew, "Milking the Sacred Cow," p. 5.

29 Grade B milk production was 33 percent of total U.S. milk production in 1960. Ibid., p. 10.

30 USDA, Economic Research Service, *Dairy: Background for 1995 Farm Legislation*, p. 21.

31 Ibid.

32 Ibid., p. 11.

33 USDA, National Agricultural Statistical Service, *Agricultural Statistics, 1999* (Washington, D.C.: U.S. Government Printing Office, 2000), available at: www.usda.gov/nass/pubs/agstats.htm, pp. VIII-26 and VIII-28.

34 Wen Li Cheng, "Producer's Surplus and Rents in the U.S. Dairy Industry," master's thesis, Montana State University, Bozeman, 1992.

35 This section relies heavily on McNew, "Milking the Sacred Cow."

36 USDA, Economic Research Service, "Features—Farm Policy, ERS Analysis of the 2002 Farm Bill, Dairy Programs," at http://www.ers.usda.gov/Features/farmbill/. The dairy program is described under the "Commodity Programs" section of the Web site.

37 Prices of other classes of milk are set in a manner similar to the setting of prices in other market order areas.

38 The compact has fixed the minimum price of Class I milk and has not varied it seasonally in response to supply and demand as is typically the case under federal marketing orders.

39 For additional information on dairy program changes in the 2002 farm bill, see the appendix on the 2002 farm bill in this book and USDA, Economic Research Service, "Features—Farm Policy, ERS Analysis of the 2002 Farm Bill, Dairy Programs," at http://www.ers.usda.gov/ Features/FarmBill/Analysis/dairy2002act.htm

40 USDA, Economic Research Service, *Federal Marketing Orders and Federal Research and Promotion Programs: Background for 1995 Farm Legislation*, AER no. 707 (Washington, D.C.: U.S. Government Printing Office, 1995).

41 Ibid., pp. 20–21.

42 Thomas M. Lenard and M. P. Mazur, "Harvest of Waste: The Marketing Order Program," *Regulation* 9 (May–June 1985): 19–26.

43 Ibid., p. 28.

44 "Sweet Deals in the Orchard," *New York Times*, May 24, 1983, Section A, p. 24.

45 Lenard and Mazur, "Harvest of Waste," p. 21.

46 A key difference between ordinary cartels and price-discriminating marketing orders, such as the now defunct California-Arizona navel orange order, is that production is artificially high in the latter case instead of artificially low.

47 Lawrence Shepard, "Cartelization of the California-Arizona Orange Industry, 1934–1981," *Journal of Law and Economics* 29 (April 1986): 83–123.

48 Lenard and Mazur, "Harvest of Waste," p. 21.

49 Ibid.

50 Ibid., p. 21.

CHAPTER 12

1 James Bovard, "Archer Daniels Midland: A Case Study in Corporate Welfare," *Policy Analysis* (September 26, 1995): 26 pp.

2 Gordon Tullock, "Where Is the Rectangle?" *Public Choice* (April 1997), p. 151.

3 See Luther Tweeten, "The Twelve Best Reasons for Commodity Programs: Why None Stands Scrutiny," *Choices* 10 (1995): 4–7, 43–45. Other estimates of the impacts of government programs on land values are in the same range as Tweeten's. Richard E. Just and John A. Miranowski, "Understanding Farmland Price Changes," *American Journal of Agricultural Economics* 75 (February 1993): 156–68, suggest that government payments may account for 15 to 25 percent of land values. Mykel R. Taylor and Gary W. Brester, "The Effects of Sugarbeet Production on Montana Land Prices," unpublished manuscript, Department of Agricultural Economics and Economics, Montana State University, Bozeman, January 2003, estimate that the sugar program may account for as much as 35 percent of the value of land used for sugarbeet production.

4 Data obtained from USDA, *Agricultural Statistics* (Washington, D.C.: U.S. Government Printing Office, various issues), and *Economic Report of the President* (Washington, D.C.: U.S. Government Printing Office, 1996), p. 346.

5 See table 6.4 in chapter 6. USDA, Economic Research Service, "U.S. and State Farm Income Data," available at: http://www.ers.usda.gov/data/farmincome/finfidmu.htm. The most current forecast and historic data on farm income can be found on this Web page.

6 *Economic Report of the President* (Washington, D.C.: U.S. Government Printing Office, 1987), p. 157.

7 U.S. General Accounting Office, *Farm Payments: Basic Changes Needed to Avoid Abuse of the $50,000 Payment Limit*, GAO/RCED-87-176 (Washington, D.C.: U.S. Government Printing Office, 1987), p. 2. In payment limitations, *persons* are broadly defined to include individuals and other entities such as limited partnerships, corporations, and estates actively engaged in farming.

8 Mandatory limits on benefits do not apply in the tobacco and sugar programs because there are no direct payments to farmers. In these programs, as in direct-payment programs, however, most of the benefits go to larger, higher-income producers.

9 See the appendix on the 2002 farm bill in this book for more information on payment limitations. For information on payment limitations under the 1996 farm bill, see Frederick J. Nelson and Lyle P. Schertz, eds., *Provisions of the Federal Agriculture Improvement and Reform Act of 1996*, USDA, Economic Research Service, Agriculture Information Bulletin no. 729 (Washington, D.C.: U.S. Government Printing Office, September 1996), pp. 7–8.

10 Ibid.

11 D. Gale Johnson, "The Performance of Past Policies: A Critique," in *Alternative Agricultural and Food Policies and the 1985 Farm Bill*, edited by Gordon C. Rausser and K. R. Farrell (Berkeley, Calif.: Giannini Foundation, 1985), pp. 27–29.

12 Bruce L. Gardner, *The Governing of Agriculture* (Lawrence: Regents Press of Kansas, 1981), p. 118.

13 Dale Heien, "Future Directions for U.S. Food, Agricultural, and Trade Policy: Discussion," *American Journal of Agricultural Economics* 66 (May 1984), p. 232.

14 The adverse effect of federal disaster relief on farmers' incentive to take out crop insurance is discussed in chapter 15.

15 For a discussion focused on the contributions of sugar interests, see Bruce Ingersoll, "Big Sugar Seeks Bailout, Gives Money to Help Get Way," *Wall Street Journal*, April 27, 2000, Section A, p. 28.

16 For an analysis of these issues in the context of the U.S. tobacco program , see Randal R. Rucker, Walter N. Thurman, and Daniel A. Sumner, "Restricting the Market for Quota: An Analysis of Tobacco Production Rights with Corroboration from Congressional Testimony," *Journal of Political Economy* 103 (February 1995): 142–75.

17 Joseph D. Coffey, "Are Government Farm Programs the Solution or the Problem?" in *Farm Policy Perspectives: Setting the Stage for 1985 Agricultural Legislation*, Senate Committee Print 98-174, U.S. Senate Committee on Agriculture, Nutrition, and Forestry, 98th Congress, 2d sess., April 1984, pp. 194–201.

18 USDA, Economic Research Service, *Cotton and Wool Situation and Outlook Yearbook CWS-2002* (Washington, D.C.: U.S. Government Printing Office, November 2002), p. 41.

19 Dwight R. Lee, "The Price Blackout," *Reason* 17 (October 1985), p. 44.

CHAPTER 13

1 Kathryn Longen, *Domestic Food Programs: An Overview*, Economics, Statistics, and Cooperative Service Report No. 81 (Washington, D.C.: USDA, 1980).

2 Based on information from USDA, *Food Stamp Program Annual Summary*, available at: www.fns.usda.gov/pd/fssummar.htm.

3 See T. M. Fraker, *The Effect of Food Stamps on Food Expenditures: A Review of the Literature* (Washington, D.C.: USDA, Food and Nutrition Service, 1990), and Betsey A. Kuhn, Pamela Allen Dunn, David Smallwood, Kenneth Hanson, Jim Blalock, and Stephen Vogel, "The Food Stamp Program and Welfare Reform," *Journal of Economic Perspectives* 10 (Spring

1996):189–98, for surveys of the empirical evidence on the effect of food stamps on food expenditures. Other data in the calculation were provided through personal correspondence with the USDA Economic Research Service, October 1997.

In 1996, food stamp purchases were $22.5 billion and total food expenditures were $692.6 billion . If each dollar of food stamps used increased total food outlays between 20 cents and 45 cents, the food stamp program increased total food expenditures by between $4.5 billion and $10.12 billion. This figure suggests that the program, at the most, increased food expenditures by 1.5 percent (10.12/692.6).

4 Data provided at the home page for the USDA Office of Budget and Program Analysis, http://www.usda.gov/agency/obpa/Home-Page/obpa.html. Program outlays for the Food Stamp, Child Nutrition Programs, and other programs of the USDA Food and Nutrition Service may be found in the USDA's *Budget Summary* for recent years.

5 Ibid. Data taken from USDA, Office of Budget and Program Analysis, *2003 Budget Summary*, p. 53 at http://www.usda.gov/agency/obpa/Budget-Summary/2003/2003budsum.htm.

6 Ibid.

7 Ronald D. Knutson, J. B. Penn, and B. L. Flinchbaugh, *Agricultural and Food Policy*, 4th ed. (Englewood Cliffs, N.J.: Prentice-Hall, 1998), p. 458.

8 Ibid., p. 457.

9 USDA, Office of Budget and Program Analysis, *2003 Budget Summary*, p. 49.

10 From author's correspondence with the Farm Credit System.

11 Data provided at the home page for the USDA Office of Budget and Program Analysis at http://www.usda.gov/agency/obpa/Home-Page/obpa.html. See USDA, Office of Budget and Program Analysis, *Budget Summary 2003*.

12 See James Bovard, "Feeding Everybody: How Federal Food Programs Grew and Grew," *Policy Review* 26 (Fall 1983), p. 42, and USDA, *Agricultural Statistics 1945* (Washington, D.C.: U.S. Government Printing Office, 1945), p. 577.

13 U.S. General Accounting Office (GAO) Testimony, February 1, 1995, GAO/T-RCED-95-94.

14 GAO Testimony, February 2, 1994, GAO/T-RCED-94-125.

15 Ronald D. Knutson, J. B. Penn, and William T. Boehm, *Agricultural and Food Policy*, p. 459.

16 Kuhn et al., "The Food Stamp Program and Welfare Reform," p. 194.

17 Sheena McConnell and James Ohls, "Food Stamp Participation Rate Down in Urban Areas but Not in Rural," *Food Review* 24, no. 1 (January–April 2001): 8–12.

18 James M. Buchanan, *Cost and Choice* (Chicago: Markham, 1969), p. 54.

19 Kuhn et al., "The Food Stamp Program and Welfare Reform," p. 193.

20 Ibid.

21 Knutson, Penn, and Flinchbaugh, *Agricultural and Food Policy*, p. 460.

22 Ibid., p. 439.

23 Ibid., p. 442.

24 Ibid., p. 441.

25 Don Lavoie, *National Economic Planning: What Is Left?* (Cambridge, Mass.: Ballinger, 1985).

26 The four pyramid groups in order of descending importance are grains and vegetables, fruits and vegetables, meat and dairy products, and fats and oil.

27 Knutson, Penn, and Flinchbaugh, *Agricultural and Food Policy*, p. 444.

28 Product labels must include calories, calories from fat, calories from saturated fat, cholesterol, total carbohydrates, sugar, dietary fiber, sodium, and a host of other nutrient information.

29 E. C. Pasour Jr. "Consumer Information and the Calculation Debate," *The Freeman* 46 (December 1996), p. 784.

30 Pauline M. Ippolito and Alan D. Mathios, "Information and Advertising: The Case of Fat Consumption in the United States," *American Economic Review* 85 (May 1995): 91–95.

31 Bovard, "Feeding Everybody," p. 44.

32 See the Office of Budget and Program Analysis home page at http://www.usda.gov/agency/ obpa/Home-Page/obpa.html. See also USDA, Office of Budget and Program Analysis, *Budget Summary 2003*, p. 49.

CHAPTER 14

1 Jack L. Hervey, "The Internationalization of Uncle Sam," *Federal Reserve Bank of Chicago Economic Perspectives* 10 (May–June 1986): 3–14.
2 *Economic Report of the President* (Washington, D.C.: U.S. Government Printing Office, 2000, p. 422).
3 USDA, Economic Research Service, *U.S. Agricultural Trade Update*, FAU-59 (Washington, D.C.: U.S. Government Printing Office, November 26, 2001), table 5.
4 "Trade Balance," *Agricultural Outlook* (December 2002), Table 25, p. 65.
5 The exchange rate determines the buying power of any domestic currency. A "strong dollar" makes it more costly for an importer to buy U.S. farm products—making it more difficult to export U.S. farm products.
6 Dallas S. Batten and Michael T. Belongia, "The Recent Decline in Agricultural Exports: Is the Exchange Rate the Culprit?" *Federal Reserve Bank of St. Louis Review* 66 (October 1984): 5–14.
7 USDA, *Agricultural Statistics, 1982* (Washington, D.C.: U.S. Government Printing Office, 1983), p. 525.
8 Clifton B. Luttrell, *Down on the Farm with Uncle Sam* (Los Angeles: International Institute for Economic Research, 1983), p. 17.
9 For data on annual exports of farm products, see USDA, *Agricultural Statistics, 2002* (Washington, D.C.: U.S. Government Printing Office, 2002), p. XV-2. See also the USDA Web site at http://www.ers.usda.gov/data/farmincome/finfidmu.htm for government payments by farm program, including emergency aid by year since 1933.
10 Clifton B. Luttrell, "Rising Farm Exports and International Trade Policies," *Federal Reserve Bank of St. Louis Review* 61 (July 1979): 3–10.
11 An enlightening discussion of comparative advantage, exchange rates, balance of trade versus balance of payments, and the harmful effects of protectionism may be found in Phil Gramm, "The Truth about Trade," *Intercollegiate Review* 23 (Fall 1987): 45–48.
12 Paul Heyne, *The Economic Way of Thinking* (Chicago: Science Research Associates, 2000), p. 147.
13 Imports may be subsidized rather than taxed. An import subsidy would have effects just opposite to those of a tariff. An import subsidy would lead to a decrease in domestic production and an increase in domestic consumption. Thus, domestic producers and taxpayers bear the cost of the subsidy. The direct cost to the government would be the quantity imported multiplied times the subsidy.
14 See "You Say 'Tomato,' Mickey Kanton Says Political Opportunity," *Wall Street Journal*, Sept. 6, 1996, p. A15, for an interesting discussion of how packaging requirements are used in attempts to provide an advantage to domestic tomato producers.
15 Organization for Economic Cooperation and Development (OECD), *Agriculture: Support Estimates, 2000* (Paris: OECD, 2001), pp. 26–27.
16 Note that this discussion presumes that with the export subsidy in effect, domestic consumers do not buy imports, either because imports are restricted or because transportation costs are sufficiently high that imports are not economical even with the $S difference between world and domestic price.
17 Brink Lindsey, *The U.S. Antidumping Law: Rhetoric vs. Reality*, Center for Trade Policy Studies, Trade Policy Analysis No. 7 (Washington, D.C.: Cato Institute, August 1999).

18 Ronald Knutson, J. B. Penn, and B. L. Flinchbaugh, *Agricultural and Food Policy*, 4th ed. (Upper Saddle River, N.J.: Prentice Hall, 1998), p. 451.

19 Kathryn Longen, *Domestic Food Programs: An Overview* (Washington, D.C.: U.S. Government Printing Office, 1981), p. 24.

20 Knutson, Penn, and Flinchbaugh, *Agricultural and Food Policy*, p. 176.

21 Luttrell, *Down on the Farm with Uncle Sam*, p. 6.

22 Knutson, Penn, and Flinchbaugh, *Agricultural and Food Policy*, p. 155.

23 W. Gene Wilson, "Government Policies: Will They Increase Farm Exports?" *Federal Reserve Bank of Atlanta Economic Review* 72 (January–February 1987), p. 22.

24 Frederick J. Nelson and Lyle P. Schertz, eds., *Provisions of the Federal Improvement and Reform Act of 1996*, USDA, Economic Research Service, Agriculture Information Bulletin no. 729 (Washington, D.C.: U.S. Government Printing Office, September 1996).

25 FSA Online, "Price Support Division Reports," "National LDP Summary Reports," available at: http://www.fsa.usda.gov/pscad/selectldpsummnat.asp.

26 Knutson, Penn, and Flinchbaugh, *Agricultural and Food Policy*, p. 168.

27 "Uruguay Round Agreement on Agriculture: The Record to Date," *Agricultural Outlook* (December 1998): 28–33.

28 Ibid., p. 28.

29 Daniel T. Griswold, "WTO Report Card: America's Economic Stake in Open Trade," Center for Trade Policy Studies, Trade Briefing Paper no. 8 (Washington, D.C.: Cato Institute, April 2000).

30 The progress of the Doha Round of trade negotiations may be followed on the Web site of the United States Trade Representative: www:ustr.gov.

31 See Paul Blustein, "Accord Reached on Global Trade; Talks Aim to Cut Farm Aid, Tariffs," *The Washington Post*, A Section, p. A01, August 1, 2004, and "Report Recommends WTO Negotiation Overhaul," *Journal of Commerce Online*, January 17, 2005, p. WP.

32 This section draws heavily on Knutson, Penn, and Flinchbaugh, *Agricultural and Food Policy*, p. 169.

33 "Uruguay Round Agreement," p. 29.

34 The average cut in tariffs for so-called developing countries is 24 percent, and the minimum cut per product is 10 percent; these countries had until 2004 to meet these less-rigorous requirements.

35 Early indications are that this new dispute-settlement process is a significant improvement over earlier GATT processes. Satisfactory settlements of several trade disputes have occurred without resort to the formal dispute process. Under the former GATT system, trade disputes often dragged on for years. See "Uruguay Round Agreement," p. 32.

36 E. C. Pasour Jr., "On Free Trade's Price: U.S. Farmers Can't Have Free Access to World Markets and Price Supports, Too" *Choices* 1 (1986): 33–35.

37 Under some circumstances, lump sum payments have no impacts on production decisions or resource allocation. The FAIR Act lump sum payments do affect production decisions and resource allocation because farmers are required to keep land in agricultural uses and to comply with conservation plans.

38 "Developing countries," under the agreement, must reduce domestic support by 13 percent, and they had until 2004 to do so.

39 "Uruguay Round Agreement," p. 30.

40 "Developing countries," under the agreement, were required to reduce the value and quantities of subsidies by 24 percent and 14 percent, respectively, during the period 1995–2004.

41 "Uruguay Round Agreement," p. 31.

42 Knutson, Penn, and Flinchbaugh, *Agricultural and Food Policy*, pp. 172–73.

43 "Regional Trade Agreements and U.S. Agriculture," *Agricultural Outlook* (September 1998): 25–28.

44 Brink Lindsey, *A New Track for U.S. Trade Policy*, Center for Trade Policy Studies, Trade

Policy Analysis No. 4 (Washington, D.C.: Cato Institute, September 1998).

45 James J. Glassman, *The Blessings of Free Trade*, Center for Trade Policy Studies, Trade Briefing Paper no. 1 (Washington, D.C.: Cato Institute, May 1998).

46 Milton Friedman and Rose Friedman, *Free to Choose: A Personal Statement* (New York: Avon, 1981), pp. 42–43.

47 G. Edward Schuh, "U.S. Agriculture in the World Economy," in *Farm and Food Policy: Critical Issues for Southern Agriculture*, edited by M. D. Hammig and H. M. Harris Jr. (Clemson, S.C.: Clemson University, 1983), p. 65.

CHAPTER 15

1 Peter Hazell, Carlos Pomareda, and Alberto Valdes, eds., *Crop Insurance for Agricultural Development: Issues and Experience* (Baltimore: Johns Hopkins University Press, 1986).

2 Barry K. Goodwin and Vincent H. Smith, *The Economics of Crop Insurance and Disaster Aid* (Washington, D.C.: AEI Press, 1995), p. 16.

3 Carlos Pomareda, "The Financial Viability of Agricultural Insurance," in *Crop Insurance for Agricultural Development: Issues and Experience* (Baltimore: Johns Hopkins University Press, 1986), Ch 16 (pp. 281–291). Indemnity claims are the farmers' claims for losses, and premium income is the income paid by farmers to obtain the insurance.

4 Peter Hazell, Carlos Pomareda, and Alberto Valdes, eds., "Introduction" in *Crop Insurance for Agricultural Development: Issues and Experience* (Baltimore: Johns Hopkins University Press, 1986), p. 7.

5 Bruce L. Gardner and Randall L. Kramer, "Experience with Crop Insurance Programs in the United States," in *Crop Insurance for Agricultural Development: Issues and Experience*, edited by Peter Hazell, Carlos Pomaredo, and Alberto Valdes (Baltimore: Johns Hopkins University Press, 1986), p. 222.

6 Harold Halcrow, *Agricultural Policy Analysis* (New York: McGraw-Hill, 1984), p. 242.

7 Ibid.

8 Ronald D. Knutson, J. B. Penn, and W. T. Boehm, *Agricultural and Food Policy* (Englewood Cliffs, N.J.: Prentice Hall, 1983), p. 235.

9 Ronald D. Knutson, J. B. Penn, and Barry L. Flinchbaugh, *Agricultural and Food Policy*, 4th ed. (Upper Saddle River, N.J.: Prentice Hall, 1998), p. 286.

10 Frederick J. Nelson and Lyle P. Schertz, eds., *Provisions of the Federal Improvement and Reform Act of 1996*, USDA, Economic Research Service, Agriculture Information Bulletin no. 729 (Washington, D.C.: U.S. Government Printing Office, September 1996), p. 30.

11 U.S. General Accounting Office, *Crop Revenue Insurance: Problems with New Plans Need to Be Addressed*, GAO/RCED-98-111 (Washington, D.C.: U.S. Government Printing Office, April 1998), p. 3.

12 Knutson, Penn, and Flinchbaugh, *Agricultural and Food Policy*, p. 287.

13 The processing fee was $60 per crop insured in 1999.

14 Kenneth L. Robinson, *Farm and Food Policies and Their Consequences* (Englewood Cliffs, N.J.: Prentice Hall, 1989), p. 100.

15 U.S. General Accounting Office, *Crop Revenue Insurance*, p. 6.

16 Goodwin and Smith, *The Economics of Crop Insurance and Disaster Aid*, p. 40.

17 Ibid., pp. 4–5.

18 U.S. General Accounting Office, *Crop Revenue Insurance*. The differences among the revenue plans are complicated. See Knutson, Penn, and Flinchbaugh, *Agricultural and Food Policy*, p. 289.

19 See USDA, Economic Research Service, "Features—Farm Policy, the 2002 Farm Bill: Title X Miscellaneous" at http://www.ers.usda.gov/Features/farmbill/titles/titleXmiscellaneous.htm for comparison of the differences between the 1996 and 2002 farm bills.

20 Nelson and Schertz, *Provisions of the Federal Improvement and Reform Act of 1996*, p. 29.

21 This section draws heavily on Knutson, Penn, and Flinchbaugh, *Agricultural and Food Policy*, p. 285.

22 Jim Phillips, "AG AID: It's a Strange Brew," *The Progressive Farmer* 113 (December 1998), p. 8.

23 The interest rate was 3.75 percent in 2002. See USDA, FSA, "Online Fact Sheet," August 2002, Emergency Loan Program, at: http://www.fsa.usda.gov/pas/publications/facts/html/emer02.htm.

24 Bruce L. Gardner, R. E. Just, R. A. Kramer, and R. D. Pope, "Agricultural Policy and Risk," in *Risk Management in Agriculture*, edited by Peter J. Barry (Ames: Iowa State University Press, 1984), p. 246.

25 Gardner and Kramer, "Experience with Crop Insurance Programs," p. 222.

26 Harold Demsetz, "Information and Efficiency: Another Viewpoint," *Journal of Law and Economics* 12 (April 1969): 1–21, addresses these issues in a general context.

27 Paul Heyne, *The Economic Way of Thinking*, 9th ed. (Upper Saddle River, N.J.: Prentice Hall, 2000), p. 532.

28 Bruce Gardner, *Agriculture's Revealing—and Painful—Lesson for Industrial Policy*, Heritage Foundation Backgrounder no. 320 (Washington, D.C.: Heritage Foundation, January 1984).

29 John E. Lee, "Observations on the Setting for Agricultural Policy," in *Farm and Food Policy: Critical Issues for Southern Agriculture*, edited by M. D. Hammig and H. M. Harris Jr. (Clemson, S.C.: Clemson University, June 1983), p. 258.

30 Michael T. Belongia, *Agriculture: An Eighth District Perspective* (St. Louis: Federal Reserve Bank of St. Louis, Spring 1984).

31 Heyne, *The Economic Way of Thinking*, p. 533.

32 Michael D. Boehlje and David A. Lins, "Risks and Risk Management in an Industrialized Agriculture," *Agricultural Finance Review* 58 (1998): 1–16.

33 Luther Tweeten and Carl Zulauf, "Post Industrial Agriculture," *Choices* 13 (1998): 30–33.

34 Charles R. Knoeber, "Contract Production in U.S. Agriculture: A Characterization of Current Empirical Research," unpublished paper, Department of Economics, North Carolina State University, February 1998. Published in French as: Charles R. Knoeber, "Les contrats de production dans l'agriculture americaine: Une caracterisation de la recherche empirique actuelle," *Economie Rurale* 259 (Septembre–Octobre): 3–15.

35 Charles R. Knoeber and Walter N. Thurman, "Don't Count Your Chickens . . . : Risk and Risk Shifting in the Broiler Industry," *American Journal of Agricultural Economics* 77 (August 1995): 486–96.

36 Alden C. Manchester, *Transition in the Farm and Food System*, paper for the National Planning Association, Committee on Agriculture (Washington, D.C.: USDA, 1992).

37 Goodwin and Smith, *The Economics of Crop Insurance and Disaster Aid*.

38 Heyne, *The Economic Way of Thinking*, p. 161.

39 J. Bruce Bullock, "Future Directions for Agricultural Policy," *American Journal of Agricultural Economics* (May 1984): 234–39.

40 H. S. Houthakker, *Economic Policy of the Farm Sector* (Washington, D.C.: American Enterprise Institute, 1967).

41 J. Bruce Bullock, *What Is the 1985 Farm Problem?* Policy Analysis no. 55 (Washington, D.C.: Cato Institute, 1985), p. 14.

42 Robinson, *Farm and Food Policies*, p. 92.

43 Gardner, *Agriculture's Revealing—and Painful—Lesson for Industrial Policy*, p. 9

44 Wayne D. Purcell and Stephen R. Koontz, *Agricultural Futures and Options: Principles and Strategies*, 2d ed. (Upper Saddle River, N.J.: Prentice Hall, 1999), chap. 7.

45 See Richard L. Kohls and Joseph N. Uhl, *Marketing of Agricultural Products*, 7th ed. (Upper Saddle River, N.J.: Prentice Hall, 1990), pp. 344–46, for more details on hedging with options.

46 David E. Kenyon, *Farmer's Guide to Trading Agricultural Commodity Options*, USDA Agriculture Information Bulletin no. 463 (Washington, D.C.: U.S. Government Printing Office, 1984).

47 Kandice H. Kahl, *Agricultural Options: An Alternative to Federal Farm Programs*, Heritage Foundation Backgrounder no. 414 (Washington, D.C.: Heritage Foundation, March 1985).

48 Ibid.

49 "The principal reason that a private-sector mechanism for hedging risks has not been developed is government's heavy involvement in agricultural affairs." Thomas Gale Moore, "Farm Policy: Justifications, Failures, and the Need for Reform," *Federal Reserve Bank of St. Louis Review* 69, no.8 (October 1987), p. 6.

50 Goodwin and Smith, *The Economics of Crop Insurance and Disaster Aid*, p. 128.

51 U.S. General Accounting Office, *Crop Revenue Insurance*, p. 3.

52 Goodwin and Smith, *The Economics of Crop Insurance and Disaster Aid*, p. 130.

53 F. A. Hayek, *Individualism and Economic Order* (Chicago: University of Chicago Press, 1948).

CHAPTER 16

1 W. Gifford Hoag, *The Farm Credit System: A History of Financial Help* (Danville, Ill.: Interstate, 1976).

2 Cole R. Gustafson, Marvin Duncan, and Jerome M. Stam, "Public and Private Policy Implications," in *Financing Agriculture into the Twenty-first Century*, edited by Marvin Duncan and Jerome Stam (Boulder, Colo.: Westview Press, 1998), p. 186.

3 This section draws heavily on Robert N. Collender and Steven R. Koenig, "The Role of Federal Credit Programs," in *Financing Agriculture into the Twenty-first Century*, edited by Marvin Duncan and Jerome M. Stam, 135–62 (Boulder, Colo.: Westview Press, 1998).

4 Gustafson, Duncan, and Stam, "Public and Private Policy Implications," p. 189.

5 Government-sponsored enterprises include the FCS and Federal Agricultural Mortgage Corporation, which serve agriculture and rural areas; Federal National Mortgage Association, Federal Home Loan Banks, and Federal Home Loan Mortgage Corporation, which serve housing; and the Student Loan Marketing Association and College Construction Loan Insurance Corporation, which serve higher education. Collender and Koenig, "The Role of Federal Credit Programs," p. 136.

6 David Freshwater, "Myths about the Farm Credit System," *Agri Finance: Profitable Lending to Agriculture* 2 (January 1998), p. 6.

7 USDA, Economic Research Service, *Agricultural Income and Finance: Annual Lender Issue*, AIS-78 (Washington, D.C.: U.S. Government Printing Office, February 2002), p. 56.

8 The farm credit programs of the FmHA, as explained later, were transferred to the newly created FSA in 1994.

9 Collender and Koeing, "The Role of Federal Credit Programs," in p.140.

10 Gustafson, Duncan, and Stam, "Public and Private Policy Implications," p. 191.

11 Housing, utility, community facilities, and other rural development programs of the FmHA were also transferred at that time to another newly created agency, Rural Development.

12 Collender and Koeing, "The Role of Federal Credit Programs," p. 140.

13 USDA, Economic Research Service, *Agricultural Income and Finance*, p. 56.

14 Ibid.

15 U.S. General Accounting Office, *Farmers Home Administration: Financial and General Characteristics of Farmer Loan Program Borrowers*, GAO/RCED-86-62BR (Washington, D.C.: U.S. Government Printing Office, 1986), p. 2.

16 USDA, Economic Research Service, *Agricultural Income and Finance*, p. 8.

17 Ibid.

18 Ibid., p. 7. Part of this difference in CCC loan debt is due, of course, to the advent of marketing loans and LDPs, which reduce the incentives to forfeit on CCC loans. Expenditures for marketing loan gain payments and LDPs in 2000, for example, were approximately $7.5 billion.

19 U.S. Office of Management and Budget, *Special Analysis: Budget of the United States Government*, 1986 (Washington, D.C.: U.S. Government Printing Office, 1985), p. F-4.

20 USDA, Economic Research Service, *Agricultural Income and Finance: Situation and Outlook Report*, AIS-71 (Washington, D.C.: U.S. Government Printing Office, February 1999), p. 17.

21 Lindley H. Clark Jr., "Interstate Banks Could Ease Farm Credit Woes," *Wall Street Journal*, January 20, 1987, p. 35.

22 Michael Becker, Steve Horwitz, and Robert O'Quinn, *Interstate Banking: Toward a Competitive Financial System*, Issue Alert no. 18 (Washington, D.C.: Citizens for a Sound Economy Foundation, 1987), p. 9.

23 USDA, Economic Research Service, *Agricultural Income and Finance*, p. 15.

24 Ibid.

25 U.S. Office of Management and Budget, *Special Analysis*, p. F-5.

26 "Program Level represents the gross value (economic cost) of all financial assistance USDA provides to the public. This assistance may be in the form of grants, guaranteed or direct loans, cost-sharing, professional services such as research or technical assistance activities, or in-kind benefits such as commodities." USDA, Office of Budget and Program Analysis, *2000 Budget Summary*, p. iii at: http://www.usda.gov/agency/obpa/Budget-Summary/2000/text.html.

27 USDA, Office of Budget and Program Analysis, *Budget Summary 2003*, p. 19, at: http://www.usda.gov/agency/obpa/Budget-Summary/2003/2003budsum.htm.

28 In the case of interest subsidies, the program level is higher than Treasury outlays because the money used for the loans might have earned a higher rate of return in an alternative use.

29 Collender and Koenig, "The Role of Federal Credit Programs," pp. 136–62.

30 Ibid., p. 151

31 USDA, *A Brief History of Farmers Home Administration* (Washington, D.C.: U.S. Government Printing Office, 1983), p. 15.

32 This example is taken from Bruce L. Gardner, *Agriculture's Revealing—and Painful—Lesson for Industrial Policy*, Heritage Foundation Backgrounder no. 320 (Washington, D.C.: Heritage Foundation, January 1984), p. 7; and Bruce L. Gardner, "Bringing a Free Market to the Farm," in *Agenda '83: A Mandate for Leadership Report*, edited by Richard N. Holwill, 29–40 (Washington, D.C.: Heritage Foundation, 1983).

33 E. C. Pasour Jr., "The Farm Credit Crisis," *The Freeman* 38 (March 1988): 108–13.

34 Collender and Koenig, "The Role of Federal Credit Programs," p. 144.

35 Ibid.

36 Ibid.

37 USDA, Economic Research Service, *Agricultural Income and Finance*, p. 56.

38 Clifton B. Luttrell, *The High Cost of Farm Welfare* (Washington, D.C.: Cato Institute, 1989), p. 84.

39 Collender and Koenig, "The Role of Federal Credit Programs," p. 155.

40 Ibid., p. 147.

CHAPTER 17

1 Frederick J. Nelson and Lyle P. Schertz, eds., *Provisions of the Federal Agriculture Improvement and Reform Act of 1996*, USDA, Economic Research Service, Agriculture Information Bulletin no. 729 (Washington, D.C.: U.S. Government Printing Office, September 1996), p. 124.

2 Water and power subsidies that reduce the cost of irrigation of agricultural crops for subsidy recipients are important in a number of western states. The inconsistency between Department of Interior irrigation subsidies that increase farm output and USDA programs that reduce farm production are further described in chapter 20. An examination of existing water rights institutions, an analysis of the role of government in distorting water use in the West through federal water projects, and proposals for institutional reform may be found in Terry L. Anderson, ed., *Water Rights* (San Francisco: Pacific Institute for Public Policy Research, 1983).

3 Terry L. Anderson and Donald R. Leal, *Free Market Environmentalism* (San Francisco: Pacific Institute for Public Policy, 1991).

4 Julian L. Simon, *The Ultimate Resource 2* (Princeton, N.J.: Princeton University Press, 1996), chaps. 20 and 21; F. A. Hayek, *The Constitution of Liberty* (Chicago: University of Chicago Press, 1960), chap. 23; Scott Gordon, "Economics and the Conservation Question," *Journal of Law and Economics* 1 (1958): 110–12.

5 Quoted in James Gwartney, "Private Property, Freedom, and the West," *Intercollegiate Review* 20 (Spring–Summer 1985), p. 42.

6 Ibid., p. 44.

7 See Charles Maurice and C. W. Smithson, *The Doomsday Myth: 10,000 Years of Economic Crises* (Stanford, Calif.: Hoover Institution Press, 1984); Simon, *The Ultimate Resource 2*, chaps. 1–16; Kenneth W. Chiton, *Are Economic Growth and a Sustainable Environment Compatible?* Study no. 152 (St. Louis: Washington University in St. Louis, Center for the Study of American Business, September 1999); Jacqueline R. Caisson, "Doomsday Every Day: Sustainable Economics, Sustainable Tyranny," *Independent Review* 14 (Summer 1999): 91–106; Julian L. Simon, ed., *The State of Humanity* (Cambridge, Mass.: Blackwell, 1995); and Ronald Bailey, ed., *Earth Report 2000: Revisiting the True State of the Planet* (New York: McGraw-Hill, 2000).

8 Dwight R. Lee and R. F. McNown, *Economics in Our Time*, 2d ed. (Chicago: Science Research Associates, 1983), pp. 145–47.

9 Simon, *The Ultimate Resource 2*, see especially chap. 11, "When Will We Run Out of Oil? Never!"

10 G. Anders, W. P. Gramm, and S. C. Maurice, *Does Resource Conservation Pay?* (Los Angeles: International Institute for Economic Research, 1978).

11 Ibid., p. 24.

12 Stephen Moore and Julian L. Simon, *The Greatest Century That Ever Was: 25 Miraculous Trends of the Past 100 Years*, Policy Analysis no. 364 (Washington, D. C.: Cato Institute, December 1999), p. 29.

13 Ibid.

14 Chiton, *Are Economic Growth and a Sustainable Environment Compatible?* p. 24.

15 Simon, *The Ultimate Resource 2*, p. 35.

16 D. Gale Johnson, "Population, Food, and Knowledge," *American Economic Review* 9 (March 2000): 1–14.

17 Ibid., p. 11.

18 Ronald Bailey, "Earth Day, Then and Now," *Reason* (May 2000), available at: http://www.reason.com/0005/fe.rb.earth.html.

19 See the section "Protection of Agricultural Land" in this chapter.

20 E. C. Pasour Jr., "Conservation, 'X-Efficiency' and Efficient Use of Natural Resources," *Journal of Libertarian Studies* 4 (1979): 371–90.

21 A transaction cost is any cost of negotiating or enforcing a contract. Steven E. Landsburg, *Price Theory and Applications*, 3rd ed. (St. Paul, Minn.: West, 1995), p. 462.

22 See the American Farmland Trust Web site at http://www.farmland.org.

23 Richard Magleby, Carmen Sandretto, William Crosswhite, and C. Tim Osborn, *Soil Erosion and Conservation in the United States: An Overview*, USDA Agricultural Information Bulletin no. 718 (Washington, D.C.: U.S. Government Printing Office, 1995).

24 Ibid.

25 Ibid.

26 Ibid., p. 3.

27 T. W. Schultz, "Dynamics of Erosion in the United States: A Critical View," in *The Vanishing Farmlands Crisis*, edited by John Baden (Lawrence: Regents Press of Kansas, 1984), , pp. 45–57.

28 Ibid., pp. 49–50.

29 Magleby et al., *Soil Erosion and Conservation in the United States*, p. 5.

30 Schultz, "Dynamics of Erosion in the United States," p. 45.

31 Ibid., p. 54.

32 American Agricultural Economics Association Task Force, *Soil Erosion and Soil Conservation Policy in the United States*, Occasional Paper no. 2 (Resources for the Future, Washington, D.C., 1986), p. 54.

33 Magleby et al., *Soil Erosion and Conservation in the United States*, p. 5.

34 Ibid., p. 38.

35 Ibid., p. 18.

36 Ibid.

37 E. C. Pasour Jr., "Agricultural Land Protection: Is Government Intervention Warranted?" *Cato Journal* 2 (Winter 1982): 739–58.

38 Walter N. Thurman, *Assessing the Environmental Impact of Farm Policies* (Washington, D.C.: AEI Press, 1995), p. 3.

39 Schultz, "Dynamics of Erosion in the United States," p. 54.

40 Crosson et al., *Soil Erosion*, p. 57.

41 *Wall Street Journal*, October 12, 1984.

42 Luther Tweeten, "The Twelve Best Reasons for Commodity Programs: Why None Stands Scrutiny," *Choices* 10 (1995), p. 43.

43 Pasour, "Agricultural Land Protection," p. 752.

44 Bruce L. Gardner, *The Governing of Agriculture* (Lawrence: Regents Press of Kansas, 1981), p. 113.

45 Nelson and Schertz, *Provisions of the Federal Agriculture Improvement and Reform Act of 1996*, p. 112.

46 See the appendix and the USDA Economic Research Service farm bill Web site for a comparison of the conservation provisions of the 1996 and 2002 farm bills: http://www.ers.usda.gov/Features/farmbill/. Further information on the various conservation programs may be found on the NRCS Web site: http://www.nrcs.usda.gov/NRCSProg.html.

47 USDA, NRCS, "Farm Bill, Conservation Programs," at http://www.nrcs.usda.gov/NRCSProg.html.

48 U.S. General Accounting Office, *Agricultural Conservation: Status of Programs That Provide Financial Incentives*, GAO/RCED-95-169 (Washington, D.C.: U.S. Government Printing Office, 1995), p. 1, and Nelson and Schertz, *Provisions of the Federal Agriculture and Improvement and Reform Act of 1996*, pp. 111–13.

49 In some instances, the increase in funding for existing programs in the 2002 farm bill were substantial. For information on these programs, see the appendix to this book and USDA, Economic Research Service, "Features—Farm Policy, the 2002 Farm Bill: Title II Conservation," at http://www.ers.usda.gov/Features/farmbill/titles/titleIIconservation.htm. The USDA site lists the differences between the 1996 and 2002 farm bills.

50 Nelson and Schertz, *Provisions of the Federal Agriculture and Improvement and Reform Act of 1996*, pp. 111–13.
51 USDA, Office of Budget and Program Analysis, *Budget Summary 2003* (Washington, D.C.: U.S. Government Printing Office, 2003), pp. 2, 24.
52 Ibid., p. 22.
53 See the USDA Economic Research Service farm bill Web site: http://www.ers.usda.gov/Features/farmbill/.
54 National Agricultural Lands Study, *Where Have the Farmlands Gone?* (Washington, D.C.: U.S. Government Printing Office, 1979).
55 See the American Farmland Trust Web site at http://farmland.org.
56 Clifton B. Luttrell, "Our 'Shrinking' Farmland: Potential Crisis?" in *The Vanishing Farmland Crisis*, edited by John Baden (Lawrence: University Press of Kansas, 1984), p. 32. See also current publications of the American Farmland Trust on its Web site at http://farmland.org.
57 Luttrell, "Our 'Shrinking' Farmland," p. 34. Lack of cropland does not appear to be a problem in meeting the demand for food by the global population. Recent research by the manager of science and engineering at the Department of Interior indicates that if annual productivity growth averages 1.5 percent, enough food and fiber can be produced to meet the rising demands of a growing world population in 2050 without increasing the amount of cropland used. (Cropland productivity increased at an annual rate of 2.1 percent from 1970 to 1980 and by 2.0 percent per year from 1980 to 1992). Indur M. Goklany, "Meeting Global Food Needs: The Environmental Trade-off Between Increasing Land Conversion and Land Productivity," *Technology* 6 (1999): 107–30.
58 Information on the rationale for and the variety of farmland protection programs by state is available from the American Farmland Trust Web site, http://www.farmland.org.
59 John Brigham, "The Politics of Tax Preference," in *Property Tax Preferences for Agricultural Land*, edited by Neal A. Roberts and H. James Brown (Montclair, N.J.: Allanheld, Osmun, 1980), p. 109.
60 Theodore A. Feitshans, "Environmental Law Update: Livestock and Poultry," *North Carolina State Economist* (July–August 1999): 1–4.
61 Referred to by the American Farmland Trust as *conservation easements*; see http://www.farmland.org.
62 F. A. Hayek, *Individualism and Economic Order* (Chicago. University of Chicago Press, 1948), p. 81.
63 Land Policy Council, *A Land Resources Program for North Carolina* (Raleigh, N.C.: Land Policy Council, 1976), p. 4.1.
64 David E. Ervin, James B. Fitch, R. Kenneth Godwin, W. Bruce Shepard, and Herbert H. Stovener, *Land Use Control: Evaluating Economic and Political Effects* (Cambridge, Mass.: Ballinger, 1977).
65 Thurman, *Assessing the Environmental Impact of Farm Policies*, p. 50.

CHAPTER 18

1 Bruce Gardner, *Agriculture's Revealing—and Painful—Lesson for Industrial Policy*, Heritage Foundation Backgrounder no. 320 (Washington, D.C.: Heritage Foundation, 1984).
2 Don F. Hadwiger, *The Politics of Agricultural Research* (Lincoln: University of Nebraska Press, 1982), p. 15.
3 Murray R. Benedict, *Farm Policies of the United States 1790–1950* (New York: Twentieth Century Fund, 1953), p. 84.

4 Hadwiger, *The Politics of Agricultural Research*, pp. 15–16.
5 Dennis T. Avery, "The Dilemma of Rising Farm Productivity," Senior Agricultural Analyst, Bureau of Intelligence and Research, U.S. Department of State, lecture before the Agribusiness Roundtable, September 10, 1984.
6 George Frisvold, Keith Fuglie, and Cassandra Klotz-Ingram, "Growth of Private Agricultural Research," *Choices* 13 (second quarter 1998): 22–23.
7 Ibid.
8 Luther Tweeten and Carl Zulauf, "Post-industrial Agriculture," *Choices* 13 (second quarter 1998): 30–33.
9 Intellectual property is a generic term for intangible personal property that includes patents and the Plant Variety Protection Act (originally enacted in 1970 and amended in 1994). Wallace E. Huffman and Robert E. Emerson, *Science for Agriculture: A Long-Term Perspective* (Ames: Iowa State University Press, 1993), p. 261.
10 Frisvold, Fuglie, and Klotz-Ingram, "Growth of Private Agricultural Research," p. 23.
11 David N. Hyman, *Public Finance: A Contemporary Application of Theory to Policy*, 6th ed. (New York: Harcourt Brace, 1999), chap. 4.
12 Vernon W. Ruttan, *Agricultural Research Policy* (Minneapolis: University of Minnesota Press, 1982), p. 182.
13 Thomas Sowell, *Knowledge and Decisions* (New York: Basic, 1980), p. 37.
14 Julian M. Alston and Philip G. Pardey, "Revitalizing R&D," in *Agricultural Policy Reform in the United States*, edited by Daniel Sumner (Washington, D.C.: AEI Press, 1995), pp. 265, 239–40.
15 "If benefits spill over beyond a particular state, from a national perspective the state is too small a jurisdiction." Ibid., p. 265.
16 However, public funding at the state level also involves inefficiencies. As discussed earlier, these services are not "public goods" and can be privatized.
17 Hadwiger, *The Politics of Agricultural Research*, p. 120.
18 Ibid., pp. 121–23.
19 Alston and Pardey, "Revitalizing R&D," p. 268.
20 Ibid.
21 Edwin S. Mills, *The Burden of Government* (Stanford, Calif.: Hoover Institution Press, 1986), p. 161.
22 William A. Niskanen Jr., *Bureaucracy and Representative Government* (Chicago: Aldine-Atherton, 1971), p. 39.
23 Vernon W. Ruttan, "Bureaucratic Productivity: The Case of Agricultural Research," *Public Choice* 35 (1980): 529–47.
24 Ibid., p. 531.
25 Julian M. Alston, Michele C. Marra, Philip G. Pardey, and T. J. Wyatt, "Research Returns Redux: A Meta-analysis of the Returns to Agricultural R&D," *Australian Journal of Agricultural and Resource Economics* 44 (June 2000): 185–215. Public-sector investment in both research- and extension-type activities is sometimes referred to in this chapter (for ease of exposition) merely as agricultural research.
26 Julian M. Alston and Philip G. Pardey, *Making Science Pay: The Economics of Agricultural R&D Policy* (Washington, D.C.: AEI Press, 1996), p. 324.
27 USDA, Economic Research Service, *Agricultural Research and Development: Public and Private Investments under Alternative Markets and Institutions*, Agricultural Economic Report no. 735 (Washington, D. C.: U.S. Government Printing Office, May 1996).
28 Ibid., p. 32.
29 Ibid., p. ii.
30 E. C. Pasour Jr. and Marc A. Johnson, "Bureaucratic Productivity: The Case of Agricultural Research Revisited," *Public Choice* 39 (1982): 301–17. Terence Kealey, *The Economic Laws of Scientific Research* (New York: William Morrow, 1996), presents a more comprehensive analy-

sis of the effects of government funding of scientific research: "As long as science is funded publicly, science lobbyists will fight a propaganda battle with the custodians of public funds. But, however much money the scientists extract, they will remain the ultimate loser. Science is nothing if it is not truth, and truth is hard to reconcile with politics" (p. 301).

31 Alston and Pardey, *Making Science Pay*, p. 209.

32 Don Fullerton, "Reconciling Recent Estimates of the Marginal Welfare Cost of Taxation," *American Economic Review* 81 (March 1991): 302–8, and Charles L. Ballard and Don Fullerton, "Distortionary Taxes and the Provision of Public Goods," *Journal of Economic Perspectives* 6 (Summer 1992): 117–31. There also are important moral costs in taxation. The inculcation of dishonest habits and the associated growth and importance of the "underground" economy in the United States is a manifestation of the moral costs associated with increased taxation—especially a progressive income tax.

33 Ballard and Fullerton, "Distortionary Taxes," p. 119, and James L. Payne, *The Culture of Spending* (San Francisco: ICS Press, 1991).

34 Payne, *The Culture of Spending*, p. 218.

35 See Ballard and Fullerton, "Distortionary Taxes," and Fullerton, "Reconciling Recent Estimates of the Marginal Welfare Cost of Taxation."

36 Alston and Pardey, *Making Science Pay*, p. 253.

37 *Economic Report of the President* (Washington, D.C.: U.S. Government Printing Office, 1988), p. 188.

38 Payne, *The Culture of Spending*, p. 186.

39 Glenn Fox, "Is the United States Really Underinvesting in Agricultural Research?" *American Journal of Agricultural Economics* 67 (November 1985): 806–12.

40 Ibid., p. 809.

41 Kealey, *The Economic Laws of Scientific Research*, pp. 233–34.

42 Don F. Hadwiger, "U.S. Agricultural Research: Utopians, Utilitarians, Copians," *Food Policy* (August 1984), p. 199.

43 Rachel Carson, *Silent Spring* (Boston: Houghton Mifflin, 1962).

44 Hadwiger, *The Politics of Agricultural Research*, p. 167.

45 Susan Offutt and Fred Kuchler, "Biotechnology: Is Safety All That Matters?" *Choices* 2 (1987): 12–15.

46 Thomas J. Hoban, "International Acceptance of Agricultural Biotechnology," paper presented at the annual meeting of the National Agricultural Biotechnology Council, June 1, 1998, in Greenville, S.C.

47 See Jim Hightower, *Hard Tomatoes, Hard Times: The Failure of the Land Grant College Complex* (Washington, D.C.: Agribusiness Accountability Project, 1972).

48 Tweeten and Zulauf, "Post-industrial Agriculture,".

49 *Economic Report of the President*, p. 183.

50 See Kealey, *The Economic Laws of Scientific Research*, especially chap. 12.

51 Ibid., p. 182.

52 See *Economic Report of the President*, p. 182, and Huffman and Emerson, *Science for Agriculture*, p. 231.

53 An analysis of the appropriate role, if any, of government in fostering agricultural research is beyond the scope of this book. Alston and Pardey, for example, suggest government-matched funding for commodity check-off levies (for research) as one possible improvement in the current system of financing agricultural research. See Alston and Pardey, *Making Science Pay*, chap. 9.

CHAPTER 19

1 For taxpayers with certain types of tax preferences, however, such as tax-exempt interest from private-activity bonds or income or losses from tax shelter farm activities, the top rate can be considerably higher than 38.6 percent. Under the 2001 tax law, the maximum rate is scheduled to be reduced to 35.0 percent in 2006.

2 James D. Gwartney and Richard Stroup, *Economics: Private and Public Choice*, 9th ed. (Orlando, Fl.: Dryden Press, 2000), p. 181.

3 Ibid.

4 Ibid.

5 Ron Durst and James Monke, "The Changing Tax Burden of Farmers," in *Agricultural Income and Finance: Situation and Outlook Report*, AIS-68 (Washington, D.C.: U.S. Government Printing Office, February 1998), pp. 33–38.

6 For other examples of the effects of targeted tax breaks that affect farmers and nonfarmers alike, see Janet Novack, "The Old Shell Game," *Forbes* (December 29, 1997): 76–81.

7 Charles Davenport, Michael B. Boehlje, and David B. H. Martin, *The Effects of Tax Policy on American Agriculture*, USDA Economic Research Service Agricultural Economic Report no. 480 (Washington, D.C.: U.S. Government Printing Office, 1982).

8 Carol D. Peterson, William Shear, and Charles L. Vehorn, "Cash Accounting Rules for Farmers: Differential Benefits and Federal Costs," *Journal of Economic Issues* 21 (June 1987), p. 642.

9 An S corporation is a regular corporation with special tax attributes. The S corporation retains the legal characteristics of the corporate form (limited liability, free transferability of interests, continuity of life, and centralized management) while obtaining taxation characteristics similar to those of a partnership. Thus, a corporation making this election would be exempt from federal income tax, but its shareholders must include in their income their share of the corporation's income. For more information, go to the Purdue tax Web site at: http://www. fnr.purdue.edu/ttax/taxstrategies/structuring activities/scorporation.htm

10 Peterson, Shear, and Vehorn, "Cash Accounting Rules for Farmers."

11 Ibid., pp. 641–42.

12 Internal Revenue Service, *Farmer's Tax Guide*, Publication 225 (Washington, D.C.: U.S. Government Printing Office, 2002), p. 12.

13 Ibid., p. 48. A 2002 tax law provides for an additional 30 percent first-year special deduction allowance (p. 50).

14 In this context, the term *capitalize* means to include certain costs in the basis of property produced or in inventory costs, rather than to deduct them as current expenses.

15 Internal Revenue Service, *Your Federal Income Tax for Individuals* (Washington, D.C.: U.S. Government Printing Office, 2002), p. 116.

16 Durst and Monke, *The Changing Tax Burden of Farmers*, p. 35.

17 Notable political efforts have been made in recent years to repeal the estate tax. Repeal of the estate tax passed both houses of Congress, but President Clinton vetoed it. The 2001 Tax Act reduces estate tax rates over a nine-year period and repeals the estate tax in 2010. If no legislation action is taken by then, however, the rate returns to 60 percent in 2011!

18 Dr. Neil E. Harl, *Agricultural Law Manual* (Eugene, Ore.: Agricultural Law Press, 1998), chap. 7, p. 9.

19 Davenport, Boehlje, and Martin, *The Effects of Tax Policy*, p. 11.

20 Ibid., p. 12.

21 See "Briefing Room, Farm Structure: Questions and Answers, Farm Organization 1978– 1997" in the USDA Economic Research Service Web site: http://www.ers.usda.gov/Briefing/ FarmStructure/Questions/Closeup.htm.

22 Ibid.

23 Ibid.
24 Ibid.
25 Ibid.
26 Durst and Monke, *The Changing Tax Burden of Farmers*, p. 33.

CHAPTER 20

1 The classification of expenditures and method of analysis in the ensuing discussion was adapted from Clifton B. Luttrell, *Down on the Farm with Uncle Sam* (Los Angeles: International Institute for Economic Research, 1983), p. 17.

2 The effects of price supports and accompanying production controls may be to decrease prices paid by consumers while increasing prices received by farmers. Prior to the 1996 farm bill, target prices on wheat, feed grains, cotton, and rice, for example, increased prices to farmers. When output of a commodity increased under these programs, however, prices paid by consumers decreased because market prices were freely established, given the program constraints.

3 M. R. Benedict, *Farm Policies of the United States, 1790–1950* (New York: Twentieth Century Fund, 1953), p. 385.

4 Bruce L. Gardner, *The Governing of Agriculture* (Lawrence: Regents Press of Kansas, 1981), p. 20.

5 The data in column 6 of table 20.1 do not include expenditures for the Conservation Reserve Program.

6 B. Delworth Gardner, *Plowing Ground in Washington: The Political Economy of U.S. Agriculture* (San Francisco: Pacific Research Institute for Public Policy, 1995), chap. 12. See also B. Delworth Gardner, "Water Pricing and Rent Seeking in California Agriculture," in *Water Rights*, edited by Terry L. Anderson (San Francisco: Pacific Institute for Public Policy Research, 1983), p. 84.

7 Randal R. Rucker and Price V. Fishback, "The Federal Reclamation Program: An Analysis of Rent-Seeking Behavior," in *Water Rights*, edited by Terry L. Anderson, 45–80 (San Francisco: Pacific Institute for Public Policy Research, 1983).

8 Vincent Carroll, "How the West Is Watered," *Reason* 18, no. 3 (July 1986): 38–40.

9 Alfred G. Cuzan, "Appropriators versus Expropriators: The Political Economy of Water in the West," in *Water Rights*, edited by Terry L. Anderson (San Francisco: Pacific Institute for Public Policy Research, 1983), p. 36.

10 David Seckler and Robert A. Young, "Economic and Policy Implications of the 160-Acre Limitation in Federal Reclamation Law," *American Journal of Agricultural Economics* 60, no. 4 (November 1978), p. 575. See also Rucker and Fishback, "The Federal Reclamation Program."

11 Gardner, "Water Pricing," p. 83.

12 A similar phenomenon occurs in the case of direct income transfers, such as the "transition payments" of the 1996 farm bill, which are tied to the land.

13 D. Gale Johnson, "The Performance of Past Policies: A Critique," in *Alternative Agricultural and Food Policies and the 1985 Farm Bill*, edited by Gordon C. Rausser and K. R. Farrell, 11–36 (Berkeley, Calif.: Giannini Foundation, 1985).

14 Ibid., p. 28.

15 Ibid., p. 34.

16 See table 6.4 and the sources cited there as well as USDA, Economic Research Service, "Farm Income Data on 'Value Added by Size Class,'" at http://www.ers.usda.gov/data/farmincome/finfidmu.htm.

17 Paul Heyne, *The Economic Way of Thinking*, 9th ed. (Upper Saddle River, N.J.: Prentice Hall, 2000), p. 532.

APPENDIX

1 The information presented in this appendix draws heavily on the short and long summaries of the 2002 farm bill provided on the Web site of the U.S. House of Representatives Committee on Agriculture (http://www.house.gov/agriculture/issues/farmbill/fbconfsum.pdf and http://www.house.gov/agriculture/issues/farmbill/2626fullsum.pdf). Additional detail is provided in the USDA Economic Research Service Web site (http://www.ers.usda.gov/Features/farmbill/analysis/).

2 The long summary of the 2002 farm bill on the House Committee on Agriculture Web site contains useful sample problems for understanding how payments under the three-piece safety net are determined.

3 The cost estimates in this table and in the other tables in this appendix represent the estimated change in spending caused by enactment of the 2002 farm bill. For useful discussions of the issues associated with these estimates, see Ralph M. Chite, *Cost of the 2002 Farm Bill*, Congressional Research Service, Agricultural Policy and Farm Briefing Book (Washington, D.C.: U.S. Government Printing Office, January 2003), or Geoffrey S. Becker and Jasper Womach, *The 2002 Farm Bill Overview and Status*, Congressional Research Service and Library of Congress (Washington, D.C.: U.S. Government Printing Office, June 2002), available at: http://fpc.state.gov/documents/organization/11277.pdf.

4 The requirement in the 2002 farm bill that labelling was to become mandatory within two years has since been rescinded.

Index

Johnson, D. Gale, 347n11, 355n16, 361n13–15
Johnson, Paul R., 332n18, 342n34
Johnson, Ronald N., 333n17, 334n28, 345n15
Jones-Costigan Act (1934), 137
Journal of Commerce Online, 350n31
Journal of Law and Economics
  "Cartelization of the California-Arizona
    Orange Industry, 1934–1981" (Shepard),
    346n47
  "Economic Effects of Federal Regulation of
    Milk Markets" (Kessel), 345n15
  "The Economic Effects of Supply Controls"
    (Rucker and Thurman), 343n56
  "Economics and the Conservation
    Question" (Gordon), 355n4
  "The Fable of the Bees Revisited" (Muth, et.
    al), 343n60
  "Information and Efficiency" (Demsetz),
    331n4, 333n29, 352n26
  "Positive Economics, Welfare Economics,
    and Political Economy" (Buchanan),
    331n5
  "Retail Price Controls in the Dairy
    Industry" (Johnson), 338n2(chap. 9),
    345n15
  "The Social Cost of Government
    Regulation of Milk" (Ippolito and
    Mason), 338n2(chap. 9), 345n15
Journal of Political Economy, 332n12, 334n10,
  342n44, 347n16
judicial branch of U.S. government, 38, 55, 333n4
Just, Richard E., 346n3, 352n24

Kahl, Kandice H., 353n47–48
Kantorovich, Leonid V., 329–30n13
Kealey, Terence, 358n30
Kenyon, David E., 353n46
Kessel, Reuben E., 345n15
Kirzner, Israel M., 330n21–25
Klotz-Ingram, Cassandra, 358n6–7
Knight, Frank, 5, 329n1
Knoeber, Charles R., 344n8, 352n34–35
Knutson, Ronald D., 344n5, 348n15, 351n8.
  See also *Agricultural and Food Policy*
  (Knutson, Penn, and Flinchbaugh)
Koenig, Steven R., 353n3
Kohls, Richard L., 353n45
Koontz, Stephen R., 352n44
Kramer, Randall L., 351n5, 352n24
Krueger, Anne, 340–41n17
Kuchler, Fred, 359n45
Kuhn, Betsey A., 347n3

labeling requirements, 141, 203–4, 213, 327,
  348n28, 362n4
labor. *See* employment
land. *See* agricultural land
land classification, 272
land-grant college, 54–55, 276, 282
Land Policy Council, 357n63
Landsburg, Steven E., 356n21
land set-aside programs, 279, 313
land use
  incentives, 271, 273
  land-use decisions, 274
  market versus central direction, 272–73,
    313
  restrictions on, 110–11, 193, 269–70, 274
Lange, Oskar, 6, 329n11
Langley, James, 345n21
Lavoie, Don, 329n2, 348n25
Lawler, John V., 344n63
LDPs (loan deficiency payments), 125–26,
  135–36, 184, 217, 321–23
Leal, Donald R., 355n3
Lee, Dwight R., 347n19, 355n8
Lee, John, 235, 352n29
legislative branch of government, 41–43, 69
Lenard, Thomas M., 346n42
Lerner, Abba, 6
Leube, K. R., 336n14(chap. 6)
Libecap, Gary D., 333n17, 334n28
liberal ideology, 40
libertarian ideology, 40
Lilie, Stuart A., 40, 333n10
Lilla, Mark, 336n5
limited-resource loan, 247–48
Lindsey, Brink, 349n17, 350n44
line item veto, 68, 69, 336n36
Lins, David A., 352n32
loan deficiency payments (LDPs), 125–26,
  135–36, 184, 217, 321–23
loan rates, 2002 farm bill, 151, 320, 322
log rolling, 43, 47, 56–57
Longen, Kathryn, 347n1, 350n19
Lord, Ron, 340–41n17
Lorenz curve, 80–81
lump sump contract payments, 125–26, 154–
  55, 224, 315, 317, 350n37
Luttrell, Clifton B., 338n11, 339n8–9, 349n8,
  349n10, 357n56–57, 361n1

Maddox, William S., 40, 333n10
Magleby, Richard, 356n23
Manchester, Alden C., 352n36

About the Authors

E. C. Pasour, Jr., is a research fellow at the Independent Institute and professor emeritus of agricultural and resource economics, North Carolina State University. Dr. Pasour received his Ph.D. in agricultural economics from Michigan State University. He is the author of *Agriculture and the State: Market Processes and Bureaucracy* and has contributed to numerous books including *Agriculture and Energy* (W. Lockeretz, ed.), *Economy, Society and Public Policy* (C. Pope and L. Wimmer, eds.), *Electric Power* (J. Moorhouse, ed.), *Environmental Ethics* (K. Schrader-Frechette, ed.), *Free Trade* (J. Taylor, ed.), *Method, Process and Austrian Economics* (I. Kirzner, ed.), and *The Vanishing Farm Crisis* (J. Baden, ed.). His many articles and reviews have appeared in such publications as *American Economist, American Journal of Agricultural Economics, Cato Journal, Journal of Farm Economics, Journal of Post-Keynesian Economics, Journal of Public Finance and Public Choice, Land Economics, Modern Age, National Tax Journal, Public Choice, Reason, Southern Economic Journal,* and *The Wall Street Journal.*

Randal R. Rucker is a research fellow at the Independent Institute and professor of agricultural economics and economics at Montana State University. He received his Ph.D. in economics from the University of Washington, and he has been associate professor of economics and business at North Carolina State University, and economist at the U.S. Department of the Interior. His scholarly articles and reviews have appeared in the *American Economic Review, Journal of Political Economy, Review of Economics and Statistics, Journal of Law and Economics, American Journal of Agricultural Economics, Journal of Law, Economics and Organization, Journal of Environmental Economics and Management, Forest Science, Journal of Applied Forestry, Journal of Economic History,* and *The Independent Review.* A contributor to numerous scholarly volumes, Professor Rucker is the author of many technical studies on natural resource and environmental issues.

INDEPENDENT STUDIES IN POLITICAL ECONOMY

For further information and a catalog of publications, please contact:
THE INDEPENDENT INSTITUTE
100 Swan Way, Oakland, California 94621-1428, U.S.A.
510-632-1366 · Fax 510-568-6040 · info@independent.org · www.independent.org